JAPAN'S NEW IMPERIALISM

Also by Rob Steven

CLASSES IN CONTEMPORARY JAPAN

Japan's New Imperialism

Rob Steven
Senior Lecturer in Political Science
University of Canterbury
Christchurch, New Zealand

M. E. Sharpe, Inc.
Armonk, New York

338.952
S84j

© Rob Steven 1990

First published in 1990.

Published in the United States by M. E. Sharpe, Inc.
80 Business Park Drive, Armonk, New York 10504.

Published in Great Britain by the Macmillan Press Ltd.

Printed in Hong Kong.

Library of Congress Cataloging-in-Publication Data

Steven, Rob.
  Japan's new imperialism / by Rob Steven.
    p. cm.
  Includes bibliographical references.
  ISBN 0-87332-756-X
  1. Japan—Economic conditions—1945– 2. Japan—Economic policy—1945–
3. Bureaucracy—Japan. 4. Japan—Politics and government—1945– I. Title.
HC462.9.S668 1990
338.952—dc20   90-34056
                                                                    CIP

Contents

Acknowledgements

It is impossible to mention all the debts I incurred in writing this book. The greatest of these are to the victims of Japan's new imperialism whom I got to know, both in Japan and in Southeast Asia. It means everything to me that you should know about one another, and I hope that this book contributes something to that.

I owe an enormous debt to my special friend Delle Small. You have helped in thousands of ways which I cannot explain here. Thank you too, Chigusa and Kenji, for looking after me. I will try to reciprocate. To Kathleen, Shaun and Bill, thanks for your time and honesty.

Some of the material included in this book was published in earlier versions by *Capital and Class* and the *Bulletin of Concerned Asian Scholars* in 1988. I am grateful to the editors for permission to use it here.

Finally, I would like to thank the Japan Foundation for the fellowship I received while doing research in Japan, and the people of New Zealand, whose taxes pay my salary.

ROB STEVEN

List of Tables

List of Abbreviations

FREQUENTLY CITED JOURNALS AND NEWSPAPERS

AS	*Asahi Shinbun*
AWSJ	*Asia Wall Street Journal*
BCAS	*Bulletin of Concerned Asian Scholars*
BT	*Business Tokyo*
FEER	*Far Eastern Economic Review*
JCA	*Journal of Contemporary Asia*
JEJ	*Japan Economic Journal*
JJTI	*Journal of Japanese Trade and Industry*
JS	*Jietoro Sensa*
JT	*Japan Times*
KTG	*Kaigai Toshi Gaido*
LJ	*Look Japan*
JTW	*Japan Times Weekly Overseas Edition*
NKS	*Nihon Keizai Shinbun*
STK	*Shukan Toyo Keizai*
TBT	*Tokyo Business Today*

Introduction

Although the current worldwide depression was first felt in Japan along with the 'oil shocks' of the 1970s, to the outside world Japanese society remained immune from the worst of it. Indeed, Japan has been seen as an example of how to avoid the economic, social and political breakdown that a faltering capitalism has elsewhere left in its wake. One reason for this myth is that most scholars who write about Japan tend to present its institutions, particularly its factories, as models for the rest of the world. Many have shared the interests of Japanese capital, which has continually shifted the burden of the crisis onto less vocal workers at home, particularly part-time women, and abroad, mainly in Asia and Latin America. The focus of this book is on the latter displacement: Japan's new imperialism in Southeast Asia.

The single most important revolutionary force which has swept through Southeast Asia this century is undoubtedly decolonisation. If there was any one point in time, or any particular event which united and unleashed the potential of the disparate liberation movements and ushered in the era of decolonisation, then that catalytic moment was the Pacific War. Spectacular Japanese victories owed a lot to the unpopularity of the colonial regimes among the peoples of Asia, and the war consolidated their struggles.

Today a new revolutionary force is sweeping through and transforming Southeast Asia. That force is capitalism, and once again the catalytic upsurge in its development is coming from Japan, from the crisis which was sparked off by the oil shock of 1973 and which has continued in one form or another to the present day. To understand the dynamism of the current capitalist revolution in Southeast Asia requires an analysis of the social forces which the capitalist crisis in Japan is jettisoning into the outside world.

A short outline of the theoretical approach which has guided this study is needed. It is necessarily brief, because this is not a theoretical work but a documentation of a process in which my theoretical knowledge has constantly interacted with my findings. Much of the theory which was used and developed therefore remains implicit rather than explicit.

1

THEORETICAL AND CONCEPTUAL CONSIDERATIONS

Marxist writing on capitalist imperialism is often flawed by econom-ism, that is, by its failure to penetrate beyond the commodity forms assumed by international capitalism and hence its inability to lay bare the social relations behind them. This is particularly true of those Neo-Marxian writers who can loosely be called 'world system' theor-ists (Wallerstein, 1979; Frank, 1967; Amin, 1974), in contrast with the 'mode of production' theorists of classical Marxism (Warren, 1980; Szymanski, 1981). At least three major areas of difference between the two schools are relevant: their units of analysis, the mechanisms through which they believe wealth is transferred and the importance they assign to international trade.

In world system theories, the unit of analysis is the world capitalist system, and what happens in particular countries depends on how they fit into this whole. They are the *dependent* variables, which change only when the independent variable, the system as a whole, changes. The latter is held together by the market, and sometimes the phrase 'world capitalist market' is used interchangeably with the term 'world capitalist system'. Essentially, the market *is* the system, and international relations are seen as the systemic effects of the functioning of the whole, whose main components are a centre and a periphery and whose moving force is commodity trade. Social rela-tions and social conflict is most fundamentally between these differ-ent parts, between nations, rather than within them between classes.

Since an international market in fact exists only for commodities other than labour power, it is easy to see why world system theories tend to be economistic. Even migrant workers do not sell their skills in a worldwide labour market, but in specific markets with local boundaries shaped by the strategies of capitalist states in concrete class struggles.

In contrast to the world system theories of neo-Marxism, the classical tradition has always seen the mode of production, charac-terised by its social relations, as the unit of analysis. Because relation-ships in the production place are most basic, the boundaries of the capitalist mode of production are set by the space within which workers move about to sell their skills. The independent variable is thus class relations, constituted in specific places and manifesting themselves in identifiable concrete forms of organisation, such as the corporation and the state, while the dependent variables comprise such developments as imperialism abroad.

Imperialism in this tradition represents the attempt of a ruling class to solve conflicts with its own working class by moving abroad to exploit foreign workers. This might involve setting itself up organisationally as the ruling class in the colony, as in the classical period when it held state power, or simply forming an alliance with the overseas ruling class, with itself as the dominant partner, as happens currently under neo-colonialism. Foreign investment, trade, aid and lending are all typical outward forms of neo-colonialism, whose economistic appearance conceals its essential social character.

International relations are thus the outwardly directed effects of internal class conflicts, of attempts by ruling classes to deal with domestic social crises by moving abroad. Imperialism, rather than a shift in the equilibrium point of a single world system, is a conflict-ridden, unregulated, consequence of contradictions within modes of production. It requires the formation of alliances with the ruling classes of its colonies, since the compliance an imperialist power gets is always mediated by the colonial ruling class, without whose co-operation, imperialist power collapses.

The two theories may also be differentiated by their methods of abstraction. In world system theories, the highest level of abstraction is the world capitalist system, whose dominant social forces penetrate the different countries, which exist and which must be analysed at more concrete levels of abstraction. In mode of production theories, however, the highest level of abstraction is the capitalist mode of production dominating the different countries, while imperialism and other contacts, conquests and alliances among the world's ruling and working classes belong to more concrete levels of abstraction.

In the long run the clash between the two theories will be settled by the evidence. And the evidence seems to be mounting that an historical moment (period) might arrive when there is a change from one to the other: from a situation in which the predominant social forces of capitalism stem from all the many capitalist societies, to one in which growing alliances among capitalist classes begin to create new regional modes of production and ultimately a worldwide (capitalist or other) mode of production. I do not think that such a transition has occurred yet. There are not yet enough worldwide institutions through which such a system can express itself and function. The capitalist state, in spite of the falling away of many of its tasks during the last decade, is still the main institution through which class relations are expressed organisationally. Before one can claim that the capitalist mode of production has a single worldwide existence, such international organisations as TNCs (transnational corporations) will need to become much more important than they now are.

Following from the central position they assign to the market, world system theories see what they call 'unequal exchange' in international trade as the chief mechanism through which wealth is transferred (from one country to another), whereas mode of production theories concentrate on the transfer of surplus value from workers to capitalists in the production place. However, contrary to most mode of production theorists, I do believe that unequal exchange has become an important, though not the pivotal, mechanism of present-day imperialism, and I discuss this more fully in the Conclusion. Here I want to emphasise that since the production place is the prime site of capitalist exploitation, foreign investment remains the most basic concrete form assumed by modern imperialism.

Foreign investment, particularly its most typical current form, the joint venture, has replaced colonial conquest as the main institutional means through which imperialism functions. The joint venture expresses an *alliance between two capitalist classes*, that of the imperialist power and that of the neo-colony, and helps each maintain its ruling position. The alliance develops when relations between capital and labour in both countries break down simultaneously, so that the position of each capitalist class *vis-à-vis* its own working class is strengthened as a result. Nevertheless, because they come with vastly different powers and resources, they get from the alliance very different benefits.

Imperialism thus does not exclude cooperation among ruling classes; it depends on it, albeit cooperation between unequal partners. However, not all foreign investment expresses imperial domination. For example, when Japanese capital forms joint ventures in the US, an alliance between more or less equal imperialist powers is cemented.

SCOPE OF THE STUDY

I have focused almost entirely in this study on foreign investment and joint ventures. Although trade and aid are also forms of capitalist domination, I have only given half my concluding chapter to a discussion of trade. Aid and international debt proved to be such a vast subject, bound up with the proliferation of Japan's indirect investments, that I had to exclude it entirely.

For the same reason I also excluded indirect (portfolio) investments, which do not give control over the production place. Most Japanese money circulating round the world today is of this type, coming and going all the time, and moving in and out of bonds, shares, foreign exchange markets, gold, real state and whatever speculative project Japanese capitalists can think of. This study focuses on direct foreign investment (DFI), that is, investment which brings with it real control in the production place: managerial, technical, legal.

Since the central motive behind the current wave of Japan's DFI in Asia is to take advantage of low wages to extract the maximum possible surplus, I have excluded the unproductive industries (commerce, finance and real estate). The latter are more concerned with surplus distribution, and Japanese investments in them are concentrated in North America and Europe. Indeed, one of the features of our times is the shift of the capitalist world's centre of surplus extraction to Asia, and the appropriation of much of this by the imperialist powers among whom it is then distributed through unproductive investments, mainly in each other's financial and commercial centres. Within the productive industries my main emphasis is also on the two which are most rapidly and thoroughly being internationalised: motor vehicles and electronics.

One last explanatory point remains. There are many different measures of foreign investment, each corresponding to a different concept. This study is not so much concerned with measuring flows, that is, the amounts of money that are actually transferred from one country to another, as with the changing value of the stock of DFI. This is because so much of Japanese capital's power in the factories of Asia stems from investments made with money, not from Japan, but raised locally: borrowed, reinvested profits or local equity. The value of these investments, rather than where the Japanese companies got the money to pay for them, is the more relevant measure.

My sources often list either simply the equity held by the Japanese company or the entire value of the investments, which might include substantial borrowings (locally or from Japan) as well as other equity. Wherever these difference are relevant I have tried to say so. However, since all the different measures of DFI are at best only very general indicators of the power of Japanese capital, I have not dwelt heavily on the differences. My concern is with broad political tendencies, and the data on DFI are in any case only imperfect guides to these tendencies. Comparisons over time and among countries on the basis of the same measures have therefore been the most helpful ways of using the data.

COUNTRIES SELECTED

Some of the other limits of this study were also set by considerations of space. For example, the single most important target in Asia today for Japanese investment is China, but the complexities of including China proved too great. Even confining myself to Asian countries which have long had substantial investments from Japan was not possible. I therefore chose to focus on the ASEAN countries, mainly because the current wave of Japanese investment has revealed a decided preference for ASEAN, as opposed to the NICs (newly industrialised countries). I selected only two of the latter, South Korea, Japan's first colony and currently its most important neo-colony, and Singapore, so that at least one of each type of NIC was discussed. Taiwan (which like the South Korea has its own hinter-land) and Hong Kong (purely a city state like Singapore) have been excluded. Because Singapore is analysed as a NIC, ASEAN countries in this study refer to Thailand, Malaysia, Indonesia and the Philip-pines (Brunei was excluded for its relative unimportance).

Because of my theoretical and political orientation, which sees present day imperialism as a consequence of some crisis in the advanced country and the conclusion of alliances with the ruling classes of the neo-colonies, I have structured my argument accord-ingly. I try to show how crises and class struggles in both Japan and its neo-colonies have resulted in alliances among their ruling classes.

The overall argument is divided into three parts. The first traces the origins and outlines the nature of the current crisis of Japan, in order to show why Japanese capital is becoming more imperialistic and why it must ally itself with capital in the advanced countries as well as Asia. In part two I look at Japan's new imperialism from a global and historical perspective, emphasising its current need to approach Asia after first attenuating its rivalries with other imperial-ist powers. Part three comprises cases studies, which show that the alliances with the ruling classes of Southeast Asia are of an entirely different order. The great technological divide is the main reason why foreign capital dominates these alliances and gets the lion's share of the surplus extracted from the peoples of Asia.

General readers might find that after reading a few case studies, which are in parts quite detailed, they can proceed to the concluding chapter without losing track of the overall argument. More specialised readers might prefer to grasp the details of each of the three different types of Asian country currently being penetrated by Japanese capital: South Korea and Singapore (NICs), Thailand and Malaysia (aspiring NICs), and Indonesia and the Philippines (for which industrialisation under capitalism is a pipedream).

Because of space I have confined the detailed argument in parts two and three to the activities of the capitalist classes. My reason for not also cutting Japanese labour out of the picture in part one is the widespread ignorance of the appalling conditions faced by the Japanese working class. Many people all over the world are responding to Japan's new imperialism in racial rather than political economic terms, and one of my chief aims in writing this book is to show that most Japanese people are also its victims. That the people of Asia are its chief victims is more widely recognised, and I felt able to omit that emphasis. What is less well known about Asia is the region's growing dominance by Japanese capital and the latter's links with the local ruling classes.

1 Origins of the High Yen Crisis

The crisis of Japanese capitalism which sent the current wave of foreign investment into Asia was widely referred to as the *endaka fukyō* (the high yen recession). Although it began in the early 1980s, it manifested itself most dramatically in the yen's 50 per cent appreciation (from ¥240 to the dollar to ¥160) from September 1985 to August 1986, its soaring to ¥120 in January 1988, and its subsequent fluctuation around the 130 mark. Although I examine the period 1980–87 in most detail, one cannot fully grasp the forces at work unless one sees this period in its historical context. I therefore briefly review the main features of the years leading up to this crisis, in particular the period after 1974.

My argument is that the course of the Japanese class struggle, notably the growing capacity of capital to break the power of organised labour, confirmed Japan as a low cost production site, particularly for the outputs of the machine industries. These were then increasingly sold in the high wage countries of Europe and North America, and Japanese capital got the best of both worlds. However, this invasion of the markets of its rivals caused strong reactions against Japanese capital, the most important of which were the pressures from the US resulting in the rise of the yen. The high yen has subsequently produced a unique situation: insofar as they represent costs, Japanese wages are now the highest in the world, certainly too high for Japan to remain an area of low-cost production. It is even cheaper to produce in the US than in Japan, not to mention Southeast Asia, and a tidal wave of DFI is sweeping across the world.

However, because of the astronomical costs of such things as housing, education and social security in Japan, the higher wages have not translated into either higher living standards or a buying power which could transform export-led accumulation into growth based on working-class demand. Japanese wages are both too high and too low: too high for capital to expand the numbers of jobs in Japan, but too low to serve as a market, the most important of which is still the US and to a lesser extent the EC. In this chapter I deal with the origins of this unique accumulation model, while in the next I discuss its adaptation during the *endaka fukyō*.

RESTRUCTURING TO 1973

Postwar accumulation has been accompanied by a continuous process of industrial restructuring, or what has been called 'scrap and build' (Ninomiya, 1987). Right up to the first oil shock in October 1973 this took the form of running down the light industries which throughout the prewar period had generated the surplus for the state to build infrastructure and subsidise heavy industry, and then building heavy industry into the dominant pillar of Japanese capitalism. Until 1973, the so-called 'miracle' was based on the heavy chemical and basic materials industries, processing imported raw materials and export-ing iron and steel, ships, chemicals and petroleum products. Its counterpart was to scrap coal mining, agriculture (in spite of its subsidisation) and textiles, a strategy which meshed well with the political alliance with the US sealed in the Security Treaty of 1952. The latter would find a market for its agricultural surplus and other raw materials, as well as another lever with which to keep the Japanese in line with its military strategy in the Far East.

Scrap and build is a normal part of capital accumulation, but since this is a socio-political process it demands appropriate forms of political organisation by the ruling class to ensure working-class compliance. I have elsewhere tried at length to analyse this social structure (Steven, 1983) and only briefly outline here some of its main features. Scrap and build requires a social structure which can accommodate the main dislocations which this process normally brings. Up to 1974, Japanese social structure allowed for a relatively efficient industrial restructuring. The secret lay mainly in the way bourgeois and patriarchal social relations worked in parallel to divide and maintain tight control over the working class.

There are two axes where these relations have overlapped and reinforced social control in Japan. First, Japanese capital could get away with providing a sizeable proportion of the working class with wages and conditions which are comparable to those in Southeast Asia only because it provided excellent wages and conditions to the minority of workers who have been unionised and able to struggle effectively. This axis divides what are called regular workers, the bulk of whom even today receive from their employers lifelong (at least until about 55) job security, annual pay increments and fairly com-prehensive social security, from the many categories of temporary and part-time workers, who receive none of these benefits and who are not generally granted union membership. Part-time workers are the worst off of this group, which also comprises day labourers, contract workers, retired workers on short-term hire and so on, and their wages are typically only a third of regular workers' wages.

All large Japanese companies have kept substantial numbers of low-paid temporary workers, so that their unit wage costs have been extremely low even though their unionised, particularly their older male, workers could be very well paid. Whatever else may be said about rapid accumulation in the postwar period – for example, that it resulted from continual technical change through high levels of debt-financed investment in up-to-date equipment – it remains true that the miserable wages and conditions of the bulk of the working class allowed for the accumulation of the maximum amount of surplus from the rising labour productivity. These were the sorts of wages and conditions which could not be imposed on organised labourers, who had after half a century of struggle finally freed themselves of that burden.

The division within the working class along the permanent–temporary axis has received an extra reinforcement because of the way it has coincided with patriarchal social relations. To an extent unknown outside Japan, regular workers have been male and irregular workers female. Even the overwhelming majority of formally regular women workers, many of whom are members of trade unions, are in reality also merely low-paid temporaries. This is because although both men and women are paid dismal starting wages in large as well as small firms, these wages, which are withheld from them when young, are returned to those who toil loyally in the same firms until retirement age. But since women are effectively retired at around 30 when they marry or have children, they never receive the wages which were withheld, and the patriarchal requirement on them to parent their children converts them from nominally regular into effectively temporary workers. It is certainly no exaggeration to say that low-paid female labour has been the Japanese bourgeoisie's chief weapon in its struggle to build new internationally competitive industries after the Pacific War.

Of course not all temporary workers in Japan have been female. The million or so day labourers who congregate mainly in the slum districts of San'ya (in Tokyo) and Kamagasaki (in Osaka) are almost entirely male, and they are joined by many elderly men, who on retirement between 55–60, if they are lucky, are kept on in their previous jobs with heavily reduced pay and the insecure status of 'temporary'. Still, of no other capitalist country could one claim that over two-thirds of the floating reserve army of labour (low-paid insecure workers who move from job to job), which itself comprises a full half of the active working class, has been female (Steven, 1983, p. 193).

The second axis which divides the Japanese working class and secures a high rate of exploitation covers the vast network of subcontracting relations that exist between large and small firms in Japan. Particularly in manufacturing, the technical division of labour involved in the production process tends to coincide with an institutional division, so that different parts of a product are made by different firms, the largest of which assemble the components which are made by myriads of scattered subcontractors. The smallest of these undertake the most labour intensive tasks, sometimes receiving their orders from firms which are only marginally bigger than themselves and which are in turn working under contract from still larger firms. Often even the employers in the smaller 'child' companies are powerless in the face of the 'parent' companies' capacity to dictate contract prices, quality standards and delivery dates. Wages and conditions deteriorate to the levels of temporary workers as one moves down the hierarchy of subcontracting and re-subcontracting. Moreover, the smaller the firms, the harder it has been for workers to organise, and very few even in medium-sized companies belong to unions.

The system of subcontracting has been of comparable importance to the temporary labour system in ensuring compliance with appalling conditions by the bulk of the Japanese working class. In fact only about one-quarter of this entire class has been well paid, had regular jobs and enjoyed comprehensive social security. If half the working class has been in the floating reserve army of labour, at least another quarter has been excluded from the well-paid labour aristocracy in large firms through having to work in smaller ones which are in varying degrees victims of the subcontracting system. However, this second axis which divides the working class has not overlapped as closely with patriarchal relations as has the first. While women are more concentrated in small firms than men, at least 20 per cent of economically active males have toiled away as employees in such establishments.

THE GATHERING STORM

The first oil shock in late 1973 triggered a crisis which marked a turning point in postwar accumulation and a qualitative strengthening of the structures of exploitation and social control which had created the 'miracle'. Even though the liberalism which swept through all Japan's authoritarian institutions (family, factory, school and state) directly after the war had never been entirely extinguished, the only trace remaining of it in the period after 1973 was an ageing and disillusioned generation who had been either educated or politically active during that interlude.

The overlapping networks of social relations which had ensured capital's profitability before the oil crisis were no longer able to do so, and widespread bankruptcies, layoffs and losses of livelihood among the ordinary people occurred. But because in the preceding decades capital had concentrated on building up the heavy and raw material processing industries, whose social counterparts were the subcontracting and temporary labour systems, what was in reality a political problem presented itself as an ecological one: a constraint of nature. What was apparently a bottle-neck due to rising oil and raw material prices was essentially a breakdown of capital–labour relations.

It was to be expected that such a crisis would present itself as a conflict between Japan and the outside world. Ever since the Meiji Restoration, competition from foreign capital in one form or another, from the gunboat diplomacy of the 1860s through the free trade imperialism of the late nineteenth century and then the Second World War, has been a greater threat to Japanese capital than have the ordinary Japanese people. Although the latter have been heavily exploited, mechanisms of social control have been sufficiently stable for domestic class struggle to have been a less dynamic force shaping Japanese history than has imperialist rivalry. Even in the postwar period, after a brief interlude of intense class struggle when it seemed that the patterns of the past were being finally reversed, Japanese capital's weakness *vis-à-vis* American capital soon assumed greater weight than any revolutionary power the trade union movement might have displayed. Because local class relations have always been less *explosive* than international rivalries, the main forms of bourgeois organisation, such as the state, have been shaped by the need to be strong in dealing with foreigners rather than with the Japanese lower classes.

For example, the state has always given most of its organisational and financial resources to coordinating the interests of capital in the face of threats from abroad, whether in the form of either superior military might or greater competitive power in the production place. MITI (The Ministry of International Trade and Industry), which is undoubtedly the most important of present-day government institutions, grew hand in hand with pressures for society-wide organisation of the bourgeoisie to deal with the constant threat of American capital's greater productive power. Non-state institutions, such as the village community, the family or the company, played correspondingly greater roles in organising capital's affairs *vis-à-vis* the masses.

The result has been that even though the power of the Japanese state did not grow primarily out of the need to wage domestic class struggles, but to manage imperialist rivalries, a result was that the state could always intervene in class struggles and give the interests of the bourgeoisie a disarmingly nationalist flavour. The problems faced by the masses could always be presented as originating in America or Europe, and it would always appear appropriate to get in behind one's employers with whatever sacrifices they might demand, all for the good of the nation. Moreover, the extraordinary power of the Japanese state, even though it did not originate out of waging domestic class struggles, could increasingly be used for that purpose.

Because the catalyst in 1973 which triggered the slump in business profits was the rise in the price of oil and subsequently other raw materials, the real creators of profit and their struggles could easily be swept aside by claims that 'Japan' had the wrong industrial structure and was too dependent on imported raw materials. The nation's survival, it seemed, rested on scrapping the basic materials industries and building something more suited to the international market which had apparently sealed their fate.

The reality was quite different. There had been forces throughout the capitalist world, including Japan, which were in varying degrees undermining capital's profitability, and the hikes in oil and other raw material prices in the mid-1970s simply expressed the usual power of rentier capital (capital which owns natural resources) temporarily to displace the effects of these forces by claiming for itself an extra share (rent) of the total available surplus.

To deal with this situation, the Japanese bourgeoisie employed a three-pronged strategy, which it would repeat in the subsequent period of crisis a decade later. First, the industries which seemed to be the cause of the crisis were run down and new ones which appeared immune from the same problems were built. Second, the run-down industries were increasingly located abroad. And finally, there was a general attack on the working class, the overall aim of which was to revive profitability through raising the rate of exploitation.

All three prongs of this offensive had already been consciously woven together in the 1960s. In response to worker's struggles for higher wages, capital in the labour-intensive light industries began to move either into the up-and-coming heavy industries or into low-wage countries in Southeast Asia, the resulting loss of jobs helping it to intensify its grip on the workers who remained. The period 1968–73 thus saw the first of three major movements of Japanese capital into Southeast Asia. Domestically, these years represented the high point in the development of heavy industry, which symbolised the 'Japanese miracle' and brought unheard of wages and conditions to the male labour aristocracy. However, it also saw a massive influx into temporary and part-time jobs by mainly married women.

The 'solution' to the problems of the 1960s provided by this restructuring (with its industrial, global and domestic dimensions) was not unexpectedly the seed and eventually the dominant form of the next crisis. The fundamental socio-political contradictions of capitalism do not disappear whenever the ruling class gains the edge in the class struggle by restructuring the forms of its control. Moreover, if as a solution to one crisis capital finds it profitable to throw a large number of eggs into a particular industrial basket and then a new crisis concentrates itself around those industries, the latter can be far more acute than it might otherwise have been.

The 'oil shock' and the capacity of rentier capital to claim an extra share of the internationally available surplus was bound to affect most acutely of all industries with the greatest dependency on rentier capital, that is, the very raw-material processing industries into which the previous restructuring had been directed. Japanese capital was caught in a vicious circle, from which constant repetition of its three-pronged strategy would offer no real escape.

In Chapter 3, I discuss the predictable relocation abroad of much of the heavy industry which was linked to raw-material processing. Here I briefly review the other two aspects of the restructuring which the class struggle propelled in the latter half of the 1970s.

First, since it always appears that profitability stems from being in the 'right' industry, rather than from the exploitation of workers, scrap and build was applied respectively to the basic materials industries and to the machine industries. The latter comprised three broad types of machinery and equipment – general, transport and electrical

Table 1.1   Labour productivity and wage costs in Japan and the US, by
manufacturing industry, 1985 (US = 100)

	Labour productivity	*Wage costs* $1 = ¥238.54	$1 = ¥140
Manufacturing average	104	68	116
General machinery	290	28	48
Ceramics	202	32	54
Transport machinery	178	43	74
Rubber	153	47	79
Electrical machinery	144	47	79
Textiles	135	60	102
Metallic products	118	47	81
Leather products	105	82	140
Iron and steel	103	72	123
Petroleum products	97	74	126
Chemicals	80	80	136
Pulp and paper	69	81	139
Non-ferrous metals	53	125	212
Foodstuffs	46	166	284
Clothing	18	327	558

Source: Rōdōshō, 1987b, sankō shiryō [reference materials]: p. 124.

– and the sign of their potential profitability was their growing
international competitiveness from the mid-1970s.

The introduction of new technologies and other rationalisations of
production, which were linked to and which exploited an intensification of the temporary labour and subcontracting systems, created a
competitive power for Japanese capital in the machine industries
which surpassed that of its imperialist rivals. Among the major
powers, only the Japanese ruling class managed to keep wage costs
from rising at all in the years 1975–80 (Nihon ginkō chōsakyoku,
1986, pp. 23–4, 145–6). Table 1.1 shows that by 1985 labour productivity in Japan tended to be higher than in America in the
machinery related industries, but lower in the raw material related
ones. At 1985 exchange rates, Japanese capital had an almost across-
the-board advantage over American capital.

In November 1986 the Japanese Ministry of Labour attempted to
quantify the difference in living standards between American and
Japanese workers. It found that the cost of living (the same basket of
consumer goods, excluding the cost of land, houses and social security) was increasingly higher in Japan than in America and West
Germany. An OECD study confirmed that in 1987 the cost of living

in Japan remained 1.48 times higher than in the US. However, by the end of 1986 the rise of the yen (to ¥156 to the $) had translated into money wages in manufacturing (Labour Ministry estimates) which were only marginally higher (1.1 times) in the US than Japan, so that US real wages were 1.64 times Japanese real wages. If one included the cost of land and social security, the difference would be even greater. For example, in Tokyo more than eight times a worker's annual income is needed to buy a condominium, while in New York a house can be bought for just over three times a worker's annual income (*NKS*, 26 July 1987, p. 8; *JEJ*, 24 September 1988, p. 8; 26 November 1988, p. 11).

The Reagan administration's monetarist solution to the American external deficit, forcing down the value of the dollar, had a disastrous effect on the Japanese working class. By reducing the dollar outlays needed to employ American workers, it made investment in the US increasingly more attractive than in Japan. Japanese employers thus once again forced down wages which in real terms were already not much more than half those in America. According to Dai-Ichi-Kangyō Bank, by 1986 wage costs in the US had become much cheaper for all industries except cars. For every one dollar of wage costs in America, Japanese employers in iron and steel and chemicals had to pay ¥200–210, those in precision instruments, general machines and electrical machines ¥180–190, while those in the motor vehicle industry paid only ¥140, which was below the exchange rate at the time (Kudō, 1987, p. 35).

FROM UNDERCONSUMPTION TO EXPORT-LED GROWTH

The minimal spending power of the bulk of Japanese workers was bound, sooner or later, to set limits to the growth of the consumer goods branches of the booming machinery industries. Capital thus naturally turned to export-led growth, which became a national panacea. Growing proportions of the machine industries' production were exported and growing proportions of exports came from these industries. For example, the proportion of motor vehicles exported rose from 20.6 per cent in 1970 to 40.0 per cent in 1974 and 54 per cent in 1980, while the share of motor cars in total exports increased from 6.9 per cent in 1970 to 12.4 per cent in 1980 (Tsūshō sangyōshō, 1987a, pp. 242, 252; 1987b, p. 822; Steven, 1983, p. 246). Table 1.2 shows the rising export dependencies in 1974–84 of some of the main

Table 1.2   Export ratios* of major outputs of machine industry, 1974–84

	1974	1984
Automobiles	43.9	56.3
Colour TVs	31.3	62.2
Stereos	42.9	75.3
Watches	57.9	84.1
Cameras	54.3	78.9

* percentage of total volume exported.
Source: *Industria*, July 1987, p. 12.

Table 1.3   Composition of Japan's commodity exports, 1960–85

	1960	1970	1975	1980	1985
Textiles	30.2	12.5	6.7	4.9	3.6
Chemicals	4.5	6.4	7.0	5.2	4.4
Metals and metal products	14.0	19.7	22.4	16.4	10.5
Machinery and equipment	22.8	46.3	53.8	62.8	71.8
Others	28.5	15.1	10.1	10.7	9.7

Source: Ministry of International Trade and Industry (MITI), 1987, pp. 148–9.

outputs of the machine industries.

On the other hand, the shares in manufacturing production and exports of the heavy and basic materials industries declined. But because this meant the destruction of jobs, some attempt was made by the state and employers to adjust the pace of the decline to the capacity of the new industries to take on the displaced workers. The changing shares of total employment absorbed by the respective manufacturing industries therefore reflected a more gradual restructuring than did their shares of output and exports. Table 1.3 illustrates the restructuring process with reference to commodity exports over the period 1960–85.

The most rapid industrial restructuring took place in 1975–80. Machinery doubled its share of equipment investment and considerably raised its share of exports, while the metals industry lost half its share of exports and the chemicals and iron and steel industries half their shares of equipment investment. The extent of capital's reliance on the machine industry massively exceeded its previous reliance on the basic materials industries, and any interruption to profit making in it could be expected to have unprecedented repercussions. Once again, as we see below, the solution to one crisis bore the seeds of the next.

In comparison with the attacks on the working class which started in the next period, the social implications of the restructuring in 1974–80 were relatively unspectacular. But there were significant job losses and cuts in living standards, as well as extensions of the temporary labour and subcontracting systems. In 1974–78 fully 170 000 jobs were destroyed in the rationalisation programmes of the top 100 firms alone, while in large firms (with over 500 operatives) in a slightly longer period (1974–79) the number was close to a million (Steven, 1983, pp. 249, 258–9). And although average real wages did rise a small amount in 1974–78, they fell after that. More important, the meagre earnings of the growing numbers of part-timers and other irregular workers whom employers used to cut costs concentrated the drop in living standards around the reserve army of labour. Finally, monopoly capital relied increasingly on the subcontracting system, so that the numbers and importance of the small component-making firms, instead of decreasing as might otherwise be expected, actually rose. Japanese society as a whole became much more rigid, and many people spoke of a revival of prewar authoritarianism.

MOUNTING CRISIS, 1981–87

If the first oil shock in late 1973 was the catalyst which triggered the restructuring of 1974–78, then the second in late 1978 confirmed for Japanese capital that the basic materials industries had to be scrapped in favour of the booming machine industries. The effect on corporate profitability and on the balance of payments of high-priced raw materials was drummed home a second time. But in the context of a reduced dependence on the offending industries and the fall in the oil price which soon followed, the consequences were not as disruptive as in 1973. The new export-led growth strategy soon began to pay dividends. From a $10.7 billion current account deficit in 1980, Japan scored a $8.7 billion surplus in 1981, which increased by leaps and bounds each year until it reached $46 billion in 1985 and $82 billion in 1986. Table 1.4 shows that the new strategy did not simply produce favourable external balances: it meant an overall revival of capital accumulation, as revealed by the relatively high rates of

Table 1.4   Real GNP growth and Current Account balances, 1970–86

	GNP growth %	Current account ($ million)	Current account (¥ billion)	Exchange rate ¥ per $
1970	9.5	437	157	360.00
1971	4.3	4 307	1 483	347.83
1972	8.5	5 120	1 577	303.08
1973	7.9	−1 384	−373	272.21
1974	−1.4	−6 574	−1 869	292.06
1975	2.7	−2 110	−625	296.85
1976	4.8	2 426	705	296.49
1977	5.3	9 686	2 516	268.32
1978	5.2	18 200	3 828	210.11
1979	5.3	−7 640	−1 714	219.47
1980	4.3	−10 721	−2 613	226.74
1981	3.7	8 740	2 005	220.54
1982	3.1	6 900	1 776	249.07
1983	3.2	20 534	4 894	237.61
1984	5.1	33 611	8 004	237.52
1985	4.7	46 099	10 871	238.53
1986	2.5	82 743	13 739	168.03
1987	4.9	79 706	11 578	144.60

Source: MITI, 1987, pp. 14, 161; Tsūshō sangyōshō, 1987b, pp. 798–9. 1988a, pp. 258, 262, 272.

growth of GNP under the emerging structure.

A lot of money could be made producing machinery cheaply in Japan and selling it in the lucrative markets of the advanced countries in Europe and America. In 1983–85 from 50–75 per cent of the increase in mining and manufacturing production stemmed from export demand (*NKS*, 18 August 1987, evening edition, p. 3). And tight social control enabled employers to introduce new technologies which affected mainly the jobs and conditions of non-regular workers. Unions in large private companies actually often helped employers single out old, infirm, or rebellious workers for redundancy when this was required, and the low wages of most manufacturing employees guaranteed that rising labour productivity translated into continually falling unit labour costs.

This 'second Japanese miracle' was as firmly based on the unique power capital possesses over labour in Japan as was the first, and the accumulation it made possible further strengthened the hold of capital and the growing authoritarianism of Japanese society. The large companies emerged prominently among the world's top twenty,

Japan's New Imperialism

Table 1.5   Japan's exports, 1985–87

	Composition (%)			Value ($ million)		
	1985	1986	1987	1985	1986	1987
Foodstuffs	0.8	0.7	0.7	1 316	1 476	1 546
Textiles	3.6	3.3	3.0	6 263	6 874	6 917
Chemicals	4.4	4.5	5.1	7 698	9 484	11 662
Non-metallic minerals	1.2	1.1	1.1	2 147	2 362	2 523
Metals	10.6	8.7	7.9	18 491	18 183	18 018
Iron and steel	7.8	6.1	5.5	13 556	12 706	12 610
Machinery	71.8	74.1	74.6	126 179	155 027	171 077
General	16.8	18.3	19.5	29 537	38 381	44 755
Motors	2.2	2.4	2.6	3 789	4 940	5 904
Office machines	4.4	5.4	6.3	7 785	11 305	14 392
Electrical	22.2	17.0	17.8	38 931	35 519	40 883
Heavy electrical	1.2	1.2	1.2	2 056	2 453	2 724
TV receivers	1.5	0.8	0.6	2 625	1 727	1 422
Radio receivers	1.5	1.3	1.1	2 654	2 756	2 464
Tape recorders	4.8	4.7	3.7	8 440	9 910	8 406
Semi-conductors	2.7	3.0	3.6	4 753	6 342	8 312
Transport	28.0	28.4	27.9	49 149	59 426	63 925
Motor vehicles	19.5	20.4	19.6	34 377	42 676	44 942
Motor cycles	1.2	1.0	0.8	2 092	2 064	1 884
Ships	3.4	2.3	1.9	5 929	4 879	4 360
Precision	4.9	5.9	6.0	8 561	12 408	13 723
Scientific/optic	3.9	4.1	4.1	6 831	8 509	9 448
Other	7.7	7.5	7.6	13 544	15 745	17 480
TOTAL	100.0	100.0	100.0	175 638	209 151	229 221
(Total value in ¥ billion)				41 956	35 290	33 315

Source: Tsūshō sangyōshō, 1987a, pp. 310–11; 1988a, pp. 262–3.

with Toyota occupying twelfth position in 1986 in terms of sales and, among non-American companies, earning a profit second only to Royal Dutch Shell. Other companies in this elite group were also from the export-based machine industries: Matsushita Electric Industrial and Hitachi Ltd in fifteenth and nineteenth positions respectively (*NKS*, 16 July 1987, p. 7). Since capital always moves to where profits are greatest, the restructuring process received a band-wagon effect and produced a new vulnerability. Table 1.5 shows that by 1985 three-quarters of Japan's exports were from the machine industries. Apart from ships and certain consumer goods which Japan increasingly exports via its bases in the Asian NICs, the shares of the machine industries in total exports continued to increase even in 1985–87 in spite of the high yen (from 71.8 per cent to 74.6 per cent). We see in the next chapter that these are the very industries whose major corporations are spearheading the new imperialism.

Table 1.6   Markets for Japan's machinery exports, 1985–86 (%)

	North America			Western Europe			Southeast Asia		
	1985	1986	1987	1985	1986	1987	1985	1986	1987
Total	44.4	46.2	43.3	15.7	19.2	21.6	14.9	15.6	18.8
General	36.9	38.1	38.1	14.9	18.5	20.3	20.6	21.0	24.9
Electrical	41.0	39.8	35.4	17.6	20.7	22.5	19.8	22.5	26.7
Transport	52.1	57.3	53.8	12.7	16.6	20.1	7.1	6.5	8.1
Motor vehicles	59.9	64.9	60.7	12.5	17.3	21.8	4.9	3.5	4.6
Precision	40.8	41.2	40.1	27.0	30.1	30.5	18.0	17.2	18.9

Source: Compiled from Tsūshō sangyōshō, 1987b–1988b.

The industrial restructuring of the production process into the machine industries was thus accompanied by a locational restructuring of the circulation process into world markets, particularly those of the advanced capitalist countries where high wages seemed to provide limitless demand. Only by doing this could Japanese capital take full advantage of the productive power which its hold over the working class provided. In its obsession for short-term profits, Japanese capital was blind to the danger of rushing headlong into such heavy dependence on the market of the world's leading imperialist power, the US. Table 1.6 shows that by 1985 44.4 per cent of the entire machine industry's overseas sales were in North American (41.6 per cent were in the US) with a further 15.7 per cent in Western Europe. Two years later, the North American share fell by only 1 percentage point, but the European share soared by almost 6 percentage points and that of Southeast Asia by almost 4. We see later how Japan has started redirecting its exports to North America via Southeast Asia.

It was one thing to rely heavily on the US for food and raw material supplies in the immediate postwar period, since this did not threaten the interests of American capital, but quite another to storm into the latter's backyard and gobble up its diminishing market. This threat to the already crisis-ridden US system had as its counterpart in Japan an unprecedented industrial specialisation, an unprecedented dependence on export markets and an unprecedented dependence on the American market. There was also a qualitative difference between the continual bickering in the 1960s and 1970s over 'excessive' textile and TV exports, in which Japan's competitive advantage posed no overall threat to American capital, and the trade friction which began in the early 1980s over semi-conductors and motor vehicles on which the US claim to world technical superiority rested heavily. Moreover, by the 1980s American labour had also more fully felt the effect on jobs of Japan's export drive and added its voice to the demands for protectionism.

GROWING CONFLICT WITH THE US

Although there were warnings of the conflicts to come in the currency crisis of 1978, when the yen soared above the value of 200 for about six months, these were not seriously heeded at the time because the US external deficit was not yet chronic and because the second oil shock undermined the strength of the yen. But by 1981 both of these blinding factors had been eroded, and in the face of a large increase in its trading surplus with the US, Japanese capital accepted voluntary limits on the export of automobiles.

However, neither this nor similar attempts in the coming years to reverse the forces which had been building up since the 1970s made much difference. Partly because of the growing deindustrialisation of America as a result of mounting US imperialism, and partly because of the close links between the military and such industry as remained, the competitive power of capital in the US in consumer goods fell behind that of Japan. The latter had not yet internationalised to anything like the same degree and had no military bureaucracy to shield it from the incessant pressures of competition to revolutionise its techniques. Among the technically advanced industries, it was only in space, aircraft and communications that US capital retained its lead, whereas in all the non-military consumer-goods industries Japanese capital moved ahead. By 1985 the situation had deteriorated to point of inevitable conflict. Following the rise of the yen its manifestations included the punitive tariff on Japanese semi-conductors in early 1987, the hysteria in the US in June and July over Toshiba's sale of silent motor technology to the Soviet Union and the 'Japan bashing' revealed in the Omnibus Trade Bill which both Houses of Congress passed at that time with almost unprecedented majorities. Table 1.7 shows how from the mid-1980s the deficit with Japan comprised a gradually increasing proportion of the total American deficit.

It is important not to be deceived by the moralism both sides have used in their propaganda war, since the main purpose has been to win nationalist support from their working classes for policies for which the latter are paying the price. As we see in Chapter 4, at the highest

Table 1.7   The US Trade Deficit with Japan, 1981–87

Year	Total US trade deficit ($ million)	With Japan $ million	share (%)	With Asian NICs $ million	share (%)
1981	39 700	18 100	45.6	7 000	17.6
1982	38 443	18 965	49.3	8 205	21.3
1983	64 240	21 665	33.7	12 647	19.7
1984	122 389	36 796	30.1	21 412	17.5
1985	133 648	49 749	37.2	24 962	18.7
1986	156 156	58 575	37.5	30 816	19.7
1987	171 216	59 825	34.9	37 745	22.0

Source: Tsūshō sangyōshō, 1988a, pp. 248–9, *FEER*, 29 September 1988, p. 25.

level of the giant corporations, there is a growing cooperation between Japanese and American capital. The real danger in the current situation is that the use of nationalism as a weapon in domestic class struggles might generate political forces which could transform inter-imperialist rivalry into something much worse. Racism is one of the ugliest social forces in both countries, and the rhetoric on both sides has at times fed that to explosive levels.

One must remember that American imperialism has been dominant for so long now that even its representatives see the rules of the game, not as reflecting the interests of the power that made them, but as the very embodiment of fairness and justice. When Japanese capital operates under slightly different rules, for example, by cutting prices in the early stages of a competitive struggle in order to win market share, as has occurred on numerous occasions but most recently over semi-conductors, this presents itself as the highly 'immoral' practice of 'dumping'. It was quite natural for the Japanese electronics firms to employ this strategy, since as producers of many other products as well as semi-conductors, they could easily absorb the costs of their loss leading tactic in that industry. It was equally natural that American companies would call 'foul', since they are all specialist companies with no sidelines to use as shields against temporary setbacks.

Although growing inter-imperialist rivalry between Japan and the US (and to a lesser extent the EC) manifests itself mainly over questions of 'fair' trade and market access, it stems most fundamentally from competition in the production place. This does not mean that 'unfair' trading practices are not used as weapons in this rivalry.

The list of these is almost endless, and over Japan's exports to the US include: textiles since 1962, iron and steel since 1966 (also with the EC since 1972), TVs from 1968 to 1980 (and then with the EC after 1983), machine tools since 1978 (with the EC since 1981), cars since 1981 (with the EC since 1983 when VTRs also entered that dispute) and of semi-conductors since 1985. Dumping charges have become commonplace, with the US bringing no fewer than seven in the first six months of 1988 alone, over such things as floppy disks, digital lead-out systems, bearings and thermostats. A dispute currently raging in Europe is over the French claim that Nissan cars from Britain with only 60 per cent local content are Japanese 'screwdriver' imports (assembled from Japanese parts) and that EC dumping duties should apply to them.

Strong US demands for fair access to the Japanese market have been more recent: over agricultural products, car parts and indirect taxes since 1985 (over sake taxes and whisky with the EC since 1986), since 1987 over bidding for construction contracts in general and public works projects such as the new Kansai International Airport in particular, over finance since 1987 (with both the EC and the US) and over rice since 1988.

It is true that the Japanese distribution system is notoriously labyrinthine, but this is more a product of Japanese history than a move against the US and Europe. Certain problems might well be solved by deregulating some of the 39 legal codes imposed on retailers, but many peculiarities will remain. But it is unlikely that many of the far-reaching recommendations of a December 1988 government report on deregulation of the retail industry will actually be implemented (Tsūshō sangyōshō, 1988a, pp. 112–24; *NKS*, 24 August 1988, p. 3; 11 October 1988, p. 5; 5 November 1988, p. 8; *JEJ*, 9 July 1988, pp. 1, 4; 26 November 1988; 3 December 1988, p. 5; *The Economist*, 8 October 1988, pp. 63–6).

The domestic political costs of clearing up the Japanese distri-bution system are likely to be too great, because they would involve radically altering the shares of the national product commanded by capital and labour. Although one might have expected the rise of the yen to put an end to underconsumptionism in Japan through cheaper imports, one of the striking features of *endaka* is that the prices of imported consumer goods have hardly fallen at all, not to mention the prices of domestic goods that rely heavily on imports. The problem even prompted a special Economic Planning Agency report. The main reason is that capital in the distribution system, which is indeed a 'non-tariff barrier', has absorbed the gains in higher profits. As the *Economist* pointed out:

> The law has not only protected small shopkeepers but also pro-longed the life of the large number of small and inefficient whole-salers needed to service them. On average, a product in Japan passes through seven pairs of hands between manufacturer and customer, compared with about three pairs in Britain. The result is Japan's famously high consumer prices (13 August 1988, p. 57).

While a bit of *gaiatsu* (outside pressure) and help from the country's large retailers (the top 200 account for only 27 per cent of sales compared to 25 per cent for the top four in Britain) could add weight to the class struggle needed to wrest this surplus from capital, Japanese labour is too weak to play its part. One of capital's weapons in the struggle is to encourage the belief that imported goods are more expensive because they are better, so that price cuts often do reduce sales. This ideology is being modified a bit now as cheap imports from Asia complement luxury imports from Europe and America. Far from conceding the gains of the higher yen to the working class, capital in the distribution system appropriated the surplus and then recycled it elsewhere, including into speculative activities which further bid up the prices of major wage goods, such as housing (*JEJ*, 2 July 1988, p. 14; 17 September 1988, p. 1).

Rather than much progress being made on this front, the trade dispute is being tackled more and more directly in the conflict over what is called intellectual property and technology trade, which still runs almost four to one in favour of the US. Since the very essence of capital's productive power lies in the technologies workers are given to use, the rivalry between Japan and the US was bound to focus on science and technology.

In America a clear distinction is made between these two, science involving basic research, which is heavily state funded and openly practiced in a number of institutions, and technology involving its application in industry, often in private corporations which patent it as soon as it is discovered. The Japanese have not, until recently, accepted this distinction, since in Japan scientific research facilities are so poor that very little basic research is carried out, whereas the bulk of what is called R&D (research and development) is really the application by private corporations of scientific knowledge from America to their production processes. The Americans are now complaining that because Japanese capital gets a free ride on American science it can put all its energy into applied technology and increasingly steal a march on American capital. The US thus wants Japan to share the burden of scientific research as well as to get access to Japanese technology in the private sector, or she will increasingly exclude Japanese nationals from American research institutions (*JEJ*, 16 January 1988, p. 2, 16 April 1988, p. 5; 17 September 1988, p. 14).

Although there is a myth that Japanese capital is technically more innovative than western capital, the former has thus far mainly absorbed and adapted rather than created new technology. For example, government appropriations for science and technology, which were about $11 billion in 1987, are still concentrated in energy development, particularly nuclear energy ($2.35 billion), and aerospace, while MITI's Research and Development Project on Basic Technologies for Future Industries, which deals with new materials, biotechnology and future electronics, received a paltry $40 million (*Look Japan*, April 1987, pp. 20–1). Of course a lot of innovation can be involved in adapting technologies to the production place, and this research is carried out by corporations rather than by government, although sometimes with government assistance. For example, five companies are currently pooling their research and development resources and participating in a government project to make robots which do submarine oil drilling (*JEI*, 1 August 1987, p. 18).

The most sensitive area is memory chips, for which the US relies heavily on Japan and in which the latter is ahead in thirteen technologies and behind in only five. The Japanese are also ahead in most production and processing technologies apart from computer software, such as mechatronics and high precision work. In opto-electronic devices, which are likely to replace electronic ones (since light travels faster than electricity), the Japanese are also clear leaders. The US remain ahead in the life sciences, electronics (except opto-electronics) and substances and materials (*FEER*, 31 March 1988, pp. 58–65).

Among the main weapons with which the battle is being fought are the two countries' totally different patent laws. For example, in the US the patent goes to the first to invent, while in Japan (and Europe) to the first to file; in the US the application is not made public until the patent is granted, while in Japan it is made public after eighteen months and any competitor can review it; in the US it takes about two and a half years for the patent to be granted, while in Japan it takes five. Although there seems to be some commitment to harmonise the different systems, little progress has actually been made. The US is claiming great urgency saying that Toshiba's alleged violation of COCOM proved that Japan cannot be trusted with sensitive technologies. And so the battle rages on, with little progress to date. Not much was resolved at the Montreal mid-term meeting of the Uruguay round of GATT talks in December 1988 (*JEJ*, 23 July 1988, p. 1; 27 August 1988, p. 1; 3 December 1988, p. 2; 17 December 1988, p. 17; *FEER*, 22 December 1988, pp. 44–5).

The most damaging blow struck by either side so far has been the American Omnibus Trade Act, signed into law by Reagan on 23 August 1988, much of which is aimed right at Japan. Super Article 301 allows retaliation against countries that run trade surpluses through 'unfair trade practices'. The Act provides for mandatory sanctions against the Toshiba group, it allows goods produced in the US by foreign firms to be targets of dumping charges, and it permits charges without evidence of lost business to be filed with the ITC (International Trade Commission), so that imports of products violating US patent laws can be banned (*JEJ*, 3 September 1988, p. 3; 13 August 1988, pp. 1, 4; *FEER*, 18 August 1988, pp. 93–4).

THE POLITICS OF EXCHANGE RATE ADJUSTMENTS

American capital can use weapons against Japanese capital which command widespread support from the other imperialist powers. One of these was its monetarist strategy to reduce its deficit with Japan by shifting much of the burden from its own to the Japanese working class. The spectacular rise of the yen, following the 'G5' agreement (among the finance ministers of the five major powers on 22 September 1985) that adjustment of the exchange rate should receive the highest priority, had just this effect.

It is important to understand how and why this was so. Before the US suspended the convertibility of the dollar into gold, when exchange rates were relatively fixed (for example, ¥360 to the dollar from 1953 to 1970), the superior productive power of the leading capitalist powers resulted in trade surpluses which created vicious circles. The deficit countries eventually had to pay in gold or some other commodity, which further weakened their productive power and strengthened that of the imperialist powers. Contrary to monetarist theory, prices in the advanced country only rise if the gold transferred is not accumulated in further productive capacity. Under the gold standard, which the dominant powers normally have an interest in maintaining, trade surpluses siphon resources from defaulting countries, allow further accumulation in the imperialist countries and further consolidate their dominance. And the more wealth that concentrates in the advanced countries, the more concessions can be made to their workers, so that eventually the latter can achieve living standards which give them a stake in imperialism.

Until around 1970 American imperialism benefited in this way from its superior productive power, but its military expenditures abroad had required such a level of borrowing that it could no longer allow the holders of that debt freely to withdraw gold from the country. Henceforth, it would cover its debt with paper dollars, and then allow these to devalue against foreign currencies if need be. But under no circumstances did American imperialism intend to allow a substantial movement of resources out of the country.

Devaluations do, of course, result in more commodities than before leaving the country for any given quantity entering it. But when this result is achieved via exchange rate adjustment rather than the movement of gold, both the dynamic effects as well as the costs borne by the various classes are different. The movement of gold does not affect the competitiveness of capital in the dominant country and there is no threat to the jobs or living standards of its working class. However, in the deficit country, capital must force on its workers far worse conditions, otherwise its technical backwardness keeps it permanently uncompetitive.

However, when the currency of a deficit county is devalued, the superior competitive power of capital in the advanced country is momentarily blocked. Because its total sales in the country which devalued can fall, the jobs and living standards of its working class might be threatened, since it must now raise productivity if it is to cut prices sufficiently to recover its lost sales. Exchange rate adjustment therefore gives the ruling class in the deficit country a chance to break out of the vicious circle, and to initiate or revive capital accumulation. Since inflation undermines the advantage received from the devaluation, strict wage controls must of course be imposed.

Although currency adjustment might only temporarily reduce the competitive power of advanced capital, it can provide a sufficient breathing space for capital in the deficit country to revive accumulation. It has been at least a facilitating factor in the massive movement of capital from advanced to underdeveloped countries since 1970, particularly of American capital into Latin America. The accumulation of debt by the US thus became all the more inevitable, because the resulting deindustrialisation of America meant that the productive power of US capital would express itself less in exports from the US and more in exports to the US from countries where this capital had located itself. A system of flexible exchange rates thus came to be championed by the US, whose deficit made its situation in some respects similar to that of its own neo-colonies.

Like capital in the underdeveloped world, US capital has an interest in exchange rate adjustment to deal with its deficit with countries such as Japan, South Korea and Taiwan. But in all of them, the living standards of workers are much lower than those in America. US capital thus hopes that devaluations can sufficiently lower the dollar price of American labour to revive both accumulation and US technical superiority in enough industries to forestall the need to slash real wages. By the end of 1987, money wages in most industries in America were below those in Japan.

An exchange rate which allows both better living standards and job opportunities in America than in Japan is indeed a happy situation to defend, although there will be tremendous pressure on these living standards if inflation is not to gobble up the price advantage so far gained. Since more than half of the eight million new jobs created during the Reagan administration's 'recovery' have paid less than $7000 a year (*South*, 4 July 1987, p. 20), the American ruling class might well succeed in keeping wages within the required limits.

It might, however, take a long time for a such a monetarist policy to rectify the Japan-US trade imbalance, which has causes other than relative prices. For example, Japan's import bill dropped almost 30 per cent in the first half of 1986, partly because of the high yen but partly because of the fall in oil prices (from $28.10 a barrel in 1985 to $16.50 in January to October 1986). Moreover, in spite of a decline in yen-denominated exports to the US in the same period, the revaluation caused the dollar denominated figure to rise by over 20 per cent. The US has become dependent on a large number of Japanese (and other) imports. Some products, such as compact disk players and VTR equipment, are not even made by American companies, while others, like motor cars and steel, are already subject to export quotas. This import dependence has a great deal to do with the deindustrialisation of America resulting from its own foreign investments.

Although in mid-1987 the rise of the yen had cut Japan's trade surplus, and although six months later the US external (but not internal) deficit also showed signs of a firm turnaround, by the end of 1988 the improvements had slowed. Japan's exports began to surge ahead once again, although the highest increases were to Asia and the EC. And though exports to the US only grew marginally, American imports from the NICs soared. In 1985 the latter were equal to 57 per cent of US imports from Japan, but in 1987 the proportion rose to a record 68 per cent and then to 74 per cent in May–June 1988. All that the currency readjustment seemed to have achieved was to redirect Japanese exports to the US via the NICs. This triangular pattern of trade is further analysed in the Conclusion (*NKS*, 4 November 1988, p. 9; 10 November 1988, p. 9; *JEJ*, 12 September 1987, p. 3; 15 October 1988, p. 14; *FEER*, 29 September 1988, p. 25).

To revive capital accumulation in the US to the degree that can correct the deficit will take, not simply radical exchange rate adjustments, but a rate of exploitation of the American working class which is much closer to that of the working classes in the countries from which the imports are coming – Japan, South Korea and Taiwan – either by slashing wages or by the monumental introduction of new technology. Whether either can be achieved depends on the course of the class struggles in the countries concerned.

Apart from its distortion of relative wages, the rise of the yen translated directly into dollar prices of Japanese goods which were 50 per cent higher than those which prevailed in 1985. Since the yen also appreciated against most other currencies as well, the trade-weighted average effective exchange rate adjustment was 37.4 per cent. In the absence of a comparable rate of inflation in the countries to which Japanese companies exported, such a price hike would have had an acute effect on sales. So the immediate response of Japanese companies was as much as possible to refrain from raising export prices, in the hope that sooner or later they might find some way to preserve their profitability through cutting costs.

But it was not possible to prevent heavy falls in sales and profitability, or a full-blown recession, known as the *endaka fukyō* (high yen recession). This recession was characterised by all the normal phenomena one has come to expect: bankruptcies, layoffs, wage cuts, restructuring and overseas investment.

2 The High Yen Crisis

The overall response of Japanese exporters to the rise of the yen was to cut costs rather than raise overseas prices. In fiscal 1986, declining raw material (particularly oil) prices enabled them to recover a full 60 per cent of lost revenue, and they got back about 50 per cent of similar revenue in fiscal 1987. Through a variety of other cost cutting measures, most of which were at the expense of their workers, they managed to limit the fall in the volume of their exports in 1986 to a mere 3.2 per cent. As far as the capitalist class was concerned, the *endaka fukyō* bottomed in the last quarter of fiscal 1986, and production was once again on the rise in 1987 (*JEJ*, 15 August 1987, p. 11; Keizai kikakuchō, 1987a–1988a, p. 442).

As far as the working class is concerned, the real depression is only beginning, because capital's strategy for solving the trade imbalance with the US is clearly not to raise wages and shift into industries for which workers provide the market, but to persist in the production of machinery for export to the US and the EC, and more and more via third countries, particularly in Asia. This means that the *endaka fukyō*, brief as it was for capital, signalled an historical turning point for labour. The accelerated outflow of capital into imperialist ventures abroad is causing the *kūdōka* (hollowing out) of Japanese industry, that is, the deindustrialisation of Japan (Aoki, 1987). At least one third of the Japanese people can expect to be acutely threatened by this process, which has already caused mounting unemployment and deepening poverty in Europe and America. Since capital's response to the recession grew out of the profitability signals it received in the various industries, it is important to examine these in some detail.

UNEVEN PROFITABILITY: INDUSTRIAL OVERVIEW

The high yen did not affect the profitability of capital in all industries to the same degree. The loss of export revenues in fiscal 1986 was about ¥7 trillion, which increased to about ¥9 trillion after the effects of the resulting industrial slowdown had worked themselves out. On the other hand, capital's import bill fell from ¥31 trillion to ¥21 trillion, so that the end result was probably a small overall *gain* of about ¥1 trillion (Takeuchi, *et al.*, 1987, pp. 7–8; Tsūshō sangyōshō, 1987a, pp. 310–13). However, the effects of the yen's rise were unevenly distributed among capitalists in the two main groups of industries. Where some 20–30 per cent of output was exported, that is, among the machinery industries, the losses were the greatest, whereas the basic materials importing industries gained most through a 20–30 per cent fall in their costs: of crude petroleum, metals, natural gas, hides, fertilisers and agricultural products. Apart from agriculture, the domestic procurement of these materials is minimal, and their importation exerted very little influence on local activity.

A survey carried out by *Nihon Keizai Shinbun* in March 1987 of 980 quoted companies (excluding finance) showed how the profitability of the two groups of industries had moved in opposite directions in fiscal 1986.[1] From 38–48 per cent declines in consolidated profits were the norm in the machinery industries, while, apart from iron and steel, the basic materials industries all registered increases. A few examples are worth elaborating.

Import-Using Industries: Profit Rise

Electric power's 30 per cent profit increase resulted from both the rise of the yen as well as the fall in oil prices, and one company, Chubu Electric Power, achieved a record 56 per cent rise. However, in 1987 and 1988 other factors, such as a cut in power prices, ended the bonanza. Profits in the pulp and paper industry rose by up to 50 per cent in 1986, with five of the big eight companies posting records the next year (*NKS*, 24 October 1987, pp. 1, 8, 13; *JEJ*, 11 June 1988, p. 16).

Chemicals registered an approximately 10 per cent rise in 1986 but even better performances in 1987 and 1988, mainly because of increased demand from the Asian NICs and a series of plant accidents in the US. Some ethylene plants which had been idled as a result of the industry's overall decline since 1973 were even revived. The collapse of oil prices in October 1988 to a 26 month low ($10.81 a barrel) gave a renewed boost to the petrochemical industry, and to Japan's trade surplus: a $3 fall pushes the surplus up by $4 billion (*JEJ*, 13 February 1988, p. 20; 18 June 1988, pp. 6, 19; 15 October 1988, p. 2; *NKS*, 8 November 1988, p. 1).

Unproductive Industries: Windfall Profits

Because many Japanese capitalists put their money into unproductive investments following the rise of the yen rather than into plant and equipment, they bid up land prices massively and gave a 30 per cent increase in consolidated profits to real estate companies. In fiscal 1986 bank loans for land ballooned by 36.2 per cent and land prices in central Tokyo rose by 76.8 per cent for residential areas and 76.2 per cent for commercial areas. Only about 30 per cent of transactions were based on actual demand, the rest representing speculative investments for resale. Today, the value of land in Japan is 3.3 times GNP, compared with the US where land is worth 70 per cent of GNP (*FEER*, 9 July 1987, p. 58; 9 June 1988, pp. 44–5; *JEJ*, 25 June 1988, p. 32; 29 October 1988, p. 13; 1 August 1987, pp. 1, 5; 19 March 1988, pp. 1, 5; *TBT*, July 1987, p. 23).

The biggest gains in fiscal 1986 were made in the financial sector: by banks, trust banks, insurance companies, life assurance firms and above all share brokers. The top 50 consolidated profit earners in 1986 saw the four major sharebrokers and leading banks all in prominent positions. Only twelve manufacturing firms were in the top 50 (*NKS*, 31 May 1987, p. 1).

The importance of *zaiteku* (fund management) in total corporate profitability is understated by what the unproductive industries themselves declare. Quite a few giant manufacturing companies are big players in the *zaiteku* stakes, and for some these non-operating profits concealed large operating deficits. For example, Nissan's huge operating loss in fiscal 1986 was only transformed into a consolidated profit which kept it in the top 50 because of its second largest *zaiteku* profit of $1 billion. Other manufacturing firms in this group were Toyota (first for the eighth year running), Matsushita (third), Sony (fifth), Sharp (sixth) and Sanyo (tenth). The ratio of interest and dividends received to total pretax profits of all listed firms (excluding finance) soared from 37.5 per cent in the half year October 1984–March 1985 to 50.2 per cent in the period April–September 1986 (*BT*, August 1987, p. 23; *JEJ*, 6 June 1987, p. 9; 23 January 1988, p. 3; *FEER*, 28 July 1988, p. 78).

In 1985–86 surplus funds flowed into every possible channel in Japan, bidding up not simply land prices, but also causing a rise in the value of shares which bore less relation to their real value. What has puzzled some observers about the crash of October 1987 is that it occurred after rather than before Wall Street and that the recovery was so rapid. Among the main reasons for this have been, not just the general strength of Japanese capital, but that in relation to the market value of company assets, shares have been no more over-valued than land, whose prices were also forced to their limits by *zaiteku* speculation, which fell and then settled. If the market value (44 per cent of assets) rather than the book value (4 per cent of assets) of company owned land is used, then share prices in Japan were relatively low: only 45 per cent of the value of net assets in March 1986. In the West, such a low value of a company's shares would make it ripe for a takeover and asset stripping (*JEJ*, 23 July 1988, p. 4).

Sunset Industries: Continued Decline

Almost as spectacular as the gains of some industries in 1986 were the losses of others. Most prominent was iron and steel, with the appreci-ation of the yen accelerating its long-term downward trend. With world production and demand in decline and imports from South Korea rising rapidly, Japanese steel makers cut back heavily on production and began one of the most radical rationalisation pro-grammes ever. It took everything from mass layoffs, a building boom in fiscal 1987, renewed foreign investment, to unexpected diversifica-tions to restore profitability to the industry. For example, Nippon Steel moved into information services in tie-ups with IBM Japan and Hitachi as well as into the leisure industry. By March 1988 the five majors were posting record profits and were being tipped to lead the list of the fastest rising profit earners in fiscal 1989 (*JEJ*, 6 February 1988, p. 20; 13 February 1988, p. 18; 21 May 1988, p. 20; 13 August 1988, p. 17; 24 September 1988, p. 30; 15 October 1988, p. 1; *NKS*, 20 September 1988, p. 15).

A similar story could be told of non-ferrous metals. For example, from a peak of over one million metric tons of aluminium produced in 1975, a decade later after the closure of many smelters this had been slashed by 75 per cent. Two years later, in 1987, another two of the remaining three smelters had closed and capacity was a mere 35 000 tons. Today only Nippon Light Metal reaps the benefit of the radical rationalisation and soaring aluminium prices. Apart from aluminium, all of the seven major non-ferrous metals companies recorded sharp profit increases in fiscal 1987, with even better pros-pects for 1988 (*JJTI*, May 1987, p. 15; January 1988, p. 22; *JEJ*, 11 June 1988, p. 16). As the *Japan Economic Journal* commented: 'The three industries – petrochemicals, steel and aluminium – have something in common: effective restructuring that has in part led to today's boom' (18 June 1988, p. 24).

Also as a result of the high yen, the stagnation of shipbuilding took a similar qualitative leap downwards in 1986, but in this case even six months after an equally major reorganisation, the industry remained in the doldrums. Korean shipbuilders for the first time outperformed their Japanese counterparts to become the world's leaders. Even the government recommended plan to scrap a further 20 per cent of capacity and a regrouping of companies did not help. Marine transportation has been equally bleak (*JEJ*, 2 May 1987, p. 4; 21 November 1987, p. 20; 11 June 1988, p. 16; 8 October 1988, p. 23; 14 January 1989, p. 20; *Industria*, May 1987, p. 28).

Export Industries: Sharp Falls

The greatest turnarounds in profitability were recorded in the export-based machinery industries. Among the car makers, dramatic declines in declared income were recorded almost across the board in fiscal 1986: Toyota by 31 per cent, Nissan by 45 per cent, Honda by 1.4 per cent, Mazda by 80.1 per cent and Mitsubishi by 7.6 per cent, although Suzuki and Fuji (maker of Subaru) recorded increases of 17.5 and 13.8 per cent. The volume of exports to the US and Europe actually increased in 1986 (by 8.1 and 17.7 per cent), but elsewhere they plunged: by 51.3 per cent to the Middle East, 27.5 per cent to Southeast Asia and 39.6 per cent to Oceania (*TBT*, July 1987, pp. 18–31; *Industria*, July 1987, p. 24; *AS*, 31 July 1987, p. 13).

The fundamental problem of 'excessive sales' in the advanced countries remained unsolved, although the form of the crisis changed. Exports to the US fell by 12.2 per cent in 1987 and by 17.4 per cent in April–September 1988, but now mainly because of increased local production. And while the numbers of vehicles exported worldwide fell by 4.5 per cent in 1987, the numbers of knockdown sets climbed by 38.2 per cent. More worrying was that the number of cars exported to Western Europe rose by 4.8 per cent in 1987 to just under a million and a half.

If diversifying export markets and increasing overseas production was one remedy sought by Japanese capital, another was to expand the domestic market. In 1987 the numbers of new cars sold in Japan rose by 5.4 (including minicars and imports) and then by a further 9 per cent in 1988. However, the special factors behind these increases are unlikely to continue. First, the price wars from mid-1987 aimed at absorbing the new wealth created by the land and stock price boom could not be sustained. Second, just as the inflation of asset prices created a new rich, willing to spend on luxury consumer goods, it also created a new poor, those without assets whose need to save out of their earned incomes was in turn boosted. The fundamental pressures which sent the car makers into overseas markets a decade ago are thus likely to reassert themselves. Over 70 per cent of households already have a car in this heavily congested country, where rent for a parking space (a compulsory requirement of car owners) in central Tokyo costs more than that for a family home in my city. In December 1988 the Japan Automobile Dealers' Association predicted a 5 per cent fall in new car sales in 1989. Yet the immediate crisis seems to be over, with Nissan's 1986 losses having been firmly reversed as the company raised the share of its sales to the domestic market from 46.3 to 60.6 per cent (*NKS*, 31 October 1987, p. 13; 29 November 1987, p. 9; 21 October 1988, p. 9; *JEJ*, 23 January 1988, p. 19; 13 February, 1988 pp. 3, 20; 5 November 1988, p. 19; 26 November 1988, p. 20; 17 December 1988, p. 21).

Exports of electrical machinery fell by 11 per cent in 1986, while the majors, Hitachi and Mitsubishi, recorded 15 per cent declines in exports and 44 and 34 per cent declines in profits. Toshiba's profits plunged 48.7 per cent event though it retained its previous level of exports. The operating profits of a large number of majors went into the red: Sony by ¥6.6 billion, Sansui by ¥6.5 billion, Akai by ¥4.3 billion, JVC by ¥4.1 billion, Canon by ¥3.6 billion and of Sanyo by ¥2.8 billion. The worst hit branches of the industry were consumer electrical and electronic products, where both exports and output fell heavily in fiscal 1986 and fiscal 1987. However, the output and exports of industrial electronic machinery and components have continued to expand, regardless of the higher yen. Table 2.1 shows the fall in major electronic consumer exports in 1986–87. Most important was the drop in VTRs, which comprise half of all consumer electronic exports (Tsūshō sangyōshō, 1987b and 1988b; *JEJ*, 30 May 1987, p. 24; *NKS*, 22 May 1987, p. 15; 9 July 1987, p. 16; 2 June 1987, p. 1; *JJTI*, January 1988, pp. 16–17).

However, largely because of the rationalisation programmes at home and abroad, the situation improved somewhat. By September 1988 recovery was firmly under way with profits over the previous six months rising strongly for the companies worst hit by the recession: Hitachi (4.3 per cent), Toshiba (8.4 per cent) and Mitsubishi (9.9 per

Table 2.1   Major electronic exports, 1986–87

	1986		1987	
	Volume	*$ million*	*Volume*	*$ million*
TVs	8 655 580	1 727	6 001 443	1 422
To US	3 282 299	611	1 353 432	306
Radios	41 689 172	2 756	28 739 119	2 464
To US	21 078 790	1 268	13 640 936	1 121
Video tape recorders	27 689 146	7 416	22 800 731	5 900
To US	17 990 092	4 524	12 380 819	2 882

Source: Compiled from Tsūshō sangyōshō, 1988b.

cent). But some, like Sansui, continued to languish well into 1988 (*JEJ*, 2 July 1988, p. 20; 10 September 1988, p. 18; 5 November 1988, p. 16).

Construction: Miniboom

Among the profit leaders in 1987–88 were the companies associated with the construction boom of those years. The production of rental housing in the three metropolitan areas increased by 50 per cent in fiscal 1986, and even homeownership expanded following tax changes and low interest rates resulting from high bank liquidity. The profits of the real estate companies which were amassed during the land boom had to be shared with the construction and building materials companies, notably aluminium. Ordinary people have had to pay for the higher priced housing. The so-called 'wan ruumu manshiyon' (one room mansion), a contradiction in terms, is in fact becoming all that many can afford nowadays. However, by the end of fiscal 1987 the bubble had begun to burst, and housing starts in September 1988 fell by 7 per cent and then again by 8.5 per cent in October. The vacancy rate for new apartments rose sharply in 1988 and frightened many developers. Capital will probably try to revive interest, particularly among the asset-rich classes, in buying their own homes (*NKS*, 30 June 1987, p. 23; *JEJ*, 29 October 1988, p. 13; 17 December 1988, p. 4).

Fiscal 1986 was the worst year for capital, particularly in the machinery industries. According to most government and business sources, the trough of the *endaka fukyō* was around November 1986. Rationalisations at home and investments abroad have since fully revived manufacturing profits, which were expected to rise by 32 per cent in fiscal 1988 (*NKS*, 4 September 1988, pp. 1, 14–15; *JEJ*, 5 November 1988, p. 11; 3 December 1988, p. 3; 10 December 1988, p. 18).

Small Firm Sector: On the Brink

By mid-1987 there was a widespread optimism within the capitalist class, or at least among the heavy weights. Small and petty capitalists have remained extremely insecure, particularly those for whom there is no escape overseas. Squeezed by rising costs from the higher yen and cheap imports from Southeast Asia, many small firms were driven to bankruptcy, which peaked in early 1987. Of the total of 963 bankruptcies resulting specifically from the high yen in October 1985 to May 1987, 50.4 per cent were small firms with less than ¥10 million capital.

From the beginning of 1986 subcontract prices fell by increasingly greater margins than orders. And even when orders began to pick up towards the end of 1987, subcontract prices kept falling. The result was that the profits of small manufacturing firms in fiscal 1986 plunged by 15.1 per cent. A typical case was that of Shoko Sangyo, a small company which had made moulding materials for Nissan cars and Canon cameras. Having prospered for some twenty years, it borrowed heavily to finance a modern factory, but under pressure from the high yen, the parent companies squeezed it for price cuts and its debt proved too crushing. In one sense Shoko Sangyo was atypical, because a feature of the recession was the *low* level of bankruptcies which actually occurred (Chūshō kigyōchō, 1988, p. 64; *AWSJ*, 31 March 1987, p. 1).

Total bankruptcies began to decline almost as the yen started to rise, by 9.7 per cent in 1985, 7.1 per cent in 1986, and then by close to 20 per cent in early 1987 (*JJTI*, July/Aug. 1987, p. 62). Neither was this relationship coincidental. The easy credit and surplus funds that characterised the recession were apparently lent to companies on the brink of bankruptcy and prevented its actual occurrence. With large corporate clients raising their capital ratios and relying more on the Eurobond market for their loans, the banks lowered their criteria for domestic lending. As a banking analyst pointed out. 'They've had to go to these effectively bankrupt companies because they're the only ones who are going to pay the premiums on the loans' (*AWSJ*, 31 March 1987, p. 7).

Teikoku Data Bank identified another limiting factor. Many small

export-dependent companies see the writing on the wall and disband
before their debts force them to. Particularly when they own some
valuable real estate, it pays to withdraw voluntarily. The tendency
has been confirmed statistically, with the numbers of voluntary
withdrawals, retirements and changes to new lines of business out-
numbering bankruptcies by nearly twelve to one. In 1987 there was a
190 per cent increase in the numbers of voluntary closures over the
year before. Firms which actually go bankrupt are also managing to
continue in business, since banks are willing to lend even to them. In
1984–87, the proportion of such bankrupt firms rose from 13.4 to 37
per cent of the total. The price has been a growing number of failures
among financial institutions, which accounted for 70 per cent of debts
of bankrupt companies in fiscal 1987 compared to 50 per cent in 1977.
Real estate firms, not just because of the demise of Nippon Land
(debts of $1.23 billion) in mid-1988, have further raised the share of
the unproductive sector (Chūshō kigyōchō, 1988, p. 4; *NKS*, 24 July
1987, p. 29; 15 October 1988, p. 5; 25 October 1987, p. 3; 14
November 1987, p. 3; *JEJ*, 25 June 1988, p. 13; *FEER*, 28 October,
1988, pp. 86–7).

CAPITAL'S THREE-PRONGED STRATEGY

The response of Japanese capital to the *endaka fukyō* was swift and
predictable: industrial restructuring of sorts, tightening the screws at
home and imperialism. I discuss the third in the next chapter, and
examine the first two here.

Industrial Restructuring

Industrial restructuring has come to mean completing the thinning
out of the 'structurally depressed' heavy and basic materials industries and eliminating those branches of machinery which cannot get
round the high yen. The latter is likely to involve more imperialism
abroad than the former.

Although government thinking on the subject is not consistent, the
most comprehensive statement of official policy was the so-called
New Maekawa Report (*JEJ*, 23 May 1987, pp. 7, 21). It recommended the expansion of domestic demand as the chief solution to
the current overproduction. But if a condition of this was to be
greater working-class spending power, it would find no favour among

capitalists other than as a desperate once-and-for-all measure to satisfy overseas criticism. The Nakasone government's 'Emergency Economic Measures' were not intended to redistribute to the working class the purchasing power for a more domestic-demand based system. Such a structural change could only result from struggles by organised labour for a larger share of the cake. The redistributed income, needed to encourage capital to treat working-class purchasing power as a potential market, would lead to lower rates of exploitation and profit. And capital would only concede that if forced to.

The Japanese working class was too weak to win such a restructuring of the system, and capital planned a course through the recession which promised the best of all worlds. It tried to retain the benefits of its competitive advantage in the machine industries, it took steps to meet the demands of its imperialist rivals and it continued to rely mainly on markets outside Japan, just as it had in the late 1970s. If there was to be greater reliance on domestic demand, then this would be in areas where spending power was on the rise, where capital rather than labour was the market: luxury consumer and investment goods.

The way of reconciling these contradictory strategies was to expand imperialism abroad, by locating outside Japan the point from which the final sale of the products occurred. Not much in the way of new industry would be built this time, only a continual running down of raw material processing. Machinery is not being scrapped, 'only' hollowed out, with growing proportions of production and employment in the consumer goods branches shifting overseas. Such a course is generating great profits for Japanese capital, quickly ending the recession as far as it was concerned, but it has cast labour into the sort of vicious circle which accompanied deindustrialisation elsewhere: unemployment and falling working and living conditions.

Although this restructuring continues the process that began in 1974, it also involves a shift back to one feature of an even older industrial structure: production of investment goods for the domestic market. On 5 December 1987 the headline that dominated the entire Japanese press was that a rate of GNP growth of 2 per cent (8.4 per cent on an annual basis) had been achieved in the third quarter of that year, with 1.8 per cent contributed by domestic demand and only 0.2 per cent by export demand. However, the 1.8 per cent broke down into 0.6 per cent from increased housing investment, 0.4 per cent and 0.2 per cent respectively from increased private and public

Table 2.2   Percentage changes in real GNE, fiscal years

	1987	1988(1)[a]	1988(2)[a]	1988[b]	1989[b]	1990[b]
Private Final Consumption	4.5	0.6	1.4	5.0	4.8	3.7
Private Housing	25.6	–8.6	6.1	1.9	–0.8	–6.1
Private Plant and Equipment	10.0	4.6	4.4	15.8	10.1	4.5
Public Final Consumption	–0.9	0.5	0.6	2.1	2.9	
Public Capital Formation	10.0	–2.4	–1.8	2.8	4.0	
Exports	5.2	–3.8	9.0	8.3	8.0	5.7
Imports	12.6	5.1	6.3	20.7	13.2	
Trade Surplus ($ billion)	94.0	–	–	93.0	88.0	
Real GNP	5.2	0.8	2.2	4.7	4.3	3.5

Notes: [a] Refers to the first and second quarters of fiscal 1988.
[b] Estimate for 1988, forecasts thereafter.
Source: *JEJ*, 17 December 1988, pp. 4–5; 31 December 1988 and 7 January 1989, p. 7.

investment and only 0.5 per cent from increased consumer spending. Moreover, the rise in consumer spending of 0.9 per cent compared with much larger increases for all the other categories: 10.3 per cent in housing investment, 2.2 per cent in private equipment investment, 3.3 per cent in public capital formation and 6.7 per cent in exports. Equally significant was that the 4.6 per cent growth of industrial production in this period centered on capital goods, producer goods and construction goods. The growth in consumer goods production was minimal. Nothing that has happened since has altered this picture, as revealed by Table 2.2 (*NKS*, 5 December 1987, p. 1; *JEJ*, 5 December 1987, p. 5).

The picture is actually much worse than might at first appear. Declining housing and public works expenditure, which had at least an indirect relation to working-class spending power, are being replaced by an increasing emphasis on private capital formation. In October 1988 the *Far Eastern Economic Review* commented:

Japanese industry may be on the verge of its biggest capital-investment boom since 1980 and possibly since the eve of the first oil shock in 1973, according to a series of recently released surveys of major companies' spending plans (6 October 1988, p. 59).

A growing trend is also for the largest increases in capital investment to be in branches producing investment rather than consumer goods and for greater shares of the investment to be directed to cost cutting and new products, rather than the enlargement of capacity as was the chief motive in the 1970s. In a September 1988 survey, 31.9 per cent of the firms which were increasing their investment mentioned rationalisation as their priority and a further 18.2 per cent the development of new products. Only 21.4 per cent mentioned the expansion of capacity to meet domestic demand. One measure of the structural change that is occurring is the growing share of equipment investment in GNP: from around 15 per cent in the period 1975–85 to 18.5 per cent in July–September 1986 and then to over 21 per cent in fiscal 1988. Only once before, in 1970, had it been above 20 per cent (*NKS*, 1988, p. 43; *JEJ*, 16 July 1988, p. 17; 6 August 1988, p. 12; *NKS*, 14 September 1988, p. 13; 16 September 1988, p. 1).

It would be a mistake to belittle the consumer spending boom of 1987–8, which played a major part in absorbing goods which could not be sold overseas. It seemed that the rise of the yen, which had made Japanese wages excessively high from the point of view of employers' costs, had at least made them an irresistible market and that at long last capital accumulation would be based on working class spending power. However, the real disposable incomes of most workers was not affected by the higher yen, for two main reasons.

First, many lower paid workers had to increase savings rather than real spending as a result of the recession. Since state welfare is notoriously inadequate, workers must themselves save for such things as their housing, old age, healthcare and children's education. The rising costs of all of these, combined with the cultural pressure to save and pass on the family's security, perpetuated the underconsumptionism inherent in Japan's low-wage system. Thus in 1987 the average savings of Japanese workers increased by 11.8 per cent, topping 10 per cent for the first time in six years (*NKS*, 9 October 1988, p. 3; *JEJ*, 12 April 1988, p. 13; 29 October 1988, p. 13).

Second, as discussed below, capital imposed a strict ceiling on wages during the recession, and the real incomes of the bottom 40 per cent of earners fell. This was not just because of pressure on money wages but also because of the failure of the higher yen to raise real wages through lower import prices. In mid-1987 the *Japan Economic Journal* pointed out that it might appear strange that personal consumption was picking up briskly when the rise in individual income had been so modest. However, it noted:

the swelling value of financial and other assets [had created a] new rich [who] buy luxury cars and clothes and take expensive overseas trips. This class of people is behind the recent upturn in personal consumption . . . [A] class division seems to be forming between those who have assets on which they can reap capital gains and those who do not (*JEJ*, 15 August 1987, p. 6).

The estimate that this class comprises some 34–40 per cent of the population is not far from my own earlier estimate of property ownership among the bourgeoisie, petty bourgeoisie and middle class (Steven, 1983). The apparent contradiction between the belt-tightening forced on the working class and the widespread spending on consumer goods disappears when one recognises that a large upper class can, after receiving windfall profits, go on a spending spree. The wealth effect of rising share prices alone raised real consumption by 0.7 of a percentage point in fiscal 1987, that is, 15.5 per cent of the increase. In the nine months to September 1987, while the spending of the top 20 per cent of earners (over ¥7.6 million) rose by 4.6 per cent, that of the bottom 20 per cent (under ¥3.61 million) rose by only 0.2 per cent. Spending by the middle three quintiles (to ¥4.67 million, ¥5.87 million and ¥7.6 million) fell by 1.8 and 0.9 per cent for the lower two and rose 0.2 per cent for the third. And there is no reason, other than its capacity to get away with this politically, why such an upper class should not continue to spend liberally. Wherever wealth is unevenly distributed, the upper class contributes the most to 'domestic demand', for both investment and consumer goods (Rōdōshō, 1987a; *JEJ*, 19 March 1988, pp. 1, 4).

Even the 1988 *White Paper on National Life* noted how the land and stock price boom had divided the country into a new rich and a new poor (*shinki shinpi*). Homeowners in the Tokyo area now have real estate averaging ¥86 million ($688 000), an impossible savings target in the lifetime of an average worker. Small wonder the new rich like to spend and the new poor face added pressures to save (*JEJ*, 3 December 1988, p. 9).

The sudden upsurge in the production of investment goods is, however, not just a way to shift towards areas of greater spending power. The move out of consumer goods production also reflects capital's global strategy of relocating these industries abroad, closer to their markets, and concentrating in Japan only the most technically advanced industries. Japanese capital will retain its dominant position in the international division of labour by focusing on the production of capital and luxury consumer goods, leaving mass consumer production increasingly to its subsidiaries in Asia.

Table 2.3   Methods of adjusting manufacturing employment, 1986 (% of firms using them)

	Iron and steel	Electrical	Motor vehicle	Shipbuilding
Cut temporaries	20.7	46.5	55.9	25.0
Cut hiring young workers	51.7	42.3	38.2	87.5
Cut hiring other workers	6.9	33.8	23.5	50.0
Temporary layoffs	31.0	1.4	2.9	25.0
Redeploy	65.5	39.4	32.4	87.5
Kibō taishoku/dismissal	13.8	8.4	2.9	62.5

Source: Rōdōshō, 1987b, reference materials, p. 129.

By late 1988, however, the predicted revival of exports also began to set in, and the 'new' industrial structure looked rather old. Economic Planning Agency officials admitted that 'Japanese industry has fully recovered the competitive edge it lost after the revaluation of the yen' (*FEER*, 17 November 1988, p. 119). The main change was that this time the leading edge came from exports of plant and equipment, materials, components, telecommunications equipment, semiconductors and video cameras, almost entirely things that capitalists buy. There is thus not much that is really new in the current restructuring of Japanese industry (*NKS*, 16 October 1988, p. 1; *JEJ*, 4 June 1988, p. 11; 10 December 1988, p. 7).

Destruction of Jobs is Newer

Wherever capacity is scrapped, workers' jobs and livelihoods are on the line. In many cases management gets workers to retire 'voluntarily', threatening them with *shimei kaiko* (designated dismissal) if they do not. The latter is usually the last resort, since workers are normally pressured in interviews to 'request retirement' (*kibō taishoku*), or seconded to subcontractors, who then lay them off. Alternatively, 'temporary layoffs' are used to induce workers to look for new jobs, new hiring is suspended and normal retirement used to ensure cutbacks, or workers are transferred to separate companies. Table 2.3 shows the results of a survey by the Economic Planning Agency in October–December 1986 on the different methods used in various manufacturing industries.

At IHI (Ishikawajima Harima Heavy Industries), the shipbuilding giant, the plans to cut 30 per cent of the 7000 workers centered on the 35–54 year olds and the infirm, while the pressures to retire included

Table 2.4 Employment in shipbuilding, September 1985 to December 1986

	Total	Employees	White collar	Blue collar	Contract
1985 Sept.	137 543	94 274	33 874	60 400	43 269
1986 Mar.	126 279	87 864	31 161	56 703	38 415
Dec.	98 349	68 789	25 966	42 823	29 560
% change	39.9	37.0	30.5	41.0	46.4

Source: Rōdōshō, 1987b, reference materials, p. 12.

threats of violence and even its actual use. Table 2.4 shows the loss of jobs in the shipbuilding industry as a whole from when the yen began to soar in late 1985 to the end of 1986. Contract workers, who are not employees of shipbuilding companies, decreased by a massive 46.4 per cent. But the redundancies have continued even into the recovery. In August 1987 Sasebo 'asked' 490 workers to retire early, a few months later shipbuilders were planning a ('temporary') cut of another 10 000 and as late as September 1988 Mitsubishi Heavy Industries announced a plan to shed 1900 workers from its shipbuilding division in fiscal 1989. Shipowners have also shown themselves equal to the task, announcing in September 1987 a further 56 per cent cut within the year of crew jobs (13 000), which had already been slashed from their peak of 39 000 in 1974 to 24 000 in 1985 and 23 000 in 1986, to be implemented through 'each firm asking the seamen to retire voluntarily' (Sasaki, 1987, pp. 8–12; *JEJ*, 26 September 1987, p. 14; 22 August 1987, p. 10; 7 November 1987, p. 19; 9 September 1988, p. 20).

Similar tactics are being used to achieve the mammoth cutbacks planned for the iron and steel industry (Sasaki, 1987, pp. 8–12). On 13 February 1987, Nippon Steel suddenly announced a plan to close five blast furnaces – at Yawata, Sakai, Muroran, Kamaishi and Hirota – in 1988–89 involving 7000 jobs, bringing the total intended cut by 1990 to 19 000. If one adds the effect on small subcontractors, the total number of jobs lost will be well over 30 000, the biggest ever rationalisation in Japanese history. Including planned reductions in March 1987 to March 1989 by the other steel majors (5500 by Kawasaki Steel, 4000 by Sumitomo Metals, 6000 by Kobe Steel and 5000 by Nippon Kokan) as well as the repercussions on their subcontracts, the total expected loss of jobs in the industry by 1990 would be over 100 000 if the original schedule was adhered to. However, the equipment investment boom of 1988 has led to a brief postponement of some of the plans, although most have been going through (Sasaki,

1987, pp. 14–15; *JJTI*, May 1987, p. 14; *JEJ*, 13 February 1988, p. 20; 24 December 1988, p. 38).

Typical of the iron and steel and shipbuilding majors is how the economies of whole towns have become dependent on them, such as the five where Nippon Steel plans to close blast furnaces, Innoshima where Hitachi Shipbuilding has a major works, and Aioi which is a stronghold of IHI.

From 1980–85, the population of Muroran fell from 160 000 to 136 000, and it is expected to fall by another 50 000. In Kamaishi, the tax paid by Nippon Steel in 1985 comprised 34 per cent of the town's company-tax income, while the total number of persons directly linked to the company was about 20 000 (2400 employees plus subcontractors and family members) out of a population of 60 000. Over the past 25 years, the town has lost 33 000 people, mainly because Nippon Steel has been transferring employees to Nagoya and Chiba, and the loss of each such employee causes a drop of ten in population. The announcement that a second furnace is to close is a total disaster for the population of this 'castle town' (Sasaki, 1987, pp. 17–18).

Innoshima is a Hitachi Shipbuilding 'castle town', with 3300 employees in 1985, but it cut these to 1800 in 1986 and laid off a further 1300 by the end of the year. Of the rest, about 300 are being moved to a new company, leaving only 200 who will repair ships for the Navy. Hitherto 70–80 per cent of the population have been linked to shipbuilding, as has 80 per cent of the town's shipments. It is difficult to find jobs outside shipbuilding, and the jobs-to-applications ratio is 0.06: only six jobs for every hundred seekers. With lay-offs concentrated among the over 45 year olds, the situation is desperate because getting second jobs has become almost impossible. Of the 739 people who left the factory in 1985, only 64 had found work by February 1987. The company has been ruthless: having pressed people to buy their own homes (from a Hitachi real estate company) and lent them money, it has been pressing them to pay back the loans. Houses which cost ¥16 million cannot be sold for ¥8 million, and the redundancy payment of ¥2 million covers only half the ¥4 million loaned (*ibid.*, pp. 8–21).

In the ten years 1976–86, 340 000 jobs have been lost in companies quoted on the first board of the stock exchange, mainly in 'structurally depressed' industries: 84 000 in shipbuilding and vehicles, 83 000 in textiles, 62 000 in iron and steel and 39 000 in chemicals. As these industries continue to be run down, the number of jobs lost multiplies to inestimable levels, particularly when large numbers of subcontractors are involved. Some recent examples from the sunset industries include the closure of 25 non-ferrous metal mines in fiscal 1985 and 1986 with the loss of 5371 jobs; the annual shedding since 1987 of almost 1000 jobs by just one textile firm, Toray, which is expected to continue at least until 1989; and the scrapping of 2800 jobs by Tokyo Gas in 1988–90. As if to rub it in, MITI announced in January 1988 that the number of workers in Japanese overseas subsidiaries had topped the million mark nine months earlier (*JEJ*, 27 February 1988; 5 March 1988, p. 19; 18 June 1988, p. 6; 10 September 1988, p. 10; *NKS*, 12 January 1988, p. 3).

In the export-dependent machinery industries the loss of jobs is only beginning, although the main cutbacks so far have been non-regulars and overtime. There are many signs of what is likely to become a continual process of attrition. For example, in April 1986 Matsushita Electric, regarded as the most competitive firm in the country, announced plans to cut its work force by 1000, while Sanyo planned to lay off 1200 temporary and part-time workers. In January that year there had been about 16 000 such workers in the motor vehicle industry, but by October they had been reduced to 7000. The car company most acutely affected by the recession, Nissan, managed to rid itself of 8000 workers by June 1988, while Toshiba cut the work force at its 27 domestic factories by 40 per cent from 24 000 (Sasaki, 1987, pp. 28–30; *JEJ*, 23 July 1988, p. 12).

In mid-1987 it was hard to pick up a Japanese newspaper without finding either an announcement by some company to cut its work force or some estimate by a public or private body of impending cuts. For example, in July the Japan Industrial Bank announced that 31 195 jobs would be lost in the car industry in 1985–90. Among the companies which at this time announced plans to scrap jobs were: NTT (1300), KDD (1000), Fuji Electric (1100), Japan Air Lines (900), Mitsui Mining (300), Nissan Diesel (1100) and Toshiba Machine (1000). In all some 400 000 factory jobs were destroyed in 1987. In some cases, such as NTT which in September 1988 agreed to a 'request by its trade union' to slash 30 000 jobs by 1990, there was worse to come (*NKS*, 28 May 1987, p. 9; 10 July 1987, p. 9; 17 July 1987, p. 3; 29 July 1987, p. 5; 31 July 1987, p. 13; 10 September 1987, p. 13; *JEJ*, 12 September 1987, p. 13; 2 April 1988, p. 23; 17 September 1988, p. 13).

Although some regular jobs had already been axed in the export industries by the end of 1986, ruling class circles estimated that there

Table 2.5   Estimated loss of jobs from cutting 1986 external surplus

	Cut exports	Expand imports
Agriculture, forestry, fisheries	55 000	962 000
Mining	5 000	36 000
Construction	7 000	7 000
Manufacturing	850 000	575 000
Consumer group (foods, etc.)	44 000	134 000
Basic materials (non-metallic)	129 000	184 000
Basic materials (metals)	63 000	35 000
Machinery	505 000	143 000
Transport, communications	163 000	142 000
Wholesale, retail	299 000	216 000
Finance, insurance, real estate	62 000	70 000
Services	148 000	186 000
Total	1 589 000	2 194 000

Source: Rōdōshō, 1987b, reference materials, p. 133.

were at that time between 6.4 and 13.8 per cent superfluous workers in manufacturing: between 778 000 and 1 686 000. The lower estimate was based on what were considered 'appropriate' levels of labour productivity, the latter on 'appropriate' personnel expenses in relation to turnover. By the end of 1987 Nomura Research estimated (productivity basis) that in manufacturing firms with over 30 regular workers alone, there would be 1.25 million (16 per cent) surplus workers. An overall picture of the coming effect on jobs in various industries of the two broad strategies (cut exports or expand imports) for correcting the external balance is presented in Table 2.5. In practice both strategies are being used. The Advisory Council on the Industrial Structure estimated a loss of about two million jobs in the period 1980–2000: 500 000 resulting from a doubling of imported intermediary goods, 500 000 from a doubling of imported final goods, and from 560 000 to 970 000 from cutting exports and expanding foreign investment (Kudō, 1987, p. 50; Rōdōshō, 1987b, reference materials, p. 31).

A large question mark hangs over how far food imports will be liberalised, since many powerful but contradictory forces are at work. On one side is the US with its massive external deficit and its surplus of agricultural products, dying to make a killing on the Japanese market. Supporting it are the financial and industrial factions of the Japanese bourgeoisie, who have long found the subsidisation of agriculture wasteful. Capital in the food processing industry is also keen to take advantage of the high yen and import more raw materials, particularly heavily protected rice, wheat and dairy products. Finally, the urban working class and petty bourgeoisie would love to buy rice for a fifth and meat for a half of their current prices.

On the other side is a coalition of interests, which has so far held the upper hand. It is brought together by Nōkyō (The Federation of Agricultural Cooperative Associations), which coordinates farmers' agricultural and political activities. The ruling Liberal Democratic Party is heavily dependent on the agricultural vote, and supports stabilising Japan's food supply, which already comprises more net imports than that of any other country.

Since 1987 there have been signs of a change in the balance of power between the two camps. For the first time in 31 years, the producer price of rice was cut by almost 6 per cent and then by another 4.6 per cent in 1988, with not as much political backlash from farmers as was expected. One reason could be that almost 60 per cent of farmers no longer sell much rice (12 per cent of the total) and are in fact mainly engaged in non-agricultural work. Nōkyō increasingly represents chiefly its 300 000 member bureaucracy, which uses farmers' money mainly for non-farming business operations. If the protection of Japanese agriculture continues to be whittled away, the burden of the adjustment will fall heavily on farmers (*BT*, August 1987, p. 535; *JEJ*, 5 November 1988, p. 2; 2 July 1988, p. 19; 16 July 1988, pp. 1, 5; 15 October 1988, p. 3; 17 December 1988, p. 3).

Estimates of actual unemployment in Japan are hopeless, capturing at most only one half of the persons who would be classified as jobless in Britain or America. The investigation is carried out the last week of each month, and even if one did part-time work for only two hours on the last day of the month, one cannot be regarded as unemployed. Furthermore, it is necessary to be actively looking for work and to have registered at an employment stabilisation office. Anyone doing however small an amount of unpaid assistance in a family enterprise can also not qualify as unemployed. Moreover, the size of the work force is overestimated compared to other countries, so that the percentage unemployed is minimised. For example, members of the armed forces are included in the work force in Japan, whereas they are not in the US.

If one combines the different ways of measuring real unemployment to form composite indices, the result is actually higher unemployment in Japan than the US, as revealed by Table 2.6. On every

Table 2.6　Indices of real unemployment in Japan and the US, 1977–86

		A	B	C	D	E	F	G	H	I	J
Japan	1977	53.43	1.27	2.4	32.19	7.58	23.5	2.43	7.5	14.5	6.6
	1982	56.85	1.47	2.6	33.45	8.39	25.1	1.24	3.7	15.1	4.7
	1986	58.41	1.64	2.8	36.35	9.87	27.2	3.92	10.8	16.9	8.9
US	1977	100.67	6.99	6.9	60.03	5.67	9.4	1.01	1.7	11.9	7.9
US	1982	111.87	10.68	9.5	62.07	6.56	10.6	1.57	2.5	14.6	10.3
US	1986	119.54	8.24	6.9	62.75	5.83	9.3	1.12	1.8	11.2	7.8

Notes:

A – labour force (million persons)　　　　　　　　　　C – B/A %
B – registered unemployed (million persons)　　　　　F – E/D %
D – not in labour force (million persons)　　　　　　　H – G/D %
E – wanting to work (million persons)　　　　　　　　I – B+E/A+E %
G – given up looking for work (million persons)　　　J – B+G/A+G %
Source: Keizai kikakuchō, 1988b, p. 122.

index except registered unemployed (C), joblessness in Japan comes out higher than in the US. There are higher proportions of people outside the labour force who are looking for work (F); higher proportions of those proportions of persons have given up trying to find jobs (H); and on both composite indices, Japanese unemployment comes out much higher. Index (I) shows the percentage of persons in the labour force plus those outside it but wishing to work who are either registered unemployed or who say they want to work, while index (J) shows the ratio of registered unemployed plus those who have given up trying to find jobs to the persons in the labour force plus those outside it who have given up trying to find work. The reasons for the not widely recognised higher unemployment in Japan than the US is that unemployed people have been taught to disappear into their families with their shame.

Even MITI recently admitted that if it used the American measure, it would almost have to double the official estimate of Japan's jobless. Nevertheless, the official figure climbed sharply to 3.1 per cent (1.86 million) in the first half of 1987, although with the equipment investment boom of 1988 it fell back to levels around 2.7 per cent (Rōdō-shō, 1988b, statistical appendix, p. 10).

There is an across-the-board-agreement among all sections of the capitalist class that joblessness will rise steadily in Japan as a result of the structural changes towards which the rise of the yen in 1985–86 became the catalytic turning point. That scrapping unprofitable pro-

Table 2.7 Industrial distribution of employment, 1970–2000 (1 000 persons)

	1970	1980	1985	1993	2000
Material production sector	26 770	25 020	25 010	24 090	22 990
Agriculture, forestry, etc.	9 060	5 880	5 180	4 440	3 500
Manufacturing	13 770	13 660	14 530	13 950	13 335
Basic materials processing	3 970	3 390	3 200	2 860	2 280
Machinery and metallic production	5 230	5 380	6 190	6 110	6 470
Other	4 570	4 890	5 140	4 980	4 600
Construction	3 940	5 480	5 300	5 700	6 140
Network sector	13 380	15 970	16 710	16 560	17 020
Electricity, gas, water	290	300	330	350	340
Transport, communications	3 240	3 500	3 430	3 540	3 290
Commerce	8 530	10 260	10 780	10 410	10 790
Finance, insurance, real estate	1 320	1 910	2 170	2 260	2 600
Knowledge service production	10 790	14 370	16 350	20 690	23 100
Management services		2 940	3 666	5 380	6 630
Medical and health services		1 800	2 110	2 840	3 190
Education services		1 840	1 980	2 280	2 320
Leisure related services		3 320	3 810	4 850	5 410
Housework substitute services		1 630	1 800	2 160	2 270
Public administration, and others		2 840	2 990	3 180	3 280
TOTAL	50 940	55 360	58 070	61 340	63 110

Source: Keizai kikakuchō, 1987d, p. 50.

duction and industries involves a substantial loss of jobs is not questioned at all, but the level of future unemployment is generally minimised by over-optimistic expectations of the industries which are to be 'built' instead. In other words, while no one denies that the high yen has signalled the start of Japan's deindustrialisation, the 'hollowing out' (*kūdōka*) of its productive industries, the social consequences are not being realistically faced, even by organised labour.

What will be Built: Pie in the Sky

Discussion of where displaced workers are meant to go has been very abstract and is difficult to describe. It has centred on two main areas of hoped-for growth: services and industries of high value added. Sometimes both are combined into what are called high-technology information-centred services, particularly for businesses. In its *Basic Strategy Towards the Twenty First Century*, the Economic Planning Agency incorporated this conception into existing industrial classifications (Keizai kikakuchō, 1987d). Table 2.7 shows how it expects the distribution of employment to change.

As far as the scrap heap is concerned, the 'basic strategy' is to preside over the hollowing out of Japanese industry right up to the end of the century. Both in terms of employment and shares of GDP, the manufacturing and primary industries will decline the most, with the biggest falls occurring in agriculture and raw material processing. Although the document admits that machinery has great potential for further growth, it notes that this will not be realised because capital will increasingly shift machinery overseas.

In contrast to its hard-headed acceptance of capital's interests in scrapping uncompetitive production, the *Basic Strategy* suddenly reveals totally unreal expectations regarding what capital might wish to build. Knowledge service industries are supposed to generate jobs for 33.7 per cent of the work force by 1993 and then 36.6 per cent by 2000, as opposed to 28.1 per cent in 1985, an increase of 4.34 million jobs in 1985–93 and another 2.41 million by 2000. The largest growth is expected to occur in management and leisure related services, but medical and health services are also supposed to provide many more jobs. This sort of pie-in-the-sky optimism is common in government propaganda directed towards workers, but it is unusual in documents which set out capital's medium and long-term strategies.

Conceptions like the following have a ring of Utopianism, particularly when they are floated in the midst of a recession in which every possible way of raising the exploitation of workers is being pressed to the full: 'expand free time and give weight to individual worth', 'create free time for foreign and domestic travel', 'shorten working hours', 'increase leisure', 'lifetime health care', 'expand domestic-labour-saving goods and services', 'expand social capital and social security', and 'improve housing' (Keizai kikakuchō, 1987d, chs 7–8).

If the service sector is to be significantly expanded, then ordinary people will need more money to pay for the improved services. However, one of the main reasons for the current skyrocketing foreign investment is the excessively high level of Japanese wages following the rise of the yen, and deindustrialisation is no more likely to lead to higher wages in Japan than it has in Britain or America. Simply to list all the things that Japanese workers have long needed but which capital has consistently denied them sweeps aside the two major political conditions on which the projected restructuring depends: redistributing purchasing power from capital to labour, and expanding the unproductive sectors of the economy. Japanese workers are simply not organised to win the first, while the second will be limited by the pace of deindustrialisation, since the wealth used by the growing unproductive sector must come from the productive sector.

The new threefold classification used by the Economic Planning Agency seems to recognise the distinction between productive and unproductive industries, as well as the latter's dependence, even parasitism, on the former. Its network sector, which resembles the circulation process, is apparently unproductive, but it wrongly includes transport, electricity, gas and water, which are productive. The difficulty of limitlessly expanding unproductive industries is recognised in appending the term 'production' to 'knowledge services'. However, most of these are either unproductive or at best only indirectly productive: they are simultaneously things which workers require, such as health and education, which normally come in for the chop in times like these.

Ever since the need for comprehensive social security became glaringly obvious following the unemployment caused by the first oil crisis, there has been a lot of official talk about expanding the virtually non-existent welfare state. Yet even in 1986, as in the two years before, the proportion of national income devoted to social security was a mere 14.0 per cent, compared to 17.9 per cent in the US, 25.8 per cent in Britain, 31.0 per cent in West Germany and 43.3 per cent in Sweden. Moreover, almost all of the increase in Japan since 1974 has been in pensions, which gobbled up 47.7 per cent of the total in 1986, and medical-insurance and related expenses, which accounted for 39.7 per cent of the total (*NKS*, 10 August 1987, p. 1).

The ideology of 'post industrialism', which grew up in the US and UK to rationalise the deindustrialisation of those countries, might explain the lack of consistency in the picture of a rising service economy as the solution to unemployment. The notion of knowledge-intensive is less appropriate to these services than it is to manufacturing, while adding the word production only further confuses the issue. And the issue is whether industries which normally grow alongside and depend on the material production sector can survive, let alone expand without apparent limit, when the latter is massively run down. Japanese capital has its eye on two ways in which this normally impossible task is to be achieved: imperialism abroad and further increasing exploitation at home.

Normally the most competitive branch of manufacturing, in this case machinery, would be the main source of the domestic surplus, but because it is being shifted it will not have much more weight than construction. So rather than any one of the material production industries being singled out to sustain the growing service sector, Japanese capital is aiming at an across-the-board tightening of the screws. The maximum possible surplus will be squeezed out of productive workers in all industries, and the drains on this surplus will be minimised by maintaining a comparable regime over unproductive workers. The extent of this attack will depend on how much material wealth imperialism can bring into the country. However, since the outflow of capital is proceeding so rapidly, the expected returns are too far away for capital to ease the pressure at home at this stage. It is raising the exploitation of both productive and unproductive workers in the standard ways: new technology, speedups and wage cuts.

Increasing Exploitation

New Technology

The Japanese media talk about *hai teku* and knowledge-intensive production as if this were something new to capitalism or peculiar to certain industries. However, competition among capitals within all industries has always compelled each to rely on technical superiority as its chief weapon against rivals. Accumulation within each industry is thus always spearheaded by knowledge-intensive production. Like the term 'modernisation' which became a fetish in the literature on underdevelopment, the term 'new technology' also obscures the never ending technical changes which capitalism propels, so that 'new technology' simply refers to capital's latest weapon against rivals.

In this sense, there are currently three broad types of 'new' technology which are spearheading change in a wide range of Japanese industries. These are microelectronics, which includes 'mechatronics', that is, its use in the machinery as in robotics; new materials, for example, fine chemicals and fine ceramics; and biotechnology, for example, in pharmaceuticals. The Economic Planning Agency recently estimated that the most important uses of all of them in the coming decade will be to produce existing goods more efficiently (Keizai kikakuchō, 1987d, p. 47).

The introduction of new technology is a highly politically charged process. Indeed the introduction of robots into motor vehicle assembly in the late 1970s and early 1980s was only accepted by workers because the expansion of the industry at that time maintained overall levels of employment. Now that the motor vehicle industry is moving abroad, the effect on jobs of its *fait accompli* automation is being bitterly felt. Much the same applies to the electrical industry, where, for example, automating circuit-board assembly often allowed one worker to replace ten or more.

However, today's ultimate production system is not one of rows of industrial robots silently welding parts together, but a flexible plant totally controlled by computers, which can respond quickly to volume and design changes. The buzz words today are CAD (computer aided design) and CAM (computer aided manufacturing) systems, the main impetus for which came to Japan only with the rise of the yen and the need to slash costs. That is what really lies behind the current capital investment boom, which according to the chairperson of the Japan Centre for Economic Research, is being propelled by a 'thrust for technological innovation, particularly in computers and communications, [which] is likely to boost the productivity of Japanese industry by 10 per cent in 1988' (*JEJ*, 12 November 1988, p. 4; 2 April 1988, p. 23; 24 September 1988, p. 1; *NKS*, 22 August 1988, p. 11).

The same forces are behind the other major priority in capital's current equipment investment drive, namely, diversification into new products and new lines of business. We have already noted the penchant of steelmakers for computer-related ventures. Computer software and information services have become favourites, and among the companies which in 1988 alone either established or announced intentions to establish subsidiaries in these fields were Hoya, Fujitsu, Matsushita, Hitachi, Sony, Mitsubishi Electric, Nippon Steel, Kobe Steel, Nippon Kokan, Showa–Shell Oil, Nippon Yusen, Bank of Tokyo, Kyowa Bank, Unitika, Sumitomo Rubber, Kyushu Electric Power, Hokuriku Electric Power, Kao and Kirin Beer (*FEER*, 21 April, pp. 72–3; *NKS*, 22 August; 7 September, p. 9; 6 November, p. 5).

The introduction of new technology is closely linked to Japan's temporary labour and subcontracting systems. Since above-average production techniques always require workers of above-average skill to operate them, they become a wedge that divides the working class. Those whose educational privileges allow them to acquire the know-how have a strategic advantage, and with luck and loyalty to their employers they can move through the middle class into the bourgeoisie. The requirement of uninterrupted length of service excludes women from this type of class mobility, since patriarchal relations allocate to them the job of childcare during an important time in a person's climb to the top, and it has discouraged women from even acquiring the knowhow.

The agents of new technology are therefore overwhelmingly men in the regular work force, while irregular workers, mainly but not exclusively women, do increasingly repetitive jobs on the production line, in offices or at home. In spite of some 36 per cent (almost 47 per cent in Tokyo) of high school graduates going on to university, there was a shortage of over half a million technical workers (4 per cent of the total needed) in fiscal 1986. At the same time there were up to a million and a half surplus workers in jobs, nearly two million officially unemployed, and as many again unofficially unemployed (*NKS*, 11 August 1987, p. 26; *JJTI*, July/Aug. 1987, p. 60).

Technology (new and old) is not, however, simply a fetish that obscures the division between regular and irregular workers, men and women, the bourgeoisie and the working class. It is also the guise under which the subcontracting system and imperialism masquerade. Under a vertical technical division of labour between parent companies and their subcontractors, the former retain control over the more technically advanced processes and subcontract out the simpler more labour-intensive tasks to the latter. Most manufacturing firms which do subcontracting work remain technically dependent on their parent companies. We can see later on how this same subcontracting system is being internationalised, either through forcing existing subcontractors to move abroad or through finding new ones on arrival.

Increased Intensity of Work

The second way capital is raising the exploitation of the working class is through speed-ups and a whole range of 'cost down' measures. For example, in a manner reminiscent of the mid-1970s, capital appended catchy slogans to its more recent campaigns. Daihatsu's 'MP 30' drive was to cut 'meetings and paper' by 30 per cent, Toyota's 'C 50' was a responding challenge to achieve a 50 per cent such cut, the 'TP Movement' was Toshiba's campaign for 'total productivity' through rebuilding the production line, the 'SV 15 Movement' was Kitashima Dock Daisei Kojo's slogan to 'survive' through a 15 per cent cost down and 'DRILL' was Mazda's slogan to cut costs by a 'drastic innovation of all'. NEC also ran a campaign to double efficiency and halve production costs (Ninomiya, 1987, pp. 68 ff.; *JEJ*, 9 May 1987, p. 4; Satō *et al.*, 1987, p. 127). The production manager at Toshiba was particularly proud of his company's effort: 'the program is essentially a top-down scheme and can be applied to foreign factories' (*JEJ*, 2 and 9 January 1988, p. 4).

The Japanese working class has long been made to toil for many more hours than its western counterparts. In 1985, the average working week in manufacturing for production workers was 43.6 hours, compared to 38 in the US, 40.7 in the UK, 36.5 in West Germany and 37.2 in France. The number of working days per year is also between 20–30 more in Japan than in these countries, all of which have about twice as many paid holidays and almost universal five-day working weeks, while only 6.1 per cent of Japanese workers regularly enjoy a five-day working week (although this latter will rise a bit with the mandatory five-day week for financial institutions from February 1989). In all, Japanese workers must put in about 200–500 more hours a year than western workers.

Moreover, in Japan overtime is in effect compulsory and comprises about 10.5 per cent of total working hours (8.9 per cent in the US, 8.2 per cent in Britain), but is is a 10 per cent which employers expand and contract with total freedom. Although overtime pay is ostensibly 1.25 times higher than regular pay, it is not supplemented by the twice yearly bonuses which accrue to the latter and so is in effect *lower than regular pay*.

All the talk of increasing leisure time is thus just a euphemism for unemployment, since regular hours in manufacturing were actually higher in 1986 than they were in 1974 and 1975, and they increased again in 1987. Overtime has also risen, by 9.4 per cent in September 1988 over the previous year, for the sixteenth consecutive month. Within the working class there are also important differences, since small firms require a total of about eight more hours a month than large firms, but five hours less overtime, giving the large firms more flexibility in regulating working hours.

Japanese workers are also under tremendous pressure not to take the holidays to which they are entitled, with Nissan recently cancelling holidays about which a great fanfare had been made. It seemed like a cruel joke to have Japan's new five-year (1988–92) economic management programme at this time predict increasing leisure and higher consumption (Rōdōshō, 1987b, p. 58; statistical appendix, pp. 60–2; 1988b, statistical appendix, p. 12; Nihon ginkō, 1986, p. 145; *NKS*, 19 July 1987, p. 8; 21 October 1987, p. 33; *JEJ*, 4 June 1988, p. 1; 9 July 1988, p. 12; 3 September 1988, pp. 3, 20; 12 November 1988, p. 17; 14 January 1989, pp. 6, 14).

The current campaign to intensify the labour process comes on top of an already strict regime, but one which likes to present itself in a benevolent light. For example, the Revised Labour Standards Act, effective from April 1989, purports to shorten the present legal working week from 48 to 46 hours (although not until 1992 for about 25 million workers mainly in certain small and medium enterprises). But in effect this Act abolishes the eight hour day. Employers will be able to force people to work for over ten hours a day for a number of days straight without overtime pay, so long as over a period of three months the hours average no more than 40 a week (or 44 for the 25 million). The flexibility which employers used to have in relation to overtime, but for which they had to pay 'extra', they will in future have free of charge. The potential fall of two hours a week in total working time will be more than paid for by the added flexibility and the savings in overtime pay (*JEJ*, 14 November 1987, p. 3; *NKS*, 3 November 1988, p. 3).

Toyota has already taken the bull by the horns and, in addition slashing overtime by a half, established its own calendar with holidays during the week so that it can take advantage of reduced power costs by bringing workers in on the weekends. The company achieved a considerable 'cost down' from this device. Many companies have also been announcing new 'flextime' systems to take advantage of the new law. Mitsubishi Electric will allow workers to choose their own hours, in order to encourage initiative and creativity, but it decided to exclude its 2000 production workers and 1000 of its non-production workers from this opportunity to be creative. However, from November 1988 all of Hitachi's 40 000 employees went on its flextime system, the largest in the industry. Sumitomo Life has exchanged an extra 40 minutes a day for six extra holidays, which the workers will probably not take, in order to cope with intensified competition in the finance industry (*JEJ*, 9 May 1987, p. 4; 7 July 1988, p. 13; 19 November 1988, p. 23; *NKS*, 12 August 1987).

The classical sources of employer flexibility to keep up the intensity of work are the temporary labour and subcontracting systems. We have seen how easily temporaries can be laid off, but employers can with equal ease hire them. A recent law restored to legality a practice which had been notorious in the prewar period and which was banned afterwards, even though in practice it crept back with the mounting recession: labour bosses as intermediaries between the worker and the actual user of the worker's time. The Labour Dispatch Act of July 1986 once again allows the hirer of workers to 'dispatch' them to hungry employers, and a number of such parasitic companies have emerged from the woodwork, dealing particularly in women workers in the industry of the future, services. These are an advance on the *paato banku* (part-time bank), which was more a source of information on exploitable workers than an agent for dispensing them. Within six months, temporary employment businesses had risen threefold to 7975 (8684 by July 1988), the fastest growing sector in the entire economy. Some companies are setting up their own temporary-staff subsidiaries to serve their temporary employment needs, for example, Canon, Kawasaki Steel, Kyodo Oil and Nippon Shinpan. The latter's subsidiary is euphemistically called 'Human Link'. A Mitsubishi official recently remarked: 'Most of the major manufacturers are operating a subsidiary in this business. A new employment system using temporary staff appears to be taking root in Tokyo' (*JEJ*, 20 August 1988, p. 9).

It was to be expected that companies, such as Nissan and Toshiba, which had only months before been laying off permanent workers, would now be recruiting temporaries of one kind or another. Hiring retired workers, as has been done by Asahi Breweries, is another favourite, since here one gets skill and experience for only 60 per cent of regular wages. A superb recent study has shown (Fujita, 1987) that another expedient, before the 'final solution' of shifting overseas, is to move to regions within Japan of particularly high unemployment, such as Kyushu and Hokkaido. Mitsubishi Corporation and Ricoh are among the companies recently to have taken this less radical step (Shiga, 1988; *JEJ*, 26 December 1987, p. 16; 2 July 1988, p. 22; 30 July 1988, p. 8; 6 August 1988, pp. 1, 5; 20 August 1988, p. 9; *NKS*, 13 September 1988, p. 1; 15 September 1988, p. 11).

Another avenue short of moving to Asia for cheap labour is to bring that labour to Japan, illegally so that workers' vulnerability keeps their wages at Asian rather than Japanese rates. Employers have admitted to paying illegals ¥100 an hour, that is, only 21 per cent of the average legal minimum (which varies according to prefecture) of ¥474 an hour for part-timers. While in the past the great majority of persons prosecuted for illegal entry were women (89.8 per cent), mainly brought in by the *yakuza* (gangsters) from Thailand and the Philippines to work as prostitutes in Japan's burgeoning sex industry, in January–June 1988 for the first time the proportion of men was greater (58 per cent). The latter, increasingly from South Korea, are used to do the sort of heavy work which can usually only be forced on Japanese day labourers, particularly in construction. Those prosecuted for illegal entry are only the tip of the iceberg: 7196 in January–June 1988 compared to an estimated total of 150 000 illegals (Utsumi and Matsui, 1988; Utsumi, 1988; *NKS*, 17 October 1988, p. 5; 30 October 1988, p. 10; *JEJ*, 17 September 1988, pp. 1, 7, 9; 29 October 1988, pp. 1, 5; 12 November 1988, p. 3; 19 November 1988, p. 19; 12).

The expansion of part-time women workers has been one of the main features of the entire recession which began in 1974: high-paid secure male jobs have been giving way to low-paid insecure female jobs. Although Labour Department statistics do not capture the full measure of this practice, they confirm the trend. Part-time women workers increased by 320 000 in 1985 to 1987. We must remember that this typically means a 30–40 hour week, but on something like ¥500–600. In 1987 23.1 per cent (3.65 million) of all women employees were officially regarded as working part-time, but in commerce the proportion was 30.6 per cent (Kaji, 1986, pp. 5 ff.; Rōdōshō, 1988b, statistical appendix, pp. 32–3; *NKS*, 31 October 1988, p. 30).

Yet another pool of cheap temporary labour are seconded workers, who fall into two groups: those temporarily seconded from their original employers and those who have been finally retired off. According to a Labour Ministry survey, in the five-year period to January 1987, 568 000 workers (3.3 per cent) had been temporarily seconded, 149 000 in 1986 alone, when another 26 000 were permanently seconded. Almost 92 per cent of giant firms with over 5000 employees were involved in 1986, and they have so far dealt with some 7 per cent of their workers in this way. One recent example is the acceptance by Toyota of 700 workers from Nippon Steel (*AS*, 12 July 1987, p. 1; 31 October 1987, p. 13).

The subcontracting system is the last great source of flexibility for monopoly capital, and workers in the smallest firms are as vulnerable to the grossest intensification of work as are temporaries. In the period 1975–85, which roughly corresponded with the restructuring out of raw material processing and into the export-dependent machine industries, the numbers of new small firms increased greatly, as did their rate of disappearance, their capacity to expand and contract production, as well as their shifting from one industry to the other. The Small and Medium Enterprise Agency proudly announced that the rate of the country's dependence on small firms (4–299 employees) to spearhead the restructuring had increased from 39.6 to 47.5 per cent in this period (Chūshō kigyōchō, 1987, pp. 39–43).

During the high yen recession, among the problems faced by small subcontracting firms were pressures from parent firms to cut contract prices. For example, in the fall of 1986 Toyota instructed its affiliated parts makers to lower their prices by 3–5 per cent, and by June 1987 it reported that its rationalisation efforts had cut production costs by ¥78 billion, about half of which came from cheaper components (*JTW*, 15 August 1987, p. 12; *JT*, 24 July 1987, p. 6; *Industria*, May 1987, p. 42; *JEJ*, 24 October 1987, p. 17; 14 November 1987, p. 19). From the ceilings of Mazda subcontractors, which were also asked to cut prices and which saved the company ¥100 billion in 1986 and 1987, one could see a sign which read (Satō, *et al.*, 1987, pp. 133–4):

V50: sakusen tenkaichū	[V50 Strategy Now Operational]
Seisansei 50 per cent appu o	[Raise Productivity by 50 per cent]
Jitsugen sase. Ikinokorō	[Let's Survive]

WAGE CUTS

The final way to increase the exploitation of workers is by cutting wages. Although wage costs are also reduced when irregulars are brought in to raise the intensity of work, employers have maintained tight ceilings on the wages of even their regular workers. From 1974 to 1986 the latter's real wages rose by an average of only 1 per cent per year, and the spring 1987 wage negotiations (one could no longer call them an 'offensive'), even in the opinion of the *Journal of Japanese Trade and Industry*, resulted in a:

complete rout for labour. The wage hikes agreed on during the annual parleys were the thinnest ever, reflecting the deteriorating exports and dwindling financial resources of Japanese industry – both factors attributable to the rapid upswing in the yen (July/Aug. 1987, p. 7).

The average increase was only 3.57 per cent, while in the steel industry it was 1.55 per cent, in metals and shipbuilding 1.74 per cent, and in commerce 1.50 per cent. Increases in bonuses had also came to a complete halt in summer 1987, with an actual average reduction in manufacturing by 1.8 per cent and by much more in machinery: 9.7 per cent in precision, 7.9 per cent in general, 7.4 per cent in transport and 3.3 per cent in electrical. In January to September 1987, the incomes of the bottom three quintile groups rose by only 0.5, 0.8 and 0.1 per cent, while those of the upper two rose by 3.6 and 1.1 per cent (ibid.; Rōdōshō, 1987a; *NKS*, 22 May 1987, p. 9; 7 August 1987, p. 5; 7 June 1987, p. 21; 27 November 1987, p. 11; 16 December 1988, p. 11; December 1987, p. 13).

Even some executives accepted pay cuts. In March 1986, the bonuses of directors at Fujitsu were reduced by 17 per cent, and their salaries by 10 per cent, while Matsushita cut directors' bonuses by 10 per cent. But cutting managerial salaries is mainly a propaganda device to help workers tighten their belts, because most members of the executive class were among the property owners whose incomes from capital gains soared in 1986–87 (*STK*, 28 February 1987; *NKS*, 31 July 1987, p. 13).

In 1988, in spite of the turnaround in company profitability, workers fared only marginally better. From the record low hike of 3.6 per cent a year earlier, all they won in the spring negotiations was a rise of 4.4 per cent, with a mere 1.78 per cent for steel workers. The first sign of any relief came with an average increase of 5.65 per cent in summer bonuses and an approximately 8.15 per cent increase in winter bonuses (*JEJ*, 4 June 1988, p. 4; 16 July 1988, p. 15; 10 December 1988, p. 17; *NKS*, 10 November 1988, p. 13).

The combined effect of all the measures associated with the second prong of capital's response to the high yen crisis, squeezing the Japanese masses, was to reduce a near doubling of the yen's value in 1985–87 to a mere 20–30 per cent increase in dollar-based unit wage costs: 19.83 per cent in electrical machinery, 26.81 per cent in transport machinery and 28.06 per cent in general machinery. In January to March 1988 another 9 per cent increase in labour productivity ensured a further drop of 4 per cent in unit wage costs. Thanks to the increased exploitation of the Japanese working class, the US accusation that Japanese companies were not raising export prices but were 'absorbing almost exactly half of the yen appreciation' was not too far from the mark. The other half, and more, would be recovered from the peoples of Asia (*JEJ*, 28 November 1987, p. 3; 4 June 1988, p. 4; *FEER*, 17 November 1988, p. 119; *Ekonomisuto*, 4 July 1988, p. 19).

I suggested earlier that imperialism always results from some crisis in the capital exporting country. What actually forces capital to move abroad is the class struggle following the crisis, or more fundamentally, the historically determined organisational strengths of the bourgeoisie and the working class. On the one hand, there was the extraordinary power of the Japanese bourgeoisie and its organisations, and on the other, a labour movement in total disarray (Steven, 1983; *Ampo*, recent issues).

It was thus the inability of the Japanese working class to oppose capital's strategy of looking for cheaper labour outside Japan while continuing to sell in the advanced country markets which lies behind the new imperialism. To get round growing inter-imperialist rivalry and the high yen, Japanese capital is relocating much of its productive industry overseas, confirming once again that major historical developments in Japan are spurred more by the organisational might of western imperialism than the Japanese working class. Such has been the course of the Japanese class struggle.

Note

1. *NKS*, 27 June 1987, part 2, p. 1. Unless otherwise sourced, the data on fiscal 1986 comes from this or the following other general surveys: *JEJ*, 15 August 1987, p. 11; *NKS*, 13 August 1987, p. 1; 15 August, 1987, p. 3.

3 Global Strategy to 1980: Focus on Asia

The movement abroad by Japanese capital is essentially the extension of a social relation, in which the Japanese bourgeoisie forms alliances with foreign ruling classes against both the Japanese and foreign working classes. There are thus two general types of assistance which the imperialist move provides: first, access to extra workers (or rent earning raw materials), who can be played off against one another and who help ensure that somewhere or other the conditions which Japanese capital has to offer are accepted; and secondly, the opportunity to bring the weight of the foreign ruling classes to bear on Japanese workers, as occurs when cheap imports are brought into Japan. If the movement is to an underdeveloped country, the neo-colonial ruling classes do not get the same benefits in return from the alliance, since while they do receive help from Japanese capital in their domestic struggles, they do not get an equal crack at Japanese workers. Only when two imperialist powers come together, such as Japan and the US, are the benefits of the alliance more reciprocal. However, there is often a lot of conflict before the spoils are evenly divided, although eventually both sides do normally get equal access to each other's domain.

Since capital is a social relation with an economic appearance, the forms of its internationalisation are often quite misleading and can even appear benevolent. For example, there is hardly a Southeast Asian government which is not clamouring for investment, trade and yen loans from Japan, claiming that these bring great benefits to their people as a whole. However, when capital is internationalised, its outward appearance is more deceptive than usual. This is because the connections between the different moments in the process of exploiting workers are more obscure when they are scattered worldwide than when they exist in the same country.

Extracting the surplus in capitalist society requires at least four distinct processes to occur without interruption. Money must be converted into means of production (machinery, materials, fuels, and so on) and labour power; these must then produce some new commodity; this latter must be sold, yielding more money than was originally spent; and the surplus must be available for further accumulation. Extracting the surplus requires each of these moments to proceed smoothly at the proper time, and together they constitute capitalist exploitation.

Whenever any one of these processes is seen in isolation from the others, its social significance is lost sight of. This is an easy thing to do, because even when they all take place in the same country, they are separated in both time and space. Money gathers in banking institutions, and its movement to the separate places where things are made, factories, is seen only by the small number of people who organise corporate lending. The shops from which the new commodities are sold are seen by all of us, but as means of acquiring the necessities of life, and so we do not observe the connection between our purchases and the making of the products in factories. The internationalisation of bourgeois social relations obscures their political reality even more, because the spatial separation of the different moments is so much greater. Even within any one of them, specialisations often involve enormous distances. For example, the production of cars nowadays involves the manufacture of parts in many different countries, while the banking system makes billions in minutes through constantly shifting money around the world.

When, as occurred before the Second World War, imperialist ruling classes took over and directly wielded state power in their colonies, their presence was also much more visible, particularly when they filled the key institutions with their own nationals. For example, when whites owned and operated the banks, the factories and the shops, and when they also ran the government, the real links that bound these institutions together were quite obvious.

However, holding state power in the colony was also a very rigid thing to do in a mode of production like capitalism, which flourishes best when the ruling class has the maximum flexibility. At times the resources needed to maintain state power were so great that the losses outweighed the gains, but it was not possible to reduce the commitment of resources to match more closely the benefits received. Under neo-colonialism, however, in which the local ruling class holds state power and maintains social control, the imperialist power can operate much more freely. It can concentrate different moments in different countries (raw material extraction in one, commodity production in another and selling in yet another), and separately expand or contract the resources it risks in each one when the returns vary. Investment, trade and lending can each be carried out in specialised areas, and each can be varied.

The more capital internationalises, the more it gains from such flexibilities and the more it demands. And since high levels of flexibility always suit the stronger party to an agreement, the alliance between the imperialist and the neo-colonial ruling classes has to be renegotiated constantly. Its terms also shift with developments in the class struggles of the countries concerned.

There is thus no particular time when one can say the Japanese bourgeoisie formed a binding agreement with any other ruling class. But at any one time it does have stronger and weaker commitments which correspond to its overall strategy for dealing with its most pressing problems. In this chapter, I examine the background to and development of Japanese capital's worldwide strategy for dealing with the current crisis. I focus on the period leading up to the rise of the yen in order to illustrate a process: the new wave of imperialism, mainly in Asia, that began in the mid-1970s but which is still to achieve its full momentum. In the next and subsequent chapters I look at the details of the current period.

Just as the *endaka fukyō* had to be understood in the context of the crises which preceded it and out of whose 'solutions' it was born, so must the current turning point for Japanese imperialism be put in the context of the same crises, since imperialism before 1980 was one of the three prongs of a strategy to deal with them. There were thus three main stages in the development of postwar imperialism, each characterised by its role in the corresponding crisis to Japan.

In the first, the forms were mainly aid (yen loans) and trade, with investment becoming important only towards the end around 1970. The main geographical focus was Asia. The second period began with the oil shock and the crisis centering on the basic materials industries. It involved a huge escalation in foreign investment, trade and yen loans, and its main geographical focus was also Asia, although increasingly the US as well. However, whereas the first wave of DFI (direct foreign investment) in Asia was almost entirely motivated by the search for lower wages, the second which began in the mid-1970s was after a wider range of cost reductions, particularly of raw materials. The third period began with the early stages of the *endaka fukyō* around 1980, and it has a much wider geographical focus and purpose. Table 3.1, which shows the accumulated value and the number of approved investments each fiscal year since 1963, outlines the three periods.

I organise the discussion mainly around the waves of foreign investment: the textile investments of the 1960s in Asia, the basic materials

Table 3.1   Accumulated value and cases of Japanese DFI, fiscal 1962–87

Fiscal year	Cases	$ million	% increase over last year	Accumulated totals $ million	Cases
1951–62	961	546			
1963	213	126	28.6	672	1 176
1964	184	119	–5.6	791	1 360
1965	197	159	R 33.6	950	1 557
1966	244	227	I 42.8 W	1 177	1 801
1967	290	275	S 21.1 A	1 452	2 091
1968	369	557	I 102.5 G	2 009	2 460
1969	544	665	N 19.4 E	2 674	3 004
1970	729	904	G 35.9 S	3 578	3 733
1971	904	858	–5.1	4 436	4 637
1972	1 774	2 338	172.5	6 774	6 411
1973	3 093	3 494	49.6	10 268	9 504
1974	1 912	2 396	–31.5 S	12 664	11 416
1975	1 591	3 280	O 37.0 H	15 944	13 007
1976	1 652	3 462	I 5.5 O	19 406	14 659
1977	1 761	2 806	L –18.9 C	22 212	16 420
1978	2 393	4 598	63.9 K	26 810	18 813
1979	2 694	4 995	8.6	31 805	21 507
1980	2 442	4 693	–6.0	36 498	23 949
1981	2 563	8 932	E 90.3 F	45 430	26 512
1982	2 549	7 703	N –13.7 U	53 133	29 061
1983	2 754	8 145	D 5.7 K	61 278	31 815
1984	2 499	10 155	A 24.7 Y	71 433	34 314
1985	2 613	12 217	K 20.3 Ō	83 650	36 927
1986	3 196	22 320	A 82.7	105 970	40 123
1987	4 548	33 364	49.5	139 334	44 707

Source: Shūkan tōyō keizai, 1973–88.

investments of the 1970s also mainly in Asia, but in Latin America and Australia as well, and the machinery investments of the 1980s in Asia and North America. This chapter provides an overview of the first two periods, while the third is dealt with in subsequent chapters.

In each case there is no suggestion that the new wave of investments, which characterises the period, is all that is important in it, since the major tendencies of each period overlap into others. For example, the mining investments of the second period already began to dominate towards the end of the first. A full 57 per cent of the $3061 million invested in mining up to 1973 was committed in the previous two years. Even a tendency of the third period is evidenced in the first. What distinguished the *endaka fukyō* was a high dependence on the North American and European markets, but this dependence was built over many years together with commercial and financial investments needed to service the export drive.

Table 3.2 Accumulated DFI, by region and industry to March 1974 ($ million)

	North America	Latin America	Asia	Europe	Elsewhere	Total
Manufacturing	587	1 056	1 211	155	252	3 260
Food	27	40	47	24	30	167
Textiles	37	183	483	6	34	743
Wood/Pulp	219	19	71	–	54	362
Chemicals	28	343	76	36	54	538
Metals	152	159	99	28	47	486
General machinery	35	93	49	37	3	217
Electrical machinery	60	69	183	7	9	328
Transport machinery	6	125	77	4	9	222
Other	22	26	126	13	9	196
Agriculture/forestry/fisheries	36	39	103	1	50	229
Mining	254	189	605	827	1 186	3 061
Construction	12	41	11	1	1	66
Commerce	824	120	74	143	70	1 231
Finance/insurance	251	211	128	237	91	918
Other	465	150	228	596	65	1 504
TOTAL	2 428	1 808	2 359	1 959	1 716	10 270

Source: Shūkan tōyō keizai, 1974, pp. 442–3.

FIRST PERIOD: 1962–73

Table 3.2 shows that in the first period, manufacturing investments centred mainly on the textile and electrical industries in Asia and Latin America. These were chiefly for the local markets. The textile investments of the 1960s grew out of the crisis of rising real wages following the revival of capital accumulation in the mid-1950s, and to some extent out of trading strategies in Asia and America. The early stages of the mounting conflict with the US were thus over 'excessive' textile exports.

In spite of the priority the Meiji state had assigned to heavy industry, textiles remained the mainstay of Japanese capitalism right into the late 1930s and then again after the war well into the 1950s. Throughout, the power of capital, revealed by its capacity to accumulate, rested heavily on the rigid gender division of the working class, not just in tandem with the temporary labour and subcontracting systems, but also with an industrial division. The men were concentrated in the rising heavy industries, the women in the labour intensive textile industries where wages were less than half those of the men. In large part, therefore, it was the high rate of exploitation of women textile workers which provided the surplus accumulated by the heavy industries (Steven, 1986).

During the 1960s, however, the power of Japanese capital which derived from its hold on low-paid workers in labour-intensive areas was threatened by Asian capital, which had an even stronger hold on low-paid workers. Japanese wages, even women's wages, had risen sufficiently to give capital in Asia the upper edge, and the Japanese ruling class as a result first developed its three-pronged strategy.

Japanese capital consciously moved out of the lighter industries, or their more labour intensive branches where it was losing its competitive advantage, into ones of higher value added. A rough order in which the levels of technology in textiles rose was weaving and knitting, the production of natural fibres (cotton, flax, jute, silk, wool), garment manufacturing (riddled with sweat shops and subcontractors), spinning (dominated by Toyobo, Kanebo and Unitika) and the production of synthetic fibres (polyester, nylon and acrylic, the technology for which was brought in from the US and Europe by Toray and Teijin). During the 1960s cotton textiles were moved to Asia, while synthetic textiles were consolidated at home. The whole strategy was well coordinated with an aggressive diplomatic policy in the region: the Japan–Republic of Korea Friendship Treaty and the Japan–Taiwan Economic Cooperation Agreement in 1965, and the establishment of the Asian Development Bank in 1966.

Capital could only retain its edge in the older labour intensive industries if it found a working class more vulnerable than its own, which it did by allying with the ruling classes of Asia and embarking on a programme of foreign investment. However, DFI in textiles was not just propelled by capital's quest for lower wages, but also to preserve its markets. Textiles had been the mainstay of Japan's exports for some time, and in order to survive the competition from the newly established cotton industries in Asia, the need arose to produce locally, alongside them. The growth of export markets in Asia were also greatly assisted by yen loans and the postwar reparations programme, so that the onslaught on Asia at this time involved an integration of the different moments in the overall process of capital accumulation.

The growth of DFI in synthetic textiles later on was part of that competitive struggle for market shares in Asia. Synthetic fibre investments started when the Japanese domestic market became saturated in the mid-1960s, with half the industry's output being exported by the end of the decade. This was the final stage of its internationalisation, which by March 1974 was already considerable. Toray and Teijin, which accounted for 83 per cent of total fibre investments, had an overseas capacity which was 30 per cent of their domestic capacity, and 60 per cent if factories under construction were included (Yoshihara, 1978, p. 104).

The major features of the textile investments were their concentration in Asia (67 per cent) and other low wage countries such as Brazil; their small average-size (median was $223 000, while only five out of 275 projects were over $10 million); their equity pattern was the joint venture (67 per cent of the 275 involved only 25–54 per cent Japanese equity); and the *sōgō shōsha* (general trading companies) were active if not leading participants. Since this was the pioneering period, the networks and resources of the *shōsha* were crucial in getting things started, and they served to tie together the different moments of the overall accumulation process. In his detailed study on this period, Yoshihara wrote:

> Trading companies act as financiers, exchange brokers, organizers, consultants, and information salesmen, but we should not lose sight of the fact that their primary operation is marketing (1978, p. 126).

The other major manufacturing DFI in Asia in the 1960s had also become an export-oriented industry following the saturation of the Japanese market: labour-intensive consumer electronics products, such as radios, TVs (first black and white, then colour) and tape recorders. Household electrical goods, like rice cookers, fans, stoves and vacuum cleaners were part of the same process, although since their weight in the electrical machinery industry as a whole was much less, I focus on electronics. Moreover, just like textiles, before their internationalisation they too first exhausted the sources of cheap labour in Japan by relocating as far as possible into remote areas. For example, in 1966–69, 91 per cent of electronics component factories built in Japan were outside major cities, and in 1970–73, the proportion increased to 98 per cent (ibid., p. 133).

However, the two industries were very different in terms of their market structures, since only in synthetic textiles did a few large firms dominate, whereas this sort of structure characterised the entire electronics industry. A few giants towered over thousands of component makers in subcontracting relationships, and there was no need for the participation of the trading companies. However, even the giants undertook mainly small investments, often just to open an assembly plant. Although joint ventures were rarer in electronics than in textiles, the Japanese were not averse to them, because the level of technology transferred was very low.

While market strategy was a major force behind the textile investments, it had little importance in promoting those in electronics, since the markets aimed at were almost entirely in the advanced countries, not least Japan itself. Of gradually increasing importance to the electronics investments was also their function in securing low-cost components for importation back to Japan. This applied mainly to the Asian NICs, and is examined in Chapter 5. Since electronics was an export industry, it was not welcomed where import substitution was being seriously attempted, such as Indonesia and to a lesser degree Thailand, which together accounted for about half Japan's textile investments in the region.

Because DFI in Asia was mainly attracted by the low cost of labour, each venture was not typically very large in terms of value. The number of investments therefore captures the importance of Asia in these two industries more accurately than does their value. Table 3.3, which presents a survey of textile and electronics ventures by country and fiscal year, confirms the central position of Asia for both industries in this period. South Korea and Taiwan were the chief targets, but as wages rose in those countries in the 1970s, the attractiveness of the poorer ASEAN countries increased. Only in the third period, the *endaka fukyō*, did electrical investments also pour into the US and Europe.

While the early years, and particularly the textile investments, were characterised by small projects and small companies, often with the help of the *sōgō shōsha*, larger companies and bigger projects took the limelight in the second period. Table 3.4, which ranks Japan's top twenty transnational manufacturing corporations according to the amounts of their overseas production at the end of fiscal 1973, shows that the electronics majors had by this time moved ahead of the big textile companies, and that the automakers had also begun to assert an importance which would predominate in the third period. However, the companies making the largest overseas investments were still mainly the *sōgō shōsha*, which in by March 1974 occupied the first five and the tenth positions. Toray, Sony and Honda were the only manufacturing companies among the top ten (Shūkan tōyō keizai, 1974, p. 2).

Table 3.3   Survey of DFI cases in textiles and electrical machinery, fiscal
1951–1987

	1951–74		1975–79		1980–87		Total	
	T	E	T	E	T	E	T	E
World total	181	258	39	115	42	252	269	641
Asia	124	184	25	69	25	116	178	379
South Korea	23	41	7	10	–	12	30	64
Taiwan	33	78	–	11	2	33	37	128
Hong Kong	8	9	1	2	8	8	18	20
Singapore	3	19	1	32	1	12	5	64
Thailand	26	7	2	3	4	12	32	22
Malaysia	5	16	5	6	1	14	11	36
Philippines	7	2	1	2	–	6	9	10
Indonesia	14	2	7	3	–	3	21	8
Latin America	24	30	4	15	2	15	30	61
United States	8	21	3	20	8	67	21	112
Europe	5	9	5	8	4	46	14	64

Note: Table excludes cases which subsequently withdrew, and totals include
cases for which the date of establishment is unknown.
T – textiles; E – electrical machinery.
Source: Shūkan tōyō keizai, 1988, pp. 16–19.

The importance of DFI to large manufacturing corporations at this
time was also revealed by the proportions of quoted ones which had
already made overseas investments. Excluding primary industry, this
was highest in electrical machinery (42.7 per cent), precision machinery (42.4 per cent), non-ferrous metals (40 per cent), textiles (39 per
cent), mining (35.7 per cent), transport machinery (33.3 per cent)
and chemicals (32.7 per cent). However, the 'good' that this did them
was still very limited: the overseas production of the top two TNCs,
Hitachi and Matsushita, comprised only 5 per cent of their total
turnover in 1973 (Shūkan tōyō keizai, 1974, pp. 4–5). Relative to
other imperialist powers, Japanese capital was also still weak, and
even in the region selected to be its 'backyard', it was the number one
investor only in Thailand. In South Korea, Hong Kong, Taiwan, the
Philippines and Indonesia it was second to the US, while in Malaysia
and Singapore it was fourth behind the US, Britain and one other
(ibid., p. 25).

Table 3.4 Overseas production of Japan's top 20 TNCs, fiscal 1973

	$ million	Cases	Main countries*	Industry
Hitachi	179	20	TW, HK, P, T, M, S, A, C, G	Electrical
Matsushita	179	45	K, TW, P, T, M, S, I, G	Electrical
Yoshida Kogyo	120	27	TW, HK, T, M, I, F, H, C, A	Fasteners
Sanyo	118	28	K, TW, HK, P, T, M, S, I, SP	Electrical
Teijin	116	25	K, TW, HK, P, T, S, I, A, B	Textiles
Toyota	93	10	T, I, PO, C, A, B, CR, PR	Motor cars
Nissan	85	12	T, M, S, TR, C, A, MX, PR	Motor cars
Mitsubishi HI	81	18	TW, T, SV, S	Ships, aircraft
Ajinomoto	75	11	P, T, M, I	Food Flavouring
Toyobo	70	25	S, I, A	Textiles
Ishikawajima Harima	69	8	M, SV, S, B, PR, AS	Shipbuilding
Unitika	61	18	TW, HK, T, M, S, I, B	Textiles
Toray	52	46	K, TW, HK, T, M, S, I, E, B	Textiles
Toshiba	51	22	K, TW, HK, P, T, M, IN, IR, C, A	Electrical
Dai Nippon Printing	45	11	HK, M, S, B	Printing
Mitsubishi Electric	41	26	K, TW, HK, P, T	Electrical
Kanebo	36	16	K, TW, HK, T, I	Textiles
Hattori Tokeiten	36	10	TW, HK, G, E, C	Watches
NEC	33	18	K, TW, IR, A, B	Communication Equipment
Teac	31	4	HK, H, A	Casette Decks

Notes:

A–America	AS–Australia	B–Brazil	C–Canada
E–England	F–France	G–W. Germany	H–Holland
I–Indonesia	IN–India	IR–Iran	K–S. Korea
MX–Mexico	P–Philippines	PO–Portugal	PR–Puerto Rico
SP–Spain	SV–S. Vietnam	T–Thailand	TR–Turkey

CR–Costa Rica
HK–Hong Kong
M–Malaysia
S–Singapore
TW–Taiwan

Source: Shūkan tōyō keizai, 1974, p. 4.

SECOND PERIOD: 1974–79

If the first period ended with the oil shock of late 1973, the second had no such clear cut off point but has merged into the third, the current period. Nevertheless, the two are distinguishable in terms of the main influences behind the DFI, its location, as well as the institutional forms it assumed. In the second period, Japanese capital restructured its production process at home and abroad primarily to recover a competitive power it had lost with the oil crisis. The emphasis was on reducing costs and raising productivity, and so it moved chiefly into areas of lower costs, of raw materials and labour power, in Southeast Asia and Latin America.

Investments in Europe and America were concentrated in the unproductive sectors of finance and commerce. The purpose here was more to sell the goods, which were cheaply made in a careful division of labour among low-paid workers in Japan and the Third World, in countries where higher wages provided better markets. There was no point in locating productive investments in the advanced countries, because high wages there would simply have made them uncompetitive.

The second period therefore continued the emphasis on labour intensive industries in Southeast Asia, but it also included a powerful new thrust into securing raw materials. The first coherent statement of this strategy came in September 1974 with the publication of the Industrial Structure Advisory Council's *Long Term Vision of the Industrial Structure* (Kitazawa, 1983, p. 51). It rationalised and urged the continuation of moves already under way, for example, the investments in logging and the production of wood chips in Southeast Asia which began towards the end of the 1960s. Particularly the primary processing stages of the basic materials industries – steel, non-ferrous metals, petrochemicals, pulp and paper – were all told to go overseas, so that Japan could concentrate on machinery, final processing and final assembly. Sophisticated high-tech industries and energy conservation should be the focus of domestic activity, while all else could move abroad. Such was to be the widely heralded 'new international division of labour'.

In this second period the investments as well as the investing companies were also noticeably larger than in the first. For example, while in 1973, 43 per cent of the parent companies were small or medium-sized firms, by 1980 only 30.7 per cent were. From the mid-1970s, giant firms also greatly expanded the scale of their over-

seas activities, and investment decisions began to be made on the
basis of their global strategies, involving a global division of labour.
Mining investments were almost exclusively by giant firms, as were
80–85 per cent of those in chemicals and metals. The *sōgō shōsha*
were particularly prominent. For example, by 1979 Mitsui and Co.
had 59 overseas subsidiaries in 25 nations covering the whole range of
basic materials industries: iron-ore in Australia, aluminium and
iron-ore in Brazil (making Mitsui Japan's top iron importer), copper
ore in Zaire, uranium in Canada, petrochemicals in Iran and South
Korea, lumber in the Philippines and rubber, lumber and cement in
Indonesia (Tsūshō sangyōshō, 1984c, pp. 21–2; Tsuchiya, 1980).

Among the largest undertakings by giant corporations in this
period were (many were only completed in the next): in Indonesia
the ASAHAN aluminium smelter (1976) and the LNG development
project; in Brazil the CENIBRA (currently being expanded into one
of the world's largest) and FLONIBRA pulp and paper projects
(1973–74), the Kawasaki Steel and Nippon Steel mills (mid-1970s)
and the AMAZON (Mitsui consortium) aluminium plant (1978); in
the Philippines the Kawasaki steel sintering plant; and four petrochemical projects: Mitsui in Iran (1973) and South Korea, Sumitomo
in Singapore (1977) and Mitsubishi in Saudi Arabia (1981) (Nakano,
1978, pp. 66–75; Tsuchiya, 1983, pp. 40–1; Watanabe, 1986, pp.
203–4; Kitazawa, 1979; Tsuda, 1978, pp. 70 ff.).

The consortium was the typical institutional form assumed by the
large-scale mining and resource-related investments. It was often put
together by one or more of the *sōgō shōsha*, whose role in the
electrical and textile investments of this period was much less than
before. In addition, a substantial proportion of the large resource
development projects went hand in glove with Japanese aid and
therefore also involved Japanese construction companies. It was not
accidental that the early 1980s was the period when most (almost 80
per cent in 1982) overseas contracts won by Japanese construction
companies were in Asia. This was when most of the projects that
grew out of the scramble for raw materials in the mid-1970s were
being completed. By 1986 the Asian share of construction contracts
would have fallen to just over 40 per cent, with another 40 per cent
coming from the US and Europe (*NKS*, 23 September 1987, p. 3).
Table 3.5 reveals that the resource-related manufacturing and mining
investments were overwhelmingly in the underdeveloped countries of
Asia and Latin America.

A large proportion of the investments made 'elsewhere' in mining,

Table 3.5   Accumulated Japanese DFI, by industry and region, March 1980

	N. America	L. America	Asia	Europe	Elsewhere	Total
Manufacturing	2 030	2 583	3 847	683	1 724	10 867
Food	180	120	139	42	51	532
Textiles	167	339	870	126	44	1 546
Wood/pulp	269	188	132	–	91	680
Chemicals	230	481	528	96	977	2 312
Metals	323	667	732	107	298	2 127
Machinery	189	225	242	104	32	792
Electrical	495	195	473	72	35	1 270
Transport equipment	71	292	238	53	149	803
Other	105	75	492	82	51	805
Agriculture/forestry/fisheries	238	183	259	2	155	837
Mining	469	1 176	2 815	859	1 187	6 506
Construction	109	134	65	11	40	359
Commerce	3 034	386	331	658	203	4 612
Finance/insurance	733	294	237	704	78	2 046
Other	1 100	799	988	878	1 118	4 883
Real estate acquired	419	19	25	31	377	871
Branches' equipment	71	8	77	67	600	823
TOTAL	8 202	5 580	8 643	3 893	5 486	31 804

Source: Shūkan tōyō keizai, 1980, pp. 554–5.

metals and chemicals in this period were in Australia, which became a major target of Japanese mining companies. The most important of these investments were in coal for export to Japan, bauxite for aluminium smelting, aluminium smelting itself and iron and steel.

Chief among them was the involvement of the Japanese consortium comprising Kobe Steel, Marubeni and Sumitomo Trading Company in Comalco, which began operations in 1970 (dates below also refer to start dates). This giant aluminium smelting company also involving the Conzinc Riotinto group now employs 8600 workers and has a paid-up capital of A$560 million. Kobe Steel was also involved, though to a limited extent, in the even larger CRA Ltd of 1985, a general mining company with over 27 000 workers capitalised at more than A$1 billion. Another Kobe Steel heavyweight was its 1980 investment company jointly formed with C Itoh and Nissho Iwai to exploit opportunities in bauxite mining and aluminium smelting but which has recently branched out into processing gold ore. Two other Japanese consortia, both led by Sumitomo Light Metal Manufacturing, have entered aluminium smelting. The first, which includes Comalco as well as Kaiser aluminium and Kobe Steel, opened in 1978 on Boyne Island in Queensland and employs nearly 1000 workers. The second is a wholly owned Japanese financial and trading venture of 1983 to exploit opportunities in the aluminium industry.

Other major ventures in Australia include the Tomen consortium's participation in the A$91 million Port Waratah Coal Services in 1976; Tokyu's wholly owned A$29 million 'leisure' project, Yanchep Sun City, in Perth in 1974; Mitsui's participation in Thiess Dampier Mitsui Coal in 1962, its wholly owned Mitsui Iron Ore Development in 1970, its 70 per cent share in Mitsui Coal Development in 1980, and its 50 per cent share (Mitsubishi has the other 50 per cent) in the A$200 million Japan Australia LNG mining company in 1984 (Shūkan tōyō keizai, 1988; *NKS*, 20 August 1987, p. 9).

In at least one respect the 1970s saw a return to the 1950s. At that time, even though DFI was only an adjunct to Japan's policy of getting raw materials via trade, it nicely complemented it. The largest portion of DFI was in mining (44.6 per cent) to secure oil, iron ore and copper ore, while the next largest was in manufacturing (36.3 per cent). But most of the latter were also resource related: lumber, pulp, steel and non-ferrous metals. The big four projects set up in these early years were Alaska Pulp (1953) in the US, the Usiminas steel works in Brazil (1957), Arabia Oil in Saudi Arabia (1958) and North Sumatra Oil in Indonesia (1960). Even though the labour

intensive textile and electrical industries overshadowed resource
procurement in the 1960s, towards the end of that decade the forces
that would dominate the 1970s had powerfully re-asserted themselves. In 1968–71 mining once again predominated, but this time the
focus shifted from the Middle East and the Americas to Asia and the
Pacific and lasted well into the 1980s: oil in Indonesia; natural gas in
Indonesia, Sarawak and Brunei; copper in the Philippines, Malaysia
Zaire and Papua New Guinea; iron ore in Australia and the Philippines (and Brazil); and coal, aluminium and nickel in Australia
(Tsuchiya, 1984, p. 33; Watanabe, 1986, pp. 207–11).

In the 1970s there was a marked shift towards mining or manufacturing which undertook primary processing of materials for export to
Japan, particularly chemicals and metals. These were now motivated
by the need for both secure raw material supplies as well as cheap
ones, and the importance of low cost labour used in primary processing. The significance of underdeveloped countries is clearer when we
examine the distribution of workers in Japanese affiliated companies
Table 3.6 shows that only about 20 per cent of them were in the more
developed capitalist countries and that about one third of those were
in commerce.

In 1980, wages in Asia were only 20 per cent of those in Japan
while those in Latin America were 47 per cent, in the Middle East 3.
per cent, in Africa 15 per cent and in Oceania 62 per cent. In Europe
they were about the same as in Japan, whereas in America they were
a good 35 per cent higher. The relocation of industry abroad in thi
period was also very closely linked to its 'hollowing out' at home
with the hiring of new workers overseas paralleling quite closely the
destruction of jobs in Japan. Even in the more capital intensive heav
and basic materials industries, which were being run down in Japan,
large number of jobs were involved. However, many more were los
as a result of the continuing relocation of the textile and electrica
industries, where labour costs played a much more central role in
capital's strategy (Steven, 1983, pp. 26, 258–9).

However, cheap labour was normally only a secondary consider
ation in the cost-down strategies of the mining companies, which
made highly capital intensive investments providing very few jobs
Textile and electronic workers in Asia therefore remained the larges
groups in overseas factories. A more important reason for locating s
much mining investment in Third World countries was that the latte
were too weak to resist the polluting side-effects of this type c
industry.

Table 3.6 Workers in Japanese affiliated companies overseas, 1980

	North America	Latin America	Asia	Europe	Africa	Middle East	Oceania	Total
Primary	1 402	1 156	11 317	282	1 885	–	2 146	18 188
Mining	516	1 024	1 098	69	2 469	3 120	1 937	10 233
Manufacturing	53 652	114 960	371 551	17 905	21 665	7 913	17 512	605 158
Food	1 537	2 452	6 721	35	855	–	374	11 974
Textiles	9 661	18 061	93 738	1 532	12 996	30	519	136 537
Wood/pulp	4 925	4 044	3 389	85	–	–	534	12 977
Chemicals	2 076	4 512	15 952	1 113	1 503	1 548	16	26 720
Iron and steel	755	31 224	10 828	2 201	1 663	1 348	6 941	54 960
Non-ferrous metals	7 270	3 013	6 013	–	250	–	1 125	17 671
Machinery								
General	2 151	13 331	19 533	1 293	–	34	150	36 492
Electrical	18 891	22 313	133 637	5 323	2 484	578	1 519	184 745
Transport	2 014	8 743	24 718	2 624	214	772	3 797	42 882
Precision	364	1 223	8 898	189	–	–	59	10 733
Other	4 008	6 044	48 124	3 510	1 700	3 603	2 478	69 467
Commerce	26 722	4 839	15 699	14 462	320	531	4 569	67 142
Other	1 650	6 127	5 017	784	781	532	233	15 124
TOTAL	83 942	128 106	404 682	33 502	27 120	12 096	26 397	715 845

Source: Tsuchiya, 1984, p. 54.

All of the giant projects mentioned earlier were highly polluting and damaged the health of workers and of people living in the areas nearby. Some even died of pollution induced illnesses. For example, iron dust has caused fatal asthma among Filipino workers at Kawasaki Steel's sintering plant at what was once the village of Nabacaan in Mindanao. The entire population of this village had been forcibly relocated eight kilometres away to a hill named Kalingagan to make room for the company. Analysis of dead fish found near the plant indicates that iron ore (from Australia) stored outside gets blown into the canal and flows into the sea. Workers who get ill are usually fired, and the company-designated hospital reportedly cooperates in suppressing information on the victims. Noel Yamada, who visited the site, wrote:

> This worker's coughing reminded me of those other victims [in Chiba] of KSC [Kawasaki Steel Corporation]. Also I remembered the secret agreement between KSC and its company hospital to bury [hush up] pollution victims. KSC does exactly the same covering up of its pollution-producing activities in Mindanao. Since I was there, one of the four fired workers has died (Yamada, 1980, p. 73).

In spite of the company's power to conceal information, in 1980 there were 700 officially recognized pollution victims and 60 deaths in the pollution area in Chiba, where the only large plant is Kawasaki Steel. In Japan, the restructuring out of light and into the heavy chemical industries, which reached its height in the 1960s, had caused many widely publicised pollution induced illnesses, such as Minamata (the main area of mercury poisoned water) disease, *itai-itai* ('painful' disease resulting from PCB poisoning) and a variety of cancers. Petitions against pollution increased sevenfold in 1960–72 (Shōji and Miyamoto, 1975, p. 4).

Copper pollution in Japan dates back one hundred years, when the Ashio copper mine claimed hundreds of thousands of Japanese victims. In the 1970s, copper pollution was taken to such places as Zaire, the Philippines, Peru and Sabah in Malaysia (by a consortium including two government agencies: the Overseas Economic Cooperation Fund and the Metal Mining Agency). The anti-pollution struggles which occurred in Japan over the years had made it very difficult for polluting companies to continue domestic operations without large pollution-preventing investments. Most of them simply decided

Table 3.7   Japan's DFI compared to that of other imperialist powers, 1986

	Stocks US $ billion 1986	% of GNP 1985	Per capita 1985	Share in world flow 1980–85	Share in receipts 1980–84	Ratio of overseas mfg production 1983
US	259.9	5.8	983	19.2	59.4	17.3
UK	139.5	25.7	2 069	21.1	10.8	n/a
West Germany	73.3	8.4	859	8.2	2.1	19.3
Holland	66.1	44.7	3 833	9.4	7.7	n/a
Japan	58.1	3.3	367	10.9	6.7	3.9
Canada	40.6	10.1	1 333	9.1	3.4	n/a
World	775.5	n/a	n/a	100.0	100.0	n/a

Source: Compiled from Nihon bōeki shinkōkai, 1987a–1988a.

to spread their muck among the vulnerable peoples of the Third World (Matsui, 1979).

Although the advance of Japanese imperialism was considerable in the second period, it was by international standards still at an early stage. Overseas subsidiaries of Japanese TNCs were no more than that, since it was only after the rise of the yen that Japanese companies began to set up bases overseas. Table 3.7 shows that, even as late as 1986, Japan's foreign investments were still comparatively modest.

However, Japanese imperialism's many tentacles were well integrated, with close cooperation between its trading and investment activities, particularly in the industries associated with the first two periods. Table 3.8 shows the results of a MITI survey measuring the degree of internationalisation of all industries except finance. The first four measures are the ratios of the capital, assets, turnover and workers of Japanese subsidiaries (with over 50 per cent ownership) to those of the domestic companies, while the next four measure trade and the links between production and trade. Export and import ratios show the proportions of turnover in each industry in Japan which is exported and the proportions of supplies which are imported. Exports to and imports from subsidiaries indicate the shares of Japanese exports and imports which are to and from the subsidiaries.

In each of mining, textiles and electrical machinery, the level of internationalisation on almost all measures was significant. However, although they revealed high levels of overseas production, sales and sources of supply, in the case of textiles the linkages were not very

Table 3.8 Measures of the internationalisation of Japanese capital, fiscal 1981 (%)

	Production						Trade Linkages	
	Ratio of subsidiaries to domestic				Export Ratio	Import Ratio	Export To subsidiary	Import From subsidiary
	Capital	Assets	Sales	Workers				
Primary	29.9	5.6	8.1	10.2	4.3	21.1	12.7	35.5
Mining	41.2	22.7	9.6	9.9	31.6	12.4	35.4	28.6
Manufacturing	15.1	4.4	3.3	5.5	24.1	17.1	13.1	25.2
Food	3.7	1.0	0.8	0.9	0.6	20.8	17.6	1.4
Textiles	36.2	9.2	5.3	10.8	15.6	10.5	3.3	7.7
Lumber/pulp	24.5	2.6	1.2	1.7	4.5	31.2	0.4	18.7
Chemicals	12.3	3.2	2.0	3.7	9.9	10.5	14.1	5.4
Iron and steel	21.7	9.4	4.3	11.3	37.6	20.4	3.2	11.7
Non-ferrous M	17.1	10.0	5.9	10.7	8.0	37.5	11.5	19.8
Machinery								
General	9.8	3.6	4.2	4.0	32.3	5.0	14.9	34.7
Electrical	21.1	7.2	8.6	12.6	31.1	4.2	19.7	35.6
Transport	21.0	5.4	3.9	6.4	44.4	0.8	5.0	13.2
Precision	7.0	2.2	3.5	3.4	47.7	5.3	56.7	67.1
Other	3.8	0.8	0.3	0.3	6.2	1.3	2.4	33.0
TOTAL	13.6	3.5	5.4	2.6	21.7	19.5	18.7	32.1

Source: Tsūshō sangyōshō, 1984c, pp. 74–5, 78–9.

close. While 15.6 per cent of Japanese textile production was exported, only 3.3 per cent of this went to Japanese subsidiaries, and while 10.5 per cent of the Japanese textile market was met by imports, only 7.7 per cent of them came from subsidiaries. However, in mining and electrical machinery the links were closer, although only 4.2 per cent of Japan's supply of electrical goods came from imports. The linkages in precision machinery were even closer, and a start had also been made in motor vehicles, which would expand in the years to come. In each of these latter, the links are made through components, in which there is a growing trade between parent and subsidiary.

Much of the linking of trade and investment was by the *sōgō shōsha*, particularly in raw material related investments. However, in the electrical and motor vehicle industries coordination was by the parent companies. Most of the majors already had impressive worldwide networks involving production bases, sales outlets and to a lesser extent component suppliers. The extension of the latter would be their main task in the third period.

From the other end, notably Asia, the importance of Japanese DFI increased enormously. Japan was now the top investor in Thailand, Indonesia and South Korea; it was second in Taiwan, the Philippines, Hong Kong and Malaysia; but it remained fourth in Singapore. It would take a few more years for Japan to claim the number one position throughout the region, including Singapore (Nihon bōeki shinkōkai, 1982a, p. 102).

The second period ended in the early 1980s with a shift in the line-up of forces opposing Japanese capital. Until then the primary confrontations had been with the working classes of Southeast Asia and the female and other super-exploited workers of Japan. Relations with the ruling classes of the advanced countries had been relatively cooperative, with conflicts over 'excessive' textile and TV exports never really becoming serious. And with a strong Japanese demand for what they had to offer, cheap labour and scarce raw materials, the ruling classes of Southeast Asia got from the alliance with Japanese imperialism enough of the spoils to keep most conflicts well beneath the surface, notwithstanding such outbreaks of nationalist agitation as greeted Prime Minister Tanaka in Jakarta in 1974. Rates of accumulation were high enough to keep both sides happy.

The end of the second and origin of the third period lay in a strategy Japanese capital had begun to adopt already in the early 1960s: as far as possible geographically to separate the points of production and sales, so that the maximum profits could be made from simultaneously exploiting both the lowest wage costs as well as the most luxurious markets. Such a strategy had been pursued by capital in the electrical industry from the early 1960s, when growing shares of output began to be exported to Europe and America. To achieve the lowest possible costs, a constantly shifting division of labour between Japan and Southeast Asia in the manufacture of electrical goods was adopted. By the end of the second period the numbers of workers in Japanese affiliated electrical factories in Asia, chiefly in assembly but increasingly also in the manufacture of simple components, exceeded the total numbers of workers hired in all industries in each of North and South America (Table 3.6). To ensure the maximum price from the sale of these products, exports to the advanced capitalist countries were supported by DFI in commerce and finance. By 1980, there was almost as much Japanese DFI in North America in these industries as there was in manufacturing in Asia.

When manufacturing investments entered the advanced countries, they focused on capital-intensive production or industries where women or black workers could be exploited, such as textiles or assembly of electrical goods. The strategy was gradually extended to other branches of machinery, particularly motor cars, and more and more manufacturing companies moved abroad. Between May 1975 and May 1980, the proportion of quoted companies which had done so increased from 32.5 per cent to 48.1 per cent, overwhelmingly in a cost-cutting drive into Asia and Latin America (Shūkan tōyō keizai, 1981, p. 8).

The top twenty companies producing overseas were not very different by the end of the second period from what they had been in the first (Table 3.4). The leaders were mainly the same electrical and textile firms, although they were now joined by the odd chemical and engineering company, such as Dai Nippon Ink Chemicals and Chiyoda Construction. Nissan and Toyota had slipped from seventh and sixth to eleventh and fifteenth places respectively. Generally the same Asian countries led the list of production sites, and Asia was as prominent as before (70 per cent in 1970–79) in receiving the bulk of Japan's new chemical investments, particularly the polluting ones (ibid., 1981, p. 11; 1986, p. 10).

We have seen how the extension of Japan's export-led growth strategy from the electrical to other branches of machinery intensified inter-imperialist rivalries and led to the *endaka fukyō*. We have also noted Japanese capital's determination to remain on the same course, by further cutting costs in Japan and by further internationalising the production of machinery. The third period of foreign investment, which began in the early 1980s, is thus characterised by extending the role of Asia in producing low cost components and in assembly, more and more for export to the advanced countries, including Japan.

However, from the mid-1980s, after the higher yen had cut US wages to levels lower than in Japan, DFI poured into the US and European machine industries. But these were still confined to their more technically advanced rather than their labour intensive branches.

THIRD PERIOD: 1980 AND AFTER

High-tech productive investment in the advanced countries is the major new development of the 1980s. It did not occur earlier because there was nothing to override the importance, when these function as costs, of the much higher wages of American and European than Asian workers. For a while, Japanese capital tried to steer a middle course in the advanced countries, by cutting wage costs through investing in automated assembly plants or by exporting to them cheaply made Japanese components. But this did not work for long, because the rising exports of components from Japan became a new source of trade friction, even leading to a special anti-dumping tariff on them by the EC. This tariff, which was directed specifically at 'screwdriver plants' which assembled Japanese components imported into Europe, required from June 1987 at least 60 per cent local content if it was to be avoided.

In practice Japanese companies can often still avoid the tariff if they bring in components from third countries, and cheap Asian parts are ideal for this purpose. However, since the interpretation of the EC regulations is still not settled, Japanese companies have had to procure more parts locally (*NKS*, 16 July 1987, 5; *FEER*, 20 October 1988, p. 106; *The Economist*, 8 October 1988, pp. 63–4).

The distinctiveness of the third period lies in the new function Asia has in this regard. If as many components as possible which are required by Japanese factories in the advanced countries could be made cheaply and imported from third countries, then Japanese capital might retain the best of all worlds. Some would have to be made in the advanced countries, but with the rise of the yen the latter's wages are less the problem they used to be. However, if the division of labour between Japanese and Asian subcontractors could be refined, and the final product (including components) could go to the advanced countries from Asia rather than from Japan, then the old strategy of producing where wages are low and selling where they are higher could be retained.

Japanese capital's current three-pronged strategy is thus very similar to what it was in previous periods. Nomura Research (Dobashi, 1986) explicitly spelt out and linked together the following: industrial restructuring at home, foreign investments abroad and 'cost-down' attacks on the Japanese working class. The industries hardest hit by the rising yen have thus been moving abroad very rapidly, with the transnationals setting up numerous subsidiaries even in the advanced countries. However, instead of importing components almost exclusively from Japan as in the past, they are now bringing in more from cheap production sites in Asia.

A new alliance of forces among the world's capitalist classes is also taking shape. At the highest level, of monopoly capital in the advanced countries, conflict is giving way to cooperation, as Japanese transnationals tie-up with US and EC transnationals. But at the next level new antagonisms are emerging, as Japanese companies in the advanced countries look for local subcontractors when cheap Asian parts are unavailable or when they cannot bring their Japanese affiliates with them. Western parts makers are not used to being treated like 'Japanese subcontractors'. New conflicts are also emerging between the governments of the advanced countries, particularly Japan, and those of Southeast Asia, as that region is transformed more thoroughly into a Japanese hinterland.

However, not all Asian countries are equally suited to the Japanese strategy. Making components for giant corporations often requires skills and technology found mainly in the NICs, and at first the poorer ASEAN countries found the Japanese less interested in what they had to offer: cheap labour and raw materials. New labour saving technologies and the collapse of commodity prices reduced their bargaining power and they felt left a bit high and dry. However, the rise of the yen, which once again made relative wages an overwhelming consideration for the machinery industries, turned the tide in ASEAN's favour. Tables 3.9 and 3.10, which provide the Ministry of Finance's latest figures on Japanese foreign investment, show the broad changes that are underway. On the one hand there is a concentration on the advanced countries for both productive and

Table 3.9 Total Japanese DFI, by major country and fiscal year

Country	1986 $ million	%	1987 $ million	%	1951–87 $ million	%	Cases	%
North America	10 441	46.8	15 357	46.0	52 763	37.9	16 408	36.7
US	10 165	45.5	14 704	44.1	50 159	36.0	15 573	34.8
Canada	276	1.2	653	2.0	2 604	1.9	835	1.9
Europe	3 469	15.5	6 576	19.7	21 047	15.1	4 861	10.9
UK	984	4.4	2 473	7.4	6 598	4.7	1 368	3.1
Luxembourg	1 092	4.9	1 764	5.3	4 072	2.9	117	0.3
Holland	651	2.9	829	2.5	3 166	2.3	425	1.0
West Germany	210	0.9	403	1.2	1 955	1.4	867	1.9
France	152	0.7	330	1.0	1 300	0.9	841	1.9
Asia	2 327	10.4	4 868	14.6	26 658	19.1	13 691	30.6
Indonesia	250	1.1	545	1.6	9 218	6.6	1 494	3.3
Hong Kong	502	2.2	1 072	3.2	4 505	3.2	2 829	6.3
Singapore	302	1.4	494	1.5	3 065	2.2	2 042	4.6
South Korea	436	2.0	647	1.9	2 765	2.0	1 559	3.5
China	226	1.0	1 226	3.7	1 740	1.2	397	0.9
Malaysia	158	0.7	163	0.5	1 446	1.0	1 073	2.4

Table 3.9 Continued

Country	1986		1987		1951–87			
	$ million	%	$ million	%	$ million	%	Cases	%
Taiwan	291	1.3	367	1.1	1 419	1.0	1 899	4.2
Thailand	124	0.6	250	0.7	1 134	0.8	1 303	2.9
Philippines	21	0.1	72	0.3	985	0.7	651	1.5
Latin America	4 737	21.2	4 816	14.4	25 189	18.1	5 930	13.3
Panama	2 401	10.8	2 305	6.9	11 146	8.0	3 059	6.8
Brazil	270	1.2	229	0.7	5 086	3.7	1 359	3.0
Cayman Islands	930	4.2	1 197	3.6	2 476	1.8	133	0.3
Bahamas	792	3.5	734	2.2	1 981	1.4	80	0.2
Mexico	226	1.0	28	0.1	1 584	1.1	250	0.6
Oceania	992	4.4	1 413	4.2	6 647	4.8	2 267	5.1
Australia	881	3.9	1 222	3.7	5 724	4.1	1 548	3.4
Africa	309	1.4	272	0.8	3 951	2.8	1 226	2.7
Liberia	289	1.3	267	0.8	3 010	2.2	740	1.7
Middle East	44	0.2	62	0.2	3 079	2.2	324	0.7
S. Arabia/Kuwait	41	0.2	54	0.2	1 363	1.0	4	0.0
World Total	22 320	100.0	33 364	100.0	139 334	100.0	44 707	100.0

Source: Ōkurashō, 1988a.

Table 3.10   Total DFI, by region and industry, March 1988 ($ million)

	North America	Europe	Asia	Latin America	Oceania	Total
Manufacturing	14 753	3 310	10 000	4 994	1 496	36 038
Food	724	112	425	207	68	1 546
Textiles	397	245	1 231	428	9	2 353
Lumber/pulp	952	2	212	200	128	1 495
Chemicals	1 449	347	1 585	562	111	5 247
Metals	1 650	276	2 064	1 764	364	6 304
General machinery	1 716	365	778	361	53	3 284
Electrical machinery	4 451	704	1 562	366	53	7 155
Transport machinery	2 221	797	1 028	995	613	5 675
Other	1 142	462	1 115	112	98	2 980
Non-manufacturing	36 858	16 794	16 286	20 126	5 131	99 365
Agriculture/forestry	260	5	262	186	171	893
Fisheries	139	3	129	104	69	538
Mining	1 440	890	6 677	1 549	1 601	12 936
Construction	510	57	254	203	49	1 134
Commerce	9 727	3 374	1 482	1 397	801	16 807
Finance/Insurance	9 149	10 508	1 447	6 913	640	28 772
Service	3 164	540	3 173	826	655	9 026
Transport	188	93	393	7 690	73	9 970
Real estate	10 130	268	846	55	658	11 958
Other	2 151	1 056	1 622	1 203	415	7 332
Branch equipment	667	905	336	45	12	3 336
Real Estate	485	38	37	23	7	595
TOTAL	52 763	21 047	26 658	25 189	6 647	139 334

Source: Ōkurashō, 1988a.

unproductive investments, on Asia (the NICs, ASEAN and China) mainly for productive investments and on the tax havens of Latin America for finance (Panama and Bahamas) and flag-of-convenience shipping (Panama and Cayman Islands). On the other hand there is a massive escalation of unproductive investments in finance, insurance and real estate, largely in the advanced countries.

One of the most striking things in these tables is the sudden escalation of manufacturing investments in the advanced countries in the years leading up to and following the rise of the yen. To understand this process requires some detailed analysis of the main industries into which this investment is moving, motor vehicles and electronics. That is the task of Chapter 4.

4 Current Global Strategy: Advanced Countries

Although the details of Japanese capital's entire current global strategy are beyond the scope of this study, I found it impossible to make sense of the new imperialism in Southeast Asia without grasping some of the finer points behind its strategy in the advanced capitalist countries of Europe and America. Here as elsewhere there are major regional and industrial concentrations: particular countries and groups of countries have specific roles to play in Japanese capital's emerging worldwide strategy. Its broad outlines were revealed in a survey of 1702 non-financial quoted companies carried out in January 1987. Of those intending to invest in the US in the next three years, 53.2 per cent aimed at sales outlets, 50.2 per cent in the production of finished products, and 26 per cent in the production of components and intermediary goods. Investment plans in Asia had almost the opposite priorities: 57.9 per cent aimed at finished articles, 41.2 per cent components and intermediary goods and only 39.4 per cent sales outlets (Keizai kikakuchō, 1987b, p. 45).

The present chapter analyses Japanese capital's activities in the advanced capitalist world, with the emphasis on the US and EC, in the two productive industries on which it is currently focusing: motor vehicles and electronics. My purpose is to highlight the different types of alliances being formed with imperialist capital and with capital in the underdeveloped countries. Japan's plans for Asia are intimately bound up with the points of common interest and rivalry which exist in its relationship with the advanced countries.

The common interest is capital's exploitation of labour all over the world, and that has required alliances which have fallen into two categories: between more or less equal partners, such as Japanese and US capital, and between unequal ones, like Japanese and South Korean capital. One of the tasks of this chapter is to assess the extent to which inter-imperialist rivalries are in practice transcended by common antagonisms towards labour. Rivalries between equals are always more explosive, since unequal power usually produces subordination rather than open struggle. The rise of the yen was the most potent recent manifestation of inter-imperialist rivalry.

One indication of the new pattern to the Japanese web is the growing willingness among the most internationalised corporations to create multiple head offices and to locate these in the strongholds of their leading allies. With the decision by Sanyo in December 1988 to set up a North American head office in New York, the number of companies which had either taken or decided to take this step, which before the rise of the yen had been unthinkable, reached ten: Kyocera (California, West Germany and Hong Kong), Uniden (Texas, Belgium and Hong Kong), Yokogawa Electric (Georgia, Holland and Singapore), Sony (New York, West Germany and Singapore), Omron Tateisi (New York, Holland and Singapore), Yamaha (California and Britain), Matsushita (Illinois and Britain), Honda (California), Toyota (US), Nissan (Amsterdam) and Sanyo (New York) (*NKS* 10 September 1988, p. 7; *JEJ*, 16 July 1988, p. 4; 24 December 1988, p. 36).

Traditionally, most Japanese investment in the advanced countries has been in the unproductive sectors, and even by the end of 1986 only 12.8 per cent of the total in the US was in manufacturing, compared to 29 per cent of British (the number one investor in the US) and 34 per cent of Dutch (number two). However, although money continues to pour into the unproductive industries, there has been a marked increase in the manufacturing share, with 25 per cent of all such investments in the US to May 1988 having been made since January 1987. And in the EC by the end of 1988 over 400 manufacturing companies were expected to have set up operations, one hundred of them in 1987 alone (*Zaigai kigyō*, no. 105, June 1988, p. 19; *JEJ*, 26 November 1988, p. 13; 24 December 1988, p. 32).

One of the strategies capital normally adopts in situations like the *endaka fukyō*, M&A (mergers and acquisitions), has seen surprisingly little use in Japan, apparently because Japanese executives still regard selling their companies as somehow shameful. But this has not deterred them from what are called 'in-out' mergers, that is, buying into or taking over foreign companies. From only 44 overseas M&A cases in 1984, the number soared to one hundred the next year, 204 in 1986, 228 in 1987 and 199 in the first eight months of 1988. Between 50–60 per cent of them have been in the US, a further 20 per cent in the Asian NICs and about 5 per cent in Britain. The rise of the yen has thus sent Japanese capital increasingly on the prowl for foreign partners to help it set up and maintain operations. The most spectacular acquisitions have tended to be in the unproductive industries, particularly real estate in the US, and are thus beyond the scope of this study. However, the two largest takeovers are relevant: Sony's

purchase of CBS Records for $2 billion in November 1987 and
Bridgestone's of Firestone for $2.6 billion in early 1988.

While takeovers in the unproductive industries are typically outcomes of speculation, those in the productive industries are often
motivated by the desire to obtain or control leading technologies.
Japanese companies have been finding that the easiest way to get a
foothold into or to retain leadership in an industry is to buy a
successful US company. Insofar as the 'merger' element predominates, the current buying spree is deepening the alliance between US
and Japanese capital, but the 'acquire' element has increased hostility
and rivalry. There is no question that many of the acquisitions in real
estate have caused a lot of bitterness. In the productive industries
most of the friction has resulted from the effect of takeovers on the
technological competition which lies as the heart of Japanese–American rivalry (*NKS*, 30 September 1988, p. 8; 3 October 1988, p. 1;
9 October 1988, p. 1; 10 October 1988, p. 1; *STK*, 5 November 1988,
p. 77; *FEER*, 18 August 1988, pp. 72–3; *The Economist*, 17 September 1988, pp. 93–4).

Japanese capital has been further upsetting the US by establishing
R&D centres all over the country and by enticing leading American
scientists to run them in order to attract the best young researchers. It
is thus being claimed that Japan is now trying to buy the world's top
brains. Of 66 overseas R&D centres owned by Japanese companies
in 1988, 23 were opened since 1987 and 42 were in Europe or
America. In the car industry, Isuzu, Nippondenso and Mazda all set
up centres in the US in 1987. However, in spite of the friction that
such actions have provoked, Japan's global R&D operation seems to
have deepened its alliance with the advanced countries, partly because it helped preserve their dominance over Asia. A number of
leading US and European companies have reciprocated by setting up
R&D centres in Japan: Dupont, Kodak, Upjohn, ICI and Henkel
amongst others (*NKS*, 8 August 1987, p. 9; 18 January 1988, p. 1;
10 September 1988, p. 11; 8 November 1988, p. 13; *JEJ*, 24 September 1988, p. 6; 26 November 1988, p. 8).

MOTOR VEHICLES: MAINLY THE US

Japanese capital in the car industry, which was the most acutely
affected of all by the *endaka fukyō*, has tried two main ways of
avoiding friction with the US. First, 'voluntary restriction' in 1981

had a lot of propaganda value, but it only reduced exports by about 5600 that year and then at most 51 200 in 1984 when the total quota was raised to 2.3 million. Second, the export of both motor vehicles and parts has been gradually supplemented by the local assembly of knock down sets as well as the domestic production of components. The ratio between knock down sets and exports rose from 0.6 per cent in 1982 to about 15 per cent in 1986, just before the launching by all the major car makers of their plans (Table 4.1) to produce 2 million cars by 1990 and almost 3 million by 1992 (and have locally produced cars exceed exports). A supply glut seems inevitable (Nomura, 1987, p. 116; *NKS*, 25 December 1987, p. 1; 25 October 1988, p. 8).

The Plot Thickens

The most relevant issues in Table 4.1 centre on the ownership of the plants, their location and their sources of parts. As is revealed by the ownership of DSM and NUMMI, there are growing signs of mergers and other forms of cooperation, not simply between Japanese and American car makers, but also between them and Taiwanese and Korean companies. The latter are brought in primarily for the low-cost subcontracting jobs they can do, particularly in certain types of assembly work and component manufacture.

The interlocking patterns of ownership thus put the Japanese and US companies on one side and the Korean and Taiwanese companies on the other. For example, among South Korean companies, Daewoo is 50 per cent owned by GM (which also owns 38.6 per cent of Isuzu and 5 per cent of Suzuki) and receives licensing technology from Nissan; Hyundai is 15 per cent owned by and receives licensing technology from Mitsubishi; Samsung, the electronics giant, is 24 per cent owned by Chrysler (which also owns 20 per cent of Mitsubishi); and Mazda owns 8 per cent and Ford owns 10 per cent of Kia Motors (Ford also owns 24 per cent of Mazda). In Taiwan, Nissan owns 25 per cent of Yue Loong Motor Co., which makes Nissan cars under licence (Nomura, 1987, pp. 94–5, 110; *Industria*, August 1987, p. 44; *JEJ*, 12 September 1987, p. 12; 10 October 1987, p. 20; 24 September 1988, p. 31; *NKS*, 10 September 1988, p. 8).

Components

The location of the various plants in the US also affects their prospects for cutting costs, particularly of parts. Such a reduction is

94

Table 4.1 Japanese car makers' DFI in the US

	Honda	Nissan	Mazda	Mitsubishi	Toyota	Toyota	Fuji
Name*	HAM	NMMC	MMUC	DSM	NUMMI	TMMU	Subaru
Owned	Wholly	Wholly	Wholly	Joint/Chrysler	Joint/GM	Wholly	Joint/Isuzu
Location	Ohio	Tennessee	Michigan	Illinois	Californ.	Kentucky	Indiana
Models and start date	Accord: 11/1982 Civic: fall 1986	Truck: 6/1983 Sentra: 3/1985	Small Capella: late 1987	Small Hatchback Sports Special: 11/1988	Nova Corolla FX 12/1984	2000cc Camri: Oct. 1988	Subaru Small truck late 1989
Capacity	510 000	240 000	240 000	240 000	250 000	200 000	240 000
Workers	4 200	3 250	3 500	2 900	2 500	3 000	1 700
Local Content	60% 66%	over 50% 60%	over 50%	50–60%	50%	60%	over 50%

Notes: *HAM: Honda of America; NMMC: Nissan Motor Manufacturing Corporation; MMUC: Mazda Motor Manufacturing Corp.; DSM: Diamond Star Motors; NUMMI: New United Motor Mfg. Inc.; TMMC: Toyota Motor Manufacturing USA; Subaru: Subaru–Isuzu.
Source: Nomura, 1987, p. 118; AS, 24 July 1987, p. 9; BT, December 1987, p. 52.

important, since the ordinary profits to sales ratios in the US have been only just over half their usual levels in Japan. Many of the US ventures have thus been situated in the so-called 'automobile corridor' extending from Michigan to Georgia, where most of the US industry is concentrated and where local parts can more easily be found. Although many Japanese parts makers have been setting up in this area, as late as 1986 there were still only 30 such firms with established production bases in the US. However, by the end of 1987, 72 had commenced production (*NKS*, 23 August 1987, p. 8; *BT*, December 1987, p. 58).

The main problem is not that parts are unavailable, since most are either interchangeable or are made by firms in related industries, such as electronics and plastics. The difficulty lies rather in the sub-contracting system to which Japanese car makers are accustomed. For example, contracts are usually made for five to six years, for the life of a model, so that the 'child' company becomes heavily dependent on the 'parent' and is forced to accept things like price cuts and fluctuating orders, which cushion the parent in bad times. Already TMMU buys parts on just such long-term contracts, as Toyota does in Japan, and it gives 'technical guidance to parts makers to improve the quality . . . and make them cost competitive'. Moreover, to avoid the costs and inconvenience of storage, Japanese companies also like to take delivery of parts on the day they use them, the so-called *kanban* system (*Industria*, May 1987, p. 42).

The importance of satisfactory component suppliers cannot be exaggerated, since Japanese car makers, unlike their US counterparts, produce very few themselves. The average Japanese car involves some 40 000 establishments with about 70 per cent of value added comprising parts brought in from them, and even primary parts (engines, brakes, lamps and electrical parts) involve an average of 168 establishments, most of which are closely tied to the parent company. The latter must carefully organise subcontractors to keep them in line, tying them to the group (*keiretsuka*). However, in the US there are not simply fewer parts makers to pit against one another, but they also tend to act independently and are difficult to control (Shimokawa, 1985, p. 22–3).

The few Japanese component makers which have been in the US for some time include some majors. Nippondenso is a Toyota affiliate which has been assembling air conditioners in Los Angeles since 1971 and now supplies Honda with heaters. Calsonic, a subsidiary of Nissan which also operates in Taiwan, South Korea and Malaysia, assembles air conditioners. Three others are giants which need to be put into an international context: Yazaki Sogyo, Asahi Glass and Yuasa battery.

By 1987, Yazaki was employing 12 000 workers in its fifteen overseas subsidiaries, that is, 2300 more than in its seven domestic affiliates. Wire harness making is highly labour intensive, and the company has a reputation for carefully selecting low wage countries for its overseas ventures. It has 1500 workers in two Mexican plants, but it plans to add another 6000 in four new plants by 1990. In 1986 it opened plants in Portugal and New Zealand, and in early 1987 it started joint ventures in the US and Canada. At the end of 1988 it also jointly set up a gas equipment research and development firm in the US (ibid., p. 103; *Industria*, August 1987, p. 45; *JEJ*, 22 October 1988, p. 17; *JEJ*, 5 December 1987, p. 20).

Asahi Glass operates throughout Southeast Asia, and its Belgian joint-venture, Glaverbel, is the third largest glass maker in Europe with over 4000 workers. While it has only recently started manufacturing in Ohio to supply Honda, it is opening a second plant in 1989 in Kentucky with a capacity of half a million, mainly to meet demand from Toyota and Mitsubishi. Asahi Glass also has joint ventures producing electronic and computer parts in the US (*NKS*, 15 August 1987, p. 8; 10 August 1987, p. 38; 24 January 1988, p. 1; *JEJ*, 16 July 1988, p. 18).

Yuasa Battery operates in fourteen countries, including Europe, America and over half a dozen Asian countries. It currently plans to raise its share of the world market threefold to 15 per cent by moving abroad from an increasingly high-tech base in Japan to its top priority regions of Asia, Britain and the EC, and North and South America, in that order. Towards the end of 1988 Yuasa decided to set up a research and development centre jointly with Exide in Pennsylvania.

In some cases car parts can also be procured by companies already established in motorcycle production. For example, Kawasaki Heavy Industries had been making motor cycles in Lincoln (Nebraska) since 1981, but a slump in demand coincided with the growing need for auto parts, which the company is now beginning to mass produce (*NKS*, 24 August 1987, p. 37; *JEJ*, 29 August 1987, p. 13; 27 February 1988, p. 21; 10 December 1988, p. 21).

Among the companies which moved to the US in 1987 was Jidosha Denki Kogyo, a Nissan affiliate, to make parts at the Kentucky plant. Diesel Kiki, another Nissan affiliate, bought a plant from Borg–Warner in Indiana which it converted into the first integrated production system by a Japanese company in the US, making a wide range of parts from compressors to air conditioners. Diesel Kiki, whose South Korean plant supplies Hyundai and Kia, is now scaling down its activities in Japan as a result of these moves. In late 1988 Nissan Diesel opened a parts centre in the US, while in 1989 Nissan joined Honda and Toyota by making its own engines, at its Tennessee factory.

In similar categories are three Honda affiliates (including Masuda Manufacturing) which began production in September 1987 in a shared plant in Ohio, and an affiliate which Honda is helping build a plant for making clutches for automatic transmissions in Portland from 1989. Mitsubishi has done likewise and brought with it a group of sixteen affiliated parts makers, the Mizushima Machinery and Metal Association. Another major move was the tie-up between Mitsubishi Corporation and United Technology Automotive in 1988 to promote joint ventures with UTA for parts.

Mazda seems to have the most advanced plans of all Japanese car makers in this regard. It has formed a joint venture with three of its subsidiaries to produce press parts in Michigan from 1988. By 1990 it expects to achieve 70–75 per cent local content from 48 component makers, of which nineteen are Japanese, eight are related to Ford (to which Mazda is introducing the Japanese system of managing components), while the rest are independent.

Toyota is the worst placed of all, having only recently secured tariff exempt status for its Kentucky plant because of opposition from US autoparts makers. In November 1987 it announced a $300 million expansion of its Kentucky plant to make engines, axles and steering components. But Toyota also has multiple strategies in the US. For example, Toyota Auto Body of California is to make converters for removing air pollutants from exhaust fumes, and in a tie up with Motorola, Toyota will develop car ICs, both for export to Japan (*NKS*, 3 September 1987, p. 1; 26 August 1987, p. 8; 17 November 1987, yūkan, p. 1; 5 January 1988, p. 8; *Industria*, August 1987, p. 45; *JEJ*, 4 April 1987, p. 17; 5 September 1987, p. 11; 5 September 1987, p. 9; 28 November 1987, p. 11; 27 February 1988, p. 23; 16 April 1988, p. 18; 28 May 1988, p. 19; 13 August 1988, p. 11; 20 August 1988, p. 18; 27 August 1988, p. 20; 8 October 1988, p. 24; 24 December 1988, p. 37; *TBT*, January 1988, p. 22).

Other companies which have recently either entered the US or expanded their activities there include quite a few car window and tyre manufacturers: Asahi Glass, Nippon Sheet and Glass (which also has a Mexican factory supplying the US market), Sumitomo Rubber (which bought Dunlop out in Europe and America in 1984–85), Bridgestone and a joint venture between Yokohama Rubber, Toyo Rubber and Gummi–Werke of West Germany, which will start production in 1991. There are also many companies in other branches of the industry which have made similar moves, for example, by steelmakers to manufacture surface-treated steel sheets (DURA) for upmarket cars: Nippon Steel, Sumitomo Metal and Nippon Kokan (*FEER*, 30 June 1988, pp. 52–4; *JEJ*, 9 May 1987, p. 4; 29 August 1987, p. 17; 26 December 1987, p. 18; 2 April 1988, p. 2; 1 October 1988, p. 18; 5 November 1988, p. 19; 10 December 1988, p. 22; *NKS*, 17 May 1987, p. 1; 1 July 1987, p. 8; 15 August 1987, p. 8; 13 December 1987, p. 4; *Industria*, May 1987, p. 41).

However, of all of the above only the Mexican plants offer the sort of exploitative possibilities to which the Japanese majors are accustomed. Wages are only 10 per cent of American wages and the Maquiladora bonded industrial zones offer the best opportunities, since duty-free imports from the US are temporarily allowed for the manufacture of products for re-export to the US. These zones stretch along the border, and a popular idea is the twin-plant system, in which the capital-intensive ones are on the US side and the labour-intensive ones on the Mexican side. Some capitalists also say that labour productivity is higher in Mexico than in the US. Nissan, which gets parts from wherever it can in North America, reports that Mexican suppliers come out on top on a ten point comparison of 300 suppliers, including Japanese ones. The factory Nissan itself opened in Mexico in 1966 now has over 6000 workers, who even produce engines for export back to Japan (Nomura, 1987, p. 121; *JEJ*, 5 December 1987, p. 20; *NKS*, 15 September 1987, p. 9).

In spring 1986 only ten Japanese plants were in the bonded zones, almost all of them electrical firms, including Matsushita, Sony, TDK, Sanyo, Hitachi and Toshiba, but a year later 21 more had made the move and another twenty were planning to do so. Mitsubishi Heavy Industries, which because of both the rise of the yen and a dumping duty imposed on it started assembling forklifts in the US in 1988, uses parts from a plant recently set up in the area.

In addition to low wages, the attractions of the area include the low price of electricity, its closeness to California where most Japanese investment is located, the Mexican government's generous debt-for-equity options and the fact that products assembled in the bonded zones are exempt from the voluntary restraints on Japanese exports to the US, even if they contain Japanese components (*JEJ*, 19 December 1988, p. 12; *FEER*, 27 October 1988, pp. 87–9; Ninomiya, 1987, pp. 80–1). The *Japan Economic Journal* concluded:

> [T]he Mexican bonded industrial zones present a unique opportunity to Japanese corporations to recover their international competitiveness, badly eroded by the appreciated yen (*JEJ*, 30 May 1987, p. 7).

C Itoh, the giant trading company with its hand in almost every pie, has obliged by setting up a consulting service in its US, Mexican and Japanese offices to entice Japanese firms into the bonded zones, while Mitsui & Co. is planning a 'Shelter Program' for the same purpose (*JEJ*, 8 August 1987, p. 18; 15 October 1988, p. 19; *JS*, September 1987, pp. 58–64).

However, even when this unique opportunity and similar ones in Asia are more fully exploited, Japanese car makers in the US will still rely on a variety of sources for their parts. Some will come from US makers, some from Japanese companies that have made the move, while the most specialised ones will probably continue for some time to come from Japan. However, since Toyota estimated that even at ¥150 to the dollar it was 30 per cent cheaper (including transport costs) to make parts in the US and ship them to Japan, this could change. In fact, imports into Japan of US-made car parts have increased enormously since 1987. For example, Honda is importing tires, headlights and carpets from the US and glass from Canada (*NKS*, 15 August 1987, p. 8; *JEJ*, 29 August 1987, p. 12; 15 August 1987, p. 8; 24 December 1988, p. 36).

In addition to their drive to cut costs, particularly of components for locally made cars, Japanese companies are also developing new strategies in order to revive their fortunes in the US following the rise of the yen. The most important is the development of new upmarket products: Toyota's Lexus, Nissan's Infiniti and Honda's Legend. They seem to recognise that the glut of cars in America and growing competition at the bottom end from South Korean imports, calls for something different from their traditional response of always tightening the screws back home. But this change of emphasis is unlikely to do much about the most imminent form of the crisis: overproduction in the advanced countries.

All the major car makers still have as their central overseas strategy the expansion of production in the US. But they come to it with different overseas experiences. A wider global view than from the advanced countries is thus needed. I discuss only the big five companies.

A World's Eye View of Japanese Car Makers

Although Toyota is the largest company with over 40 per cent of the market in Japan, it has been the slowest to establish overseas production centres. Until its recent investments in the US and Canada, among the few countries where it both assembled vehicles and had some affiliates providing parts were Thailand, Australia and Taiwan. Apart from these, there was a small plant making engines in Indonesia and a number of assembly plants: a joint venture in India for about 15 000 knockdown trucks, a large-scale joint venture (3700 workers) in Malaysia, a 21 per cent share in the Lotus Group plant in Norwich in England (542 workers), a joint venture in Portugal (2000 workers) and three small plants in Latin America: joint ventures in Costa Rica and Peru, and a wholly owned plant in Brazil. Other important tie-ups in Europe are with Volkswagen, for which it recently began producing pick-up trucks in West Germany, and in Spain with that country's national car maker to assemble Hi-Ace knockdown vans under licence. Nevertheless, in spite of its late start, by March 1986 Toyota had 31 overseas subsidiaries (44 two years later) and was only behind Honda and Matsushita in terms of the total value of its overseas production. In 1988 it asked about 50 of its affiliated component makers to build their own assembly plants in Taiwan (Shimokawa, 1985, pp. 156–65; Shūkan tōyō keizai, 1988; Nihon zaigai kigyō kyōkai, 1988, p. 78; *NKS*, 4 November 1987, p. 9; *BT*, January 1988, p. 31).

Nissan, by comparison, has more developed and larger-scale overseas operations, since over the past ten years, under Ishihara's leadership, an aggressive foreign strategy was one of the company's top priorities. Also, unlike Toyota which developed within a single Japanese prefecture and formed close relationships with local subcontractors, from the beginning Nissan sought suppliers from all quarters, however far afield, usually with the eye on cost. It set up in Peru (400 workers) and Thailand (250 workers) around the time it started making engines in Mexico, where it now produces 87 000 cars a year. It was well established in Australia (now with 2363 workers making 43 000 cars) and New Zealand (957 workers) by the mid-1970s, and in the early 1980s it moved into Spain (with Motor Iberica, currently employing 6033 workers making 70 000 vehicles), established its plant in Kentucky and formed its tie-up with Alfa Romeo in Italy. In 1983 it opened assembly plants for cars, buses and trucks in the Philippines, and in 1986 its large British factory, which consolidated its position as the only Japanese company with a direct stake in Europe.

Producing 40 000 cars to start with, the British venture was to reach its capacity of 100 000 in 1991. But the company has now planned to double this by 1992, and with its usual sharp eye for low-cost labour, will make Spain, where it will double production of commercial vehicles by 1990, its other main production base in Europe. The target is 5 per cent of the European market with 600 000 vehicles, only about half of which will be imported from Japan. The whole operation is to be coordinated from a European head office probably in Amsterdam. With 350 000 vehicles sold in 1987 and 2.9 per cent of the market, Nissan was already the top Japanese car maker in the area.

But the company has also had difficulties in Europe of late, and not just from workers. Both French and Italian car manufacturers, which, unlike the British, command large shares of the European market, are objecting to this English back door through which Japanese cars are entering duty free. The French claim that cars with less than 80 per cent local content are 'screwdriver' imports, since that is about the level reached if an engine, gearbox or chassis is locally produced. Nissan has responded by aiming at 80 per cent local content by 1990.

A new avenue of expansion throughout the advanced countries is Nissan's growing cooperation with Ford. Plans have already been made to build Ford's jeep-type sports utility vehicles in the Spanish factory and to join hands in design and production at Ford's Australian subsidiary. There is even growing speculation that Nissan might try to absorb Mazda, which has even closer links with Ford. Other recent moves by Nissan include the ventures in Pakistan to assemble large trucks, India to make parts and assembly in Turkey. In late 1987 it was planning to ship thin steel sheets to its Taiwanese affiliate and having them stamped into body panels for export back to Japan as well as to Nissan's plant in Mexico. Together with Nissan Diesel, as we see in Chapter 6, the company is also planning to make engines in Thailand.

Yet of Nissan's currently 32 overseas subsidiaries, the most important remains the American venture, with the most modern automated equipment, robots and all. In January 1988 it decided to boost production to 400 000 by 1992, and from July it started using CAD systems, which link its plant at Atsugi in Japan to its Research and Development Centre in Michigan.

Nissan's international strategy is increasingly to produce upmarket cars in Japan, and to concentrate elsewhere, even in the US, on lower-priced models. In 1985 it claimed 6 per cent of world car output, of which 11 per cent was produced overseas. It has the fifth largest overseas assets of all Japanese companies, three times more than Honda, which in nineteenth place is the next manufacturing company on the list. Nissan strongly believes in the 'international division of labour', and it is currently instructing up to one hundred of its affiliated parts makers to locate themselves in Asia, particularly ASEAN and China. The 'aim is to set up a "global buying network" for parts and materials' (*JEJ*, 31 December 1988 and 7 January 1989, p. 5). At its central research base in Yokosuka, it concentrates on high-tech developments, such as gas turbine engines, new ceramic materials and electronics. It even has a finger in space aircraft production (Shūkan tōyō keizai, 1988; Shimokawa, 1985, pp. 137, 166–75; *JEJ* 12 September 1987, p. 12; 26 December 1987, p. 17; 2 January 1988, p. 11; 16 January 1988, p. 19; 21 May 1988, p. 18; 8 October 1988, p. 24; 19 November 1988, pp. 23–4; 26 November 1988, p. 25; 10 December 1988, p. 20; *FEER*, 14 July 1988, pp. 68–74; *NKS*, 15 December 1987, p. 8; 21 January 1988, p. 1; 4 November 1988, p. 13).

Honda's international strategy has come to centre even more heavily on the North American projects, where its sales (700 000 in 1987) are nearly double what it sells at home (400 000) and where it earns over 80 per cent of its consolidated profit. Honda plans to stop exporting the Civic altogether and aim increasingly at the top end of the market by developing 'superior' products involving the highest levels of technical skill. The company sees the key to success in its Acura sales network handling the Integra, Legend and a new $30 000-plus model to be developed by 1992. The Acura network is growing by leaps and bounds, from 150 outlets in 1986 to 300 the next year and targeted to reach 600 by 1990. When its new plant to build the Integra is completed in August 1989, Honda will have the largest production facilities of all the Japanese car makers in the US. Together with the expansion of its engine plant in Anna (Ohio), these will raise Honda's total investment in the US to over $1.7 billion. While in the past it had exported as many knockdown sets as possible for local assembly and tried to encourage assembly under licence, it now aims to achieve higher local content and to promote Americans to top levels of management. Like Toyota, it has a head office in the US from where it plans full-scale re-exports to Japan. The company will enlarge its R&D staff from 80 in 1987 to 500 by 1991.

Partly because of its strength in motorcycles, Honda has the widest network of overseas production centres, including component makers, of all Japanese car makers. It currently produces cars and motor bikes in Taiwan and Thailand; cars, car parts and particularly motor-bike engines in Malaysia; everything for motor bikes in the Philippines; motor-bike parts (including engines) and car parts in Indonesia; motor bikes and electrical engines but soon also cars and a second motor cycle factory in India; motor bikes in Pakistan; motor bike knockdown sets in Iran; motor bikes in Belgium; motor-bike engines in France; cars, car parts and motor bikes in the US; motor bikes in Peru; motor bikes and parts in Brazil; and motor bikes in Nigeria. In Europe the company only has the Austin Rover Group producing its Concerto, eventually using engines from the Honda plant currently being constructed at Swindon, west of London. It hopes that engines from the same plant will raise to 80 per cent the local content of the small cars to be jointly developed and manufactured from 1989. The output of Honda's 71 overseas production bases is worth more than that of any other Japanese company, and it is also one of the growing numbers of them which puts money into flag of convenience shipping in Latin American tax-havens, notably Panama (Shūkan tōyō keizai, 1988; Shimokawa, 1985, pp. 180–5; *Industria*, August 1987, p. 45; *JEJ*, 5 September 1987, p. 11; 10 October 1987, p. 11; 17 November 1987, p. 11; 9 July 1988, p. 18; *NKS*, 18 September 1987, p. 9; 26 September 1987, p. 1; 25 September 1988, p. 4; *BT*, December 1987, pp. 53–4; *TBT*, January 1988, p. 15).

Capital in the rest of the Japanese car industry has to pursue less independent international strategies. Mazda moves around the world with Ford, benefiting greatly from that giant's access to components and sales outlets. Both should be important to Mazda's prize project, the wholly owned factory in Michigan. The company's tie-up with Kia Motors, the number two in South Korea, has also helped it develop an international division of labour, which it sees as the solution to the high yen. Mazda exports nearly 70 per cent of its cars, the highest of all the majors, but setbacks in the US have been compensated by expanded knockdown exports to Ford affiliates in

Taiwan and Mexico as well as to their common affiliate in South Korea, Kia Motors. The latter has been equally important to Mazda's cost down efforts through overseas sourcing of parts, particularly for trucks, which account for 42 per cent of Mazda's exports to the US. In addition to South Korea, Mazda maintains a procurement office in Taiwan, to which it sent a mission from its Toyukai (92 affiliates) in 1987 to sound out new ventures to make parts. Other important overseas subsidiaries, of which there were 24 in 1988, include assembly plants in Thailand, New Zealand, India and Colombia. The only progress Mazda has made in Europe has been the agreement by which Saab, the Swedish producer of military equipment, will assemble Mazda compacts (*NKS*, 23 October 1987, p. 9; 8 November 1988, p. 8; *JEJ*, 31 October 1987, p. 22; 23 January 1988, p. 5; 29 January 1988, p. 24; Shūkan tōyō keizai, 1988; Shimokawa, 1985, pp. 186–94; *BT*, January 1988, pp. 30–1).

Mitsubishi's international strategy complements that of Chrysler, its partner in its single largest undertaking recently opened in Bloomington Illinois. Aiming at the top end of the US and Japanese markets, Diamond Star will begin producing the sports type Eclipse in early 1989.

Of equal if not greater importance is the development of Mitsubishi's 'Asian Car', made from low cost parts which are supplied to and from Mitsubishi subsidiaries throughout the region. In October 1988 Mitsubishi's proposals to ASEAN governments to slash tariffs on and to treat parts made anywhere in ASEAN as locally made were accepted by all except Indonesia. Mitsubishi Motors Australia, which was acquired from Chrysler in the late 1970s, produces cylinder heads and other components made from cheap local aluminium; ATC (Asian Transmission Corporation) in the Philippines supplies transmissions (with parts from Japan); through Hyundai a number of components come from South Korea, such as small pressed body parts, Pony Excel engines and transmission gears; Thailand supplies bumpers, Malaysia doors and steering systems, Indonesia engine assembly and Singapore radios; assembly is undertaken almost everywhere, including Taiwan (China Motor Co.), but vehicles destined for Canada are put together by MMC Sittipol in Thailand.

Exports to the US and to Japan are the task of Hyundai, whose Pony Excel, which is patterned after the pricier Mirage, is Mitsubishi's not-so-secret weapon in the growing struggle for the lower end of these markets. Other strings to Mitsubishi's bow of 21 overseas subsidiaries include an assembly plant for cars in New Zealand and one for small trucks in India. Its only links with European capital in the industry are with Daimler Benz through technical and sales agreements (*JS*, July 1988, pp. 56–60; *FEER*, 25 December 1986, pp. 64–5; 10 November 1988, p. 79; *JEJ*, 12 September 1987, p. 12; *NKS*, 10 November 1988, p. 10; *JT*, 12 November 1988, p. 9; Shimokawa, 1985, pp. 195–9; Nihon zaigai kigyō kyōkai, 1988, p. 78; Maruyama, 1987, p. 306).

While the Japanese car industry is not the threat in Europe which it is in the US, simply because cars similar to the ones imported from Japan are made by local companies, Japanese car exports to Europe have been increasing in spite of the rise of the yen. But unlike the US, whose market demand is much larger than the local producers can supply, Europeans produce more cars than they buy, and like the Japanese are net exporters always on the hunt for markets. And while the US absorbed 3.5 million (48 per cent) out of the 7.2 million vehicles exported from Japan in 1985, another 1.37 million went to Western Europe and some 300 000 to each of Canada and Australia. However, in 1986 exports to Western Europe leapt by 17.7 per cent to 1.61 million and then by another 4.8 per cent to 1.69 million in 1987, their value (because of the rising yen) soaring by almost 72 per cent in 1986 and a further 32 per cent the next year. It thus became necessary to agree to 'voluntary' limitations on exports, and Japanese car makers realised that the only long-term solution was also *genchi seisan*, local production, mainly in cooperation with European capital (*NKS*, 16 August 1987, p. 4; 21 June 1987, p. 1; *Industria*, September 1987, p. 20; *JEJ*, 23 May 1987, p. 15; 31 December 1988 and 7 January 1989, p. 3; Tsūshō sangyōshō, 1987b, p. 140, 1988, p. 124).

In conclusion, capital in Japan's core manufacturing industry has been under enormous pressure to relocate abroad. The chief target has been the US, where almost half its exports have been going but with which conflict had escalated to unacceptable levels. Japanese capital happily responded to this pressure after it took the form of a steep rise in the value of the yen, since production costs even in the US and Europe became cheaper than in Japan. Asia's role in this strategy is to help further reduce the costs of operating in the advanced countries. But the class alliances involved are quite different. The tie-ups with US and European capital involve more or less equal power and mutual exchanges of technology. But in Asia Japanese capital normally confronts, not just technologically weaker capitals, but with itself additionally strengthened through inter-imperialist tie-ups, very isolated and vulnerable partners. The inequality is thus multiplied. It seems that rivalry among the imperialist powers is giving way to cooperation. The *Japan Economic Journal* aptly captured the mood: '"Cohabitation" is in fact the current buzzword among industrialists throughout the world' (30 April 1988, p. 5).

Table 4.2 shows a survey of DFI cases in transport machinery (overwhelmingly parts for cars and motor cycles) as well as in motor vehicle manufacture (also mostly car parts), by country and date (fiscal years). It is significant that Asia remains the main overseas centre of component making for Japanese cars, although as revealed by Table 4.3, since 1986 there was a greater rush into the US than into the two older Asian suppliers.

ELECTRICAL MACHINERY: ROUGHER WATERS?

The Japanese electrical industry has moved through many stages of development and internationalisation, and in some branches such as household electronic appliances it has become technically superior to the US. It has also gradually developed a complex international division of labour, which began with the location of the simplest labour intensive activities in countries like Taiwan and South Korea. Later, this function was taken over by the poorer ASEAN countries, and the NICs became centres of intermediate technology, now even producing VTRs under licence. But throughout, the division of labour in Asia was consciously directed towards lowering the costs of producing things which, like cars, were to be sold in the higher wage countries of Europe and America.

And as with the car industry, the final stage of internationalisation, production in the advanced countries themselves, is occurring in joint ventures with the latter's leading corporations. In both cases too, the rise of the yen became the main catalyst promoting this final stage, because it significantly altered the relative costs of production in Japan and the other advanced countries. However, since costs in the latter have not fallen sufficiently for Japanese capital to receive its customary profits, the new role for the peoples of Asia and Latin America in Japan's increasingly global electrical industry is the same as in the car industry: to supply cheap components for factories in Europe and America. The purpose behind the tie-ups with capital in the advanced countries is to consolidate the advantages of imperialist capital through further development and control of technology.

Table 4.2   Survey of DFI cases in transport machinery and motor vehicles

	1951–74		1975–79		1980–86		Total	
	TM	MV	TM	MV	TM	MV	TM	MV
World total	48	19	41	26	123	78	216	128
Asia	34	12	26	21	40	19	120	74
Latin America	22	8	8	4	6	1	18	4
Europe	–	2	1	1	13	7	14	10
North America	3	1	2	1	38	24	44	28
Oceania	2	–	3	2	5	2	10	5

Note: TM – transport machinery; MV – motor vehicles. Totals include cases for which date is unknown.
Source: Shūkan tōyō keizai, 1988, pp. 16–20.

Table 4.3   Numbers of car parts makers to undertake DFI, by country, year and affiliation

	North America			South Korea			Taiwan		
	Total	–1985	1986–7	Total	–1985	1986–7	Total	–1985	1986–7
Type of Parts									
Engine	3	2	1	4	4	–	13	12	1
Electric	10	6	4	3	3	–	7	6	1
Driving force	11	7	4	4	4	–	4	2	2
Connecting system	9	2	7	–	–	–	5	4	1
Body	22	4	18	2	1	1	12	7	5
Miscellaneous	9	5	4	1	1	–	5	3	2
Total	64	26	38	14	13	1	46	34	12
Affiliation									
Toyota	9	4	5	2	2	–	8	3	5
Nissan	12	5	7	1	1	–	10	6	4
Honda	9	4	5	–	–	–	5	4	1
Other makers	7	1	6	2	1	1	–	–	–
Independent	27	12	15	9	9	–	23	21	2
Total	64	26	38	14	13	1	46	34	12

Note: 1986–8 ends in April 1987.
Source: Maruyama, 1988, p. 60.

The electrical industry can be broadly divided into electronics and non-electronics, with the former replacing the latter during the 1960s as the leading high-tech sector. In Japan today the non-electronic branches (such as white goods) of the electrical industry absorb about one-third of the total of 1.6 million workers and also provide about one-third of total value added. However, in terms of their shares of

Table 4.4   World's major general electrical companies (1985/86[b])

	Turnover abroad ($ billion)	(%)	Workers	R&D as % of turnover	Two main branches
GE	28.29	8	304 000	3.8 (9.0)[a]	HA:24%; HE:18%
Philips	18.14	94	345 600	6.7	HA:37%; IE:28%
Siemens	17.84	47	348 000	9.3	HE/FA:45%; ICE:31%
Hitachi	22.67	30	164 117	5.9	ES:29%; HA:21%
Matsushita	20.88	50	133 963	4.8	HA:61%
Toshiba	15.26	31	120 000	5.6	ES:33%; HA:31%
Westinghouse	10.70	8	124 935	2.2 (9.1)	HE/FA/M:40%; IM:34%
Mitsubishi	9.55	28	71 479	4.2	HE:28%; HA:29%
Thorn EMI	4.58	40	80 484	3.5	HA:26%; IE:25%
Thomson CSF	3.56	61	62 100	9.2	M:67%; ES:15%
Sansho Group	2.47	–	33 514	NA	HA:30%; CE:9%

Notes:
HA – Home appliances   HE – Heavy electrical machinery
IE – Industrial electronics   FA – Factory automation
ICE – Information/Communication   ES – Electronics/semiconductors
    equipment   IM – Industrial machinery
M – Military
CE – Communications equipment
[a] Figures in brackets includes state contribution
[b] Different times in 1985–86 for the different firms.
Source: Nomura, 1987, p. 67.

equipment investment in Japan's manufacturing industry, the electronics branches are vastly more important, absorbing 25.0 per cent in 1985 as opposed to the 18.4 per cent of the entire motor vehicle industry. Electronics itself comprises three main sub-branches: industrial electronics, which in 1985 comprised 62 per cent of world production, consumer electronics (colour TV, VTR, audio equipment), which comprised 13 per cent of world production and components (23 per cent). They had similar weights in Japan. But shares of manufacturing equipment investment revealed the overwhelming importance in Japan of component manufacture, which took a whopping 15.4 per cent share, followed by industrial electronics with 5.3 per cent and consumer electronics with 2.4 per cent (Shimura, 1986, p. 56).

Conflict with the US has occurred mainly in branches of the industry in which there was a substantial trade imbalance, that is, consumer appliances (audio and video equipment), components (semi-conductors) and communications equipment, in that order. In industrial electronics, which commands the largest share of world production, the US still enjoys a substantial surplus. Table 4.4 lists

Table 4.5   World's top ten electronics companies, 1984

	Country	Turnover (IBM = 100) Electronics	Total	Electronics share (%)
1. IBM	US	100	100	80
2. Matsushita	Japan	37	44	68
3. Philips	Holland	31	33	75
4. Hitachi	Japan	30	43	56
5. AT&T	US	22	72	23
6. Siemens	West Germany	21	33	51
7. NEC	Japan	20	16	100
8. General Electric	US	19	60	25
9. Toshiba	Japan	19	29	51
10. ITT	US	18	43	33

Source: Nomura, 1987, p. 68.

eleven of the world's major companies which operate generally throughout the electrical industry, showing their scale as well as the two major branches they concentrate on. Table 4.5 ranks the world's top ten electronics companies, showing the degree to which they specialise in electronics.

Although even in the 1970s there was a large US trade deficit in consumer electronics, this spread to semi-conductors in the late 1970s, to other components in the early 1980s and to communications equipment in 1984. The imbalance was exacerbated by the large increase in the deficit in consumer appliances due to the huge influx of VTRs, which are not manufactured at all by US companies. Yet a major underlying factor was the global strategy adopted by US capital to cut costs by moving into Asia. For example, 70 per cent of IBM's manufacturing costs came to comprise components made in Asia, including Japan. So although the US retained its trade surplus in industrial electronics, import dependence even in this industry rose from 4.3 per cent in 1980 to 13.6 per cent in 1985. But in consumer electronics it soared from 48.2 to 71.6 per cent, and in components (including semiconductors) from 21.8 to 32.5 per cent, with predictable effects on the trade balance. Although most Japanese companies operate in all branches of the industry, they do so in different degrees and face different US competitors, as revealed by Table 4.6, which ranks, by their turnover in 1984, the top five Japanese and US companies in those branches of electronics where rivalries have been greatest (Nomura, 1987, p. 74).

Table 4.6 Ranking of US and Japanese majors in disputed industries

Computers		Communication Equipment		Semi-conductors		Household electrical[a]	
US	Japan	US	Japan	US	Japan	US	Japan
IBM	Fujitsu	AT&T	NEC	Motorola	NEC	GE	Matsushita
DEC	Japan IBM	ITT	Fujitsu	TI	Hitachi	Whirlpool	Sanyo
Sperry[b]	NEC	Motorola	Hitachi	Intel	Toshiba	NAP	Hitachi
Honeywell	Hitachi	IBM	Oki	NS	Fujitsu	RCA	Toshiba
Burroughs	Toshiba	GTE	Toshiba	AMD	Matsushita	WC	JVC

Notes:

[a] Includes whitegoods

[b] Following the merger of Burroughs and Sperry into Unisys, the latter became the US number two computer maker.

IBM – International Business Machines
NEC – Nippon Electric Company
AT&T – American Telephone and Telegraph
ITT – International Telephone and Telegraph
TI – Texas Instruments
GE – General Electric
NS – National Semiconductor
NAP – North American Phillips

DEC – Digital Equipment Corporation
GTE – General Telephone
AMD – Amdahl
RCA – Radio Corporation of America (taken over by GE in 1986)
JVC – Japan Victor Company
WC – Westinghouse Corporation

Source: Nomura, 1987, p. 76.

Conflict with the US has been much more bitter over electronics goods than motor cars, mainly because Japanese competition has been increasingly extended into communications, one of the remaining fields where the US is technologically ahead. And since competition among the Japanese majors spearheads the technical progress, US attacks have been directed one by one at particular companies. In each case, the Pentagon was either directly involved or was lurking in the background, to safeguard American 'industrial security' in the face of threats from Japan. The attack on individual high-tech electronics firms was stepped up after the FBI caught Mitsubishi Electric and Hitachi employees in the 1982 IBM 'industrial espionage' incident.

The first heavy gun in this battle was fired when pressure from the Pentagon forced Fujitsu in March 1987 to end its acquisition bid for Fairchild. About the same time Oki Electric was singled out as the culprit which 'dumped' semiconductors in the US via Hong Kong, triggering off the row in early 1987 and punitive tariffs of 100 per cent on $300 million worth of Japanese goods using semi-conductors. Not to lose an opportunity like this, Margaret Thatcher threatened to withdraw the licences of Japanese banks and insurance firms operating in London unless the British firm, Cable and Wireless, was offered a substantial stake in the consortium building a second telecommunications system in Japan. Many issues got mixed up and were used interchangeably as evidence of Japanese treachery: telecommunications, supercomputers, participation in building the new Kansai International Airport, automotive parts and even liquor imports from the EC. Clearly, the specifics were not the issue (*LJ*, August 1987, pp. 16–17).

And then came the renewed uproar over a Toshiba affiliate's alleged violation of COCOM, a product of the cold war which has become so vague, because of conflicts among members and special exemptions, that no one seems to know much about it. In 1971–77, the US received 51 per cent of the special licences for computer exports, so that IBM has the largest number of after-sales service employees of any computer maker in Moscow. The allegation that Toshiba machines were responsible for a reduction in the noise levels of Soviet submarines, thus endangering US antisubmarine forces, does not bear examination. Since Toshiba Machine exported the lathes in December 1982 and June 1983 and delivered their computer programmes in July 1984, they could not have been operable until the end of 1984 at the earliest. But all the Soviet submarines which the

Pentagon claims greatly reduced their noise levels with the help of Toshiba lathes had been launched by then. In fact as early as 1983 the Pentagon had found the new generation of Soviet submarines harder to detect. Moreover, signature reduction in submarines is a key military technology, requiring long development, so that one factor could not bring about such a remarkable change. Finally, it is claimed that two of the machines were installed in the Leningrad Baltic Dockyard, but according to the Pentagon's own publication, *Soviet Military Power*, this has not built submarines since 1950 (*BT*, September 1987, pp. 22–3).

Clearly, the hysteria over Toshiba's 'betrayal' was part of a long line of attacks on individual Japanese high-tech electrical firms. It was not surprising that NEC, one of the few which had not yet faced a US attack, was also being rumoured in mid-1987 to have violated COCOM. With the close links between the Pentagon and US electronics firms, it is natural that conflict in this industry assumes a quasi-military dimension and generates a siege mentality on both sides.

Japanese capital's overseas strategy is thus being shaped by two dominant goals: to make peace with the Americans and to fend off growing competition from the NICs, both leading to the same line-up of class forces we found in the car industry. While the rise of the yen gave the Japanese a cost advantage in the US which they never before had, it also raised the competitive power of South Korean and Taiwanese firms, which have since become a serious threat, particularly in some branches of consumer electronics. Foreign investment is thus going mainly into these two parts of the world, in a carefully planned division of labour. A large part of the motivation to link up with US capital is to consolidate technical superiority in existing industries or to develop it in new ones.

Consumer Electronics

Japanese electronics companies face the challenge of internationalisation with already well developed overseas networks, chiefly in consumer appliances and components in Asia. Until the *endaka fukyō* the main US operations were in colour TVs and some components which service them. The largest capacities were possessed by Sanyo (1.2 million sets), Matsushita (1 million), Sony (750 000), Sharp (700 000), Toshiba (400 000 sets), Hitachi (250 000) and Mitsubishi (150 000). Video recorders and video cameras have been

supplied to US companies on an OEM (Original Equipment Manufacturing) basis. For example, in 1985 RCA got 13.8 per cent of the
US VTR market with supplies from Hitachi, which also provided the
5 per cent share claimed by Sears (Yamauchi, 1985, p. 86; Nomura,
1987, p. 78).

From 1976 to 1980, the proportion of total Japanese VTRs which
were exported rose from 48.3 to 77.6 per cent, where it has remained. But the US share of the exports soared from 32.3 per cent in
1981 to 54 per cent in 1984 and 65 per cent in 1986, although the rise
of the yen then slashed it back to 54 per cent in 1987. Competition
from South Korean VTRs made under licence from the Japanese
majors also helped cut the volume of Japanese exports by 36 per cent
that year. But the European share had been falling over the years,
from 44.4 per cent in 1981 to 22.5 per cent in 1984, mainly because
Japanese companies began to set up operations there but partly
because of the production of the V2000 system (mainly by Philips).
However, following the rise of the yen, the decline was reversed and
the European share stabilised at around 20 per cent. But the 38 per
cent increase in the volume of exports to the Asian NICs (excluding
South Korea) in 1987 raised their share from 5.3 per cent in 1986 to
9.3 per cent. Table 4.7 shows the enormous capacity which had been
created in Europe in the few years 1982–87 (Tsūshō sangyōshō,
1987b, p. 138, and 1988b; Yamauchi, 1985, p. 53).

The West German plant of the JVC joint venture with Telefunken
(owned by Thomson of France) has been expanding production
beyond all expectations, although the British plant was closed in
April 1988. One of the most recent to open – NEC in the UK – will
also produce car phones for the EC market in order to get round the
dumping duty this product faces. Finally, Sony has decided to produce VHS type recorders both in Japan and in France from November 1988. The company has been particularly aggressive in Europe.
Already 90 per cent of its TVs and 70 per cent of its cassette tapes
sold in the region, which accounts for 22 per cent of its total sales, are
locally made, and at the end of 1988 it was employing 7200 European
workers (*JEJ*, 13 February 1988, pp. 18–19; 24 December 1988, p.
36).

Recalling the rush into the US by TV makers in the 1970s, the rush
into Europe by the VTR makers in the 1980s was primarily motivated
by the need to secure these markets in the face of mounting criticism
over excessive Japanese exports, the location of the plants once again
being chiefly determined by market considerations. However, the

Table 4.7   DFI in Europe by Japanese VTR makers, 1982–87

Company Share	Partner Share	Country of DFI	Start Date	Production (000)
Matsushita (56)	Bosch (35)	West Germany	2/1983	250
Matsushita (100)	–	Spain	1/1987	100
Matsushita (100)	–	France	8/1987	30
JVC (50)	Thomson (50)	West Germany	5/1982	400–750
JVC (50)	Thomson (50)	UK	10/1982	150
Sony (100)	–	West Germany	5/1982	40
Toshiba	Toshiba UK (100)	UK	4/1984	120
Toshiba (100)	–	West Germany	4/1987	120–400
Sanyo (100)	–	West Germany	(7/1987)	230–350
Sanyo (90)	Sanyo Marubeni	UK	1983, but stopped VTR to	
Marubeni (10)	UK (10)		concentrate on West	
			Germany	
Mitsubishi (100)	–	UK	9/1983	150
Hitachi (100)	–	UK	7/1985	60–120
Hitachi (100)	–	West Germany	7/1983	360–480
Sharp (100)	–	UK	2/1985	240
NEC (100)	–	UK	7/1987	120
Akai (62.7)	Mitsubishi (30)	France	(4/1986)	35–100

Note: Start date in brackets denotes the date production was boosted.
Compiled from: Yamauchi, 1985, p. 88; Nihon yushutsu yunyū ginkō, 1988, p. 21.

popularity of the UK as a production base stems mainly from its lower wages, the policy of the Thatcher government which encourages foreign investment and Britain's capacity to serve the entire European market. Spain, where Japanese companies employ the largest number of workers in Europe (over 19 000 compared to 11 000 in each of Britain and Germany) is often selected for the same sorts of reasons. A very similar pattern accompanied the investments in Europe to make microwave ovens. All of the latter but one (Toshiba's joint venture with Thomson in France) were in Britain: by Toshiba, Matsushita, Hitachi, Sharp and Brother.

The success of the European ventures, the intolerable trade friction with the US and the rise of the yen all finally pressed Matsushita, Hitachi and Toshiba to open VCR plants in the US in 1986. However, they have been operating in the red, with costs up to 15 per cent higher than in Japan, mainly because of the absence of qualified parts suppliers. But MITI has been urging them to raise their production from some 60 000 units to 3 million by 1991, which would about equal their sales in the US in 1987. Table 4.8 shows that it was not just colour TVs and VTRs which were increasingly, by leaps and bounds

Table 4.8   Overseas production of consumer electronics goods, by region, 1979–87 (million, units and %)

Domestic and Overseas Production

	Domestic			Overseas			Total Production		
	1979	1986	1987	1979	1986	1987	1979	1986	1987
Audio (units)	23.8	33.1	18.9	12.1	22.1	38.4	35.9	60.0	65.0
Shares	66.0	55.0	29.0	34.0	37.0	59.0	100	100	100
Colour TVs (units)	9.4	15.0	11.7	4.0	18.7	23.5	13.4	33.9	35.5
Shares	70.0	44.0	33.0	30.0	55.0	66.0	100	100	100
VTRs (units)	2.2	35.2	35.2	–	2.7	5.7	2.2	38.8	41.9

Regions of Overseas Production

	Southeast Asia			North America			Europe		
	1979	1986	1987	1979	1986	1987	1979	1986	1987
Audio (units)	11.6	22.1	38.3	–	–	–	–	–	–
Shares	96.0	99.0	99.0	–	–	–	–	–	–
Colour TVs (units)	1.2	6.6	9.1	2.0	7.5	8.6	0.3	2.6	3.3
Shares	29.0	35.0	39.0	50.0	40.0	36.0	8.0	14.0	14.0
VTRs (units)	–	0.9	2.1	–	0.1	0.5	–	1.6	2.9
Shares	–	35.0	36.0	–	2.0	8.0	–	60.0	51.0

Source: NHK, 1988, p. 61.

after the rise of the yen, being produced abroad rather than in Japan, but audio equipment (radio cassettes and 'head' stereos) as well. It also shows that while the US and Europe were major production sites for the higher-tech colour TVs and VTRs, audio equipment was almost entirely produced in Asia.

And so the rush around the advanced capitalist world to find suitable production sites for new and old products continues. Among some of the most recent developments are Matsushita's decision to start producing CD players in West Germany in a joint venture with Bosch and Phillips from August 1988; JVC's mid-1988 plans for an audio factory to make miniature CD players in France, along with its plans to boost TV production in 1988 in the US by 50 per cent and to open a new factory in Glasgow to boost production in Britain; and Toshiba's decision to start producing large colour TVs (and braun tubes) in the US from late 1989, the first Japanese company to do so (*NKS*, 4 June 1987, p. 1; 4 September 1987, p. 9; 7 October 1987, p. 23; 13 October 1988, p. 9; *Industria*, August 1987, p. 23; *JEJ*, 12 September 1987, p. 14; 14 November 1987, p. 21; 26 December 1987, p. 16; 28 May 1988, p. 19; 23 July 1988, p. 18; 5 November 1988, p. 4; 12 November 1988, p. 21; Nihon yushutsu yunyū ginkō, 1988, p. 23).

The division of labour between the advanced and the underdeveloped countries in consumer electronics is clearly illustrated by

Matsushita's current global strategy. The company plans to locate outside of Japan 25 per cent (as opposed to 12 per cent at the end of 1986) of its total production to cater for 50 per cent of its overseas sales (33 per cent in 1986), in particular the exchange-rate sensitive consumer goods which it can no longer afford to make in Japan: small colour TVs, electric fans and small refrigerators. Domestically it will concentrate on industrial products and high-tech lines, for example, digital VTRs and its 43-inch TV set (1 inch bigger than Mitsubishi's).

Offshore, Matsushita sees the future in ASEAN rather than the NICs, and it intends to double its ¥50 billion DFI in the region (plus Taiwan) over the next five years in an attempt to preserve the 45 per cent contribution by Asian factories to its overseas production. Each country has a definite function for the electronics giant: Malaysia focuses on colour TVs and electric irons (half for export), Singapore on semi-conductors (90 per cent for export), the Philippines on dry-cell batteries as well as floppy-disk drives and electrolytic capacitors (the latter mainly for export), while factories in Thailand and Indonesia are predominantly for the domestic markets. In the past, the exports were mainly to third countries, but following the rise of the yen there will be a switch to the Japanese market, for example, of audio equipment from Taiwan and Singapore. The company will import components both from its own subsidiaries as well as Asian companies which have supplied them. In fiscal 1987 imported components were boosted by 50 per cent.

The growing focus on Asia has not, however, meant a scaling down of the US operations, only of the domestic ones (exports to total sales falling from 37 to 27 per cent in 1985–87). On the contrary, TV production in particular has been massively increased in the US under the direction of Matsushita's new 'North American TV Division', although the local content in 1988 was still only 50 per cent with many parts coming from Asia and Mexico. Picture tubes will be added in 1989 as the company tries to raise its local content to 70 per cent by 1990, and re-imports back to Japan will also be stepped up, particularly of the larger sets. In late 1987 Matsushita Electrical Industrial and Matsushita Electrical Trading decided to merge, so that they might better coordinate the group's rapidly expanding overseas subsidiaries: 59 manufacturing units, 37 marketing units and four credit services in early 1988 (*FEER*, 25 December 1986, pp. 66–7; *JEJ*, 12 September 1987, p. 14; 23 January 1988, p. 18; 30 January 1988, p. 4; *NKS*, 27 November 1987, p. 9; 16 December 1987, p. 9; 15 October 1988, p. 8).

Hitachi is another company with a similar international strategy, even proclaiming that it is switching from an exporting to an import-ing company: the value of foreign-made parts was expected to soar by 45 per cent in fiscal 1988 to exceed $1 billion. Currently buying parts from over 1000 companies abroad, it plans to select one hundred of them as prime suppliers who will account for half the total within three years: 60 of them in Asia, twenty in the US and twenty in Europe. Already in 1986 it responded swiftly to the rise of the yen by transferring the production of medium-class audio equipment from its Toyokawa plant (in Aichi) to Taiwan and other NICs. It also moved part of its CD manufacturing to its subsidiary in Taiwan, and part of its colour TV production from its Gifu plant to California, West Germany and Britain. From August 1987, the company started to implement its comprehensive restructuring plan, so as to consoli-date in Japan its high-tech activities. The Yokohama plant is being converted into an engineering centre responsible for design and experimentation (*JEJ*, 12 September 1987, p. 5; 31 December 1988 and 7 January 1989, p. 5).

Electrical companies used to concentrate their offshore production of colour TVs and VTRs, which involve the highest levels of skill and technology, almost entirely in the advanced capitalist world where these products are also mainly sold. But now with new wage struc-tures following the rise of the yen, not only will consumer goods like stereo equipment be normally be produced in the NICs, but even colour TVs might go that way. Some Japanese makers have been arranging OEM supplies from companies like Goldstar and Samsung, whose TVs are almost identical in quality to their own but which are 30 per cent cheaper (*NKS*, 21 July 1987, p. 3; 15 August 1987, p. 9; *JEJ*, 29 August 1987, p. 15; *BT*, September 1987, p. 28–9).

Information Communication Equipment (ICE)

If the locus of consumer goods production is moving towards Asia, then the opposite is occurring in those branches of electronics related to what the advanced countries are carving out for themselves, information communication. The total market of this industry in the US is expected to double from $216 billion in 1983 to $422 billion in 1990 and then again to over $1 trillion by 2000. A strategy of using existing production bases combined with tie-ups with leading US corporations is how Japanese capital has entered the ICE manufac-turing industry, the potentially most lucrative branch of all (Nomura, 1987, p. 75).

ICE manufacturing, however, is a field heavily dominated by IBM

Table 4.9   Leading information communication equipment makers, 1984/85

Market shares of computer makers			Market shares of large-scale Communication-equipment makers
Large	Mini	Personal	
IBM: 76	IBM: 42	IBM: 27	AT&T: 31
Burroughs: 5	DEC: 28	Apple: 8	ITT: 12
Armadale: 4	Data General: 6	Commodore: 4	Siemens: 11
Sperry: 4	Prime: 6	Tandy: 4	GTE: 7
Honeywell: 3	Wang: 3	NEC: 4	NEC: 7

Source: Nomura, 1987, p. 75.

and AT&T, not simply in the US, but throughout the world. Table 4.9 shows that NEC, the top Japanese company, barely figured in world shares of the major ICE manufacturing branches in 1984/1985.

To help it take on the challenge, NEC decided to open in the fall of that year a research centre in San Jose for household information equipment and in July 1988 a Europe Business Coordination Centre in London. The latter will function as a head office for the company's sixteen European subsidiaries (five in the UK, three in Germany, two each in France and Italy and one each in Holland, Ireland, Finland and Sweden) as they prepare for 1992.

NEC currently has a total of 48 overseas subsidiaries, of which thirteen are in Asia and eight each in North and South America. Of these, 25 are production bases: only three each in Asia (Taiwan, Singapore and Malaysia) and Latin America (Mexico, Brazil and Argentina), all overwhelmingly making parts, with the rest mainly in Europe, the US and Australia. At the end of April 1987 the company also had 23 sales and service outlets in fifteen countries, 26 offices in 25 countries and 17 000 overseas employees. It has adopted an aggressive overseas policy and plans to raise its share of overseas production from 30 per cent in 1987 to 50 per cent by 1989, having already lifted it from 20 per cent since 1984. As a result of 'its first year of globalization' in 1987, an 8 per cent drop in exports was compensated by a 12 per cent increase in the turnover of its overseas subsidiaries and an 8.9 per cent increase in overseas production.

Since 1980 NEC has adopted a system of what are called 're-entry bosses' to watch over the performance and personal lives of every Japanese overseas employee, including their families, with educational consultants to help with children's education. The company has also pioneered a register of all the skills and abilities its employees might require overseas, so that everyone's language ability, negotiating skills, 'vitality', problem-solving capacity and so on can be known, and the most suitable people sent to deal with the most delicate situations (*NKS*, 31 July 1987, p. 9; 13 August 1987, p. 9; 12 August 1987, p. 8; 15 August 1987, p. 9; 17 August 1987, p. 1; 28 December 1987, p. 7; 6 January 1988, p. 8; 9 January 1988, p. 13; 9 November 1988, p. 11; *JEJ*, 30 January 1988, p. 4; 5 November 1988, p. 4; *TBT*, January 1988, pp. 16–17; Shūkan tōyō keizai, 1988).

As one of the companies thrown into the red by the rising yen, Canon has stepped up its overseas activities in an attempt to build a comprehensive worldwide operation. With its eye on the twenty-first century, it has set up R&D bases in the US and France, and it is vigorously concluding technical tie-ups. The company's overseas production ratio was expected to rise from 12 per cent in 1987 to 17–18 per cent in 1988 as a result of a drastic programme to cut exports from Japan and raise production abroad. It hopes to reduce its 1988 export ratio of 74 to 30 per cent by the end of the century.

Canon's main overseas production of office equipment has been in West Germany and France, where it has been boosting its output of fax machines and copiers as well as starting to make laser printers. More recently it has set up joint ventures with Olivetti (1987) in Italy and with Lotte (1985) in South Korea, where it also has a technical agreement with Goldstar in camera production. Canon has also supplied Eastman Kodak (US) and Agfa-Gevaert (Germany) on an OEM basis. In March 1987 it commenced production of photocopiers in Virginia, where even with 80 per cent of components coming from Japan costs are 15 per cent lower than at home, and it intends to branch into other OA equipment within the year.

Canon also recently decided to transfer its entire electric type-writer business (including design and managerial decision making) to its US subsidiary. In the field of computers, the company has agreements with Siemens and Apple amongst others and with a number of US semiconductor makers (including Motorola). But Canon remains one of eight Japanese companies whose photo copiers are subject to a 20 per cent EC dumping duty, made permanent in February 1987.

Another company in the same boat is Oki Electric, which has been selling about 200 000 printers a year in Europe. It has now decided to produce printers in England for the entire European market, beginning in December 1987. The English plant in Cumbria will be its third outside Japan, the other two being in Atlanta, where it will start making portable car phones from 1989, and Taiwan.

Other copier makers that were spurred (*hakusha*) into Europe in the mid-1980s were Ricoh into Britain in 1983 and into France in 1988; Minolta, Konica and Matsushita into West Germany in 1986–7; and Toshiba into France and Sharp into Britain in 1986. By 1990 their overseas capacity is expected to exceed that of their exports. Already in 1987 Ricoh could meet 70 per cent of its demand in Europe with local production. Once these and its three US plants (the third opened in 1988) become fully operational in 1990, it will have moved 50 per cent of its entire OA equipment capacity overseas. But it would still be short of its goal of 70 per cent.

A similar story could be told of dot-matrix and laser printer makers like Fujitsu, Seiko-Epson and Kyocera. In the case of fax machines there is a slight difference, since Japanese makers currently enjoy 90 per cent of the world market, with the sole competition coming from Thomson of France and a few licensed South Korean and Taiwanese makers. But the motive for moving to the US and Europe is much the same: to avoid trade friction. And with Sharp's commencement of personal computer production in the US in January 1988, the last of the majors transferred production to America in this industry. But Seiko Epson's launching of personal computer production in Britain from September 1988 was the first step of its kind into Europe, taken *before* any company might become the target of dumping charges (*TBT*, January 1988, p. 19; *NKS*, 5 June 1987, p. 9; 27 October 1987, p. 9; 19 November 1987, p. 9; 17 December 1987, p. 9; 30 December 1987, p. 7; 4 January 1988, p. 7; *JEJ*, 6 June 1987, p. 13; 3 July 1987, p. 6; 23 January 1988, p. 19; 12 March 1988, p. 15; 16 April 1988, pp. 17, 22 July 1988, p. 22; 20; 1 October 1988, pp. 16–17; *Industria*, May 1987, p. 41; Nihon yushutsu yunyū ginkō, 1988, p. 23).

Like other branches of the information communications industry, equipment manufacture is overwhelmingly concentrated in the advanced countries. This means that relations among the corporations of the major powers are characterised by both intense competition and by a commonality of interest against labour as well as against capital in the underdeveloped world. An important indicator of this alliance are the large number of tie-ups among leading players on both sides. The more successful ones not yet mentioned have included NEC, which is teaming up with Honeywell and a French computer company; Fujitsu, which is establishing a joint venture with GTE to serve the US data-communications market; Oki Electric, which has entered the AT&T camp through its merger with UNIX; Matsushita, which has joined with DEC to supply equipment to

NTT; and Hitachi, which is cooperating with National Semiconductor after acquiring the latter's subsidiary, National Advanced Systems (*NKS*, 13 January 1988, p. 8; 31 November 1988, p. 8; *JEJ*, 21 November 1987, p. 22; 26 November 1988, p. 27).

Components

Apart from a few service related components which were locally made in advanced capitalist countries, before the rise of the yen it had generally been cheaper to bring in parts from Japan and Asia. This industry therefore reflects the concentration in the advanced countries of certain consumer electronics goods and information equipment. The latter's increased local production caused a flood of Japanese component imports, which then caused new friction on both sides of the Atlantic. Japanese capital has thus had to shift some component production into the advanced countries while continuing to import others from Asia, including Japan. Fortunately, the rise of the yen greatly reduced the costs of making electronics parts in Europe and America, just as it had for car parts. The dollar exchange rates at which unit wage costs of productive workers in Japan and the US were the same in 1984 was ¥138.9 in ICE, ¥141.5 in computers, ¥115.3 in consumer electronics and ¥150.5 in electronic components. *Endaka* thus made the latter cheaper in the US than in Japan (Nomura, 1987, p. 82).

Nevertheless, Japanese capital's basic strategy remains to combine Japan's 'productive power' with Europe and America's 'commercial power', Asia's function being unambiguously to assist the former through its lower wages. Matsushita's sales agreement with GM to supply VTRs on an OEM basis and its productive agreement with Goldstar to secure parts epitomise the desired international division of labour. Table 4.10 shows the regional distribution of DFI cases in the three main branches of the industry in 1974–84, confirming how Asia became Japanese capital's overseas centre for making components. Around this time overseas components comprised 24.6 per cent of total components made by Japanese companies, with South Korea providing 6.6 per cent, Taiwan 12.3 per cent and all others combined only 1.5 per cent. The table also shows that the overseas production of industrial electronics goods, which are mainly sold in Asia, is also concentrated in that region, while consumer electronics are produced mainly where they are sold, in the advanced countries (Nomura, 1987, p. 86; Yamauchi, 1985, p. 90).

Table 4.10   Cases of DFI in electronics, 1974–84

	Industrial	Consumer	Components	Total
Asia	17	21	63	101
Latin America	2	9	5	16
United States	3	11	18	32
Europe	6	18	12	36
Other	0	5	1	6
TOTAL	28	64	99	191

Source: Shimura, 1986, p. 153.

Table 4.11   Planned DFI in electronics, as of July 1986

Company	Country	Investment	Product/Production start
Matsushita	West Germany	¥2 billion/100%	VHS video mechanisms/1986
	West Germany	¥10 billion/50 %	Electronic parts/end 1986
Sanyo	US	¥6 billion/3 years	Optical disks, CD soft/June 1987
	Taiwan		Linear ICs/early 1987
Toshiba	US	¥20 billion/WH	100 000 braun tubes/1986; 160 000/1989
Hitachi	US	¥10 billion/100%	Magnetic disk equipment/April 1987
	US	100%	Motor vehicle parts/June 1986
JVC	US	¥9 billion/JVC US	Video tape; 10 million CD soft/1987
Columbia	US		1.2 million CD soft/January 1987
Fujitsu	US	¥3–4 billion	Semicustom ICs/mid-1987
Pioneer	US	¥1.4 billion	Speaker systems, etc./1987

Source: Kitada and Aida, 1987, p. 72.

Since 1984 growing trade friction and the rise of the yen produced a new rush of investment plans in both consumer goods and components. Table 4.11 summarises the main decisions which had been announced by July 1986.

Although quite a few more components factories have since been set up in Europe and America, most of these also centre on higher value-added products or are intended to strengthen the servicing of customers. The move by Matsushita Electronic Components into Germany and the US in 1984/5 and by Alps Electric into Britain in 1985 to make VTR parts are typical examples of how, what was originally a marketing strategy, was accelerated by trade friction, anti-dumping actions and the rise of the yen. In 1988 both companies were expanding their operations in the other's territory. Alps set up a parts factory in Germany to make VTR heads as well as parts for computers and mobile phones, while Matsushita moved into Britain to make components for microwaves and started making copier parts in Germany.

Fujitsu responded very quickly to the rise of the yen and set up a large magnetic disk equipment factory in Billsborough in 1986. It now intends to expand the range of components produced there, doubling or even tripling its capacity. Some of the drives will be shipped to Spain to help the company boost printer production there from 3000 in 1987 to 20 000 by 1989, partly for export back to the US as well as to Japan (*NKS*, 12 August 1987, p. 8; 30 October 1987, p. 9; 26 November 1987, p. 1; Shūkan tōyō keizai, 1988; Shimura, 1986, p. 152–5; *JEJ*, 19 December 1987, p. 19; 26 December 1987, p. 16; 23 January 1988, p. 18; 21 May 1988, p. 17; *FEER*, 25 December 1986, pp. 64–5).

Before the electronics branches of the electrical industry began to predominate, over half of all components were 'passive' (as opposed to 'active' ones like semiconductors and microprocessors and braun tubes), and their overseas manufacture was almost entirely in Asia. But then a movement by capital which we saw in textiles was also made in the electrical industry: the simplest most labour intensive branches went to the poorer ASEAN countries, while the intermediate ones shifted to the NICs, where some infrastructure and skill had been developed.

However, now that electronics is itself being increasingly applied even to the production of electronics components, low wages are not of themselves the attraction they used to be, and components closest to the cutting edge of technological change tend to be made where that edge is sharpest. It is thus not so extraordinary to find that almost all of the current foreign investment plans to make components in the advanced countries centre on high-tech ones, particularly for ICE. The examples are too numerous to mention (*JEJ*, 16 January, pp. 17, 19; 23 April, p. 17; 4 June, p. 22; 25 June, p. 23; 2 July, p. 23; 1 October, p. 17; 8 October, p. 23; 15 October, p. 20; 22 October, p. 17; 10 December, p. 21).

Semiconductors

The lion's den of semiconductors is a very young industry, mainly because technology in its required raw materials is relatively undeveloped, with huge scope for advancements. There is also great room for improvement in the production process, for example, in the technology of etching, and unlike motor cars, there seems to be no limit to the output's final use, which extends from household, office, factory and into outer space.

Because technical change in the industry is so rapid, it is difficult to set out even a general picture of the international technical division of labour that is not out of date. However, there seem to be three main levels of technology which are associated with three groups of countries. Right at the top is the technology involved in making microprocessors, a type of semiconductor which receives its instructions in '4-bit' chunks and which performs complicated tasks like controlling laser printers and computers. The world's leaders in this technology are the US companies Intel and Motorola, and Japanese companies must make microprocessors under licence. Although they also design their own, these are the simpler 4-bit or 8-bit controllers found in many consumer products, like VTRs. But the US companies are now refusing to licence their latest 32-bit designs, and although new types of chips are constantly being developed (RISC, TRON), the US monopoly of 90 per cent of the world market is unlikely to be affected because new products require new software. Today's third generation of machines are running essentially the same software based on Intel designs, and to compete with that would require an extra $12 billion investment.

The type of semiconductor with which the Japanese have had the greatest success is the memory chip used in computers (dynamic access memory or D-RAM), for which they now control over 75 per cent of the world market. But making chips always involves two processes. The higher-tech task of writing patterns on the wafers is concentrated in the advanced countries, chiefly Japan and the US, whereas the finishing process is a labour-intensive assembly job being moved increasingly to underdeveloped countries.

The manufacture of memory chips is an extremely competitive industry, and the Japanese majors have thrived on it. While Texas Instruments, Motorola and Philips were clear leaders in the field in the early 1980s, by 1985 NEC had moved to first position. Hitachi, Toshiba and Fujitsu had overtaken Phillips, and Hitachi and Toshiba were right on the heels of the two American giants.

This competition among the world's majors extends worldwide, and the Japanese firms seem to have made Malaysia their main low cost area for the labour intensive finishing process to complement their investments in wafer fabrication in the US. NEC has an aggressive strategy to establish a global production system, including Asia (Malaysia and Singapore), the US and Europe (Scotland and Ireland). This centres on its integrated production base (wafer processing as well as assembly) for 256KDRAMs in the US (Roseville, California), and facilities for the finishing process in Scotland and Ireland. To minimise foreign exchange losses, the company is shipping chips from Britain to the US and from the US to Europe, while to minimise trade conflict it is considering importing some of the US-made chips to Japan. In mid-1986 NEC was also constructing integrated production facilities for 8-bit microprocessors in Britain. The role of Singapore and Malaysia in this scheme is in the finishing process of bipolar ICs and transistors, although Singapore also serves as a consumption and distribution centre.

All the other majors have made or implemented similar plans. Hitachi complements its integrated facilities in the US making 256KDRAM and 64KDRAM chips with its finishing process for MOS memory chips in Germany; the finishing of linear ICs, transistors and 256KDRAM in Malaysia; and the finishing of transistors (100 per cent for export) in Taiwan. In 1989 Hitachi will complete its front-end wafer processing facilities at Dallas, where it will make 1-megabyte DRAMs as well as ASICs (Application Specific Integrated Circuits).

When it opens its new plant in Oregon in 1989, Fujitsu will be the third Japanese company to start integrated production of 256KDRAM chips in the US, which it complements with assembly in Ireland. Toshiba has been planning to set up such facilities in the US to complement its assembly in Germany, Malaysia and South Korea. However, from May 1988 it began to entrust production of its 1-megabyte DRAMs to Motorola under licence in order to reduce trade friction. With a view to producing ASICs in the US, all the major companies have also been establishing design centres in various parts of the country. By September 1987, Fujitsu already had five in operation and one in the pipeline for completion by the end of the year, NEC the same number in operation and two in the 1987 pipeline. Hitachi, Toshiba and Mitsubishi had only slightly less ambitious plans (*JEJ*, 30 May 1987, p. 19; 21 November 1987, p. 13; 28 November 1987, p. 26; 13 February 1988, p. 18; 17 September 1988, p. 30; 22 October 1988, p. 17; *NKS*, 14 September, 1987, p. 9; 14 November 1987, p. 1; 1 December 1987, p. 8; 7 September 1988, p. 1; 19 September 1988, p. 9; 11 October 1988, p. 11; *FEER*, 7 July

1988, pp. 43–6; 18 August 1988, pp. 80–3; Nomura, 1987, pp. 51–62).

Cooperation at the top is also integral to monopoly capital's strategy in the semiconductor industry, because none makes the whole range of ICs by itself. All the American majors have been operating in Japan since the mid-1970s, as have the Japanese majors in the US, although chip manufacturing is a more recent undertaking. But the ground has been fertile for tie-ups of one sort or another. The most significant is the growing cooperation between Toshiba and Motorola, which the Pentagon, it seems, has been trying to undo with its hysterical campaign over COCOM. Toshiba has the most extensive network of high-tech foreign partners of all Japanese electrical firms, and seems to pose the greatest threat to the Americans. Apart from Motorola, they include Sun Microsystems, United Technologies, Rhone–Poulenc, Siemens, AT&T, Visa International, Westinghouse Electric (at least until late 1988 when the merger was dissolved), LSI Logic and Computervision. Toshiba has also built up an impressive range of productive bases in the US, covering white goods, audio and video equipment, motors and ICE (TVs, electric (braun tubes) (*JEJ*, 1987, p. 20; *NKS*, 10 September 1987, p. 9; 29 October 1988, p. 8).

To sum up the common features of all the different branches of the electronics industry, astronomical technical change continued to throw Japanese and US companies into one another's arms, perhaps because of rather than in spite of the intense worldwide competition in the industry. So although the competition has at times generated a lot of heat, this has quickly subsided in the wake of new tie-ups among capitalists. The politicians, on the other hand, seem to thrive on the racism that can be generated and give a misleading impression of what the real dangers are. Where distances have grown substantially, however, is between the technological progress of the Asian countries, including the NICs, and that of the advanced countries.

CONCLUSION

Cars and electronics were the two industries most closely associated with the export-led boom of the late 1970s and early 1980s, and they were also the two which were most severely affected by the rising yen and the inducement it gave to globalisation. Space has not allowed me to examine capital's strategies in other manufacturing industries, where DFI has also been seen as a solution to current problems in

Table 4.12   Tie-ups between Japanese and US companies in 1986

	Technical Exchange	DFI Cases Total	in US	in Japan	Grand Total
Manufacturing	399 (343)	317 (162)	276	41	716 (505)
Hi-tech	181 (185)	100 (57)	67	33	281 (242)
Semiconductors	50 (29)	43 (22)	26	17	93 (51)
Computers	52 (46)	17 (13)	9	8	69 (59)
Biotechnology	13 (26)	9 (4)	5	4	22 (30)
Communication equipment	15 (7)	11 (4)	10	1	26 (11)
New Materials	12 (21)	5 (4)	4	1	17 (25)
Robots	10 (24)	4 (2)	4	0	14 (26)
Other	29 (32)	11 (8)	9	2	40 (41)
Electrical machinery	49 (19)	62 (16)	60	2	111 (35)
General machinery	50 (38)	50 (23)	49	1	100 (61)
Motor vehicles	36 (27)	42 (36)	42	0	78 (63)
Metals	16 (19)	8 (3)	7	1	24 (22)
Chemicals	33 (27)	18 (8)	15	3	51 (35)
Textiles	6 (3)	5 (1)	5	0	11 (4)
Food	11 (8)	14 (8)	14	0	25 (16)
Other manufacturing	17 (17)	18 (10)	17	1	35 (27)
Finance	12 (16)	16 (12)	14	2	28 (28)
Construction/real estate	16 (16)	47 (13)	47	0	63 (29)
Communications	15 (36)	10 (7)	8	2	25 (43)
Other	20 (37)	15 (10)	14	1	35 (47)
TOTAL	462 (448)	405 (204)	359	46	867 (652)

Note: Figures in brackets denote 1985.
Source: *JS*, May 1987, p. 64.

Japan. Among them is iron and steel and non-ferrous metals, but fully eighteen out of the 22 investment projects in metals in North America which were made in 1985 to mid-1986 were related to motor vehicles and semiconductors. And the tendency towards cooperation rather than unmanageable conflict between Japanese and US capital that we found in motor vehicles and electronics has also been industry wide. Table 4.12 shows the numbers of tie-ups that were publicly announced in 1986 alone.

As we saw in the case of motor vehicles, the production of a limited range of electronics goods in Europe and America does not mean there has been any real deviation from the fundamental strategy of using these regions as essentially consumption rather than production centres. Although it might appear that the rise of the yen changed this situation, the only modification was to refine the production strategy so that it could continue to complement the marketing strategy, which has remained almost entirely unaltered. *Endaka* raised production costs in Japan, and adequate compensation could not be found by letting plans to *produce* goods in the advanced countries continue to be guided purely by a *marketing* strategy which was itself faltering. That could only work so long as production costs were inconsequential and so long as the advanced countries kept their markets totally open.

However, following the rise of the yen and mounting protectionism, new expedients have had to be found to restore that happy state of affairs. The Maquiladora bonded zones in Mexico are proving ideal for combining the production and marketing strategies, since cheap Mexican labour makes parts right where they are most needed. Elsewhere a combination of different strategies is in the process of being worked out to ensure low cost production without intensifying inter-imperialist rivalry. In most cases unit costs are being kept down by using only the most advanced technologies in the production process, so that the numbers of workers who need to be paid the higher wages is kept to the minimum. Since this usually involves cooperation with capital in the advanced countries, it simultaneously helps keep rivalry within acceptable bounds. Equally widespread are the attempts to find the most vulnerable workers in the advanced countries – women, blacks, migrants, areas of high unemployment – or to use the notorious techniques of 'Japanese management' to create low paid workers through temporary labour and subcontracting systems.

But the inter-imperialist cooperation does not simply solve a problem for Japanese capital in its traditional markets. It is spurring a technological revolution and sends Japan into Asia as part of an increasingly powerful imperialist alliance, whose real power rests on a technological lead which has become impossible to bridge so long as capitalism is the motor of technical change.

5 Investment in Singapore and South Korea

We have seen how inter-imperialist rivalry has been giving way to cooperation as Japanese transnationals tie-up with their American and European counterparts and shift high-tech production to the advanced countries. But this is producing new contradictions, since Japanese companies are confronting more technically backward capital in Asia not as equal partners – they already have those in Europe and America – but with offers to produce low value added products or simply to assemble components brought in from elsewhere.

The main conditions which force the Southeast Asian ruling classes to cooperate with the Japanese are their historically determined 'backward productive forces'. Because capitalism is a system of production for profit or not at all, capitalists are in constant competition with one another and must continually renew their techniques to keep up with rivals. Their survival thus depends on the 'level of their productive forces', on whether they can earn the profits needed to keep on investing in 'new' technology. The power of imperialist capital rests ultimately on its ability to do this, to ruin rivals instead of falling behind them.

Possessing the leading technologies is normally a legacy of the past, of having started off with a leading edge which was then maintained through constantly reinvesting the profits which it made possible. The power of capitalist imperialism is thus a product of timing, of the weakness of the competition when it first entered the fray. The first capitalist powers have tended to make the largest profits which enabled them to develop the most competitive technologies, thereby ensuring they earned the largest profits. Special historical circumstances have been needed to counteract this most basic feature of capitalism.

Although classical imperialism was driven by military as well as economic rivalries, colonies that became sources of wealth had something which compensated for their technical backwardness, usually some natural resource. Special raw material deposits, water for power generation or climate for growing crops enabled colonies with backward productive forces to generate wealth, and even after the transition to neo-colonialism foreign capital has invested in them for this reason.

The notion of 'newly industrialised' recognises that capitalist development in the Asian NICs has occurred, only later than elsewhere. This timing would have precluded development had not capital found areas of investment in which lateness was not a disadvantage. In the ASEAN countries, this was mainly in industries associated with raw materials and food. But apart from South Korea and to a lesser extent Taiwan, the NICs do not have natural endowments, since they are artificial products of the cold war and the struggle for decolonisation: the broken off urban centres of colonial resource-rich hinterlands. So although their original capitalist development was related to processing or trade in raw materials, which imperialism concentrated in the urban centres, this is not possible any more. Since their separation from their hinterlands, they no longer have direct access to raw materials, only relatively skilled workers. With about a quarter of its people in Seoul, even South Korea shares this feature of the NICs.

To survive competition with capital in the advanced countries, capital in the NICs had to carve out a niche for itself. It had access to almost as cheap but relatively more skilled workers than were available in the hinterland, but few raw materials to serve as a leading edge. Competition came from two quarters: more productive working classes in the advanced countries and cheaper ones in the hinterlands. NICs capital could only afford to trail technically behind the advanced countries so long as its workers were paid less. And it could only concede higher wages to its better organised workers than the average in ASEAN if it was technically superior. And so it found its niche in an alliance with the imperialist powers, including Japan. The latter got access to its low paid workers and it got just enough technology to give it a leading edge over ASEAN.

So while ASEAN countries remained mainly centres of resource extraction and processing, the NICs became sources of cheap labour for the Japanese manufacturing industry. They have had to combine draconian controls over their working classes with never-ending quests for newer technology. Hong Kong and to a lesser extent Singapore have had the added functions of commercial and financial clearing houses for Japanese companies throughout Asia. In the case of Hong Kong, Japanese capital's main interest has been in finance, commerce and services, although in the others, notably Taiwan, the focus has been almost entirely on manufacturing. Electronics and automobiles have been the main targets. However, since the rise of the yen there has been a general revival of interest in the unpro-

Table 5.1   Composition of accumulated Japanese DFI in Asia by country, 1987

	Total value $ million	Distribution by industry (%)			
		Manufacturing	Machinery	Resources	Unproductive
North America	37 406	26.5	14.6	4.4	69.1
Asia Total	21 790	38.2	11.9	31.2	30.6
NICs					
Hong Kong	3 433	8.7	2.1	0.9	90.4
South Korea	2 118	51.4	19.1	1.0	47.6
Taiwan	1 051	90.9	52.9	0.3	8.8
Singapore	2 571	60.2	27.9	0.2	39.6
ASEAN					
Indonesia	8 673	27.2	2.5	68.8	4.0
Malaysia	1 283	66.7	18.5	13.9	19.4
Philippines	913	40.4	14.9	47.6	12.0
Thailand	884	70.1	20.7	2.4	27.5

Source: Ōkurashō, 1987b, pp. 54–7.

ductive sectors as well. In fiscal 1987 unproductive projects in Asia skyrocketed by 136 per cent to $2866 million, overwhelmingly in the NICs: real estate in Singapore and Hong Kong and hotels in South Korea. Table 5.1 shows how by March 1987 only Taiwan among the NICs was still almost purely a production base.

The reasons for the different patterns of Japanese DFI in ASEAN and the NICs lie in the conditions and class struggles of each country, which form the context and shape the terms of the alliances between the local and Japanese ruling classes. Table 5.2, which shows the cases of DFI as of July 1987 in the most favoured manufacturing industries in the NICs, outlines the process over time.

A significant feature of the current wave of manufacturing DFI in Asia (NICs and ASEAN) is the new emphasis on securing cheap supplies for Japan. Traditionally the main markets aimed at by Japanese subsidiaries were either local or third countries, with less, compared to US subsidiaries, being sold in the home market. Since the rise of the yen, a firmer link is being forged between investment and trade, particularly in electronics and motor vehicle components.

Table 5.2 Survey of DFI cases in NICs manufacturing by year started, to July 1987

	Total	Textiles	Electric	General machine	Chemicals	Other manufacturing	Commerce/Finance
Asia	3 338	178	379	159	293	849	936
to 1969	449	48	63	25	51	139	84
1970s	1 597	101	190	80	153	388	457
1980s	1 207	25	116	51	84	305	372
Singapore	535	5	64	22	40	90	214
to 1969	26	2	1	–	6	10	6
1970s	260	2	50	13	15	47	86
1980s	228	1	12	8	19	30	113
Hong Kong	621	18	20	5	12	65[a]	391
to 1969	83	3	5	2	3	17	41
1970s	317	6	6	2	4	25	221
1980s	204	8	8	1	5	21	120
South Korea	343	30	64	34	51	121	16
to 1969	8	1	1	1	1	2	1
1970s	228	29	50	21	33	75	6
1980s	98	–	12	10	16	41[b]	9
Taiwan	565	37	128	54	69	193	53
to 1969	170	22	42	20	26	57	2
1970s	190	11	47	24	20	66	16
1980s	190	2	33	10	23	66	34

Notes: Excludes firms which have since withdrawn. Totals include cases for which date is unknown.
[a] includes 18 in precision machinery.
[b] includes 10 in automobiles.
[b] includes 28 in motor vehicles and transport machinery.
Source: Shūkan tōyō keizai, 1988, pp. 16–17.

SINGAPORE

History of Struggle

Singapore, which was once the entrepôt and manufacturing centre of British imperialism in Malaya, is today unquestionably the most heavily overseas-dominated of all Southeast Asian countries. However, the importance of Japan among the foreign allies of Singaporean capital has, until recently, lagged behind that of the US. We need to trace the history of the struggles which led this island's ruling class into such an unequivocal alliance with foreign capital.

In 1945 Singapore was the centre of the most advanced working-class organisation in Malaya. The militant struggles of 1946 and 1947 challenged the whole system of political economic management, since they involved all possible issues from abolition of the contract system of employment through equal pay regardless of sex or ethnicity. By March 1947 the Malayan labour movement was at the peak of its strength: 1 173 000 working days had been lost in Singapore alone during the preceding year. The Pan-Malayan General Labour Union (which included the Singapore General Labour Union) was founded in February 1946 with good connections with the Malayan Communist Party and included over half the total work force and 85 per cent of trade unions.

The British Military Administration dealt with this labour unrest in ways many of which have since become normal practice in Singapore. In 1945 two Chinese newspapers were closed down, their staff and editors sentenced to prison terms for using the term 'economic exploitation'. Japanese prisoners of war were widely used as strike breakers (20 000 in Singapore alone), and 'agitators' were excluded from future employment. Demonstrations were banned, troops were used against demonstrators, militants were banished, anti-communist trade unionists were sent out from Britain as advisers and an elaborate system of restrictive trade union legislation was used to destroy the militant organisation. In 1948, the Pan-Malayan Federation of Trade Unions (formerly the PMGLU) was banned, as was the May Day demonstration in Singapore. Legislation restricted union officials to persons without criminal records and with three years experience in the industry (effectively excluding militants and seasonal workers), and it also prohibited inter-industry or inter-occupational federations such as the PMFTU. With the declaration of the state of Emergency, a further array of repressive measures, arrests, purges of 'undesirable elements' and even the hanging of PMFTU leaders finally sealed the fate of militant working-class organisation in Singapore (Stenson, 1970; Morgan, 1977).

The only legal outlet for an all-embracing genuine anti-colonial movement in the 1950s was the People's Action Party, which was based on the working-class movement, but which included a group of English educated intellectuals. It was this latter group, under Lee Kuan Yew, who with considerable help from the British eventually took over the party and systematically smashed its militant socialist wing using the very tactics the British themselves had found so successful. The British shrewdly recognised in Lee someone who would eventually work with rather than against imperialism.

Although Britain had more at stake economically in Peninsular Malaya, its strategic interests made it more reluctant to concede full independence to Singapore; only self-government in 1959. Lee favoured the proposed Federation, because it promised a larger market, control over leftist forces and guaranteed independence from Britain, but in 1965 Singapore was expelled because of Lee's intransigence. This was another major turning point in the PAP's journey towards a thorough-going alliance with imperialism. Deprived of the larger market needed to achieve a degree of economic independence, the PAP had to rely on what had generated wealth in the colonial period: foreign capital, disciplined workers and access to the Malayan hinterland for materials and a reserve army of labour. Socialist strategies to real political-economic independence having been firmly rejected, the vulnerabilities of the small city state narrowly circumscribed the attempt to achieve it under capitalism.

The Singapore model was consciously developed at this time: industrial and political stability at any cost, vast infrastructural facilities, incentives in priority industries, and key state-owned institutions to assist private profit making, all to be systematically maintained in order to attract foreign export-oriented investment. There has never been any deviation from it; only adaptations and extensions to meet new situations. Throughout the aim was to ensure that Singapore always remained the most favoured outlet for foreign investment in Southeast Asia.

For example, the high wages policy of the early 1980s was intended to stimulate labour saving technologies, raise labour productivity and so guarantee Singapore's attractiveness to foreign investors over its neighbours. When this and other problems led to a recession and a decline in foreign investment, the government cut wage costs by 12 per cent simply by slashing employers' contributions to the national pension scheme, suspended some other taxes and levies, imposed a wage freeze and launched a special drive for low-paid Malaysians: 'to recruit electronics industry workers in order to prevent wage awards in the sector from cracking the government's pay freeze' (*FEER*, 12 June 1986, pp. 114–15). Japanese companies in Singapore have found the hinterland most useful in this regard: nearly a quarter of Matsushita's work force is now Malaysian and Aiwa contracts out mechanical assembly jobs to companies in Malaysia. Then after a two year wage freeze the government started encouraging companies to introduce a Japanese-style system in which bonuses could be cut to allow greater wage flexibility in bad times. By September 1988, 38 per cent of companies monitored by the Labour Ministry had complied. The PAP and Lee have expressed unbounded admiration for Japan and have implemented a number of additional measures to further Singapore's emulation of the Japanese model, particularly its industrial relations system (*The Economist*, 22 November 1986, p. 10; *SCMP*, Business Post, 20 February, 1987, p. 3; *Business Times*, 20 February 1987, p. 1).

The same faithfulness to the interests of foreign capital applies to the widespread use of state power to aid private industry. For a long time it was recognised to be crucial to this end, but more recently there has been a worldwide ideological reaction by transnational capital against it, and true to form Singapore has launched a programme of privatisation (*FEER*, 8 September 1988, p. 141; 2 April 1987, pp. 50–1).

But the campaign to restructure into areas of higher technology is more urgent, because Singapore is surrounded by low-wage countries into which foreign capital is continually shifting. For example, even some of the top US companies in Singapore's prize industry, disk drive manufacturing, have recently taken this step: Seagate Technology and Micropolis Corporation have transferred part of their production to Thailand (*JEJ*, 1 October 1988, p. 6).

Iain Buchanan summed up the Singpore model rather well (Mirza, 1986, pp. 45–6):

Singapore's essential role as focus and clearing house for foreign economic interest in the Malay world remains the same: capital and enterprise gather in the island state, and spread outwards; a colonial pattern of trade persists with Singapore as the middlemen; the region's markets and raw materials are exploited through

Singapore. The republic's relationship with its Malaysian and Indonesian hinterland remains a colonial one, but the structure of colonial influence is changing: from British and Dutch Domain into an American and Japanese one.

Foreign Investment

Actually, American and Japanese investment led the way from the beginning, the former in petrochemicals and electronics, the latter in electronics and shipbuilding. But because petroleum requires such large investments (absorbing 55 per cent of DFI in 1970), the relative money values of US and Japanese investments overstate the former's importance. The Japanese do have one large stake in this industry, the Sumitomo consortium's 50–50 joint venture with the Singapore government (whose share is to be taken over by Shell), Petrochemical Corporation of Singapore (PCS). PCS and four other foreign-owned refineries (Shell, Esso, BP and Mobil) have made Singapore the Asia-Pacific's premier entrepôt refining centre (*NKS*, 19 January 1988, p. 9; *FEER*, 26 May 1988, pp. 86–8; *JEJ*, 5 March 1988, p. 15; 29 October 1988, p. 24).

Table 5.3, which presents DFI in manufacturing (excluding petro-chemical projects) by country of origin in 1970–86, shows how in recent years Japanese investment came to equal and then in 1986 surpass US investment. Since then Japan has retained the lead: in the first half of 1987 commitments soared 3.7 times over the same period in 1986 to S$339 million, the year ending with Japan ahead of the US for the second time running. And then in January to June 1988 commitments from Japan leapt by a further 13.3 per cent over the same period in 1987 to S$377 million, which was 45.8 per cent of the total S$823 million. Japan claims sixteen of the top 50 foreign corporations in Singapore, while the US and UK have nine each. The gross investment of the 1000 odd Japanese firms operating there now constitutes about one third of the total investments in the country (*JS*, November 1988, p. 52; *JEJ*, 3 September 1988, p. 19; Iwasaki 1988, p. 89).

Table 5.4 measures the contribution of local and foreign capital to Singapore's manufacturing sector. Because the classification is according to the majority shareholder, it tends to understate the shares of foreign firms, particularly Japanese ones which have a higher incidence of minority holdings than those from other countries. The foreign dominance indicated is thus all the more staggering.

Table 5.3 Accumulated DFI in Singapore manufacturing by main country of origin, 1970–84: commitments 1985–86 (excluding petrochemical projects)

	U.S.		Japan		Britain		Holland		Total	
	S$ million	%	S$ million	%	S$ million	%	S$ million	%	S$ million	%
1970	343	34.5	68	6.8	199	20.0	183	18.4	995	100
1975	1 118	33.1	454	13.4	481	14.2	473	14.0	3 380	100
1980	2 215	29.5	1 185	15.8	1 227	16.3	1 216	16.2	7 520	100
1981	2 599	30.2	1 372	16.0	1 412	16.4	1 310	15.2	8 593	100
1982	3 236	33.7	1 584	16.5	1 581	16.5	1 423	14.8	9 607	100
1983	3 736	33.5	2 236	20.1	1 759	15.8	1 478	13.3	11 123	100
1984	3 649	30.0	2 874	23.6	1 590	13.1	1 558	12.8	12 180	100
Commitments:										
1985	432	47.8	244	27.0	76	8.4	75	8.3	904	100
1986	444	37.3	494	41.5	93	7.9	57	4.8	1 190	100

Source: Reports of the Economic Development Board and Nihon bōeki shinkōkai, 1988a, p. 402.

Table 5.4   Shares of foreign and local firms in Singapore manufacturing, 1985 (%)

	Local	Foreign	US	Japan	Total
Establishments	79.1	20.9	3.8	5.5	3 504
Workers	47.0	53.0	16.8	16.2	253 510
Output	37.5	62.5	21.0	11.7	$38 505 505
Value Added	36.3	63.7	23.8	13.5	$10 687 326
Direct Exports	25.9	74.1	25.8	12.7	$24 276 303
Capital Expenditure	37.1	62.9	29.2	11.8	$1 977 205

Source: Department of Statistics, *Report on the Census of Industrial Production, 1985*, January 1987, p. 6.

Similar data could be presented to show the overwhelming weight of foreign capital in banking, finance and services, which are all major sectors, as well as Japan's growing importance in them. For example, SIMEX (Singapore International Monetary Exchange), which is Asia's first financial futures market, has been developing a wide range of new financial products very much with an eye on plugging Singapore into Japan's as yet untapped power in world finance. One of these is the sale of Nikkei Stock Average futures in September 1986. When the Tokyo and Osaka Stock Exchanges began selling these two years later, SIMEX promptly slashed its commission rates by up to 72 per cent. The decision in July 1988 by the Government of Singapore Investment Corp. to locate its second overseas office in Tokyo (the first was in New York) underlines the importance of the Tokyo–Singapore axis in Asian capital markets (*JEJ*, 2 July 1988, p. 21; 3 September 1988, p. 20; 10 September 1988, p. 6).

It is striking that after more than twenty years of this type of capitalist development under the guidance of a nominally independent state, there are still few signs of local ruling class developing any independence of foreign capital. Nigel Holloway, formerly the *Far Eastern Economic Review*'s bureau chief in Singapore, wrote recently:

In a country where gross savings comprised more than 40 per cent of GDP last year, net investment commitments in manufacturing by local companies contributed 0.7 per cent of GDP. Local manufacturing commitments have averaged a feeble 21 per cent of total commitments since 1972. The rest has come from foreign investors.

There has been no sign of improvement in recent times. The local share has fallen every year since 1982 . . . The island republic is little more than a sub-contractor of the rich countries (16 July 1987, p. 60).

In the state sector this subservience to foreign capital is all the more remarkable, because if anywhere this is where thinking about the 'national interest' (the way ruling classes express their interests) is most prominent. Very recently there have been one or two signs of an attempt by the Economic Development Board, 'which has basically acted as a foreign-investment agency since its inception' (ibid.), to promote local entrepreneurs. But it is looking for them among the 25 000 local managers currently working for foreign companies. And while there are some emerging local capitalist enterprises, not least in shipbuilding (thanks to one of the rare cases of technology transfer by Japanese firms like IHI), they too show no inclination to depart from the Singapore model. So it seems that the tie between the ruling class of Singapore and those of the US and Japan is more than an alliance, because that term denotes negotiation and a boundary that shifts with changing conditions.

Electronics Investments

Particularly since it began restructuring into higher-tech production, Singapore has become ideally suited to the Japanese strategy of increasing the manufacture of sophisticated electronic components in Asia. Of all the Asian countries with Japanese DFI, Singapore receives the fewest complaints for the levels of technical skill possessed by its workers. Registering a whopping 33.5 per cent growth in the first half of 1988 over the same period in 1987, electronics has spearheaded a revival of foreign investment and a rate of economic growth in 1988 of 10.9 per cent (8.8 per cent in 1987) following the very sharp recession of 1984–86 (*FEER*, 3 November 1988, p. 115).

In an attempt to revive accumulation in the only way it knew how, that is, by attracting foreign investment, Singapore's Economic Development Board (EDB) came up with a whole set of new incentives for foreign capital, especially small businesses, which had hitherto been ignored in favour of the multinationals, and services, which had taken second place to manufacturing. The EDB now has separate divisions for services and small businesses, and it offers a special corporate tax rate of 10 per cent (as against 33 per cent, cut from 40 per cent) for firms which set up their operational headquarters (OHQ) in Singapore. To be granted OHQ status, a company needs to have manufacturing facilities, R&D, distribution and a sizeable network of overseas companies. In addition to the concessionary tax rate of 10 per cent on their service income, companies with OHQ status get other incomes such as dividends tax free (*FEER*, 4 September, 1986, p. 64–5).

The frills to the already flash red carpet laid out for foreign capital have caught the attention mainly of Japanese and US electronic firms. In early 1987, among those which announced significant investment commitments were a large number of Japanese majors, such as Sony, Aiwa, Matsushita, Toshiba, Unizon, Fujitsu, Isetan, Sogo, Tokyu and Yaohan. Close behind were a growing number of small and medium-sized subcontractors.

Some of the Details

The first Japanese company to be granted OHQ status in November 1987 was Sony, which selected Singapore as one of the four pillars of its new global strategy to establish 'worldwide head offices' in Japan, Europe, North America and Asia. Earlier that year the company had opened its new plant to produce die castings for precision machinery for its Asian subsidiaries, it had set up a design centre (Sony Precision Engineering Centre) for household electric appliances and it had opened a distribution centre, what the Singapore government calls an International Procurement Office (IPO). Along with thirteen other Japanese companies (including Fujitsu and Uniden) which also have IPOs in Singapore, Sony now ships materials, components and products to and from its eight factories in South Korea, Thailand, Malaysia and Singapore. Its one hundred staff (recently expanded from 30) also procure parts from the same number of local parts makers in the region.

Sony's current plans (including the Thai video tape factory and the Malaysian audio and TV factory opened in 1988) are to raise its overseas production ratio from 23 per cent in 1987 to 35 per cent by 1990, with Asia supplying 10 per cent. The routine assembly functions which used to be allocated to Singapore are being shifted to ASEAN, as Singapore becomes Sony's Asian high-tech production base, making a wide range of precision components for VCRs and CDs, such as optical mechanical decks (*AS* 25 November 1987, p. 11; *JEJ*, 3 October 1987, p. 5; 26 December 1987, p. 17; 5 December

1987, p. 21; 16 April 1988, p. 7; 3 September 1988, p. 19; 5 November 1988, p. 7).

Aiwa, which is a subsidiary of Sony, has decided to make Singapore its worldwide production centre, which will account for over half the company's total output and which will house its research and development and product design work. The decision to relocate in Singapore follows with indecent haste on the closure, one after another, of production lines in its main Japanese factory. It will produce two of its newest high-tech products in Singapore, the digital audio tape recorder and the 8 mm video camera, mainly for export to Japan. According to a company representative, 'If the yen continues to hover in the 120s, it will make more sense for us to buy almost all parts from abroad than to procure them at home' (*JEJ*, 2 and 9 January, 1988 p. 5; *Straits Times*, 7 February 1987, p. 1; *Financial Times*, 3 February 1987).

The Matsushita group, which operates six wholly owned factories in Singapore and which in 1986–88 alone invested some $250 million in the island, will in April 1989 open an Asian OHQ as part of its four-block global network. The new company will oversee the entire manufacturing and marketing operations of Matsushita's Asian subsidiaries. Among the major recent developments in Singapore were a Technical Centre opened in 1987 (to make dies and moulds as well as to design and make automation equipment); expansion of capacity by Matsushita Refrigeration Industries (which makes compressors); and the addition of CDs, digital tuners and 256KDRAM chip assembly to the existing activities of Matsushita Electronics. The latter plans to triple IC capacity and to take over the production of radio and cassette recorders, which are being shifted out of Japan.

Matsushita Electronics also intends to enlarge its R&D department to have 45 per cent of total products designed in Singapore. As one of the group's two major exporters in Asia (the other is in Taiwan), this company's importance has greatly increased with the rise of the yen. Matsushita Graphic Communication Systems chose Singapore for its first overseas production base (1987), where it plans to produce 40 per cent of its exports of telefaxes by 1990. Finally, Matsushita Kotobuki opened a factory in Singapore in August 1987 purely to supply its US subsidiary with colour TV print bases (*Business Times*, 20 and 27 February 1987, p. 1; *NKS*, 31 July 1987, p. 9; *JEJ*, 3 October 1987, p. 5; *NKS*, 31 July 1987, p. 9; *JEJ*, 3 October 1987, p. 5; 15 October 1988, p. 18).

Toshiba announced in November 1986 that it would eventually

transfer from Japan to Singapore a full 50 per cent of its domestic production of colour TV sets (equivalent of 400 000) as well as a substantial share of its audio equipment. This was described as the most significant attempt in 1986 by a Japanese company to move its domestic operations abroad. Singapore is to be upgraded in Toshiba's global strategy, and the 150 000 TV chassis that used to be produced for export to the Toshiba factory in Tennessee will be shifted from Singapore to a new factory where labour is much cheaper, in Mexico (*Straits Times*, 11 November 1986; *LA International*, 1987a, p. 178).

Unizon, a major maker of sophisticated electronics components which the high yen forced to shift abroad for the first time, selected Singapore for a $50 million investment to supply mainly the Japanese market. Yokogawa Electric Corporation, which controls more than half the world market of the Centum (a sophisticated process-control system used mainly in oil refining plants), chose Singapore as its first offshore site, beginning production in July 1987 but planning to double this by early 1988 (*Business Times*, 6 April 1987, p. 1).

Other majors in the electrical industry have also either recently expanded their activities in Singapore or indicated their intentions to do so. Sanyo is now producing car stereos and compressors for air conditioners, JVC is making low-priced radio cassettes and tape recorders, while Tokyo Electric is into low-priced electronic cash registers. Mitsubishi Electric is another Japanese company which will open a parts centre (IPO) for all its Southeast Asian plants.

In computers, towards the end of 1987 NEC began to build a new plant to double its monthly chip production and Fujitsu, which had hitherto supplied most parts to its overseas units from Japan, announced the opening of an IPO centre. Today the centre buys parts and materials for ICE from all over Southeast Asia and distributes them to Fujitsu plants worldwide. In August 1988 the company also opened a new factory in Singapore to make digital switching systems and circuit boards for the first time outside Japan (*NKS*, 16 October 1987, p. 9; 9 December 1987, p. 8, 17 December 1987, p. 9; *JEJ*, 3 October 1987, p. 5; 27 February 1988, p. 21; 21 May 1988, p. 17; 20 August 1988, p. 7; Dobashi, 1986, p. 16).

Among the other almost endless examples of major electrical firms which rushed into Singapore after the rise of the yen were Asahi Techno Vision, Teraoka Seiko, Kobe Steel and Sumitomo Bakelite. Noteworthy developments outside electronics include the 62-story 'Republic Plaza' (the world's tallest building outside the US) to be built in the island's financial centre by a consortium led by C Itoh; Seiko's decision to shift the majority of watch-making facilities to Singapore, Hong Kong, China and Thailand; Pokka's decision to triple its beverage capacity in Singapore and expand exports back to Japan; and a wave of new projects by Japan's leading retailers: Isetan, Yaohan, Sogo and Tokyu (*NKS*, 17 July 1987, p. 9; 12 August 1987, p. 11; 31 October 1988, p. 15; *Industria*, July 1987, pp. 43–4; *JEJ*, 8 August 1987, p. 19; 20 February 1988, p. 20; 27 February 1988, p. 8; 17 September 1988, p. 30; Nihon Bōeki Shinkōkai, 1987a, pp. 123–4; *FEER*, 7 July 1988, p. 81).

Links with Local Capital

Japanese capital has not found it necessary in Singapore to form joint ventures in order to win cooperation from the local ruling class, since this is secured primarily through the state, with which there have been some important tie-ups. The main ones include two refineries (the previously mentioned PCS with Sumitomo in 1977, and Polyolefin in 1980 also with a Sumitomo consortium), although the government now intends to sell its shares in both to Shell; two shipyards (Jurong Shipyard in 1963 with IHI and Mitsubishi Singapore Heavy Industries in 1973); and one company to make braun tubes (Hitachi Electric Devices in 1978). Rather, joint ventures have been sought in areas where Japanese capital felt unable to succeed without local partners, overwhelmingly in commerce and finance, although the 'local' conglomerates in these industries have been widely linked to British and American capital. In manufacturing, Japanese companies have typically set wholly-owned subsidiaries (Iwasaki, 1988, p. 91).

The largest conglomerate in Singapore, the Overseas Chinese Banking Corporation, has deep ties with British and American capital. The top bank in the country and the centre of the George Lee family empire, it helps hold together a group which began in rubber and pineapples during the colonial period, and was subsequently extended to the unproductive sector and into some manufacturing. Its network extends throughout Southeast Asia (it owns 9 per cent of Sime Darby) and includes the US and Australia (Inoue, 1987, pp. 213–21; Iwasaki, 1988 pp. 94–6; Yoshihara, 1988, p. 216).

Even more confined to finance and related services (insurance, securities, real estate and hotels) is the Wee family empire centering on the United Overseas Bank and stretching overseas into Hong

Kong, Malaysia, Australia and the UK. Starting in the 1930s in banking and trade, UOB grew primarily through absorbing rival banks and through joint ventures with foreign firms, such as America's Chase and Japan's Orient Lease. More recently it has been diversifying into high-tech manufacturing, partly through acquiring 31 per cent of Haw Par Brothers, a conglomerate including some 60 companies in such fields as pharmaceuticals and electronics, some, like Toyotron (50 per cent owned by Toyo Plywood) linked to Japanese capital (Inoue, 1987, pp. 221–7; Iwasaki, 1988, pp. 96–9; 104; *FEER*, 1 September 1988, p. 48; Yoshihara, 1988, pp. 222–3).

Very much in the same boat but with its centre of gravity less in banking than in hotels and real estate is the Khoo Teck Puat family empire, which extends through Malaysia into Hong Kong, the UK, Australia and New Zealand. Sometimes known as the Goodwood group, it has no industrial base to speak of and receives its overseas allies through British capital. Other major groups operating in Singapore include the Kwek family's Hong Leong group (also of Malaysia) and the 'British' Inchcape group of Hong Kong. Hong Leong has a number of joint ventures in Singapore with Japanese companies, such as Rheem (Far East), which is a S$33 million project with Mitsubishi Corporation making metal containers, three ventures with Mitsui & Co., including a S$10 million real estate firm and a leasing firm with Marubeni (Shūkan tōyō keizai, 1988; Inoue, 1987, pp. 227–33; Iwasaki, 1988, pp. 98 ff.).

On the whole, Japanese companies in Singapore have not cultivated the sorts of links with leading local capitalists that they had to elsewhere in Asia where varying degrees of nationalism (leading to restrictions on 100 per cent ownership) demanded local participation in foreign investment projects. But apart from the comprador culture enforced by the Lee regime, Singapore also from the beginning attracted larger companies than the other NICs, and they possessed the resources to establish wholly-owned subsidiaries. In South Korea and particularly in Taiwan the investing companies have been smaller, and joint ventures were formed to tap local sources of capital and not just to accommodate nationalistic pressures and regulations (Yoshihara, 1978, pp. 28 ff.).

The larger industrial DFI projects in Singapore thus tend to be either fully Japanese owned or 'national' ones with the Singapore government as the local partner whose cooperation was thereby secured. It is almost entirely in trade and services that examples are found of large projects (over 500 employees or S$20 million) with local partners other than the government (Shūkan tōyō keizai, 1988).

Conclusion

In its desperation to attract foreign capital, the Lee regime has always been willing to pour public money into private profit making, and it has functioned as the single most important local 'receptacle' for Japanese companies. In the increasingly strategic electronics industry, most large projects are also either wholly Japanese owned, or have the government as the joint venture partner. For example, NEC, Fujitsu, Mitsumi, Mitsubishi Electric, Hitachi, Victor, TDK, Tamura and many others all have wholly-owned subsidiaries. There is unquestionably no greater haven for foreign capital in Asia than this island.

What remains to be considered is how the growing Japanese presence is affecting the line-up of class forces in the country as a whole, particularly with reference to working-class struggles. Most important is that Japanese capital has replaced other foreign capital, chiefly from Britain and the US, rather than local capital, in the alliance which dominates the country. From the point of view of both local capitalists and workers, the advance of Japan has neither caused nor even extended the neo-colonialism under which they live. Neither was Japanese capital much of a force behind the almost total transformation of local capital into a comprador class. Rather, it has simply become the recipient of the latest red carpet because of its technical and financial power in the region.

The Singaporean working class was also not the creation of Japanese capital, although much of the core of the industrial proletariat in electronics has grown knowing no other employers or employment system. It is here that the influence of Japan on the Singaporean class struggle is most important. It was not just that the quirks of the Lee regime found Japanese style authoritarianism attractive and wished to emulate it, but that Japanese techniques for controlling Singaporean workers were manifestly succeeding in Japanese factories. It was thus due to more than Lee's idiosyncrasies that so many of Singapore's institutions of social control have Japanese counterparts and that Lee has been consciously adding to them. This is where the influence of Japanese capital is likely to be felt most acutely by the people of Singapore. The real danger from Japan will therefore be found in one of the last places where one might look for it: in the forms of working-class organisation.

SOUTH KOREA

History of Struggle

Throughout Korea's capitalist history, the class struggle has been intimately connected with Japanese and later on also US imperialism. The colonisation of Korea was planned almost immediately following the Meiji Restoration, and it was implemented in stages corresponding to the growth of Japan's military power. But only during the Russo-Japanese War did the almost total absorption of Korea by Japan begin, when Japanese military superiority forced on the Korean government a series of treaties which culminated in the establishment of a Japanese protectorate in 1905 and the annexation of Korea in 1910. Thereafter, until the end of the Second World War, the Korean people had to submit to such ruthless repression and rule by the Japanese that even the most reactionary of the postwar military dictators had in public at least to feign a certain anti-Japanese stance (Kim and Kim, 1967; Nahm, 1973).

Even more so than in any other Asian country apart from China, the national liberation movement in Korea matured during the Pacific War and with the final defeat of Japan was poised to assume power. However, increasing US military intervention against the nationalists culminated in the division of the country, the Korean War of 1951–55, and the consolidation of the very type of military rule in the South to which the Korean people as a whole had long endured under Japanese occupation (McCormack and Gittings, 1977; Cumings, 1981).

Nominally independent governments were headed by a series of dictators who were essentially representatives of the US military, the local bourgeoisie and, from the mid-1960s, Japanese capital as well: Rhee Syngman in 1948–60, Park Chung Hee in 1961–79 and Chun Doo Hwan in 1980–88. Although the new President, Roh Tae Woo, is still beholden to the same interests as his predecessors, the popular democratic movement which has been building over the years could by 1987 force relatively fair elections, in which Roh won with a minority of votes only because the left opposition had failed to unite. On each occasion except the last, the changing of the guard was preceded by an intense period of strikes and popular agitation which was used by the military as a pretext for the imposition of martial law that followed. But without exception, after each internal crisis the Korean ruling class bolstered its position by relying more and more on foreign capital, increasingly Japanese. Foreign investment was first allowed in 1962, but only under extreme restrictions, which were modified in 1970 and then again more thoroughly in 1984. Although there have been lags, crises in Korea's class struggle have always been met by increased dependence on foreign capital.

So far, the mounting trade union struggles which began in autumn 1987 have resulted in an advance for Korean democracy (Foster-Carter, 1987) rather than imminent military intervention, although Korean capital is once again looking for foreign allies. Wage rises of over 20 per cent were won by workers whose hours had been the longest in the world (54.3 a week) and for whom a major grievance had been delayed payment of wages (often over two months). The main beneficiaries of Korea's first minimum wage which the strikers also won were 6.5 million women workers. A large proportion of them are in the industry on which the postwar boom was built, textiles, and their wages had been less than half those of male workers. Above all, for the first time in Korea's capitalist history, major industrial unrest was not squashed by military terror. On the contrary, so powerful had the democratic movement become that the state actually compelled Hyundai, which had never allowed unions in any of its factories, to recognise workers' rights to organise independently. Previously, the state would send in troops to break strikes.

Rapid Accumulation

The high rates of capital accumulation which are associated with postwar Korea resulted from more than the repression of the people by the military, which has existed widely throughout Asia. The recipe was not found in the current orthodoxy of free trade, unrestricted foreign investment, reliance on the private sector and a concentration on exports. Rather, it was the opposite of each of these which laid the basis for the so-called 'South Korean miracle', producing average growth rates of industrial production of over 14 per cent in the takeoff period of 1954–62 and nearly 17 per cent in the next decade. A high level of protection to promote ISI (import substitution industrialisation), one of the strictest sets of regulations for foreign investors in the region and widespread state regulation all helped local capital organise and consolidate its strength. Even when in the 1970s pressure from Japanese capital helped swing the tide towards export-led growth and Free Trade Zones (FTZs) for such industries as electronics and motor vehicles (not to mention textiles), this occurred only after an ISI phase had built up a certain productive power to compete in export markets. But even then, ISI and state protection were maintained in the less developed heavy and chemical industries throughout the 1970s, as the state guided capital along a path of heavy industrialisation. Japanese capital was keen to take part in this task, since it was at the time moving out of heavy industry in Japan and relocating it abroad. Import substitution and export growth were not competing alternatives in South Korea, but complementary strategies which followed one another in each of a range of industries (Kuznets, 1977).

The ability of the ruling class in South Korea to get away with greater independence from foreign capital than elsewhere in Southeast Asia owed a lot to US fear that concessions had to be made to Korean nationalism. Otherwise, the anti-communist alliance on which the American military strategy rested would collapse. The South Korean bourgeoisie could thus extract from its US ally terms which would consolidate its strength, not simply in the face of the popular struggle, but which would enable it to win some independence from the US itself. So although South Korea's geography and prewar history might have made it the most submissive of all Japan's neo-colonies after the war, US military interests helped its ruling class become one of the most powerful and independent in capitalist Asia.

Japanese DFI

The Japanese had to wait until two years after diplomatic ties were restored in 1965 before the first postwar DFI project could be undertaken, and until the first major crisis of South Korea's predominantly ISI strategy had forced a series of concessions to foreign investors and export production in 1970 before the first major wave could get under way. Table 5.2 showed that the 'rush' into South Korea to escape rising wages in Japan took place in the early 1970s. In 1973 alone 290 projects were approved, that is, more than in all the previous years combined. Many entered the Masan FTZ to take advantage of the concessions Japanese capital had won there (Yoshihara, 1978, p. 18; Sunoo, 1978).

The 1970s rush was mainly undertaken by small unlisted firms, in contrast to the entry into Singapore which was spearheaded by large quoted companies. The targets were textiles, electronics (where US capital already had a large presence) and other light manufacturing,

Table 5.5 Korean technological imports, by main country of origin,
1962–86

| | Japan | | United States | | Total | |
	Cases	$1 000	Cases	$1 000	Cases	$1 000
1962–79	890	139 883	337	105 274	1 504	350 598
1980–83	596	130 091	273	223 775	1 137	479 527
Total	1 486	269 968	610	329 049	2 641	830 124
1984–86	710	320 248	370	462 050	1 408	979 137

Source: For 1962–83, *Kaigai tōshi kenkyūjōhō*, June 1988, p. 15, and for
1984–86, *Korea Business World*, December 1987, p. 17.

mainly for export but outside the FTZ for the local market as well.
Japanese firms also entered into more joint ventures with local
capital than did US ones, often together with a large trading company.

The attitude of Korean capital to DFI from the US and Japan has
always been to prefer loans to DFI, and to acquire technology under
licence rather than through direct investment. DFI has never, in the
last 20 years, exceeded 5 per cent of all foreign loans. However, both
overseas debt and royalty payments have been a heavy burden which
has helped tip the balance in favour of ever more liberal foreign
investment laws, particularly after 1984. Since 1962, at least $1.7
billion has left the country in royalty payments, of which $411 was
lost in 1986 alone. Table 5.5 shows that the number of agreements
from Japan has always exceeded those from the US but that more
money has gone to America. But in 1986 the value of technology
imported from Japan also exceeded that from the US.

The main attraction of Korea to Japanese capital in the early years
was the proximity of its cheap labour force at a time when Japanese
textile wages began to pinch. However, a mutual interest was served,
since the influx of Japanese capital played a major role in the export
boom of the 1970s and an average rate of real economic growth of 7.8
per cent. The state helped use the surplus form the textile and other
light industries to build up the heavy chemical and basic materials
industries (Nihon nōritsu kyōkai, 1987a, p. 124).

But the 1970s also saw two 'oil shocks' and increasing shortages of
labour, which workers managed to translate into higher average
wages. Capital responded by raising prices and higher balance of
payments deficits. In 1980 the deficit peaked at $5.3 billion and South
Korea's international debt approached the $50 billion mark, the

Table 5.6   Comparative manufacturing hourly wages and indices, 1978–87

	1978 ($)	1978 Index	early 1985 ($)	early 1985 Index	at Y160 ($)	at Y160 Index	1987 Index
Japan	5.81	100	6.99	100	10.42	100	100
US	6.17	106	9.52	136	9.52	91	
South Korea	0.84	14	1.31	19	1.29	12	20.2
Taiwan	0.66	11	1.54	22	1.60	15	20.5
Singapore	0.99	17	2.04	29	2.03	19	24.5
Hong Kong	n/a		n/a		n/a		22.0
Malaysia	n/a		n/a		n/a		10.2
Thailand	n/a		n/a		n/a		8.4
Indonesia	n/a		n/a		n/a		6.5
Philippines	n/a		n/a		n/a		6.3

Source: The money wages and indices to 1985 come from Nihon nōritsu kyōkai, 1987, p. 13; the 1987 indices are Jetro estimates, in *JS*, November 1988, p. 36.

highest in Asia. Finally, growing protectionism in Europe and America ended the decade together with its associated export boom.

However, the two oil shocks confirmed the Korean government's resolve to restructure out of the basic materials industries and into machinery. But since this could only become competitive if it took a giant technological leap forward, the state realised it had to give foreign capital a much freer rein. The Foreign Capital Inducement Act (1984) created an automatic approval system for all projects not specifically prohibited, and in 1985 the Negative List was slashed so that 97.5 per cent of the manufacturing industries were liberalised. In late 1988 the government even announced a timetable for opening the stockmarket to foreign investment.

Recalling the rush of 1972–73, the rise of the yen in 1985 produced a similar tide in 1986. Table 5.6 shows how it lifted Japanese wages above US wages but made South Korean wages even more attractive than they had been in the late 1970s. It also shows how much more attractive ASEAN wages had become by 1987.

The 40 per cent fall in the value of the won against the yen helped to revive the boom of the 1970s, with Japanese capital leading the way. In 1986 the number of projects by Japanese companies skyrocketed, even though the value of DFI from Japan fell. A Korean observer noted that 'Japanese investors have been increasingly oriented toward small and medium-sized joint ventures with Korean firms, mainly centered on the parts and components industry (Kim,

Table 5.7   Approved DFI in South Korea, by main country of origin, 1962–June 1987

	United States		Japan		Total	
	Cases	*$1 000*	*Cases*	*$1 000*	*Cases*	*$1 000*
1962–66	25	25 000	5	8 300	39	47 400
1967–71	84	95 300	241	89 700	349	218 600
1972–76	78	135 000	739	627 100	851	879 400
1977–81	67	235 700	132	300 900	244	720 000
1982–86	168	581 600	276	875 200	565	1 766 500
1985	43	108 007	58	364 253	131	531 956
1986	49	125 128	109	137 654	205	353 740
1987 (June)	34	88 500	100	190 200	164	423 600
TOTAL	456	1 161 100	1 493	2 091 400	2 263	4 056 100
% of Total		28.6		51.6	100	100
1987[a]		255 000		494 000		1 060 000

Note: Kim, Il-Hwan, 1987, p. 5; Nihon bōeki shinkōkai, 1988a, p. 400:
[a]Incomplete data for 1987 from *FEER*, 18 February 1988, p. 54.

Il-Hwan, 1987, p. 4). But in 1987 the value of Japanese investment soared to $494 million, up from $138 million in 1986 (*FEER*, 18 February 1988, p. 54). This time the balance of payments moved into the black, but only in relation to Europe and America. The inflow of Japanese DFI as well as technical tie-ups between Japanese and South Korean capital in the mid-1980s continued to suck in imports of machinery, components and materials, whose value far exceeded that of the moderate exports which South Korean companies made to Japan. Japanese capital tended to use South Korea as an offshore production site for export to third countries, in contrast to US companies which exported mainly back to America.

Table 5.7 shows how Japanese DFI surpassed that from America during the first boom of the 1970s and then leapt ahead again even further in the second export boom of the mid-1980s. However, while Japan accounted for two thirds of DFI in the early 1970s, a decade later its share had fallen to just over a half, still a predominance unequalled elsewhere in Asia.

With only a few exceptions, the most favoured industries have also been ones targeted by the US. However, Japanese firms account for the overwhelming majority of DFI in textiles, the third most favoured manufacturing sector ($214 million in 1962–87). In chemicals, the second most preferred manufacturing sector ($504 million), US investments were much larger than Japanese ones, while in electrical machinery, the top manufacturing sector targeted by foreign capital ($635 million), their shares were more similar. The industry which attracted most Japanese money, particularly since 1985, has been hotels, partly to service the stream of tourists that pour into Seoul, partly to take advantage of the Olympics. In all, 66 foreign investments in hotels worth $995 million had entered South Korea by mid-1987, $207 million in 1986 alone (Kim, Il-Hwan, 1987, p. 6).

The Rise of the Won

The export boom of the mid-1980s depended heavily on foreign investment, with the share of exports claimed by foreign ventures rising from 18.7 per cent in 1977 to 29 per cent 1986. It produced rates of economic growth of over 12 per cent and a current account surplus of $4.3 billion in 1986, enabling the government to reduce foreign debt by $1.4 billion to $45.3 billion by the end of the year. However, the $7 billion surplus with the US eventually led to the revaluation of the won, whose rate had been one of the legs on which the boom had rested, as well as increased US pressure further to liberalise the Korean market. A recovery in the price of oil and continued mass struggles for higher wages chipped away at the other two supports of the boom: cheap oil and cheap labour (*FEER*, 18 February 1988, p. 54; Nihon nōritsu kyōkai, 1987a, pp. 125–6).

South Korean Capital Moves Abroad

South Korean capital responded to the high won with a three-pronged plan similar to one so successfully used by its imperialist ally: foreign investment 'to counter [its] weakening price competitiveness against the US dollar and to avoid the mounting protectionism from the advanced countries' (*Korea Business World*, October 1988, p. 12), industrial restructuring and belt-tightening at home. Because low-wage ASEAN countries appeared more attractive to foreign investors in labour-intensive industries, capital in South Korea has tried to restructure into high-tech areas, to relocate its labour-intensive ones, such as electronics assembly and apparel, in China and ASEAN, while also attempting to keep the lid on the growing power of organised labour. Capital throughout the NICs has adopted a similar strategy (Lim and Teoh, 1986).

However, the ability of South Korean capital to emulate in this regard the ruling class on which it remains heavily dependent for technology is limited. Some of the larger *chaebol* (business groups) might succeed, but most smaller firms will find it difficult to challenge the Japanese *zaibatsu*, which are spearheading the move by their affiliated component makers into Korea and elsewhere.

Between 1986 and June 1987 a total of $412 million (half in manufacturing) was sent abroad, almost as much as had been invested in the entire period 1968–85 ($476 million). In addition to the electronics investments listed in Table 5.8, 1988 saw Goldstar extending its activities into Mexico and Thailand, and the completion of Daewoo's refrigerator factory in China. Other overseas investments by Korean capital have been influenced more by natural endowments and market strategy: 39 per cent of the total of $633.3 million at the end of 1986 was in mining and 8.4 per cent was in trade in North America (*Korean Business World*, October 1988, p. 12; Kwag, Dae-Hwan, 1987, p. 5; *KTG*, No. 70, May–June 1988, p. 5).

Korean capital has had to find foreign allies willing to welcome it into their domain, just as it has to entice allies into its domain. The function of the Seoul Olympics, apart from the nationalism they fostered to counteract growing class consciousness, was to announce the appropriateness of Korean capital as an ally of the advanced powers, particularly in high-tech industries. This means further reliance on Japan and the US for technological imports and foreign investment, the Singapore way. The alliance with Japanese capital is thus being extended by Japan's growing need for cheaper components and South Korea's needs to produce more sophisticated ones.

Quest for High Technology

Particularly since the strikes of fall 1987 and then spring 1988, the South Korean state has come to depend heavily on further tie-ups with foreign capital to solve its 'high won' and higher wage crisis, in the hope of obtaining greater technological transfers. There is no question that some progress has been made, since while in the 1970s Japanese firms would relegate to South Korea such tasks as assembly or the making of peripheral parts, the projects now increasingly involve making the entire product, with relatively high levels of local content even for some core components. This is even true of industries which led Japan's export-boom of the early 1980s, cars and electronics, both of which are pivotal to the current accumulation strategies of South Korea's *chaebol*. Tie-ups with the Japanese (and US) majors continue to be essential to these strategies.

Table 5.8 Korean DFI in Electronics, August 1988

Investor	Country	Approved date	Korean share	Amount ($1 000)	Main products
Goldstar	AL, US	4/1981	100	3 500	Colour TV, microwave
Samsung Elec.	Portugal	7/1982	55	275	Colour TV
Samsung Semi. & Tele.	LA, US	7/1983	100	8 000	Semiconductors
Samsung Elec.	NJ, US	12/1983	100	3 000	Colour TV
Daewoo	CA, US	3/1986	58	2 800	Microcomputers
Samsung Elec.	CA, US	4/1986	99	2 435	Computer related
Goldstar	West Germany	9/1986	100	2 932	Colour TV, VCR
Samsung S & T	ID, US	10/1986	3	5 000	Semiconductors
Oriental Nylon	CA, US	7/1987	30	2 500	Hard disk drive
Goldstar	Turkey	8/1987	25	597	Microwave
Daewoo Elec.	Hong Kong	8/1987	50	1 750	Refrigerators
Samsung Electromechanics	Japan	1/1988	75	805	Computer peripherals
Rinnai Korea	Indonesia	4/1988	8	80	Gas range
Goldstar	Thailand	5/1988	49	439	Colour TV, washers
Korea Marvel	Thailand	7/1988	100	2 130	Electronic parts
Maxon Elec.	Thailand	7/1988	76	950	Consumer products
Trigem Comp.	West Germany	8/1988	100	880	Computer related
Daewoo Elec.	France	8/1988	51	478	Microwave

Source: Korea Business World, October 1988, p. 12.

However, the very problems which have sent South Korean capital into ASEAN have reduced the interest of Japanese capital in Korea. In addition to the high won and higher wages, these include the anticipated difficulties of importing parts and materials because of the Korean government's renewed attempts to redress the trade balance with Japan, the 'deteriorating' industrial relations situation, high interest rates, a strict system of taxation and divided control and Korean nationalism. The only new developments on the plus side are some revisions of the foreign investment law (freer profit repatriation and access to the domestic market) and Roh's election (Nihon nōritsu kyōkai, 1987a, pp. 129 ff.; Ishida, 1987).

Korean nationalism remains a potent force even within the giant *chaebol* which have spearheaded capital accumulation and with which Japanese capital has had to ally. Table 5.9 lists the top ten groups at the end of 1986. In sharp contrast to most conglomerates in ASEAN (including Singapore), South Korean groups have focused on the manufacturing industry rather than simply on commerce or finance, and they have to an unequalled degree built up independent industrial bases. They also dominate their strongholds more thoroughly than anywhere else in the region, including Japan. However, while the mass of small Japanese firms use sophisticated technology and serve the *keiretsu* in tight subcontracting relationships, the small firm sector in South Korea is underdeveloped and technically backward. Small and medium firms in Japan absorb 71.8 per cent of the labour force, but they attract only 57.3 per cent of South Korean workers. A 1982 survey saw the *chaebol* claim a full 25 per cent of GNP and an almost total monopoly of technology imports, which involved only 1300 firms (*Korean Business World*, December 1987, p. 42; *FEER*, 17 March 1988, p. 67).

Electronics Industry

Electronics is unquestionably the most important industry in South Korea today, with exports finally overtaking those of textiles in 1988. But the boom depends heavily on three main products (microwave ovens, VTRs and colour TVs) and on the overwhelming dominance of the *chaebol*, which, lacking their own small-firm subcontractors, rely heavily on Japanese capital for parts and technology, even in electronics where they boast their greatest independence (Table 5. 10).

The same problems of dependence on foreign capital and the

Table 5.9 Top ten South Korean business groups, 1986

Group name	Turnover W billion	Member companies	Main Industries
Samsung	13 711	31	Trade, electronics, construction, textiles, sugar refining, machinery, heavy industry, commerce, insurance
Hyundai	12 768	43	Construction, heavy industry, cars, steel, aluminum, cement, electronics, trade
Lucky–Goldstar	9 127	46	Chemicals, electronics, electrical machinery, oil, trade, insurance
Daewoo	7 149	25	Trade, heavy industry, cars, electronics, construction, chemicals, securities
Sunkyong	5 285	13	Trade, textiles, chemicals, oil
Ssangyong	2 949	16	Cement, oil, construction, trade
Korea Express	2 113	12	Air line, construction, transport, securities
Hyosung	2 106	19	Trade, textiles, tyres, hides, heavy industry
Korea Explosive	1 780	20	Chemicals, food, trade, insurance, securities
Lotte	1 447	26	Food, commerce, hotels, petrochemicals

Source: Inoue, 1987, p. 107.

chaebol, which characterised the 1970s boom (based on textiles, chemicals, iron and steel, ship building), plague the current Korean 'miracle' centering on electronics. The *chaebol* produce mass consumer products for export rather than intermediate and industrial goods, which are imported from Japan. So because the rise of the yen simply inflated costs, the export-led boom produced both an increasing trade deficit with Japan and a protectionist reaction in the US.

All these structural problems came together in 1986: textiles gave way to electronics as South Korea's top performer; electronics exports rose by 53.7 per cent to comprise 63 per cent of production and 19.3 per cent of total exports; the top ten electronics items comprised 70 per cent of electronics exports with 60 per cent going to the US; and the electronics trade deficit with Japan soared by 98.6 per cent to

Table 5.10 Rates of local content and dependency on Japan in electronics, 1985

	% Local content	Dependency on Japan as % of total imports	Main parts
Consumer Electronics			
VCRs	65	100	Head-drum, motor
Colour TVs	90	95	Integrated circuits
Cassette recorder (for export)	50	95	Deck, motors, ICS
Cassette recorder (home)	85	95	ICs
Microwave ovens	75	100	Switches, magnetron
Industrial Electronics			
Facsimiles	60	100	Thermal printer head
Personal computers	40	100	ICs
Printers	35	100	Dot matrix impact head
CRT terminals	50	90	ICs
Telephones	90	95	Resonator, piezo buzzer
Other Parts and components			
Colour braun tubes	80	95	Electronic gun, electronic Colour TV tuner
Speakers	70	95	NA
Switches	50	80	Various functions
Condensers	60	95	Various functions

Source: *Business Korea*, November 1986, p. 39.

comprise 39.1 per cent of the total deficit with Japan. In 1986 a third of all royalty payments were also in electronics, as were the great bulk of foreign investments (Park Soon-Pong, 1987, pp. 5–6; *Korean Business World*, December 1987).

Table 5.11 provides measures of the levels of foreign domination of the Korean electronics industry in 1980–84. In spite of what appears to be a rapid erosion of certain types of overseas control, foreign capital retains its lead and power by moving into ever newer areas of higher value added, so that the technological gap does not change much over time. A frequent complaint made by Korean capitalists is that their Japanese allies often transfer outdated technologies, specifically to ensure that they retain their technical lead. In the

Table 5.11   Degree of foreign domination of Korean electronics
                production, 1980–84

	Local (%)		Joint (%)		Foreign (%)		Total value ($ million)	
	1980	1984	1980	1984	1980	1984	1980	1984
Household	76.0	87.4	6.0	4.2	18.0	8.4	1 147	2 425
Industrial	38.0	61.0	54.0	26.8	8.0	12.2	364	1 213
Components	27.9	47.1	37.9	27.6	34.2	25.3	1 340	3 531

Source: Yamauchi, 1985, p. 102.

case of VTR technology, for example, which JVC and Sony have
transferred to the three South Korean leaders (Samsung, Goldstar
and Daewoo), strings are attached for this reason. Korean capital in
turn transfers to such places as Indonesia and Malaysia technologies
which preserve its lead over them, using similar sorts of conditions
(*NKS*, 26 July 1987, p. 4; Ishida, 1987, p. 108).

Nevertheless, even though there have been some successful transfers of technology through foreign investment and technological
imports, in neither the design, manufacture, nor the quality control
of such general components as condensers, magnetic tape, speakers,
PCB and resistors is Korean capital internationally competitive. Only
in the assembly of these components does it achieve international
standards (*KTG*, July 1987, p. 2).

Korean capital thus still specialises in the more labour intensive
assembly branches of the electronics industry, which is partly why it
was hit so hard by the rise of the won. Any Japanese capital can still
use South Korea as a cheap production site, since the rise of the yen
was even greater. Table 5.12 shows some of the recent moves by
Japanese electronics (and car) majors to secure component supplies
in Korea.

Similar moves, apart from tie-ups with the *chaebol* (which are
discussed below), include the following. In 1987, Fujitsu decided to
double output of disk drive heads at its Korean joint venture (FKL
Dongwa), and to start making printer heads for export to Japan. In
mid-1988, Yokogawa Electric decided to transfer all of its electronic
device lines and most of its industrial recorder lines to its joint
venture with POSCO (Hankuk Yokogawa), which supplies the Japanese and Korean markets. Other more established firms, such as
Korea TDK, have been quietly expanding their operations to take
advantage to the high yen and the need for sophisticated components

Table 5.12   Recent sourcing of components in South Korea

Japanese company	Agreement
Matsushita Electric	Household goods parts from Lucky–Goldstar group
Hitachi Manufacturing	Microwave parts from Goldstar
Akai	VTR parts from Goldstar
Yamatake–Honeywell	Regulator parts from Goldstar–Honeywell
Canon	Copier parts from Lotte Industrial
Dainichi Machinery	Precision and industrial robot parts from Samsung
Mitsubishi Motors	Car bodies and transmissions from Hyundai
Mazda	Passenger car and small truck parts from Kia
Sanyo	Colour TV braun tubes from Daewoo
Tokai Rika Electric	Car parts from Shinchang Electric
Kayaba	Pressed parts and steel covers for car shock absorbers from Dongwoo Machinery
Tabuchi Electric	Large increase in transistors from Korea Transistor
Mitsubishi Electric	AM radio and electronic parts from Mando Machinery?

Source: Ishida, 1987, p. 205

by the *chaebol* (*NKS*, 18 August 1987, p. 8; *JEJ*, 19 December 1987, p. 7; 20 August 1988, p. 7).

Motor Vehicles

All four of the big car companies in South Korea are offshoots of Japanese and American makers, on whom they remain heavily dependent for components and technology. The top three are also partly owned by the foreign majors, which use them mainly to produce low cost models for the domestic market and the highly competitive North American market. Hyundai is 15 per cent owned by Mitsubishi, and its Pony Excel has become the top selling imported subcompact in the US, with 264 000 in 1988. Daewoo Motors is 50 per cent owned by GM, and it has made GM's world car, LeMans, for the domestic market since 1986 and for export to the US since 1987. Daewoo also has technical agreements with Isuzu to manufacture small trucks and Nissan to make 9-seater vans. Kia Motors, which used to concentrate on buses and trucks, is 8 per cent owned by Mazda, 2 per cent by C Itoh and 10 per cent by Ford, and is now producing cars for the home and US markets. The Festiva (Pride in Korea), was designed by Mazda and is made by Kia on an OEM basis for Ford, with Japanese parts comprising 40–50 per cent of input value and with robot-manufacturing technology from Kawasaki

Heavy Industries. Kia has a 100 per cent interest in Asia Motors, which also makes buses and trucks. Dong-A, which was taken over by the Ssangyong group in 1987, makes 4WD vehicles (jeeps and tanks) in cooperation with Fuji Heavy industries, and also has technical agreements with Nissan Diesel (Nomura, 1987, pp. 108–12; Kwon, Yong-Soo, 1986; *Business Korea*, February 1987, pp. 16–20; *FEER*, 24 March 1988, p. 97; *JEJ*, 6 August 1988, p. 11).

South Korea's car industry has grown enormously since 1983, but from one which aimed primarily at the domestic market into an export industry, all under the guidance of the foreign partners but no less profitable for their local allies. Exports of vehicles and components have skyrocketed, but so has the trade deficit in components, because of continued dependence on Japanese companies for sophisticated functional parts. In 1983 only 8 per cent of car parts made in Korea were exported, less than 1 per cent of imported parts left the country in exported cars, and 11 per cent of cars were exported. By 1985, the proportions had risen to 12, 34, and 32.6 per cent. By 1988, almost 70 per cent of Korean-made cars were being exported, mainly (85 per cent in 1986) to North America. Mitsubishi and Mazda had found an alternative to *endaka*: as in the electronics industry, Korean car companies have been importing parts from Japan (70 per cent) and selling cars to the US (Kwon, Yong-Soo 1986).

But because the higher yen made Japanese parts more expensive, Japanese car makers have had to find cheaper supplies abroad. Everywhere except in North America, the strategy has been to shift the emphasis from direct investment in parts production to technical tie-ups. The reason for the opposite tendency in the US is because (often wholly owned) Japanese companies have to raise local content to avoid renewed trade friction and because they cannot sufficiently control the more independent US parts makers. Elsewhere, notably in Asia, parts are being made either for export back to Japan or to the US, or for use by joint-venture companies in cars most of which are exported. In 1968–84 there were 79 technical tie-ups with Japanese companies by Korean car parts makers (nine with US firms), and the number increased to over one hundred by July 1987.

Yet out of twelve joint ventures authorised in the first six months of 1987 in auto parts, eight were Japanese. They included a project between a Hitachi group and Daeyang Trading to make crankshafts, one between Sumitomo Electric and Korea Tungsten Mining to make metallurgical parts, one between Yokohama Rubber and Hankook Tire to make tires and tubes, and agreements involving Sanshu Press,

Table 5.13   Japanese DFI and technical tie-ups in car components (cases), 1962–87

	Before 1977		1978–82		1983–85		1986–87		Total	
	DFI	*TTI*	*DFI*	*TTI*	*DFI*	*TTI*	*DFI*	*TTI*	*DFI*	*TTI*
Asia	64	8	31	43	28	95	18	40	141	186
South Korea	8	1	3	4	4	26	5	14	20	45
Taiwan	19	0	9	12	7	20	8	10	43	42
Thailand	18	3	5	10	1	5	1	5	25	23
Indonesia	7	2	4	6	2	8	0	4	13	20
North America	15	0	6	5	18	9	39	3	78	17
Latin America	6	3	8	7	1	15	4	3	19	28
Europe	3	1	3	6	4	25	3	4	13	36
TOTAL	92	16	51	73	53	168	66	54	262	311

Source: Matsui, 1988, pp. 88–9.

Fukoku, Daikyo, Wabasto and Nagase. Other car parts makers to set up joint ventures in Korea in 1987, all partly to supply Hyundai, included Hiroshima Press (metal moulds), Fuji Kinko (pulleys for engines), Mitsubishi Densen (wire harness) and Mitsubishi Corporation. The latter's partner was Dana, an American company operating in South Korea, Taiwan and Indonesia.

In some cases the links between the Japanese parent and the Korean supplier are more indirect. For example, Mando Machinery, which is a joint venture with GM, is Hyundai's largest supplier of components, and Mitsubishi has secured access to them through its links with Hyundai. More recently, Mando has received technology from Tsugami to make screws and from Mitsubishi Heavy Industry to make absorption chilling units (*NKS*, 23 July 1987, p. 9; 23 October 1987, p. 9; *Business Korea*, July 1987, p. 27; *Business Tokyo*, July 1987, p. 29; *JEJ*, 30 May 1987, p. 23; 19 September 1987, p. 10; 2 and 9 January 1988, p. 25; 6 August 1988, p. 15).

Since functional parts like carburettors, alternators and automatic transmissions are being imported into Korea to raise the quality of cars for the export market, there are pressures on both sides to improve the standard of component manufacture in Korea by means of technical tie-ups and joint ventures (Table 5.13). Exactly the same pattern was observed in the electronics industry.

Links with the Top Three Chaebol

Samsung

The largest *chaebol* in terms of turnover, Samsung, also has the deepest roots in tie-ups with Japanese capital. Its founder, Lee Byung Chull (died in November 1987), went to Waseda University and remained a lifelong advocate of mergers with Japanese interests. In the 1970s, taking advantage of the government's third Five-Year Plan to build up the chemical and heavy industries, Samsung established many key firms by merging with leading Japanese companies, such as Samsung Heavy Industries (with IHI, which later withdrew), Samsung Electric Tubes (with NEC), Samsung Electronic Parts (with Sanyo), Cheil Synthetic Textiles (with Toray), Samsung Precision Industries (with Minolta) renamed Samsung Aerospace (the prime contractor for the F-X fighter programme), and Samsung Petrochemicals (with Mitsui and Amoco Chemicals of the US).

The Japanese were never as keen to share their latest technology as the group was to acquire it, and when Samsung looked to Japan in the early 1980s for LSI technology, it was refused:

> Japanese companies do more than attach strings; often they even totally refuse any transfer. According to an official of Samsung Electronics, they rejected Korea's request for transfer of technology relating to VCR design, the manufacture of certain kinds of integrated circuits, and certain ceramic materials. Other strings include a 'much higher' rate of royalty payments and a ban on independent development of the technology (*Business Korea*, November 1986, p. 39).

So Samsung deepened its ties with US capital instead: IC technology from Intel, computer technology from Hewlett Packard, entry into aircraft parts as well as pharmaceutical machines in cooperation with GE and technology to make DRAMs from Texas Instruments. But the *chaebol* also relies heavily on in-house research, with 5000 (7.3 per cent of total) employees being involved in R&D in fifteen research centres in Korea and two abroad. At times the group has had to pay dearly for its progress, as in 1988 following a successful copyright suit by Texas Instruments and an out of court settlement with Hitachi.

However, Toshiba has formed a joint venture with Samsung Electronics to make VCRs, heralding 'a new age of industrial cooperation between Japan and South Korea'. The new incentive has been the high yen and the desire to ward off trade friction: 'Toshiba will secure cheaper VCR parts needed for local production in the US, and Samsung will obtain Toshiba technology for value added VCRs' (*JEJ*, 26 March 1988, p. 20). Amongst other things, Samsung will make decks and circuit boards, mainly for export. Samsung Semi-conductor and Telecommunications is also getting 'leading edge technology' from NTT, and Samsung Electronics will joins hands with Sanyo to make copiers, fascimiles and laser printers, some for export back to Japan (*NKS*, 3 October 1988, p. 9; *JEJ*, 20 August 1988, p. 12; 27 August 1988, p. 7; 15 October 1988, p. 17 *FEER*, 9 June 1988, p. 105).

In the car industry as well, Samsung hopes to rely more on Japanese car parts makers and technology as it takes its first steps into this field in cooperation with Chrysler in 1988. In July 1986, Three Star Co., a joint venture with Nippon Radiator, began making car heating systems, but the group has a lot of catching up to do in this field to Korea's number one, Hyundai (Inoue, 1987, pp. 106–15; *Business Korea*, July 1987, pp. 25–38).

Hyundai

The largest *chaebol* in terms of group members, Hyundai, has traditionally been the strongest champion of Korean bourgeois nationalism ('pure bloodism'), and it has relied most on the alternative growth strategy to tie-ups with foreign capital: reliance on the state. When it has entered joint ventures with foreign capital, it has conceded the lowest possible equity holdings to its partner, for example, Mitsubishi's 15 per cent in Hyundai Motors and Kawasaki Heavy Industries' 5 per cent share in Hyundai Mipo Dockyard, both core group members. Hyundai's rise to prominence was through state contracts in the chemical and heavy industries in the 1970s, including the servicing of tanks and construction associated with the US military. Among its core companies, the only joint venture with Japanese capital was its dockyard.

Although heavy industry has been in decline since the early 1980s, Hyundai Construction and Hyundai Heavy Industries remain the top two group members. They are closely followed by the shining light of the 1980s, Hyundai Motors. The latter was established in 1967 in cooperation with Ford, but it was not until a series of reorganisations culminating in the tie-up with Mitsubishi in 1982, that the group shifted into the passing lane of this industry. In 1983 it developed a new model, the Pony Excel, in 1984 it commenced exports to Canada, in 1985 it decided to produce cars in Quebec from 1988 and in 1986 it started exporting to the US.

The rise of the yen made Hyundai's costs soar in 1986, and its dependence on Japanese parts was so high that much of the trade deficit with Japan can be traced to Hyundai Motors alone. The company is thus desperately looking for cheaper suppliers, not least Mitsubishi ones in low-cost areas of Southeast Asia. As a Mitsubishi Motors official pointed out:

> In the past the ratio between our supply of auto parts for Hyundai and procurement from it was 10 to one, but the ratio will probably be five to one in 1987 and three to one in 1988. In the future, cheap auto parts will be shipped from Southeast Asia to South Korea where ASEAN national cars will be manufactured (*JEJ*, 16 January 1988, p. 8).

A recent move in this regard was the joint venture between Mitsubishi Electric, Robert Bosch (West Germany) and Hyundai Motors to supply, not just the Hyundai group, but also Kia and Daewoo with car electronics parts.

The Hyundai group lives under the authoritarian control of its founder, Chung Ju Yung, who had resolved never to negotiate with the new union leaders. But just as he had to back down when faced with workers commandeering forklifts, bulldozers and heavy trucks, he also gave way to increasing pressure for tie-ups with Japanese capital. Today, Hyundai has the closest ties with Japan of all the *chaebol*: twelve of its 42 members even have branch offices in Japan. The 16 per cent wage rise won by its workers in 1987 has added urgency to the group's drive for new technology and its willingness to work with the Japanese (Inoue, 1987, pp. 116–24; *Business Korea*, November 1986; *JEJ*, 31 October 1987, p. 9; 2 April 1988, p. 12; *NKS*, 7 August 1987, p. 7).

Lucky Goldstar

The third largest *chaebol*, Lucky Goldstar, is the best suited to the vagaries of international capitalism. Its founding families (Koo and Huh) have not provided it with overbearing leadership, either in terms of managerial control or share ownership in core companies; it has the most flexible approach towards labour; it has more tie-ups with high-tech foreign firms than any other; it spends more on R&D than any other; and it has itself internationalised more widely than all the others combined. Although still heavily dependent on its founding companies, Lucky Chemicals (which started out in toothpaste) and Goldstar (which started out in household electrical goods), the group has diversified into a wide range of industries, including finance, usually together with a foreign partner. In 1987 it was thoroughly reorganised to streamline its decision making.

Goldstar has long relied on technical agreements with Hitachi, with which in 1962 it established Goldstar Cable, today the third largest core group member in terms of employees (4500). Other major tie-ups include two with Alps: Alps Electronic (1970, 5000 employees) and Alps Electric Korea, one of the highlights of 1987 which makes printers, modulators and floppy disk drives. In 1979, when the *chaebol* moved into telephones, it established a joint venture with Siemens: Goldstar Communications. In March 1986 Goldstar Precision made a technical agreement with Canon, in an attempt to take on the near monopoly of the Samsung–Minolta combination. And in 1988 Mitsubishi Electric agreed to supply Goldstar Electric Equipment with technology for laser pickups, the first such tie-up of its kind. Other core group members with foreign partners include Goldstar Electric, which makes OA equipment in a 3000 worker joint venture with NEC, Goldstar Semiconductor, which is 44 per cent owned by AT&T, and Honam Refinery, a highly profitable project with Caltex. Other major joint ventures include Goldstar Instrument and Electric (with Fuji Electric, 2100 workers) Shinyoung Electric (with Mitsubishi), Lucky Securities (with Nikko), Goldstar Foster and Goldstar Honeywell.

Lucky-Goldstar is the most highly internationalised *chaebol* in terms of its overseas sales, its access to overseas technology, as well as its own overseas investments. Fully one-third of profits depend on exports, and a large proportion of its DFI (30 overseas production and marketing outlets in 1985) is in Japan and the US in such areas as biotechnology and high-tech engineering. But like many Japanese companies, it has also entered the US in order to get round growing protectionism, for example, its colour TV factory in Alabama (*FEER*, 19 November 1987, 80–6; Inoue, 1987, pp. 124–33; Ishida, 1987, pp. 94 ff.; *Korea Trade & Business*, July 1987, p. 14; April 1987, p. 13; *JEJ*, 15 August 1987, p. 4; 4 April 1987, p. 18).

Conclusion on South Korea

The interests of Japanese and Korean capital have moved much closer since the rise of the yen in 1985, because each was given an overwhelming incentive to ally with the other: the Japanese desperately needed cheaper electrical and motor vehicle components, but many of these could only be produced with partners who could absorb the appropriate technology. And by 1985 South Korea's manufacturing industries badly needed to produce more of their own parts. Otherwise the twin problems of excessive imports from Japan and excessive exports to the US would upset their fragile prosperity. A vast increase in technical tie-ups and joint ventures was thus the most distinctive form in which the common interests of Korean and Japanese capital expressed themselves.

These developments have intensified the importance of Japanese capital to the Korean class struggle. Unlike Singapore, Japanese capital has long been a leading force behind South Korea's neo-colonial status, so that what local capital and the Korean working class have in common is a nationalism which is directed primarily against Japan. The US military presence is the most visible reminder of the deepest wound inflicted by colonisation, the nation's division into North and South, and so of the other leading imperialist power. However, the recent strike activity suggests that the battleground is shifting from the US zone to the Japanese zone.

The industrial proletariat, which was born and raised in factories jointly developed by the two ruling classes with among the most authoritarian (and patriarchal) traditions in Asia, is beginning to take on its creator. As it does so, bourgeois nationalism will lose its thunder, and one can expect Korean capital to cooperate less and less reluctantly with the Japanese. Long prevented by the triple alliance – US, Japanese and local ruling classes – from expressing its aspirations organisationally, the South Korean industrial working class has learnt to find ways round even that mighty combination. The real target is thus coming into sight.

NICS CONCLUSION

The main 'rush' by Japanese capital into the Asian NICs was on the crest of the first two waves of DFI, in the 1960s as a result of rising Japanese wages and in the 1970s following the oil crises. However, these investments produced a bandwagon effect which lasted well into the 1980s. The more companies that invested in the NICs the better became their capitalist infrastructures and so the opportunities for other Japanese companies.

However, Nomura Research recently discovered that major changes in the Asian production sites for consumer electronic goods had already occurred in a single year from mid-1985. In each of colour TVs, radio cassettes, stereos, car stereos, audio and other similar products, the shares of Japanese companies operating from Japan in Asia's total production fell considerably. The fall was only equalled by the corresponding rise in the share of Japanese subsidiaries located in Asia: by 100 per cent in the case of colour TVs. But it was also only in TVs and car stereos that Japanese subsidiaries in the NICs managed to increase their shares, indicating a gradual shift out of the NICs into ASEAN for the production of the remaining lower-value-added products (Nomura, 1987, pp. 86–7).

By 1987 the tide had firmly turned away from the NICs towards ASEAN and China, because by then the forces in the US which had compelled a revaluation of the yen had begun to raise the exchange rates of the other Asian countries from which Japanese (and local) capital had mounted successful export drives, particularly Taiwan and South Korea (by 22.9 and 16.4 per cent against the $US in 1987 alone). Even Singapore, after doggedly denying that its currency was undervalued, allowed a 10 per cent appreciation in 1987 and a crossing of the barrier of S$2 to the US$. Increasingly, it was not only Japanese wages which the currency adjustments of the mid-1980s made too high, but also those of the countries into which Japanese capital had once moved in order to escape the domestic wage rises of the 1960s and 1970s. By late 1987, lower ASEAN and Chinese wages had begun to attract more Japanese capital in labour intensive manufacturing than the better NICs infrastructures, and their respective rates of real economic growth in 1988 converged for the first time in many years, with the former rising and the latter falling (Table 5.14). By early 1988 the *Japan Economic Journal* noted unambiguously that 'recently the Japanese firms have been increasingly shifting their production bases from NICs to ASEAN countries in order to cut costs and make greater profits' (2 and 9 January 1988, p. 6).

Japan's New Imperialism

Table 5.14   Real rates of economic growth of ASEAN and NICs, 1960–87

	60–65	65–70	70–75	75–80	80–85	1986	1987	1988[a]	1989[a]	Per capita income in 1986 ($)
Indonesia	1.8	5.8	8.0	7.9	−0.6	3.2	3.4	4.5	4.4	430
Malaysia	–	–	7.4	20.7	5.1	1.2	5.2	7.4	6.5	1 600
Philippines	5.6	4.8	6.4	6.3	−0.6	1.5	5.1	6.5	5.8	540
Thailand	7.3	8.6	6.3	7.6	5.3	3.5	7.1	10.5	8.0	760
Singapore	5.8	12.8	9.5	8.7	6.1	1.9	8.8	10.0	7.0	6 900
South Korea	6.5	12.6	8.8	7.7	7.6	12.5	12.0	11.5	8.5	2 300
Taiwan	9.5	9.8	8.8	10.5	6.0	10.8	11.0	7.1	7.0	3 800
Hong Kong	–	–	–	12.3	5.7	11.0	13.5	6.0	2.5	6 800

Note: [a] estimates for 1988, forecasts for 1989.
Source: *KTG*, May–June 1988, p. 2; *NKS*, 4 October 1988, p. 7; *JEJ*, 24 December 1988, p. 8.

6 Investment in Thailand and Malaysia

When Japanese capital first responded to the rise of the yen by favouring the NICs as suppliers of low-cost components for its machinery industries, its interest in ASEAN seemed to fall together with declining commodity prices. By mid-1987, however, the situation had changed, as the higher yen combined with revalued currencies and rising wages in the NICs to force Japanese companies to look for cheaper labour. There was thus a shift from the NICs towards ASEAN, where totally different wages offered opportunities to recapture the competitive power Japanese capital had lost. DFI has thus been flowing into ASEAN in torrential proportion, and double-figure rates of growth are being anticipated.

For a long time after independence, capital accumulation in ASEAN countries continued to be based mainly on food production and the extraction of raw materials. Natural endowments remained the chief sources of profit for capital, both local and international. Cheap labour was increasingly used to process these resources in a variety of manufacturing activities as well, but ASEAN's backward productive forces limited these to the most labour intensive industries and tasks. The establishment of accumulation processes which reinvested surpluses in infrastructure and improved technology was extremely late in these countries, because surpluses had been shipped off to the imperialist countries in the colonial period. Some industries never really got off the ground, because no natural endowments could prop them up, and capital elsewhere had such a long history of accumulation and technical advantage that late entry in effect meant exclusion. Often the only way to entice capital to invest in them was to offer a labour force so miserably paid that eventually technical backwardness ceased to be a disincentive. In desperate attempts to create some 'comparative advantage', ASEAN governments have been even more dictatorial than in the NICs and enforced far worse wages and conditions.

Japanese capital has long succumbed to this temptation and located labour intensive production in ASEAN. However, in the past it did not normally bring in its most up to date plant and equipment, and often produced for local markets goods which had become dated

Table 6.1 Total approved DFI in Asia, 1986–88 ($ million)

	1986 Value	1986 % Change	1987 Value	1987 % Change	January–June 1988 Value	January–June 1988 % Change[a]	January–June 1988 Japan Share
Thailand	1 380	67	6 345	360	4 175[b]	193	44.2
Malaysia	211	61	301	43	491[b]	205	30.8
Philippines	77	−35	165	114	300[b]	404	13.1
Indonesia	826	−4	1 484	80	2 392[b]	318	8.3
China	2 834	−52	3 709	31	2 021[b]	130	
Singapore	592	34	720	22	412	1	45.8
South Korea	354	−34	1 060	200	640	51	

Notes: [a] Change in January–June amount over same period in 1987.
[b] amount in January to August.
Source: *NKS*, 30 October 1988, p. 7; *JS*, November 1988, p. 52; February 1989, p. 59.

in Japan. Now even that is changing, as intensified competition forces capital to use its most potent weapon of all: the lowest wages in the region *combined with* the most advanced technologies. Herein lies ASEAN's current attraction.

However, in spite of this merging of Japan's productive forces with Asia's human misery, very little technology is being transferred, certainly nothing like what has occurred in any of the NICs, so that productive forces in ASEAN are not being greatly affected. Almost totally dependent on the imperialist powers for the technology required to survive growing capitalist competition in the region, the ASEAN ruling classes cannot avoid prostituting their people to attract the allies needed to maintain their position.

Even NIC capital has recognised this and has been shifting into ASEAN, in some cases overtaking investors from Europe and North America. So although in the mid-1980s falling commodity prices seemed to cause a stagnation of Japanese and other DFI in ASEAN, in 1987 manufacturers from all over the world began their 'rush' into the region. By 1988 even that image was inadequate, as rates of increase soared over the 300 per cent levels. Table 6.1 shows that the shift of DFI to ASEAN and China after 1986 was worldwide.

But as in the case of the NICs, the alliances at the top can only be understood in the context of the crises and struggles to which they promised solutions. This chapter examines the two ASEAN countries where recent Japanese DFI has soared most rapidly and where it has focused more on manufacturing than resource extraction, Thailand and Malaysia. The next looks at the two where resources are still the main attraction and where the amounts of DFI are less: Indonesia and the Philippines.

THAILAND

History of Struggle

Thailand is the only ASEAN country whose ruling class enjoyed an alliance with the Japanese during the Pacific War. Afterwards and well into the 1970s the Japanese could not provide what the Thai ruling class most needed: military assistance. That came from the US, and for a long time, even after the end of the Vietnam war, this military alliance remained the central feature of imperialism in Thailand. However, substantial investments from Japan, mainly in textiles, were welcomed in the early 1960s in an attempt to boost the country's backward productive forces.

Although Thailand had never been formally colonised, it had in effect been treated by Western imperialism as part of Malaya, and capital had poured into industries where profits depended more on natural endowments than on past accumulations: rice, tin, rubber and teak. Money could be made in industries like these without much reinvestment, so little was undertaken, and most of the profit left the country in the typical neo-colonial fashion. There was thus very little development.

In spite of attempts to reverse this legacy by means of nationalised industries after the war, the situation was so desperate by the early 1960s that the military government launched its *First Development Plan* (1961–66). This promised to provide for capitalists the minimal infrastructure they needed: power, transport and communications. The Investment Promotion Act of 1962 established the most liberal climate for foreign capital anywhere in Asia. Industrialisation by means of import substitution (ISI) spearheaded by foreign investment through protective tariffs and tax concessions was envisaged (Igusa, 1988, p. 169; Wonghanchao and Ikemoto, 1988, pp. 85 ff.).

It was at this point that the interests of Japanese capital and those of the Thai ruling class coincided most closely, and Japanese investment entered mainly the textile industry. This became the second most important branch of manufacturing (behind food processing) by the end of the decade. Half a dozen Japanese joint ventures dominated it, gradually transforming it into a modern and very profitable export-oriented industry. The total amount of direct investment from Japan was twice that of its nearest rival, the US, and comprised a third of all DFI in the country.

Since ISI produces for the domestic market, that is, makes things the Thai people themselves buy, it can in practice favour local capital, which has at least some experience doing just that. But because local capital and even foreign capital operating in Thailand, cannot always produce goods for this market as cheaply as they can be imported, tariffs and subsidies are required to support ISI. However, throughout Southeast Asia, the logic of capitalist development, as repeatedly pointed out by the World Bank and the IMF, has found this wasteful. It might create a more *even* development, but 'artificially' protecting relatively backward industries contradicts profit making and 'allocative efficiency'. As if to underline the urgency of heeding this advice, 45 000 American troops arrived in the country in 1968.

And so by the early 1970s the notoriously corrupt Thanom government edged towards favouring export industries. Coinciding with a boom fed by military spending for the Vietnam war and the start of the Third Development Plan (1972–76), the New Investment Promotion Act signalled the switch to export-led growth. However, the final burial of import substitution followed a series of crises that threw the Thai ruling class more fully into the arms of foreign capital: the slump in military demand after the end of the Vietnam war, skyrocketing prices of oil, which Thailand imports, and an intense period of mass struggle, which for the first time in modern Thai history had real revolutionary potential. But the 1977 military coup resolved the crisis by means of sheer force and a deal in which the Thai ruling class was thrown at the mercy of foreign capital (Suehiro and Yasuda, 1987, pp. 48 ff.).

Among the new incentives created by the ultra-rightist Tanin regime were a series of tax breaks (on profits and imported machinery and materials) and guarantees (against nationalisation or competition from state monopolies) for foreign investors. Local producers would be forced by the winds of international competition to team up with foreign capital or to become efficient on their own: they would have to produce profitably or be wiped out. But one should not, as recently noted by the *Far Eastern Economic Review* (7 July 1988, pp. 80–1), exaggerate the importance of the fiscal incentives over other things that matter more to foreign capital:

Table 6.2 Foreign control in Thailand's top 1066 companies, 1980

	Sales (B million)	Number of companies	Foreign share of sales (%)	Foreign share of companies (%)
Mining	1 889	20	50.3	45.0
Food, beverages, tobacco	50 212	137	32.1	32.1
Textiles and apparel	22 836	93	71.6	54.8
Wood and wood products	1 515	15	11.6	26.7
Paper and printing	4 971	26	52.8	30.8
Chemicals, rubber	73 085	104	95.0	66.3
Ceramic and glass	18 304	32	28.6	40.6
Iron and steel, metals	20 277	22	84.1	40.9
Machinery	31 702	96	82.2	55.2
Other manufacturing	724	3	5.7	33.3
General trading	85 697	169	70.1	29.0
Agricultural wholesaling	12 869	53	4.6	5.7
Food wholesaling	24 294	75	9.7	6.0
Other wholesaling	37 892	221	32.0	13.6
TOTAL	386 267	1 066	59.3	32.7

Source: Tambunlertchai and McGovern, 1984, p. 81.

[T]he rival incentives tend to cancel each other out. Thailand's promotional privileges, Singapore's Pioneer Status, Malaysian, Taiwanese, or South Korean tax holidays – all offer similar benefits. More important, from the investor's point of view are questions such as: how much does labour cost; does the country offer a stable political environment; how well developed is the infrastructure?

In at least the first two respects the new regime proved very attractive to foreign capital, and by the early 1980s considerable export-led growth had occurred, with manufacturing as a whole expanding by about 10 per cent in the 1970s. This development concealed much unevenness, however, since most of the growth was in textiles, apparel and motor vehicles. In all industries foreign capital spearheaded the process, often in joint ventures (Utrecht, 1978). Table 6.2 shows the sales of the top 1066 companies in 1980 in mining, manufacturing and trading, indicating the shares of companies which were partly or wholly foreign owned.

Japanese Capital

Although foreign capital from different countries was concentrated in different industries, for example, the US in mining and the EC in pharmaceuticals, Japanese capital was strong in almost every sector. Iron and steel was dominated by three Japanese joint ventures, motor vehicles by half a dozen joint ventures, and household electrical appliances (fridges and radios) also by about the same number. Most of them had been set up through the offices of one or other *sōgō shōsha*, mainly Mitsubishi and Mitsui (*LA International*, 1987b, appendix; Utrecht, 1978; Suzuki, 1986; Phongpaichit *et al.*, 1986).

It would be wrong, however, to conclude that Thai capital has become a simple puppet of outside interests. In a number of industries it remains the predominant force and in finance, where the state has limited the entry of foreign capital, it is still the sole force. It also has independent forms of organisation, not least the military, which at times enable it to function independently. Rather, what must be grasped is the existence of a continually shifting *alliance* from which both sides have benefited.

For example, when class struggle in Thailand exploded in the early 1970s and the military rule which had existed in one form or another since 1932 was replaced by a brief liberal interlude, the balance of power moved in favour of the local ruling class. But a bloody coup, with barely concealed US complicity, restored the military government and with it the previous preponderance of influence exercised by American imperialism (*BCAS*, July–September, 1977).

The more recent crisis of the mid-1980s, which was precipitated by the fall in commodity prices, greatly increased Thai capital's dependence on Japan, which had been carving out a major role for itself in Thai affairs. The collapse of rice, wheat, tin and rubber prices, still the main exports and source of local capital's strength, caused a sharp decline in business activity, including foreign investment (not to mention the living conditions of the peasantry and the urban working class). However, by 1986 the partial recovery of commodity prices, the continued cheapness of oil and the rapid rise of the yen all helped to revive foreign investment. Phillip Bowring of the *Far Eastern Economic Review* pointed out that the interest of Japanese capital alone 'could be worth at least one percentage point on the growth rate for the next three years or so' (25 June 1987, p. 68). A year later the world was witnessing the 'Thai economic miracle', as rising wages and exchange rates in the NICs forced capital, foreign and local, to

Table 6.3   Registered capital of firms promoted by the BOI, 1960–86 (B million)

	100% owned	*Joint venture*	*Total B million*	*%*
Thai	16 967	11 298	28 265	72.2
Foreign	1 821	9 077	10 898	27.8
Japan	965	1 870	2 836	7.2
US	273	1 589	1 861	4.8
Taiwan	24	963	987	2.5
UK	11	721	732	1.9
Hong Kong	0	549	549	1.4
Holland	180	131	311	0.8
TOTAL	18 788	20 375	39 164	100.0
Total investment	–	–	207 465	100.0

Source: BOI (Board of Investment).

Table 6.4   Total value of BOI approved investments with foreign participation, 1960–88 (B million)

Main Investor	1960–82	1983–85	1960–85	1986	1987	1–6 1988	1988
Japan	36 754	10 311	47 065	14 421	23 548	28 032	70 000
US	13 305	6 445	19 750	904	5 025	8 406	n/a
Taiwan	10 739	2 810	13 549	2 331	7 309	6 924	20 000
UK	13 354	1 705	15 059[a]	5 185	6 901	18 798	n/a
Holland	11 137	−1 138	10 000[a]				
Hong Kong	n/a	n/a	7 100	1 966	3 335	2 516	n/a
Singapore	n/a	n/a	7 113	397	1 711	2 952	n/a
TOTAL	156 836	37 055	193 892	25 211	54 400	75 740	190 000

Note: [a] figures for Europe after 1986.
Source: BOI; *Asian Finance*, October 1988, p. 34; *FEER*, 12 January 1989, p. 58.

mount the Japanese bandwagon. The rate of GDP growth had to be revised upwards on numerous occasions, eventually reaching close to 11 per cent in 1988.

Tables 6.3 and 6.4 present some recent data on foreign investment, confirming the qualitative leap in Japanese capital's importance to Thailand after the rise of the yen. Table 6.3 lists the total registered capital of promoted firms by their country of origin. Although it reasonably indicates Japan's relative importance among foreign investors, it exaggerates the weight of local relative to foreign capital. This is because, while about half the *registered* capital in joint ventures is Thai, much less *paid-up* capital is local. Table 6.4 shows the total value of the investments with foreign participation in 1960–85 and then each year after that. Although the figures up to and after 1985 are not strictly comparable (because of changes made along the way and slightly different bases), they show that the value of Japanese-backed projects in 1988 alone was equivalent to the total of those undertaken in the entire period up to the end of 1986, when the rush into Thailand started.

The balance of influence between local and foreign capital has thus shifted further in the latter's favour, as it always tends to in times of crisis in countries with backward productive forces. If investment and overall accumulation was to be revived, this had to be led by stronger, more technically advanced capital.

Joint Venture Partners

Before we examine these investments in more detail, it is important to look first at some of the local partners the Japanese have cultivated over the years for their joint ventures. Most of them belong to the leading elements of the Thai ruling class, particularly its foremost business groups and families, of which there are two (partly overlapping) types: a few centering on major banks and about two dozen industrial ones. The most important are listed in Table 6.5. To illustrate how the alliance functions, I briefly discuss only the leading bank and three of the industrial groups, concentrating on their links with Japanese capital.

By far the largest of these conglomerates is the Bangkok Bank group controlled by the Sophonpanich family. Bangkok Bank itself was set up in 1944 by Chin Sophonpanich out of wealth accumulated from exporting lumber and building materials, and it has since become the largest bank in Southeast Asia with Chin, until his death in 1987, as its chief shareholder and probably the richest individual in the region. Mutual stockholdings bind over 60 companies into the group, but because of the weak capital base of most Thai manufacturing firms, the bank's lending power raises the number of companies under its influence to over 140, including the Saha Union and SPI groups as well as the CP group (Charoen Pokphand, the largest agri-business group in the country with 49 members).

It is hardly accidental that Japan's top company, Toyota, should

Table 6.5   Leading Thai business groups and families

Group	Family	Ethnicity	Main industries
Bangkok Bank	Sophonpanich	Chinese	Banking, finance, textiles, plastics
Siam Cement	Royal family	Thai	Cement, iron & steel, pulp and paper
Siam Motor	Phornprapha	Thai	Cars and parts, musical instruments
Thai Farmers Bank	Lamsam	Chinese	Banking and finance
Bank of Ayudhya	Ratanarak	Chinese	Banking, finance, cement, flour
Metropolitan Bank	Tejapaibul	Chinese	Banking, liquor, sugar, chemicals
SPI	Chokwatana	Chinese	Soap, cosmetics, clothing, food
Saha Union	Darakanand	Chinese	Textiles, plastics, clothing
Sukree	Pothirattanangkun	Chinese	Textiles, synthetic textiles

Source: Inoue, 1987, p. 154.

have linked up with the Bangkok Bank group to produce the single largest Japanese presence in Thailand, Toyota Motors Thailand. Set up in 1962, the company had two factories producing 20 000 cars in 1986, the largest market share (27 per cent). However, by 1988 total car sales had almost doubled to 135 000, and Toyota was in the middle of a large expansion programme to raise its share to 30 per cent by 1990.

A new company, Siam Toyota Manufacturing, was recently set up in partnership with Siam Cement, Thailand's largest manufacturing corporation, to produce diesel engines and components for export. This extended the already considerable swapping parts with other Toyota subsidiaries in Asia. One of the new company's tasks has been to supply metal moulds to Indonesia, Taiwan and Malaysia, all for the production of cheap pressed parts. Because the company since 1978 also had a joint venture with Hino making Hino and Toyota engines, Thailand had a well proven record of success. Today all of the Japanese majors have assigned central roles to Thailand in their relocation of parts production and assembly in ASEAN. Small wonder the motor industry is rapidly developing into one of Thailand's top money spinners (*NKS*, 9 October 1987, p. 8; *JEJ*, 17 October 1987, p. 6; *Business in Thailand*, March 1988, p. 29 ff.).

Toyota's partner in this new factory is the giant which towers over all others in the Thai manufacturing industry and which absorbs the top elite from the nation's universities. With the royal family as its chief share holder, Siam Cement is Thailand's most desired joint-venture partner and is about as close as one gets to a national bourgeoisie. The Crown Property Bureau and the Siam Commercial Bank help bind the fifteen subsidiaries and twenty associated companies together by means of often quite small share holdings.

Siam Cement, the only non-foreign firm among the country's top ten, was founded in 1913 in an attempt to bolster self-sufficiency. Its core members include the country's top iron and steel firm (Siam Iron and Steel) as well as leaders in building materials, machinery, pulp and paper, tyres, trading and plastics. More recently, the group has branched into electronics and further into motor vehicles, where its main allies have been Japanese.

Apart from its agreement with Toyota, since 1980 Siam Cement has had a major joint venture with Kubota and Marubeni, Siam Kubota Diesel, which makes diesel engines for agricultural machinery. Also in line with government support for engine manufacturing is the recent agreement between Hino and Thai Engineering Products to make auto parts for the local as well as the Japanese and US markets. Siam Cement's other links with Japanese capital include two joint ventures with Toto and one with Asahi Glass to make glass tubes for TVs for export from 1991.

A major new development is Thai CRT, a joint venture between Siam Cement (40 per cent), seventeen local electrical companies (30 per cent) and three foreign ones (Toshiba, Mitsubishi, with which it has had a long-standing relationship, and Philips) to start making braun tubes for colour TVs from 1989. TVs themselves will be made and marketed respectively by two Siam Cement affiliates which have just teamed up with NEC: Conception Industry and Home Electronics. The coup of the year in 1988 went to Siam Tyre, a joint venture with Firestone which, since Bridgestone's takeover of Firestone, gives the Japanese giant and its affiliates 70 per cent of the Thai market. Bridgestone and Siam Cement decided soon afterwards to set up a styrene butadiene rubber (SBR) plant (*The Nation*, 1 April 1987, p. 19; Inoue, 1987, pp. 241–6; Shūkan tōyō keizai 1988; *JEJ*, 25 September 1987, p. 12; 21 November 1987, p. 8; 12 March 1988, p. 19; 3 December 1988, p. 25; Suehiro and Yasuda, 1987, pp.

86 ff.; *LA International*, 1987b, pp. 65 ff.; *FEER*, 30 June 1988, pp. 53, 60–3).

Minebea is another Japanese behemoth that wangled an alliance with this most favoured group around the same time. More than a decade ago Minebea saw its future in Asia, where it now makes most of its bearings, the rest in the US. By the mid-1980s it had three large wholly owned manufacturing subsidiaries in Thailand, the second of which, opened in 1984, is its main source of computer components (keyboards, printers, fan motors), which are in heavy demand from Japanese assemblers. Minebea's joint venture with the Crown Property Bureau, in which Bangkok Bank also has a small stake, was set up in May 1987 to make ferrite heads. In 1988 its third electronics parts subsidiary began making magnetic heads and switching systems.

Today Thailand is Minebea's world production centre, with 12 000 workers compared to only 3500 in Japan, while its Singapore plant has been made supplier of technology and parts. A company Boeing 727 flies parts and personnel between Japan, Thailand and Singapore twice a week. Minebea also has the most developed propaganda apparatus of all Japanese companies in Thailand. It includes a constant stream of trainees (140 at any one time) being sent to Japan and a scholarship fund for Thai students. In August 1988 even the US Commerce Department came to see Minebea's operation in Thailand as a sort of Japanese enclave, and slapped a 17.83 per cent duty on bearings imported from Thailand, allegedly because they were subsidised by export incentives. The company responded by returning to the Thai government the tax breaks it had received for the bearings (*JJTI*, May 1986, p. 21; Shūkan tōyō keizai, 1988; *NKS*, 29 September 1988, p. 11; 15 October 1988, p. 8; *JEJ*, 24 September 1988, p. 7; 8 October 1988, pp. 9, 24; 29 October 1988, pp. 1, 23).

Siam Motors is another major Thai *zaibatsu* having extensive links with Japanese capital. Including its chief banker, Bangkok Bank, the group comprises at least 36 members held together mainly by Siam Motors, which markets Nissan cars and owns 40 per cent of group assets. Siam Motors was founded by Thaworn Phornprapha, who remained its president for 34 years until his retirement in 1984. Having visited Japan on numerous occasions, he was an early Japanophile and began importing Nissan trucks in 1948. By 1962 he had set up a wholly Thai-owned company to assemble Nissan vehicles under licence, Siam Motors and Nissan. Since then, Siam Motors has become the dominant local force in the industry, but it has relied totally on joint ventures and licensing agreements with a large number of Japanese companies: Nissan, Mitsubishi, Isuzu, Suzuki and Yamaha.

In 1964 Thaworn set up Siam Yamaha to assemble motor cycles under licence and in 1965 he formed Prince Motors, a joint venture with Nissan to assemble trucks. Two years later in a joint venture with Suzuki he founded Thai Suzuki Motors, also to assemble motor cycles. A number of joint ventures (such as Siam GS Battery and Siam Auto Parts) were also set up in such fields as batteries, piston rings, spark plugs and clutches.

The rise of the yen had a dramatic effect on the Siam Motors group, which was badly hurt by more expensive imported components. It has thus taken advantage of the government's new export subsidies as well as Japanese capital's search for cheap parts. Major expansions in component production, particularly engines, are underway, for both local use and export to Japanese companies all over the world. Nissan sees Siam Motors as pivotal to its global strategy to make Thailand a major low cost production base. In October 1986 it announced a new expansionary plan to supply Taiwan, Malaysia, Bangladesh and Pakistan. In June 1987, a new joint venture began to produce small trucks, and a year later, partly to supply it, another one (also involving Mitsubishi Motors), Thai Automotive Industry, began making 2500cc diesel engines. Exports of the Sunny to Brunei commenced in 1988. Siam Motors has also been planning a joint venture with Yamaha to make motorcycle engines for export, as well as one with Mitsubishi's Sittipol Motor Company.

This latter is both a major presence in the Thai motor industry and contributor to Mitsubishi's 'Asian Car', for which its main task is assembly and the contribution of 30 per cent of components, to double to 60 per cent when engines are added. In late 1988 the company decided to build two new plants (one to make engines, the other a second assembly plant) and intentionally to neglect the domestic market, so that it might prepare for full-scale exports. A trial of 2000 cars a month to Canada began in 1988 as a precursor to the real target, the US.

Another car Siam Motors has recently contracted to assemble is the Subaru Leone, made by Fuji Heavy Industries. The latter's presence in Thailand is also being felt through its participation, along with Mitsubishi and Isuzu, in a number of interrelated projects to make engines, mainly for pick-up trucks. These account for over half the country's vehicle sales, a hotly contested market in which Isuzu was a clear leader until 1987. But Thailand is now rapidly becoming a base for the production of most Japanese pick-up trucks, engines for which involve slow technological change and few sophisticated parts.

Of the 43 companies in the Siam Motors group, fully nineteen are related to motor vehicles, and almost all are linked in one way or another to Japanese capital. Many of the others also owe their existence to agreements with Japanese interests, for example, with Komatsu in construction machinery, with Hitachi in lifts and with Daikin in compression engines. In all, eleven of them are in trading, twelve in manufacturing, four in finance and real estate, five in raw materials and two in Thailand's notorious 'leisure' industry, a euphemism for prostitution (*NKS*, 17 July 1987, p. 9; 26 December 1987, p. 8; *JEJ*, 20 February 1988, p. 8; 11 June 1988, p. 18; 16 July 1988, p. 18; 27 August 1988, p. 19; 12 November 1988, p. 6; *Business in Thailand*, March 1988, pp. 29–41; Ikemoto 1988; *The Nation*, 30 March 1987, p. 1; Inoue, 1987, pp. 155–61; *FEER*, 25 June 1987, p. 69).

Although the Thai car industry is overwhelmingly linked to one or other of the groups discussed so far, there have been some other important developments. One is the sudden rise of Honda from near obscurity a few years ago to claim the second largest market share for passenger cars in 1988. Honda has, along with Suzuki and Kawasaki, produced motor cycles for some time in Thailand, and they are all now taking advantage of this: Honda and Kawasaki started importing their bikes to Japan in 1988, while Suzuki is rapidly expanding production and will set up a new parts facility in 1989 (*NKS*, 2 November 1988, p. 11; *JEJ*, 9 July 1988, p. 18; 10 September 1988, p. 20).

The Saha group, like the other manufacturers I have discussed, owes its origin and success to substantial links with Japanese capital. It consists of two sub-groups centering on the two core companies, Saha Union and SPI (Saha Pathanapibul Investments). Its specialty is to produce and sell Japanese consumer goods, such as sports shoes, films, cosmetics, clothing and pharmaceuticals. The textile manufacturer, Saha Union, has some twenty companies under its umbrella, notably Union Textiles, while SPI brings together about 70. Together they comprise the country's top private conglomerate.

The founder of SPI is Thiam Chokwatana, who is still the chairperson of Saha Pathanapibul, the firm he set up in 1943 to import consumer goods from Japan. Later, when he moved into manufacturing, he entered into joint ventures with foreign capital, particularly from Japan. In 1961 his brother-in-law, Damri Darakananda, joined with Japan's YKK to form Union Yoshida Industries to make metal zips. Damri then diversified into textiles, rubber products and plastics, forming the Saha Union group. In 1962 Thiam went to Japan and linked up with Lion Fat & Oil to form Lion Bangkok, a soap manufacturing company. The 1960s and 1970s saw many new joint ventures by both Saha sub-groups mainly with Japanese capital, for example, Saha Union with Unitika and Kanebo, and SPI with Mitsui, their respective specialties continuing to be textiles and household consumer goods. Chokwatana holds the SPI sub-group together by means of his wholly-owned holding company, Chokwatana Co., as well as through the public company Saha Pathanapibul. The Union side is bound together by the stockholdings of Saha Union and by its vertically integrated structure: member companies gin its cotton, weave garments, package and market them.

The same vertical integration applies to its other main line, footwear, although here the ties are with US capital. The group has recently been trying to diversify and has found willing foreign partners, such as Japan's leading thermos maker, Zojirushi. A joint venture with Tomita will contribute stainless steel tube and pipe, while one with Komatsugawa Plastics will create Japan's first metal-mould facilities in Thailand, which is to become a major Japanese supplier. The family links between Saha Union and SPI are complemented by mutual stock holdings (Inoue, 1987, pp. 162–67; *FEER*, 27 October 1988, pp. 88–90; *JEJ*, 12 March 1988, p. 7; 24 December 1988, p. 36).

Clearly, there are long-standing ties between the Japanese and Thai ruling classes, and these have contributed much to Thailand's current most-favoured status among ASEAN countries for Japanese companies fleeing the high yen. Because the *shosha* were important in organising joint ventures in the early ISI phase, large ones like Mitsui and Mitsubishi remain major presences. Thailand is Mitsui's largest DFI venue after the US, with 27 joint ventures, including a sugar factory set up in 1986 with the Bangkok Bank. Mitsui has links with a large number of leading Thai conglomerates, for example, Metro (MMC International), Sukree (Siam Resin & Chemical) and Saha Bangkok Nylon), and it is now planning to produce tapioca pellets and flour for export in association with the Metro group (*Asian Finance*, 15 August 1987, p. 66).

Table 6.6   Recent export-oriented investments in Thailand

Company	Products	Market
Sharp	Electric stoves, fridges	US, Europe
NEC	Colour TVs	Nearby countries
Mitsubishi Electric	Compressors for air conditioners	Japan
Toyo Sash	Aluminum sash window frames	Japan, China, SE Asia
Nippondenso	Metal moulds	SE Asia
Fuji Spinning	Garments	Europe, US
Bandai	Toys	US
Yamaha	Skis	Japan, US, Europe
Aderansu	Wigs	US
Nichiden Kagaku	Starch	Japan

Source: *NKS*, 25 September 1987, p. 23.

Shift to DFI for Export

Some recent developments not directly related to the major conglomerates are also worth looking at. Associated with the more than
doubling of Japanese investment in 1988 was a major shift from ISI
investments for the local market to export oriented ones. This has
coincided with the encouragement given to export companies by the
Sixth Development Plan (1987–91). The reason for the new emphasis
is strikingly evident in the move in 1987 by Pioneer and Minebea
from Singapore, where monthly wages averaged $300, to Thailand,
with its average of $75, as their main production base for export to
Japan, the US and Southeast Asia. Some other recent export-
oriented investments in Thailand are listed in Table 6.6.

The venture by Toyo Sash is its first big overseas project, which
will eventually 'dwarf the existing Thai aluminium building-materials
industry' (*FEER*, 18 June 1987, p. 66). It is to be 100 per cent for
export and is 100 per cent Japanese owned, requiring little more from
Thailand than 1000 workers and the generous incentives offered by
the Thai government. Another first is the wig factory of Aderans
which opened in June 1987. This is larger than its Korean or Chinese
ventures, and it uses young women in their teens for the extremely
labour-intensive work of setting each hair one by one. The women
work a nine hour day for six days a week for B2100 ($84) a month.
The Yamaha venture is interesting for the eighteen-month search

that went into selecting its first ski-making facilities overseas. The Philippines, where wages are even lower, narrowly lost out because of its political climate.

Another example of the same process is in toy manufacturing, which is moving from such strongholds as Hong Kong and Singapore to become one of Thailand's fastest growing industries. Toy exports have increased by 50 per cent annually in recent years. Even though 75–80 per cent of inputs (moulds, motors, gears, safety paints) must be imported for the largest segment of the industry, plastic toys, Thailand's low wages more than compensate. Tomy, known as the toy maker with the largest overseas facilities, opened its biggest plant in 1988 in Thailand, rationalising its Hong Kong and Singapore operations to specialise in precision products (*JEJ*, 12 September 1987, p. 17; 12 December 1987, p. 7; 25 June 1988, p. 8; 8 October 1988, p. 7; *FEER*, 7 May 1987, pp. 125–6; 7 July 1988, p. 80).

Electronics

The emerging division of labour between the poorer ASEAN countries and the NICs is most clearly illustrated in the current plans of Japan's leading electrical companies, which are concentrating chip manufacture in Singapore and Malaysia but household consumer goods in Thailand, although the latter is receiving a wide range of investments in electronics as well. For example, Hitachi is expanding its production of fridges, colour TVs and rice cookers, while Toshiba and Sharp have plans with macro-economic implications.

After shifting its production of rice cookers to Thailand, Toshiba received approval in August 1988 for its ¥30 billion investment plan (previously rejected by the Board of Investment for fear it would drive out local competition) to produce 1.6 million picture tubes, about 15 per cent of the company's world wide output. A condition of approval was that the entire output be exported, including goods to be produced later by the new company: fridges, washers, air-conditioners and microwaves.

Sharp is currently relocating its production of microwave ovens and fridges, 'in some cases moving whole factories out of Japan, or even Taiwan, as part of a global reorganization' (*FEER*, 25 June 1987, p. 69) and bringing with it a whole range of component makers. Half the parts came from Japan when production started in April 1987, but the company hopes to procure 80 per cent locally with the arrival of nine more support companies in early 1989. Within a year of its opening, the company reached its production targets and commenced work on product design and on its second and third facilities for air conditioners and audio-visual equipment. In 1989 it will add cassette recorders, facsimile machines, word processors and electronic typewriters, eventually aiming to integrate the entire production process from design to manufacture and become Sharp's largest offshore production base; 80 per cent of output will be exported to Europe and the US. Average daily wages for the mainly women workers in 1988 were a mere B61 ($2.44), barely above the minimum of B63 for the locality North of Bangkok (*NKS*, 16 October 1987, p. 9; 7 October 1988, p. 11; *JEJ*, 28 May 1988, p. 8; 20 August 1988, p. 17; 17 December 1988, p. 18; 24 December 1988, p. 8; *Asian Finance*, 15 August 1987, p. 67).

Also of major significance is the current move by Mitsubishi Electric of its production of floppy disk drives from its Koriyama plant in Japan to a new firm in Bangkok which is fully owned by Mitsubishi group members. When the second plant is completed in April 1989, the Thai operation will account for 60 per cent of the company's total FDD production. The quality of drives made by this company's women workers, whose average age is not even eighteen, is said to be 'even better than that of FDDs made in Japan' (*JEJ*, 10 September 1988, p. 7). Circuit boards are imported from Singapore, magnetic heads from Taiwan and it is hoped that only microchips and precision motors will continue to come from Japan.

Other electronics companies to have invested recently in Thailand include Crown Corporation (B2.6 billion to make components, 80 per cent for export), Fujikura Cable Works (two new factories from 1989), Sony (its first overseas semiconductor subsidiary), NEC and Matsushita. The latter is adding to its already large presence in Thai white goods production a new venture to make a wide range of components from April 1989 for the group throughout the region (*NKS*, 29 September 1988, p. 8; 1 November 1988, p. 11; *JEJ*, 16 July 1988, p. 17; 30 July 1988, p. 18; 27 August 1988, p. 19; 10 September 1988, p. 7; 12 November 1988, p. 21; 10 December 1988, p. 20; 17 December 1988, p. 23; 24 December 1988, p. 37).

Many important projects other than motor vehicles and electronics have also been undertaken since the rise of the yen, but space permits only a brief mention of a few. Citizen has set up an export venture to produce clocks and watches from 1988. And in the biggest agribusiness project ever led by a Japanese company in Thailand, Topy will grow and process cocoa and asparagus for export to Europe and

186   *Japan's New Imperialism*

Japan (*NKS*, 17 May 1987, p. 4; 1 August 1987, p. 17; 23 December 1987, p. 9; 27 January 1988, p. 9; 14 October 1988, p. 11; *JEJ*, 19 March 1988, p. 20; 2 April 1988, p. 23; 2 July 1988, p. 23; *Asian Finance*, 15 August 1987, p. 66; *FEER*, 25 December 1986, pp. 63–4).

Conclusion

Capital accumulation in Thailand was revived with a vengeance in the late 1980s because of the mounting interest of foreign capital, particularly Japanese, in using cheap labour to produce goods for export which the rise of the yen made too costly to make elsewhere. While agriculture and the livelihood of peasants and most urban workers continues to stagnate, capital accumulation in ASEAN's largest food exporting country is increasingly being propelled by manufacturing, which already contributes 22 per cent of GNP compared to agriculture's 19 per cent. But agriculture must sustain 70 per cent of the population. The currently overburdened infrastructure – ports, roads, telecommunications and power – will probably receive government attention only when it begins to choke off foreign investment, leaving little for the social infrastructure so desperately needed by the Thai people.

The current export-led boom, which is sucking in an even greater amount of imports (chiefly capital goods), is both a symbol and an outcome of an ever more intimate alliance between the Japanese and Thai ruling classes. However, since most of the foreign investment for export has been in the component and assembly industries, with few linkages to existing manufacturing, the enormous technological power of Japanese capital makes it the overbearing partner, leaving the Thai side constantly having to woo it with incentives and propaganda. Phillip Bowring commented:

[T]he surge of foreign investment, while bringing short-term gains, will swamp nascent local manufacturers which have been so important to the growth of self-sustaining industrial groups in South Korea and Taiwan (*FEER*, 25 June 1987, p. 68).

One recent example of such conflict is a promoted joint venture between Sumitomo and CH Autoparts (which makes bodies for Toyota) to produce rolled steel sheets. The 50–60 jobs to be created are expected to destroy 1400 jobs in 67 local companies. However, although many members of the Thai bourgeoisie are now speaking of an 'overpresence' of Japanese investment, there is little chance that bourgeois nationalism will become a stronger force. The importance of Japanese technology is too essential for local capital, which is becoming more rather than less of a comprador class, to do more than grumble occasionally. The future will thus be shaped primarily by the contradiction between Japanese-led foreign capital and its local allies on the one hand, and the Thai masses, on the other (*NKS*, 17 May 1987, p. 4; 8 July 1987, p. 12; *The Nation*, 31 March 1987, p. 17; 1 April 1987, p. 17).

In the immediate short term, it might appear that the election of the Chatichai Choonhaven government in July 1988 has solved this contradiction. That appearance is one factor behind the confidence of foreign investment pouring into the country. But the facade of stability and harmony is belied by at least three ghosts from the past. First, although there has been a small shift within the Thai power bloc from the military to private sector capitalists, the centre of gravity has remained with the former, the repressive apparatus. Second, the growing predominance of Japanese capital in Thai affairs makes it harder, not easier, for the regime to implement the reforms needed to contain the real time bomb, the oppression of the Thai masses. The year of record DFI, 1988, was also a year that saw the revival of the third ghost, major activity within both the student and labour movements. These still hold the key to the future. At least one thing is certain, the more foreign capital predominates in the alliance with local capital, the less compromising the regime will be in meeting the demands of the masses.

Japanese capital is spearheading the transition of Thailand from agriculture and raw material production to labour intensive manufacturing. It is thus the leading force behind the creation for the first time of a sizeable industrial working class and the addition of a new site of political struggle. Hitherto, revolutionary political organisation has had to centre on the peasantry, although once before, after the repression of student and trade union struggles following the 1976 coup, history had announced the need for a change of emphasis. From now on, forms of working-class organisation experienced in dealing with Japanese employers will become more crucial. Proletarian nationalism and internationalism will thus need to be combined if Japanese imperialism is to be challenged.

MALAYSIA

History of Struggle

The Japanese occupation of Malaya had a more ambiguous effect on decolonisation than elsewhere in Southeast Asia. On the one hand, it cruelly persecuted the Malayan Chinese upon taking over the country, massacring thousands of individuals in the *sook ching*, or 'purification' programme, but on the other it gave moderate encouragement to Malay and Indian nationalism. The latter was intended to strike as much against western imperialism in Indonesia and India as against the British in Malaya. The Japanese relied on the same means as the British and encouraged ethnic conflict.

The British failed to see that they had been expelled in 1941 partly by forces which had gained momentum during the war, and they used every means available to regain their position afterwards: unprecedented military force during the 'Emergency' period and as cynical a campaign of racist divide-and-rule as had ever been employed outside South Africa. But the best they could hope for was some sort of neo-colonial set-up, and they bolstered the pro-British tendency within Malay nationalism under the leadership of the Sultans, repressing the anti-imperialist tendency along with its counterparts among the Chinese and Indian populations. To the present day, the United Malay Nationalist Organization (UMNO) has maintained a close alliance with imperialism of one form or another (Amin and Caldwell, 1977).

The only way to check postwar revolutionary nationalism was to portray it as an ethnic struggle, in order to transform it from an anti-imperialist into an anti-Chinese movement. History had left much of the Malay community open to such manipulation. With the vast majority of its members in a peasantry which was even worse off than the working class, a popular base was provided on which the traditional ruling class could safely raise a nationalist banner. Working class interests have since been presented as 'foreign', while peasant interests have been sacrificed with equal impunity, on the pretext that the state is the champion of the Malay people. By framing every policy and every statement in terms of the ethnicity of the people affected, rather than of the situations they are in, UMNO gets away with serving only the upper class, as well as with shifting members of the traditional ruling class from their old to their new positions of power.

Even though the working class now includes at least as many members of the Malay as of the Chinese and Indian communities, UMNO still wins support from poor Malay workers and peasants. This is because it promises to move them out of their desperate situations, as opposed to dealing with the situations themselves. Political movements that address the circumstances of the poor, who comprise members of all ethnic groups, are successfully branded as being opposed to the indigenous people. This was again recently demonstrated in a country to which the British bequeathed a tragically similar heritage, Fiji (Brennan, 1982; Stenson, 1976; Lim, 1980; Halim, 1982).

The way the class struggle has been communalised in Malaysia crucially affects the form in which foreign and local capital cooperate. Both sides know their interests depend on feeding chauvinistic ethnic nationalism, not with policies which improve the lot of the poor, but ones which alter the ethnic composition of the rich. Both sides accept the logic of the New Economic Policy (NEP), which is not to transfer wealth from one class to another, but to ensure that by 1990, Malay individuals and institutions would own 30 per cent of share capital, other Malaysians 40 per cent and foreigners 30 per cent (compared to 4, 34 and 62 per cent in 1971) (Khor, 1983, pp. 73–4).

The Chinese and Indian members of the upper class, organised in the Malaysian Chinese Association (MCA) and the Malaysian Indian Congress, go along with the communal strategy and play comparable roles within their communities. If Malay workers and peasants vote UMNO because it supposedly helps them out of desperate situations, then many Chinese and Indian members of the lower classes vote along ethnic lines for similar reasons. The causes of poverty, rather than who will stay poor, are always excluded from the agenda.

Only when the rich cannot get from the National Front what they want, as was the recent experience of MCA over the government's decision to allow non-Mandarin speakers to assume senior positions in Chinese primary schools, is the coalition threatened. In that respect, the division between *bumiputra* (indigenous Malays) and Chinese is similar to the division in Indonesia, having salience within the upper class. However, unlike Indonesia, a large proportion of Malaysian workers is Chinese, so that the division also exists within the lower classes.

Communalism serves the power bloc because, while it rarely threatens upper class unity, particularly *vis-à-vis* the masses, it frustrates the latter's ability to build united organisations. However, precisely because the masses are ethnically diverse, the use of communalism by upper class fractions in their jostlings for advantage can unleash explosive political forces, as occurred in the riots of 1969 and threatened to occur in late 1987. In the recent case, Prime Minister Mahathir's position within his own party had been shaky for some time, and his UMNO enemies naturally seized on any issue to unseat him, including ones over which grass roots organisation had assumed communal forms.

What seemed to be an indiscriminate use of the Internal Security Act, namely the detention in October 1987 of over one hundred people covering almost the entire political spectrum, was in fact a logical outcome of the communalisation of politics in Malaysia. To assert his control over the dissidents within his party, who had filed a case questioning the legitimacy of his election, Mahathir needed to act against the very militant ethnic chauvinism on which he and his entire regime depends. And he could only get away with that if he simultaneously defended that chauvinism against the Chinese 'threat', in this case the unprecedented show of unity in opposition to having non-Mandarin department heads in Chinese schools. So the swoop covered the entire political spectrum, and the ban on rallies applied equally to UMNO and the MCA. In spite of eventually splitting his party, Mahathir emerged from the whole affair, not simply stronger within the new UMNO (Baru), but by knocking the leadership of the tiny legal left for six, he also reaffirmed the authority of the ruling class as a whole under the guise that he forestalled the possibility of ethnic violence on the scale of 1969. Like the British before him, Mahathir and his party are simultaneously the main propagators of communalism and the sole present force preventing its explosion (*FEER*, October 1987, ff.).

Neither *merdeka* (independence) nor even the NEP had much real effect on what was in ASEAN the most uneven development spearheaded by unequalled foreign domination. Well after independence two commodities still dominated production (for export), and European companies controlled most of it: 83 per cent of rubber estates, 62 per cent of tin output and 60 per cent of commerce. DFI was intended to remain the motor of growth, the 1968 Investment Incentives Act providing extremely attractive incentives for firms in pioneer, export and labour-intensive industries. The government also provided 21 industrial estates as well as four FTZs, where foreign export companies could get tax-free use of local resources (Khor, 1983).

However, although NEP was not conceived as a strategy of national against foreign capital, but one of comprador capital against the peasantry and working class, it had effects along the former lines. Since too few Malay individuals could buy shares, the government set up public companies to act in trust for the *bumiputra* community, eventually selling their shares to *bumiputra* individuals. During the rapid growth of the 1970s, these trust agencies, notably Perbadanan Nasional (PERNAS), aggressively bought shares in, merged with or totally took over established foreign companies in the estate and mining industries as well as in trading. One of its creations, the Malaysian Mining Corporation, became the World's largest tin company, but this later came under the wing of a newer and potentially more powerful trust agency, the Permodalan Nasional Berhad (PNB). By 1982 the government had invested $2.4 billion for PNB to acquire companies, almost $1 billion getting majority shares in Guthrie Corporation, one of the largest of the estate groups (ibid., p. 75).

By 1985, the NEP has not just shifted the proportions of *bumiputra*, other Malaysian and foreign share ownership to 21.9, 48.4 and 29.7 per cent (Ibrahim, 1987, p. 197), but created institutionally-based indigenous capitalists with their own vested interests. The similarities with Indonesia are striking. In both cases the state served as the organisational base for the rise of a national bourgeoisie, high oil prices ensured the availability of funds for state spending and the collapse of oil and other commodity prices, which plunged both governments into serious fiscal crises and dangerous levels of international debt, sharply swung the terms of their alliance with imperialism in the latter's favour.

It is important not to exaggerate the independence achieved before the bubble burst in 1985. The power of foreign capital is not limited to the share holdings of foreign residents, and even minority holdings in joint ventures preserve foreign control. Moreover, government appointed directors are often politicians with little understanding of the businesses concerned, whereas the foreign directors are experienced company people.

Japanese DFI

Since the British were still in Malaya when reparations agreements with the Japanese were concluded, they claimed the bulk of the indemnity. But when the mass graves of Chinese victims were discovered in Singapore in 1962, the question of blood obligation was raised. The Japanese refused to recognise it and matters dragged on until 1967 when they finally offered two ships. Although a few investments had occurred before then, such as the large joint venture with Yawata Steel (Malayawata), most of the characteristic DFI in textiles and electrical components took place afterwards (Chee and Lee, 1979).

From the outset NEP suited Japanese capital, which willingly set up joint ventures with *bumiputra* (and other) interests. Because the targets of the takeovers and mergers were British, Mahathir's policy of 'Look East' was seen as pitting different foreign interests against one another. But his real message was to workers: submit to the Japanese system rather than to the 'English sickness' (class struggle). Nevertheless, a major consequence of NEP was a shift in the relative strengths of British and Japanese capital.

Although major investments were also made in the early 1970s, particularly in raw material extraction and processing, the 'rush' into Malaysian manufacturing occurred in the late 1970s and in the 1980s, as the forces culminating in the high yen crisis gained momentum. Each of the three waves of DFI focused on a range of industries and was related to obstacles to accumulation in Japan. Table 6.7 shows a survey of cases by year of commencement, but should not be read too mechanically in relation to developments in Japan.

The first wave was in the labour intensive industries threatened by rising wages in Japan towards the mid-1960s, chiefly electronics and textiles. As in Indonesia, these could only get under way after the political climate had been cleared in 1967. However, within a decade Japanese capital was the leader in both industries: ten out of 21 foreign-controlled electronics companies were Japanese, as were fifteen out of 22 foreign-controlled textile firms. In the forefront were Toray (two 100 per cent owned polyester factories in FTZs), Toyobo, Kanebo, Matsushita (six projects, mainly in FTZs), Sanyo, Toshiba and NEC. As elsewhere in Asia, the investments were in labour-intensive areas, and came to exploit Malaysia's highly disciplined and under-paid workforce (Chee and Lee, 1979, pp. 10–15; Shūkan tōyō keizai, 1988).

About the same time a second wave arrived to exploit Malaysian resources. It gained momentum in the 1970s following the oil crisis and then tapered off in the 1980s. The projects range from Mala-yawata Steel (1962) through a whole series of investments related to timber (Daishowa Pulp, many commercial investments in Sabah and Sarawak for importing logs, and a few ventures in furniture), food,

Table 6.7 Survey of DFI cases in Malaysia, by industry and commencement year

	Total	to 1969	1970–74	1975–79	1980–84	1984–87
Total	325	30	76	68	105	39
Agriculture/forestry/ fisheries	6	3	1	2	–	–
Mining	4	2	–	1	–	–
Construction	40	–	5	2	31	1
Manufacturing	177	23	46	39	41	25
Resource related	93	16	26	26	15	8
Food	4	1	1	–	1	1
Textiles	11	1	4	5	1	–
Wood/pulp and paper	16	3	5	5	2	–
Chemicals	31	5	8	11	4	2
Rubber/ceramics	16	3	4	4	3	2
Iron and steel	10	2	4	–	3	1
Non-ferrous metals	5	1	–	1	1	2
Machinery related	80	6	20	12	24	17
Metal products	10	1	4	–	3	2
General machinery	7	1	1	–	4	1
Electrical machinery	36	3	13	6	6	8
Transport machinery	14	–	1	3	6	3
Motor vehicles	8	1	–	–	5	2
Precision machinery	5	–	1	3	–	1
Other manufacturing	4	1	–	1	2	–
Commerce/finance/real estate/services	92	1	22	23	32	12

Note: Totals include cases for which year is unknown.
Source: Shūkan tōyō keizai, 1988, p. 17.

mining and Malaysia's richest resources, rubber and palm oil. A number of investments in chemicals, particularly polluting ones, accompanied the quest for raw materials, as Japanese capital moved its heavy industry out of the country and concentrated on machinery (Chee and Lee, 1979; Nihon bōeki shinkōkai, 1987a, pp. 135–36.

The current wave of investments in the machine industries was drawn into Malaysia, as it was into Thailand, by cheap labour, although a state-led building boom was an additional attraction for the many construction companies that entered in this period. While falling commodity prices and Malaysia's worst ever recession put an end to the building boom, the merits of cheap labour increased with the higher yen. Making and assembling parts for the car and electronics industries were thus the typical targets of the current rush into Malaysia. But as late as the end of fiscal 1986 most of the Japanese money was still in resource extraction or processing, as revealed by

Table 6.8 Total cases and value of Japanese DFI in Malaysia, by industry

	To end of fiscal 1984 $ million	Cases	To end of fiscal 1986 $ million	Cases
Resource extraction	149	86	178	88
Agriculture/forestry/fisheries	29	54	30	55
Mining	120	32	148	33
Manufacturing	759	466	856	544
Basic materials	529	248	565	275
Food	22	32	33	43
Textiles	137	47	137	49
Wood/Pulp	52	71	52	72
Chemicals	180	46	189	54
Metals	138	52	154	57
Machinery	194	134	237	173
General	11	20	15	25
Electrical	94	91	127	116
Transport	89	23	95	32
Other manufacturing	37	84	55	96
Construction	19	82	25	95
Other (mostly unproductive)	111	209	214	245
TOTAL	1 046	879	1 283	1 009

Source: Ōkurashō, 1985b, 1987b.

Table 6.8. Manufacturing projects in machinery were still relatively small compared to the mining and processing projects associated with the second wave.

The crisis of falling incomes and GNP in 1985 all but shattered the new-found independence of the Malaysian ruling class. September 1986 saw a new set of conditions for DFI permitting 100 per cent ownership for large exporting companies and providing generous fiscal incentives. Although the response was not as swift or on the same scale as in Thailand, there was a dramatic turnaround in 1987 (*Business Times*, 1 October 1986, p. 1; *NKS*, 31 August, 1987, p. 9).

According to MIDA (Malaysian Industrial Development Authority), Japan has been the largest foreign source of paid-up capital in manufacturing since the early 1980s. If the large Dutch petrochemical project in 1986 is ignored and the higher total value (equity plus loans) of Japanese than Singaporean projects is recognised, then Japan's predominance is even more striking, as revealed by Table 6.9. More significant has been the steady fall in the total value of manufacturing investment because of local capital's withdrawal from

Table 6.9 DFI in Malaysian manufacturing by country, paid-up capital in approved projects (M$ million)

	Up to 1985[a]	1984	1985	1986	1987	June 1988
TOTAL INVESTMENT	n/a	3 801.1	5 686.9	5 165.0	3 933.0	8 330.0[b]
Paid-Up	n/a	1 213.4	1 823.7	1 879.8	1 529.3	1 285.7
Malaysian	n/a	938.0	992.8	707.3	778.6	532.6
Foreign	n/a	275.4	324.9	524.8	750.7	753.1
Japan	774.6 (2 106.3)	67.3	81.8	58.1	230.8	231.9
Singapore	1 263.7 (1 461.8)	38.5	47.2	90.0	135.4	n/a
UK	720.9 (2 195.9)	9.3	10.7	19.1	24.6	n/a
US	287.6 (479.3)	21.3	36.8	17.1	61.3	n/a
Holland	148.2 (152.7)	5.0	0.0	180.3	n/a	n/a
Hong Kong	261.1 (378.5)	9.5	18.4	27.5	27.8	n/a
Taiwan	23.1 (54.7)	14.0	14.7	5.0	118.5	n/a
South Korea	3.4 (3.4)	0.0	0.0	1.6	2.0	n/a
TOTAL	4 170.2 (7 666.3)	275.4	324.9	524.5	750.7	753.1

Notes: [a] Foreign paid-up capital (and in brackets the total value of investment) of companies in production by the end of 1985.
[b] January to July.
Source: MIDA; *JS*, November 1988, p. 52; *La International*, 1988, pp. 145, 173; *FEER*, 1 September 1988, pp. 54–5; 24 November 1988, p. 95; *Malaysian Business*, 16 May 1988, p. 14).

the industry. By 1987 about half the paid-up capital in approved projects was foreign, and in the first half of 1988 this soared to 65 per cent. The total value of manufacturing investments (M$8.3 billion) were as a result more than double the total for 1987.

Although a bit later than in Thailand, foreign capital mainly from Japan has also revived accumulation in Malaysia, with real economic growth reaching nearly 8 per cent in 1988. The 1989 budget cut corporation tax by a further 5 per cent and slapped a 5 per cent sales tax on food, because 'the Malaysian Government has decided to compete head on with Thailand and Singapore for the foreign-investment dollar' (*FEER*, 3 November 1988, p. 90). The *Japan Economic Journal* commented that 'investment in Malaysia is growing at a faster rate [than in Thailand], indicating that Japan is once again shifting emphasis to Malaysia' (1 October 1988, p. 21).

Joint Venture Partners

Since the main form in which Japanese capital allies with the Malaysian ruling class is through the state's NEP and associated institutions (PNB, PERNAS and HICOM, the Heavy Industries Corporation of Malaysia), its closest ties are with the *bumiputra*-bureaucratic capital rather than with private Chinese capital. Prestige state projects, such as in the heavy and resource-related industries, are thus the main ones in which this type of alliance is found, although the difficulties many of the projects have faced has strained it. I only mention a few examples.

An early case was Malayawata Steel, which although it began as a private undertaking led by Yawata Steel (which became Nippon Steel) in 1961, had by 1967 become the first industrial project in which the government had a stake. Later on PERNAS Engineering acquired a controlling 46 per cent of shares. The largest single Japanese project in the country is Malaysia LNG, the M$600 million joint venture between Mitsubishi Corporation, Shell and PETRONAS (Petroliam National Berhad, the state's petroleum company) of the late 1970s in Sarawak. The same three partners are currently planning the world's first plant to produce liquid fuel directly from natural gas, also in Sarawak, from around 1992. Another current energy project is the contract between Nippon Oil and PETRONAS for joint oil exploration off Sarawak beginning in mid-1988. The M$150 million Perusahaan Otomobil Nasional is Mitsubishi's 1983 venture with HICOM to make the national car, Proton Saga. Among the component makers associated with the latter is Nippondenso's venture also with HICOM, which is also the Malaysian partner of a number of motor cycle projects, with Honda, Yamaha and Suzuki (Chee and Lee, (1979) pp. 46 ff.; Jetro, 1982; Shūkan tōyō keizai, 1988; *JEJ*, 28 November 1987, p. 28; 20 February 1988, p. 19).

Proton Saga has faced a mountain of problems. The recession coincided with the vehicle's first appearance, and each car is now subsidised to the tune of M$15 000 mainly because the 100 000 capacity plant is only turning out 40 000 cars. A plan to ship 40 000 to the US in late 1988 was delayed by at least a year, leaving only sluggish sales to Japan's traditional dumping grounds: Bangladesh, Malta, Brunei, Sri Lanka, Papua New Guinea, Jamaica and New Zealand. There had once been rumours that Mitsubishi would not be updating the design of the car, and all the company seemed good for was to become a cheap source of components, particularly body panels, for export to Mitsubishi plants elsewhere in Asia. Losses in 1987 were M$68 million before extraordinaries and a ¥12 billion loan from its Mitsubishi shareholders had to be refinanced.

By mid-1988 even Finance Minister Daim Zainuddin described the project as a failure, upon which its executive director was replaced by Iwabuchi Kenji, former managing director of Mitsubishi Motors (MMC), and Fujioka Kyo, another MMC manager, was made head of a new corporate planning division. Now that Malaysia's most prestigious project of the 1980s is firmly under Japanese managerial control, the car will be distributed through Mitsubishi's network. With a 46.8 per cent share in 1986 of a passenger car market which had slumped from 86 772 in 1984 to 47 028, MMC is expected to attempt driving its Japanese competitors further out of the running. If one includes commercial vehicles, Toyota's 21.8 per cent share of the 126 000 vehicles sold in 1984 fell to 11.2 per cent of the 56 500 sold in 1987, while Nissan's share crashed from 26.7 per cent to 13.6 per cent. Toyota and Mazda even suspended production in November 1986. The crisis of overcapacity is likely to continue until Mitsubishi decides to go ahead with large-scale exports.

A similar tale of failure could be told of Perwaja Trengganu, a large venture between a Nippon Steel consortium and HICOM formed in 1982 to make billets and briquetted iron. The plant was shut down soon after it opened in February 1985 for failing to produce the output specified in the contract, and the M$485 million it received from Nippon Steel in compensation helped it cope with a M$118 million loss in 1987. To bail this prestige project out, a

Malaysian Chinese from UMW (United Motor Works, which assembles Toyotas) Holdings was selected to replace the Malay general manager in mid-1988 (*JJTI*, May 1986, p. 20; *La International*, 1988, pp. 102–3; *FEER*, 23 April 1987, pp. 73–7; 7 July 1988, p. 97; 1 September 1988, pp. 52–6; *JEJ*, 9 May 1987, p. 11; 21 May 1988, p. 7; *NKS*, 7 October 1988, p. 11; Shūkan tōyō keizai, 1987; Harian Perintis, 1986, pp. 87–9 74).

Because of a phenomenon also found in Indonesia whereby Chinese interests often have Malay front persons in order to receive advantages from the state, it is harder to be certain of the degree to which private capital which appears to be *bumiputra* is genuinely so. Even in the case of Sime Darby, the ex-British conglomerate which amassed its wealth in rubber and palm oil plantations but which the NEP managed to convert into a mainly indigenous empire, this is not unproblematic. The company's colonial past reveals strong ties with Chinese interests, many of which it still has. So the threat to Malay control of Sime Darby, the country's top private firm which is second only to the state's PETRONAS, comes not simply from its British colonial past, but also the Chinese bourgeoisie. With over 150 companies under its umbrella, including major ones in Singapore, Hong Kong, Thailand, Britain and the Philippines, as well as an obsession to penetrate China, the conglomerate will never really be fully under Malay control. Nevertheless, Japanese capital does have a few links with it in Malaysia. Kubota Agricultural Machinery manufactures engines, Sime Diamond Leasing is a joint venture with Mitsubishi Bank and Diamond Lease, and Sime Inax is the first overseas venture of Japan's satellite porcelain maker, although Inax has licencing agreements in South Korea, Taiwan and Indonesia. The only genuine private *bumiputra* business group, Promet, recently went into liquidation (Inoue, 1987, pp. 280–5; Shūkan tōyō keizai, 1988; *LA International*, 1988, pp. 203–4).

Among the Chinese business groups, the largest and most representative is Kuok, which comprises 23 major companies in Kuala Lumpur alone but well over one hundred worldwide. Its main activities are in finance and services in Malaysia, Singapore and Hong Kong, but it also has influence in Thailand, Indonesia, the Philippines, Fiji, Australia and China.

The rise of the Kuok empire began in 1949 with the establishment of the trading company, Kuok Brothers, which dealt mainly in rice and sugar. In the 1950s the leading light of the Kuok family, Robert, formed a joint venture with Mitsui & Co. and Nisshin Sugar Manufacturing. Thus began an intimate relationship with Mitsui as well as the very profitable development of Malayan Sugar Manufacturing, which by the 1960s had given Robert Kuok the title of 'Sugar King'. Today he controls 80 per cent of the Malaysian market and 10 per cent of the world market. From its base in sugar, the Kuok group expanded into manufacturing (wheat, flour, synthetic woods, cement and chemicals), shipping, finance, real estate and hotels. Along the way it accumulated an impressive list of joint ventures with Mitsui (such as Perlis Plantations, Malayan Adhesives and Chemical and Bulk Chemical Terminal); with other Japanese giants like Sumitomo Heavy Industry (Malaysia Shipyard and Engineering), Tosco (Century Chemical Works, Rasa Sayang Hotel and Hong Kong's Shangri-la Hotel); as well as with other giant Malaysian companies like Malayawata Steel, Sime Darby and Malaysian International Shipping (Inoue, 1987, pp. 199–205; Shūkan tōyō keizai, 1988; *FEER*, 30 October 1986, pp. 54–64).

Other leading Chinese groups are also well linked to Japanese capital, although they also have ties with other foreign as well as with *bumiputra* interests. An important example is the Kwek family's Hong Leong group, whose main base is in Singapore but which also has an impressive network of companies in Malaysia and Hong Kong. Although its specialty is finance, where the main overseas linkages have traditionally been with British rather than Japanese capital, it has entered a number of joint ventures with Japanese manufacturing and trading companies. Examples include Steel Pipe Industry of Malaysia (with C Itoh and Kawasaki Steel) and a few ventures in its main area of growth during the construction boom: with Mitsubishi in construction machinery, with Takasago in tile manufacturing, with Mitsui and Onada Cement in the M$150 million Tasek Cement set up in 1962 and with Marubeni in leasing and selling construction equipment. Hong Leong also has a few ventures with Yamaha, making and selling motor cycles (including engines), as well as a joint venture with Mitsui making paper bags (Inoue, 1987, pp. 206–12; Shūkan tōyō keizai, 1988).

United Motor Works, one of the big-four Chinese groups operating in Malaysia and Singapore, sells and leases construction machinery in a few ventures with Marubeni and assembles Toyota vehicles through Sejat Motors. The latter is also Kayaba's partner in its components factory. UMW's main competition for sixth position among Malaysia's corporations, Tan Chong Motor Holdings, is Nissan's chosen partner in its enormous 3300 worker factory. Of the other Japanese motor vehicle majors, Honda is well linked to Chinese capital in a number of joint ventures with Oriental Holding (Shūkan tōyō keizai, 1988).

Electronics

Japan's main presence in Malaysia's electronics industry has been through Matsushita, Sanyo, Sharp, Toshiba, NEC, Mitsumi, Hitachi and Fujitsu. Many of them have long enjoyed the flexibility associated with 100 per cent Japanese ownership, located as they are in FTZs in Kuala Lumpur and Penang. Fujitsu's factory is wholly owned by its Singapore subsidiary, Toshiba's is wholly owned by the parent in Japan, both Mitsumi's factories are also wholly owned, Hitachi and NEC have only minor local shareholders (although NEC has recently formed two joint ventures with PERNAS), and apart from the 52 per cent Matsushita Electric's shares which were sold to the public, the Matsushita group's massive presence is almost entirely Japanese owned. Both companies which do have local partners, Sharp and Sanyo, are allied to Chinese capital, Sharp to the Roxy group of Hong Kong and Singapore (Shūkan tōyō keizai, 1988; *FEER*, 1 December 1988, p. 66).

The growing number of small and medium firms moving to Malaysia, mainly to make parts for the majors, has not meant the latter are less active. Concentrating heavily on export production, they remain prominent among the many companies which because of higher yen are either shifting to Malaysia or expanding their activities. Already in 1985, some 74 per cent of investment in the Malaysian electronics industry was foreign, 25 per cent from the US and 21.2 per cent from Japan. Japan dominated its first two branches, the US the third:

1. fridges and air conditioners, in which twelve firms with 3367 workers made an output of M$349.5 million in 1986;
2. TVs and radiocassettes, in which 11 144 workers in fifteen firms produced an output of M$792.3 million;
3. semiconductors and IC parts, in which 57 459 workers (down from over 68 000 in 1984 because of the world glut) in 55 firms produced a M$5694.3 million output.

In the first of these, Matsushita has continued to lead the way with its M$140 million investment plan to increase its production of gas equipment, cleaners, dry batteries and air conditioners. The large investment in air conditioners which came onstream in late 1987 has transferred control of production from Japan to Malaysia, which along with Singapore and to a lesser extent Taiwan is the company's production base for export to Japan and the US. The six export factories (plus one sales firm) in Malaysia constitute a veritable 'semi-Matsushita' among the company's 60 overseas production bases, of which 41 per cent are in Southeast Asia. One of the foundations of the group's new (1988) slogan, 'Resolutely carry out our vision in the world' (*shiya o sekai ni kaka ni dōkō*), is to create a global supply network for components, in which its Singapore–Malaysia, setup has a major role. One of Malaysia's key tasks in this is to supply compressors and motors for air conditioners (*JS*, July 1988, pp. 45–51; *Malaysia Industrial Digest*, Vol. 4, 1986, p. 6; *LA International*, 1988, p. 222).

Although most of the Japanese companies are active in more than one branch of the industry, Sharp has concentrated on radiocassettes and TVs in Malaysia, where it has led a field of fourteen Japanese firms since the early 1980s when it started exporting TVs to the US. Even more so than Matsushita, Sharp has made its three production subsidiaries in Malaysia and its supply centre in Singapore its main overseas production base, largely in tie-ups with the Roxy group. In Southeast Asia this base is served by and serves one production venture in each of South Korea, Taiwan, Thailand and the Philippines, as well as a sales outlet in Hong Kong. Sharp is now making nearly half a million colour TVs and as many printer bases for export to Europe and the US. The output of its third factory, opened in December 1986, specifically replaced what had been retrenched in Japan (*JS*, July 1988, pp. 51–3; *Malaysia Industrial Digest*, Vol. 3, 1985, p. 4).

Other firms have also stepped up their TV and audio production. Matsushita Television, a new company which will begin making colour TVs in 1989, is to become one of the company's four bases for TV production worldwide and serve as its Asian supply centre. JVC opened an audio factory in 1988, which it plans to boost to the size of its largest overseas operation (in Singapore), while in 1989 it is also opening its second overseas video production facility (the first was in Europe with Thomson) to make printed boards and other parts for worldwide use. Canon also selected Malaysia for its second Southeast Asian venture (first was in Taiwan), to make video lenses from 1989. NEC, another to make Malaysia the centre of its Asian operation (in semiconductors), has also begun producing colour TVs. Finally in

1988 Sony opened two major factories in Malaysia, because 'We realized we couldn't survive unless we started taking advantage of the lower labour costs in Southeast Asia' (*FEER*, 16 June 1988, p. 120; *Malaysian Digest*, October 1988, p. 9).

Sony's new global calculations led it to change its old policy of locating production facilities near their US and EC markets and to raise Southeast Asia's share of off-shore production from almost nothing before the rise of the yen to at least 50 per cent. Complementing the new design centre in Singapore and the magnetic products factory in Thailand, Sony TV Video in Kuala Lumpur and Sony Electronics in Penang will make colour TVs, CD players, radiocassettes and other stereo equipment, all for export. Other reasons for selecting Malaysia were the new equity guidelines allowing 100 per cent foreign ownership for exporting companies (*NKS*, 11 November 1987, p. 9; *The Star*, Business Section, 25 March 1987, p. 1; *JEJ*, 19 September 1987, p. 11; 21 November 1987, p. 22; 11 June 1988, p. 17; 17 September 1988, p. 30; 5 November 1988, p. 17; 24 December 1988, p. 36; 31 December and 7 January 1989, p. 28; *FEER*, 16 June 1988, pp. 120–1; *Malaysia Industrial Digest*, July–September 1988).

The largest branch of the electrical industry in Malaysia is semiconductors, which became the top export item in 1986, even exceeding crude oil, and made Malaysia the world's third largest producer behind Japan and the US (whose companies have won Malaysia this honour). Plants in the FTZs of Penang and Kuala Lumpur already form a version of Silicon Valley, but with a difference. Of the two major production processes, only assembly and testing has been significantly transferred to Malaysia. Until recently, the more technically advanced wafer fabrication process had remained entirely in the home countries of the investing companies. But while America's National Semiconductor recently opened in Penang the first wafer fabrication plant in Southeast Asia outside Singapore and Intel is about to open the second, Japanese capital has showed no willingness to transfer the higher technology.

Although not yet on the scale of the sixteen US companies in the field, the five Japanese ones have made very rapid advances since the rise of the yen. Partly because of the world wide chip shortage following the cutbacks in Japan to ease friction with the US in 1987, the industry is currently enjoying a boom. NEC has four factories in Malaysia, its production base in Asia (plus one each in Taiwan, Thailand and Singapore). Specifically to reduce conflict with the US, both Hitachi and Toshiba planned large investments in 1987 to assemble 256KDRAM chips. Hitachi began 1MDRAMs in 1988 and planned to have these comprise over 70 per cent of its total overseas production by 1989. Toshiba has been massively boosting its transistor and IC output to meet the skyrocketing demand from Japanese companies in Southeast Asia, where it sells 85 per cent of its output. Finally, Fujitsu Microelectronics which had only just opened a new plant to make keyboards and relays, opened another in January 1989 to start making semiconductors (*NKS*, 16 October 1987, p. 9; *JEJ*, 19 September 1987, p. 14; 19 March 1988, p. 21; 30 April 1988, p. 21; 4 June 1988, p. 22; 17 September 1988, p. 30; *FEER*, 26 November 1987, pp. 69–71; 25 August 1988, pp. 72–3; *JS*, November 1987, pp. 75–7; July 1988, pp. 60–3).

Although Japanese capital's main interest in Malaysia following the rise of the yen has been in electronics, there have been new investments elsewhere. Examples in 1988 alone include Nippon Pigment's plant to make synthetic resin, Kawasaki's resumption of motorcycle production after a two-year hiatus, Seiko's decision to make watch parts in Johore instead of Thailand (due to tightened regulations on industrial waste), Minolta's move into Malaysia to make parts and 15 per cent of its cameras, Fuji Oil and C Itoh's 100 per cent owned palm-oil refinery for export to Japan and Singapore, and Towa Glove's joint venture producing factory gloves out of natural rubber for export to Japan. In the unproductive sector the main recent interest has been in large-scale retailing by such giants as Jusco, Chujitsuya and Yaohan (*Industria*, July 1987, pp. 44–5; *JEJ*, 12 September 1987, p. 17; 11 June 1988, p. 18; 23 July 1988, p. 20; 24 September 1988, p. 32; 15 October 1988, p. 20; 24 December 1988, p. 36).

It was thus mainly the exports of semiconductors and consumer electronics goods by Japanese and US companies in Malaysia's FTZs which have made the electrical industry Malaysia's top exporter, with 54 per cent of manufacturing exports in 1987. But like the commodity bubble which burst before it, this one is also fragile. The ban on trade unions in the industry, which for the past fifteen years removed organised working-class struggle from the concerns of capitalists, was lifted in late 1988, apparently because of an AFL-CIO petition to have Malaysia removed from the US's generalised system of preferences (GSP) because the ban violates workers' rights (*FEER*, 6 October 1988, p. 80).

Conclusion on Malaysia

The rush into Malaysia in the 1980s added new dimensions to what was still quite a fragile alliance between the two countries' ruling classes in the 1970s. In particular, the rise of the yen which forced Japanese capital abroad in search of ASEAN partners coincided with the collapse of commodity prices, Malaysian capital's traditional source of independence, resulting in the most serious political econ-omic situation since the riots of 1969. After a brief fall-off in DFI because of this crisis, Japanese capital seized the advantage and swamped the country with new projects from 1987.

The turning point that year had an important new feature. Whereas (according to one survey), only 43 out of 316 projects in Malaysia up to the end of 1986 were 100 per cent Japanese owned, twenty out of 34 were in 1987 and all twenty were in the first four months of 1988 (*LA International*, 1988, p. 164). The new investment regulations dovetailed with a new strategy that Japanese capital had been evolving. In the past the main factors determining the locality of DFI had been the whole range of conditions in each country, from production costs to possible markets. But since 1987 Japanese capital has increasingly looked at projects from a global rather than a local perspective, choosing countries on the basis of their relationships to one another. For example, Johore became a favourite because of its proximity to Singapore, and increasingly Malaysia is being selected to make electronic and motor vehicle parts which complement company strategies elsewhere in Asia.

So while joint ventures might have been more suitable in the past, Japanese capital now requires the greater flexibility offered by 100 per cent ownership. Their political dangers, however, are not con-cerning Japanese companies, which see themselves following the examples of the US and European TNCs. They forget that the latter could afford to ignore local conditions when the task of keeping the world safe for capitalism fell on the US military.

Japanese capital's effect on the class struggle in Malaysia has features in common with its effect in Thailand and Singapore. As in Thailand, its technological weight in the new manufacturing indus-tries which are gaining over Malaysia's traditional sectors is under-mining the independence the local ruling class had begun to assert during the years of high oil prices. But unlike Thailand, communal-ism in Malaysia keeps alive the potential of bourgeois nationalism to deflect, onto the Japanese, attacks from the masses which are directed at the ruling alliance as a whole. So long as it can do that, and bourgeois nationalism remains a stronger force than proletarian nationalism, it will be difficult for the growing industrial working class to struggle effectively against that alliance.

In some ways paralleling changes in both Thailand and Singapore, the struggle in Malaysia is shifting from the American and British zones into the Japanese zone. As the industrial focus shifts from raw materials to making and assembling parts for car and electronics companies, as Japanese DFI replaces British and American, so do the sites where the main contradictory forces clash most explosively begin to move from rural to urban centres. British methods of containing revolutionary struggles that were appropriate in the 'emergency' period will also give way to 'peacetime' Japanese methods.

There are many signs within the country that the government's capacity to keep the lid on mass aspirations purely by decree, force and intimidation is reaching its limit. New types of grassroots organisation, less leadership orientated than their predecessors and so less responsive to the old methods, are springing up everywhere, including workplaces and around particular issues in both urban and rural areas. Among the ones associated with the old industrial structure that have hit the international headlines have been the struggle by tribespeople in Sarawak against logging companies and by the residents of numerous villages against the dumping of radioactive waste by Asia Rare Earth, a Mitsubishi joint venture which produces thorium hydroxide as a radioactive byproduct when it extracts trace elements and yttrium from tin trailings (*FEER*, 21 May 1987, p. 49; 28 April 1988, pp. 44–8).

However, as in Thailand, new working class organisations qualified to take on Japanese-style repression will need to develop out of the experiences workers gain in Japanese factories. It is extremely difficult to do this in Malaysia, because the myriad of ranks and divisions among workers which the Japanese are so good at creating, in the context of the communalist culture fostered by the state, tends to intensify racism within the working class. That is the real challenge facing the peoples of Malaysia, particularly workers in the electronics industry whose right to organise has only just been won. The hold that Japanese imperialism eventually gets on their country will thus depend heavily on them.

CONCLUSION ON ASEAN'S NICS SUBSTITUTES

The massive influx of Japanese capital into Thailand and Malaysia, which is both an expression and a consequence of the growing alliances between their respective ruling classes, has considerably revived capital accumulation following the recessions of 1985. In both cases the current boom seems to signal a transition of capital's primary dependence from raw material extraction and processing to low-wage manufacturing. The boom is thus all the more fragile, because it will increasingly involve mobilising within Thailand and Malaysia the very forces which have caused capital to favour them over the NICs: working-class struggle for better wages and conditions at best, for revolutionary change at worst. Perhaps the Japanese government's current negotiations with Malaysia (*JEJ*, 5 November 1988, p. 13) to provide protection to Japanese firms is a good sign of what will be needed in the future. As these forces build within countries like Thailand and Malaysia, there is increasingly nowhere else to go, except to Indonesia and the Philippines.

7 Investment in Indonesia and the Philippines

Although Indonesia and the Philippines are in many ways very different, Japanese capital has increasingly thrown them into the same (sinking) boat. Both were primary targets of Japan's raw material scramble in the 1970s, and Japanese capital's primary interest in both remains in food production and raw materials. In spite of offering the lowest wages in ASEAN, neither Indonesia nor the Philippines has been able to rekindle much interest from Japan following their crises in the mid-1980s, resulting respectively from the slump in oil prices and the growing political-economic crisis that ended in the fall of Marcos. Both countries have thus been excluded from the surge of interest in ASEAN that started in 1987. Instead, Japanese capital has remained cautious, apparently still licking some of the wounds resulting from its excessive zeal in the 1970s and early 1980s, when it led rather than followed the example of the other powers.

INDONESIA

History of Struggle

The towering presence in the Indonesian class struggle today, the military, owes its unique position as much to Indonesia's pre-colonial and colonial as to its neo-colonial past. What distinguishes the role of the military in Indonesia from that in Thailand or even the Philippines is its monopoly of so many functions which are at least partly carried out by other institutions elsewhere. The tendency in Indonesia is for the military simultaneously to be, not simply the 'repressive apparatus' of the state, but also the institutional framework around which the bourgeoisie organises both capital accumulation and the legitimation of its rule.

Each of the three great epochs in Indonesian history has contributed to this result. In the pre-colonial period, from the eighth to the end of the fifteenth centuries, the mode of production approximated most closely to what Marx called 'Asiatic', in which the ownership of land and the extraction of the surplus from the peasantry was in the hands of the state and its administrators. The peasants paid taxes to the state, whose functionaries comprised the ruling class. This contrasts with feudalism, where private ownership of land requires each lord to rule through grants of land to 'private' vassals, who as the direct expropriators of the peasantry constitute the ruling class. Both the Thai monarchy and the Sultans of modern Indonesia and Malaysia were, in the precolonial period, organisers more of Asiatic than feudal relations of production. Their tasks were simultaneously to expropriate the surplus from the peasantry and to enforce and legitimate their regimes.

Colonialism in Indonesia bequeathed a legacy opposite to that in Thailand or Malaya, due to the different strengths of their respective colonial rulers: the Dutch and the British. More technically advanced capital in Britain favoured free trade and private penetration of Malaya and her surrounds, while less advanced Dutch capital could survive the competition only through protection and state monopolies. The culmination of the latter was the notorious 'Culture' system (1830–70), the 'most successful Dutch stage of "Asiatic" exploitation whose impression still lingers in Java' (Gordon, 1979, p. 132), in which the colonial administration used forced labour to produce mainly sugar for its monopoly export trade. While there was a transition afterwards to a modern plantation system, the already powerful Asiatic foundation in Indonesia had been greatly reinforced (Gordon, 1979; Utrecht and Caldwell, 1979).

Although the Indonesian nationalism which eventually won independence from the Dutch was spearheaded by a broad popular movement and political party centering on the person of Sukarno, a combination of historical legacies and contingencies soon created a modern, bourgeois, quasi-Asiatic state. When the grassroots anti-colonial guerilla fighters returned to their land after winning independence, the professional soldiers who remained in the forces received two powerful nudges in this direction. First, for some time after independence the Dutch still tried to preserve their interests by encouraging a division of the country, and the military was thrust to the fore to defend the fledgling nation. Second, following Sukarno's nationalisation of Dutch properties in 1957, the only institution in the wings ready to take over their administration was the military bureaucracy.

From then until 1965, Sukarno tried through a careful balancing act to merge into a coherent government three antagonistic social forces: the increasingly bourgeois military bureaucracy, the multi-class but still fairly progressive nationalist party (PNI) and the peasant-based Communist Party of Indonesia (PKI). But with backward productive forces and continued *de facto* dependence on the imperialist powers, it was not possible to combine into a single national development policy the antagonistic solutions of socialism and crony capitalism. By the time the nationalists and communists realised the degree to which the military had recaptured the ground lost by the Dutch, it was too late, and hundreds of thousands of communists and their supporters were massacred in the Suharto-led military takeover of 1966.

The disappearance of the PNI along with the PKI has left Suharto's GOLKAR party as the sole legitimate political broker in the country. But GOLKAR is not really a political party, since it exists simply as the electoral machine of the generals whenever they need to extract popular approval for one reason or another. And so today the military has become a multi-purpose and all-pervasive institution comparable to the Asiatic state: political broker and legitimator of bourgeois rule, owner of the nation's resources (particularly oil) and organiser of bourgeois national projects, and war machine against its own people and those of its neighbours.

Although the Japanese were a positive influence on Indonesian nationalism at the outset of the Pacific War, their subsequent actions dissipated whatever goodwill they might have won, and they faced massive demands for reparations. After they whittled away the original claim to some $223 million, $400 million in aid and a cancellation of trade debt, diplomatic relations were eventually restored in 1957. However, it was only after the downfall of Sukarno, who had nationalised all foreign property, and the extermination of the communist movement that the Japanese saw opportunities for themselves, anticipating that one day Indonesia would be the most important part of the region to them.

Following the political failure of a non-capitalist solution to Indonesia's underdevelopment, the new Suharto regime resolved to tackle the crisis within the constraints of capitalism. Alliance with US imperialism was its sole expedient, and massive injections of capital flooded in from the US, the World Bank and the IMF, together with a clear set of instructions on how to operate a capitalist outfit as well as vast amounts of American military aid. Liberal foreign investment laws were passed, and from 1968 Japanese capital began to enter the country.

The free-market policy and near subservience to World Bank and

Table 7.1   Total approved non-oil/gas capital investments in Indonesia, by industry and approving law, December 1973

	Foreign $ million	%	Domestic $ million	%
Forestry	495.5	58	356.8	42
Agriculture and Fisheries	113.0	33	232.5	67
Mining	860.5	95	46.2	5
Manufacturing	1 045.1	38	1 740.9	62
of which, textiles	436.9	37	749.0	63
Tourism, hotels, real estate	195.9	50	200.0	50
Other	118.3	37	207.0	63
Total approved	2 823.3	49	2 978.5	51
(Total realised)	1 131.2	56	876.0	44

Source: Robison, 1986, p. 142.

IMF orthodoxy, which persisted until 1974, was attenuated only by the great emphasis on import substitution in the First Five Year Plan (1969–74). But as in Thailand, ISI did not deter Japanese investors in Indonesia, since their strategy was to capture the largest possible market shares in the industries they favoured. Besides, they could enjoy the advantages the Plan provided in such priority sectors as fertilisers, chemicals, cement (all relating to agriculture) and textiles (basic needs) (Robson, 1986).

There were (and still are) three categories of investment in Indonesia: that which came under the Foreign Capital Investment Law No. 1 of 1967 (almost entirely foreign investment); that which came under the Domestic Capital Investment Law of 1968 (almost entirely domestic investment); and investment in oil and gas (overwhelmingly foreign and normally about twice the other two combined). Table 7.1, which lists the total amounts of approved non-oil/gas investment by industry and by the law under which it was approved up to December 1973, shows the enormous weight foreign capital had achieved throughout the economy.

The Japanese Rush In

If the rush into Thailand and Malaysia by Japanese companies was a phenomenon of the late 1980s, a consequence of the *endaka fukyō* and the quest for cheap labour, then the corresponding onslaught on Indonesia in the early 1970s was a result of rising Japanese wages and the mounting resource crisis which reached its climax in 1973. Of 286 projects undertaken by the end of 1986, 156 occurred in 1970–74 and a further 54 in 1975–80. Table 7.2 shows their distribution by date of approval and by industry. Three points in particular need to be emphasised. First, in the period 1975–80, the $870 million initially invested in 1975 in the Asahan aluminium project (the value of which has since almost trebled) towers over all else. Second, a full $905.6 million (88.2 per cent) of the $1027.3 million invested in machinery in 1981–86 occurred in 1982–83 (a point returned to later). Finally, the table excludes investments in the financial and oil/gas (mining) sectors, which, according to figures from the Japanese Ministry of Finance (MOF) were $70 million and $5261 million respectively by the end of March 1986.

Sukarno's nationalist regime had delayed the influx into Indonesia of the textile investments which rising Japanese wages had sent into other parts of Asia in the 1960s. So when the forces which culminated in the oil crisis began to raise a new tide of DFI in the 1970s, the two currents combined into a tidal wave of unequalled proportions. Immediately after the new Foreign Investment Law was passed, the two companies that received licences in 1967 were in fisheries. Six of the nine licenced the next year were also in resource exploitation (including Ajinomoto, which became a word in the local language), as were seven of the seventeen licenced in 1969. When the Suharto government revised the investment laws in 1970 to establish twelve priority categories, however, the lure of Indonesian wages attracted a flood of manufacturing investments, including textiles. That year saw 27 companies licenced (22 in manufacturing), while the next year there were another 27, in 1972 there were 22 and in 1973 the peak of 45 was reached (*Ampo*, 1980, pp. 10, 17; Jetro Jakarta, 1987).

By 1974 only South Korea was still preferred to Indonesia by Japanese textile companies, with Thailand easily the third choice, although in synthetic fibre production Indonesia led the field by a long way. Textile investments in Indonesia as elsewhere in Asia apart from South Korea were made by large listed textile companies and *sōgō shōsha*, typically in concert: 50 per cent of the latter's DFI in the industry was in Indonesia, while two *shōsha* (Mitsui and C Itoh) and two textile companies (Toray and Teijin) contributed close to 50 per cent of the Indonesian total (Yoshihara, 1978, pp. 110, 123).

Today textiles are Indonesia's top manufacturing industry, accounting in 1987 for 10.3 per cent of non-oil exports (themselves just under half the total) and surging again by 53 per cent in the first five

Table 7.2 Japanese non-financial and non-oil/gas DFI in Indonesia, by date of approval and industry

| | Initial Investments | | | | | | | | Grand[a] Total | |
| | To 1969 | | 1970–74 | | 1975–80 | | 1981–86 | | | |
	Cases	$ million	Cases	$ million	Cases	$ million	Cases	$ million	Cases	$ million
Agriculture	2	4.8	4	3.9	4	12.4	4	5.9	6	20.0
Forestry	5	8.0	8	39.7	3	12.2	–	–	4	33.0
Fisheries	5	7.2	10	26.0	2	2.2	2	3.4	16	61.4
Mining	1	75.9	–	–	–	–	–	–	–	–
Manufacturing	11	24.7	106	800.9	35	1 035.0	39	1 169.9	159	4 917.4
Food	2	2.2	6	7.7	1	6.0	–	–	7	50.0
Textiles	3	15.5	28	355.2	–	–	–	–	24	663.0
Wood/paper	–	–	10	17.0	1	6.5	2	9.9	12	57.9
Chemicals	2	0.8	20	210.1	12	52.6	7	243.3	36	546.6
Not-metallic mining	–	–	3	60.1	3	12.8	–	–	5	267.7
Basic metals	–	–	8	89.5	2	879.0	3	38.3	11	1 805.2
Machinery	4	6.2	28	59.5	16	69.1	25	1 027.3	62	1 509.8
Other manufacturing	–	–	3	4.5	–	–	–	–	2	17.2
Construction	–	–	14	14.1	5	3.0	1	1.0	1	22.1
Other	2	14.0	14	80.6	4	35.4	2	51.5	17	196.9
TOTAL JAPAN[b]	27	134.6	156	965.2	54	1 088.2	49	1 426.7	221	5 251.4
TOTAL FOREIGN	176	1 865.0	599	3 073.5	200	2 543.8	250	6 557.1	905	15 808.8

Notes: [a]includes changes, particularly withdrawals, since projects were approved.
[b]includes small participations from third countries.

Source: Figures from BKPM (Badan Koordinasi Penanaman Modal), as cited in Jetro Jakarta, 1987; Himpunan Bulletin, Sept.–Oct 1987, pp. 22–3.

months of 1988 (over the same period the year before). Electrical appliances, the next most important manufactured export, contributed a mere 0.7 per cent of the non-oil total, compared to almost 60 per cent for agricultural products, 8.2 per cent for minerals and 1 per cent for fertiliser. In summer 1987 monthly wages for Indonesia's spinning workers were a paltry $50–70, while in Thailand they were $140 and in Malaysia $240. Small wonder that by March 1987 the value of Japanese textile investments in Indonesia was 2.7 times that in Thailand, the second most favoured location. Of the 24 large joint ventures in Indonesia which employed over 800 workers in 1987, half were in textiles and one more made zippers. All except two of the 24 had commenced operations by 1976, but both of these had been approved before then (*FEER*, 8 September 1988, pp. 132–4; 6 October 1988, p. 81; *KTG*, No. 72, 1988, p. 1; Ōkurashō, 1987b, pp. 54, 56; Skūkan tōyō keizai, 1988; Jetro, 1982).

Japanese capitalists had worked closely behind the scenes with leading generals and proved themselves equal to the graft and corruption demanded by the Indonesian bureaucracy. It was therefore natural that they would be the targets for the periodic outburst of protest against foreign capital and corruption, as occurred with considerable rioting in 1974. The burning down of Toyota's joint venture company was the most conspicuous of the many signs that the Japanese 'rush' into Indonesia had revived a popular nationalism which would remain a permanent problem for Japanese capitalists.

What Oil Crisis?

The political events of 1974, together with the oil shock which overnight skyrocketed the Indonesian state's finances at every level into unheard of surpluses, heralded a considerable shift in the balance of power in favour of the Indonesian ruling class. Foreign capital was given strict limits within which to work, but these were waived when the scale and technical requirements were too great for local capital to do the job. There were specific requirements to achieve 51 per cent Indonesian ownership within ten years, to have all investments take the form of joint ventures, to favour *pribumi* (indigenous Indonesians) and to exclude foreign capital from sectors where domestic capital might take over. Priority was given to major resource processing projects, but in ways which established forward and backward linkages to promote even development.

All this was feasible only because oil revenues provided an

unprecedented independence from foreign capital. Around 60 per cent of government revenue and 70 per cent of export earnings in this period came from oil. The result was almost a decade of rapid accumulation centering on a number of domestic conglomerates under the protection of the state, such as Liem (one of the wealthiest empires in the world), Astra, Rodamas, Bakrie, Mertju Buana and Berkat. Industry (manufacturing, mining and construction) grew at a rate of 12.6 per cent in 1972–80 and realised domestic investment exceeded realised foreign investment, reversing the trend of the previous period.

In spite of the cooler climate towards foreign investment, a regular flow of joint ventures consolidated the alliance between the Japanese and Indonesian ruling classes. The former's restructuring out of the basic materials industries following the oil crisis preserved its interest in Indonesian resources, while the latter needed the technology and financial strength of Japanese capital in the heavy and chemical industries it was building. The liberal oil revenues, however, enabled the Indonesian side to assert its own interests more forcefully, so the terms of the alliance moved in its favour.

Throughout this period, Japanese capital was involved at various levels, principally in joint ventures in resource development, chemicals, construction and machinery (particularly car assembly), but also in loans for major projects in petrochemicals and natural gas which had been recently discovered. Pertamina, the increasingly corrupt state-owned (military-controlled) oil monopoly, borrowed heavily from public and private sources in Japan, partly so that the new natural gas liquefaction plants would remain under Indonesian ownership. By 1976 Japan's energy related loans were twice her other foreign investments, and it was admitted that Pertamina's overseas debts topped $10 billion.

Japanese capital also moved more prominently into high-tech contracts within the framework of other major government projects many of which were financed by official 'aid' from Japan. The most outstanding example was the Asahan aluminium smelter, for which borrowing from Japan comprised 79 per cent of the total investment reducing the Indonesian government's 25 per cent of capital to a mere 5 per cent of the investment. Other projects included a number of iron and steel ventures between Pertamina and Japanese interests (*Ampo*, 1980; Robinson, 1985).

Today Indonesia is the world's largest producer of liquid natural gas and the source of 52 per cent of Japan's LNG imports. The

Table 7.3   Japanese DFI in Indonesian oil and natural gas, 1975–86
($ million)

	1975–76	1977–78	1979–80	1981	1982–83	1984	1985	1986	1975–86
Oil and Gas	1 021	491	263	2 067	400	254	298	176	4 970
Oil	374	222	251	230	400	254	298	176	2 205
LNG	647	269	12	1 837	0	0	0	0	2 765
Non-oil/gas	499	544	416	367	384	120	110	74	2 514
TOTAL	1 520	1 035	679	2 434	784	374	408	250	7 484

Source: *Exim Review*, March 1988, p. 95: Ōkurashō, 1987b, pp. 26–7; Watanabe, 1986, p. 208.

Japanese stake in the industry is also considerable, mainly in the form of loans but also in joint ventures which import and transport the gas, such as ones involving Nissho Iwai (*NKS*, 3 December 1987, p. 8). In the 1980s oil and LNG also absorbed the bulk of Japanese investment in Indonesia, as shown by Table 7.3.

Links with Local Capital

Each of the major Indonesian conglomerates which rose to prominence in the 1970s developed on the basis of tie-ups with foreign capital, mainly Japanese, although not to the same extent as in Thailand. In some cases state patronage was more important in a group's early development than were connections with foreign capital. The most notorious of these latter is the Liem group, whose influence not only traverses the entire Indonesian economy, but extends worldwide. At least 200 companies are bound to it by a variety of complex ties.

There are three main tentacles to the Liem power network: the Kencana group, which is directly controlled by the Liem family; the Bank of Central Asia (BCA) group, which cooperates with the Suharto family; and the Lippon group, which is controlled by Liem's right-hand man, Mochtar Riady. The Liem empire also has close connections with the up-and-coming Bimantara group, founded by one of Suharto's sons and now said to be among the country's top five. Deep and complex connections between Liem, the President's family and leading members of the Chinese community are forged by interlocking directorships and mutual stockholdings in the companies of the different sub-groups. For example, the president and holder of 10 per cent of the shares in Liem's Bogasali, the nationwide giant which monopolises flour manufacturing, is Suharto's younger cousin. Moreover, according to Bogasali's articles of incorporation, 5 per cent of profits go to a foundation set up for the wives of the President and the generals.

The empire of Liem Sioe Liong (alias Soedono Salim) really developed only after Suharto came to power and gave him lucrative government concessions. In 1968, Liem was given the monopoly right to the highly prized clove trade, while the next year he received the monopoly right to manufacture flour. Still in the 1960s, he entered the textile business by obtaining bulk supplies of cloth from the military and finding subcontractors to do the work. In 1975 he established a cement factory, which grew rapidly in the development boom of the decade to make the Indocement group the supplier of over half the country's cement. Towards the end of the decade, Liem branched into real estate and, in cooperation with Marubeni, developed land for upper class housing.

Liem's closest ties with the Japanese have been in motor car assembly, which he started in the mid-1970s with Volvo and to which he later added Suzuki, Hino, Mazda and Ford as well as diesel engines. In 1983 he acquired a majority share in Suzuki's motor cycle assembly plant, and the three Japanese companies remain closely linked to Liem group members in the auto industry: National Motor, Unicor Prima, Indo Mobil Utama and Indohero. In 1985 the Liem-linked Bimantara group set up a joint venture with Daikin, in the Japanese clutch maker's first Asian project.

Overseas, the Liem empire has long had close ties with the top conglomerates of Taiwan, Hongkong, Singapore and Thailand (in particular the Sophonpanich family). Although it has achieved an independence from foreign capital which is rare in Southeast Asia, it does not have the technical-industrial base that is vital to real independence. Cement and flour have been its central productive activities, but both rely heavily on state concessions and government projects. Liem's own foreign investments have been in commerce and finance rather than in manufacturing. In fields requiring a technical-industrial base, such as motor vehicles, he has had to work closely with foreign capital (Inoue, 1987, pp. 168–76; *FEER*, 7 April 1983, pp. 44–56; 24 November 1988, pp. 80–2; 2 February 1989, pp. 52–3).

A similar conclusion applies to Astra, the second largest group in Indonesia. Although its manufacturing in high-tech industries is much more important than in the Liem group, so too is its dependence on foreign capital and technology, overwhelmingly Japanese. Having once experienced the bankruptcy of a joint venture with Pertamina, the Astra group has tried to remain independent of the state and has looked for allies elsewhere. It was not accidental that Astra Motor (Toyota) and Japanese cars were targeted in the riots of 1974 sparked off by Prime Minister Tanaka's visit.

The group's core company, Astra (later Astra International) was founded in 1957 by William Soeryadjaya (Chinese name Tjia Kian Lion), whose first business was in selling soft drinks and exporting agricultural products. But in 1962 he reconstituted GM's previously nationalised factory and established a car assembly company, Gaya Motor, hoping to assemble GM cars. When this did not work out, he looked east and began a very profitable series of joint ventures with Toyota (three), Daihatsu (two) and Honda (two). Today, car, truck and heavy equipments sales account for three-quarters of Astra's revenue.

Following the ban in 1974 on fully assembled imported cars and on the entry of foreign capital into car assembly, Japanese capital had to find local partners to assemble the parts it exported from Japan together with the ones it made locally. The result was a stream of investments in motor vehicle components, comprising much of the wave of DFI into the machinery industry in 1982–83 noted in Table 7.2.

Encouraged by the protection it received in assembly, the Astra group expanded into motor vehicle components in cooperation with Toyota affiliates Nippondenso, Kayaba and Japan Storage Battery. Recent moves towards its goal of a national car include projects to make engines with Toyota and Daihatsu, which claim 45 per cent of total car sales in the country. Some of the Toyota engines, which are to be made in a $75 million plant currently under construction, will be exported to an affiliate in Taiwan, the company's first transfer of engines between two overseas subsidiaries and a shift in policy from its 'domestic-oriented stance to active global operations' (*JEJ*, 21 November 1987, p. 22). Toyota's Kijang van, which was designed for Indonesian conditions, will become an almost wholly Indonesian-made product, soon to be exported throughout Southeast Asia and China (*NKS*, 10 November 1987, p. 8).

The collapse of oil prices, which slashed domestic demand by more than a half from its peak in 1983, badly affected Astra's ISI-related fortunes. The rise of the yen had a similar effect, because it lifted the costs of imported parts. The group is thus now poised to make a major shift into export production, which suits Japanese capital's quest for new low-cost production sites for motor vehicle parts, although not always. For example, Federal Motor, which assembles Honda motorcycles and which is Honda's partner in a number of joint ventures making parts (including engines), has been exporting motorcycles to China, thus competing with Honda's own Chinese-assembled vehicles.

Of the seven core companies in Astra's total of 200 (180 domestic), six are closely linked to Japanese capital: Astra Graphia (licenced Fuji Xerox dealer), Astra Motor Sales (Toyota dealer), Federal Motor (Honda motor cycle assembly, parts and sales), Daihatsu Indonesia (Daihatsu car and parts maker), United Tractor (Komatsu dealer and partner in truck assembly), and Multi Astra (Toyota assembly). The seventh, Midas Oil, is an offshoot of the US giant, Caltex. Other major joint ventures with Japanese interests include PT Kutai Timber Indonesia, which was set up in 1970 with Sumitomo Forestry (Inoue, 1987, pp. 177–84: *FEER*, 17 November 1988, pp. 100–2; Shūkan tōyō keizai, 1988; *NKS*, 4 January 1988, p. 7).

A *zaibatsu* worthy of the Japanese term with an even greater dependence on Japanese capital is the Rodamas (literally 'gold exporter') group, founded and still personally managed by Tan Siong Kie (Indonesian name Hanafi), the sixth wealthiest person in the country (behind three members of the Liem family). Tan made his fortune mainly in PT Asahimas Flat Glass, a joint venture with Asahi Glass set up in 1973, and its offshoot in 1976, PT Asahimas Jaya Safety Glass (for cars), both of whose success derived from a combination of state concessions and the power of foreign capital. Until the government liberalised imports in October 1986 and removed restrictions on competition in 1987, Asahimas controlled the entire Indonesian market, but by mid-1988 its share had fallen to 55 per cent. The company has thus started exports to South Korea and plans to extend these elsewhere.

Today the Rodamas group comprises 29 companies, mainly in manufacturing but also in finance, insurance and real estate. The most important of these, PT Asahimas Subentra Chemical, was given formal approval by the BKPM (Board of Investment) in 1985 and will commence production of plastics (PVC, EDC, VCM) in 1988. Capitalised at $190 million with Asahi Glass providing 70 per cent and Rodamas and Subentra 15 per cent each, the project represents the largest investment from Japan for eight years. Other core companies in the group include Summitmas Property, a joint venture with

Sumitomo & Co., and PT Salompas Indonesia, one with Hisamitsu Pharmaceuticals.

Rodamas also has links with Hong Kong and Taiwanese capital (actually mainly British and American), for example, the joint venture with Liverpool Industrial, PT DINO Indonesia Industrial, which produces detergent in fierce competition with Unilever's Rinso. Recently Rodamas has been trying to strengthen its position in the industry by cooperating with Japan's Kao. More so than any other *zaibatsu* in Indonesia, the Rodamas group owes its origin and continued strength mainly to Tan's tie-ups with Japanese capital (Inoue, 1987, pp. 184–91; Shūkan tōyō keizai, 1988; *JEJ*, 15 October 1988, p. 7).

With the partial exception of the Liem group, which has depended on both state concessions and foreign capital, *pribumi* groups have developed more through the former dependence and *cukong* (Chinese) ones more through the latter. Bakrie, the largest of the indigenous groups but still small compared to the Chinese ones, is a good example. Out of the seventeen companies in the group, not one has Japanese participation, although the core manufacturing activities in steel pipes have been in cooperation with foreign capital, lately from Taiwan and Hong Kong. The group's most recent venture is 39 per cent ownership in PT Seamless Pipe, by far the largest venture to have been approved in 1984 but due to commence production only in 1990. Hong Kong's Asia Pacific Pipe Investments owns 20 per cent, and 30 per cent is owned by Pertamina. But Bakrie has managed to purchase 100 per cent ownership in such major ventures as PT James Hardie Indonesia, its maker of fibre cement pipes. State concessions, such as cheap loans from state financial institutions, have helped indigenous groups to expand by means of M&A activities.

The largest proportion of the Bakrie group's turnover derives from its wholly owned plantations, on whose exports it has come to rely more heavily since the recession. Steel pipes are to be exported for the same reason, but only because Bakrie can secure steel from the state company (Krakatau) well below the normal domestic price (Inoue, 1987, pp. 247–55).

Bakrie is the largest of the indigenous capitalist groups, the ruling families and core activities of which are outlined in Table 7.4. While in general it is true that indigenous groups have fewer ties with Japanese capital than Chinese ones, the Bakrie group has an unusually limited number. Bakrie has also relied less on state contacts and concessions than the others, which have much closer ties with the

Table 7.4   Indigenous Indonesian business groups

Group	Family	Activities
Bakrie	Bakrie	Steel pipes, plantations, electronic parts, real estate
Samudera	Soedarpo	Marine and land transportation, insurance, shipping
Kowara	Kowara	Construction materials, foodstuffs, machinery, trade
Poleko	Baramuli	Plantations, lumber, textiles
Gobel	Gobel	Electrical appliances, batteries, lumber
Mertju Buana	Probosutedjo	Commerce, poultry, construction, cars, glass utensils
Krama Yudha	Said	Motor vehicles

Source: Inoue, 1987, p. 248; Yoshihara, 1988, p. 188.

military. There are thus plenty of examples of joint ventures with Japanese capital, although not many which constitute the core of the group's strength (Gobel and Said are exceptions), as is the case among quite a few of the Chinese groups throughout Southeast Asia.

Of the exceptions, the Gobel group's core company, the largest household electrical appliance firm in the country, is a joint venture with Matsushita which began in 1970. Gobel tied up with another large Japanese company in 1982, Osaki Denki Kogyo, and then formed a second venture with Matsushita in 1987. Its leader, Th. M. Gobel, was the Chairperson of the Indonesia–Japan Entrepreneurs Association in 1983–85.

The leading light of the Krama Yudha group, Sjarnoebi Said, worked for the Japanese military during the occupation where he learnt Japanese. Later he joined the Indonesia army and ended up in Pertamina, working for General Ibnu Sutowo, the person most responsible for its financial crisis in 1976. The capital for his motor vehicle businesses, notably the joint venture with Mitsubishi, came from 'savings' acquired while at Pertamina. From Mitsubishi's point of view, the tie-up with Krama Yudha has provided a major production base in Asia of components (particularly engines and pressed parts), not just for its licensed assemblers of commercial and passenger vehicles, but for export to the rest of Asia for use in its Asian car project. A second joint venture, PT Colt Engine Manufacturing, opened in 1985.

The Japanese ties of the other groups are not as pivotal to their existence. Poleko has operated a large synthetic textile factory jointly with Toray since 1973, a plywood adhesive factory with Mitsui since 1976, and a chemical factory with Kao since 1978. The Samudera group has had a long association with Tokyo Senpaku and Nippon Yusen. Finally, the Mertju Buana group has an impressive list of local Chinese and foreign, including Japanese, partners in its manu- facturing and other activities. Examples include agreements in the car industry involving the Astra group, Peugeot, Renault, GM, Chrysler and Isuzu (making diesel engines); a joint venture with Japan Gasoline Company and one with C Itoh and Showa Lease (Inoue, 1987, pp. 255–61; Shūkan tōyō keizai, 1988; Yoshihara, 1988, pp. 173–83; *JS*, July 1987, pp. 58–9).

While the distinction between *pribumi* and Chinese capital in Indonesia reflects a real fractional difference within the ruling class, one must remember that this is an intra-class division which does not affect inter-class relations. It does not extend to the Indonesian masses, from whose point of view it matters little whether capital is *pribumi* or Chinese. In fact, apart from the state enterprises, which are unambiguously *pribumi*, and the business groups, which can be identified one way or the other, it is very difficult to tell whether a company is *pribumi* or not. A large number of Chinese interests are so-called 'Ali-Baba' firms, which often have important government officials or military officers as their representative executives in order to secure favourable treatment from the state.

A group of researchers who tried to identify whether Japanese capital favours joint ventures with Chinese or *pribumi* elements in the ruling class eventually gave up in despair. Having discovered so many layers of linkages among military officers and Chinese and *pribumi* capitalists, they concluded that the class forces which bind these three fractions of the Indonesian ruling class together vastly overshadow the ethnic and institutional forces which divide them (*Ampo*, 1980, p. 37).

Indonesian Oil Crisis

The oil revenues of the 1970s were inflated by prices that were bound to collapse, although the enormity of the crisis, which seems to grow by leaps and bounds almost daily, was less predictable. From provid- ing over 70 per cent of exports during the boom years, in the first five months of 1988 the share of oil and gas had fallen to 46.4 per cent. The state has faced an enormous fiscal crisis in an attempt to maintain

Table 7.5   Total approved non-oil/gas Japanese DFI in Indonesia,
              1967–88

	Japanese		Total foreign		Japanese share	
	No.	$ million	No.	$ million	No.	Value
1967–1980	222	2 082.8	975	7 482.3	22.8	27.8
1981	5	76.3	37	577.3	13.5	13.2
1982	11	532.2	34	1 290.9	32.4	41.2
1983	12	457.5	55	2 520.1	21.8	18.2
1984	2	31.1	24	857.1	8.3	3.6
1985	9	63.0	50	698.7	18.0	9.0
1986	9	239.8	50	613.0	18.0	39.1
Jan.–July 1987	20	274.3	65	623.6	30.8	44.0
Jan.–July 1988	22	168.0	89	2 032.0	24.7	8.3
1988	n/a	256.0	n/a	4 500.0	n/a	5.7

Source: BKPM (Board of Investment), *JS*, November 1988, p. 52; *FEER*, 23
February 1989, p. 82.

government expenditure and to cover the trade deficit. The government's foreign debt stood at $35 billion in early 1988 (bumped up by
$1.5 billion simply because of the rise of the yen), requiring some 36
per cent of the country's overseas income to service it. Foreign
capital's leverage, stemming from the loans it has provided and its
sudden elevation to the predominant source of investment, is reminiscent of the immediate post Sukarno years. DFI regulations have
been liberalised, export-oriented industrialisation has finally been
accepted, state projects have been transferred to the private sector,
interest rates have been decontrolled, imports have been liberalised
and the currency has been massively devalued. In fact, almost all the
recommendations in a World Bank report on Indonesia, which was
published in 1981 but largely ignored at the time, have now been
implemented (*FEER*, 7 January 1988, pp. 48–9; 21 January 1988, pp.
50–1; 8 September 1988, pp. 132–4; 1 December 1988, pp. 61–3;
NKS, 25 December 1987, p. 1).

Japanese Capital Hesitates

New Japanese direct investments in Indonesia slowed down as a
result of this crisis, which was partly why such liberal regulations
were drafted in August 1986: to implement the government's aggressive mining development and export policy. Table 7.5 shows that
in 1984 approved Japanese non-oil/gas investment fell to a paltry $31

million, Japan's smallest share (3.6 per cent) of the total ever. Although this recovered to a 39 per cent share with the $240 million approved in 1986, figures from the Japanese MOF (Table 7.3) showed a continual decline in non-oil/gas investment to the end of fiscal 1986. The trend since then is not yet clear. MOF figures show that the total invested in Indonesia in fiscal 1987 rose by 118 per cent to $545 million, while the Investment Board (BKPM) in January to July 1987 approved non-oil/gas investments worth $274 million (raising Japan's share to 44 per cent). But, in the same period in 1988, Japan's share fell to a mere 8.2 per cent of approved non-oil/gas investments. The year ended with Japan in sixth position with only 6 per cent of a total which had trebled to $4.5 billion. In Indonesia, it seems, Japan is now trailing well behind other foreign investors.

There are, however, some indications among large Japanese companies already in Indonesia that switching to export production promises to be more rewarding in the long run than their ISI activities, which were disrupted by the end of the oil bonanza. For example, PT Ajinomoto Indonesia, the Japanese company's main overseas producer, is establishing a large-scale factory to make monosodium glutamate for export to China, Taiwan and Africa. In June 1987 a new subsidiary was established, PT AJINEX International, to make glutamin-acid soda. Inoue Rubber is rapidly making its Indonesian subsidiary its base for export to the US in place of South Korea and Taiwan. PT Asaminas Flat Glass is planning to invest another $90 million to increase its capacity by 40 per cent within two years, making it the largest supplier in Southeast Asia. The company will export worldwide, including to Japan. Similarly, Honda set up a new venture in late 1986 with its agent, Prospect Motor, to make automobile engines.

Also noteworthy in this context are the previously mentioned plans by companies in the Liem, Astra and Krama Yudha groups to export motor vehicle parts, particularly engines. With 80 per cent of vehicles sold in the Indonesian market comprising commercial vehicles and a local content ratio of only 35 per cent in 1988, there is plenty of potential for further investment to make Indonesia a major supply centre of low cost parts for the entire Asian region.

Other companies recently to expand or start up export activities in Indonesia are Teijin (to increase the exports of apparel), Toto (to make high quality baths for export to Southeast Asia, Japan and Europe), Eisai (to expand its capacity to produce medicines for the Japanese market) and Hitachi Shipbuilding. This is Hitachi's first venture in Indonesia, and it intends to make components for chemical plants, to be exported throughout the world. The Japan Pulp & Paper Company, which has been exporting paper to Indonesia but which recently decided to close its Jakarta office due to falling demand, suddenly realised Indonesia's potential as a cheap production site and reversed the decision. The largest Japanese pulp and paper maker will now use Indonesia as a base for export production. One company which had been exporting to Japan and the US for years is Tokai Kagu Kogyo's furniture-making joint venture in Jakarta's Pulogadung Industrial Estate, 'the mecca of Japanese business activity'. It is now doubling its capacity to take advantage of the high yen (*NKS*, 19 July 1987, p. 9; 13 September 1987, p. 4; 25 September 1987, p. 23; 30 September 1987, p. 9; 9 October 1987, p. 8; *JEJ*, 2 April 1988, p. 8; 17 September 1988, p. 31; 24 September 1988, pp. 1, 4; 22 October 1988, p. 7; *KTG*, July 1988, pp. 8–9; Shūkan tōyō keizai, 1988).

Conclusion

The Indonesian ruling class has lost enormous ground in its struggle for independence from foreign capital as a result of its oil crisis. It has had to go begging for foreign investment to create an export sector to replace the oil and gas exports which low oil prices have failed to revive. Although the Japanese have not yet responded clearly, its current vulnerability and their need for cheap supplies suggest that they will not worry very much longer about that sleeping giant (Indonesian nationalism) which from time to time takes a swipe at them. In the meantime Indonesia will remain more useful as a source of raw material and food supplies than as a low-cost production centre, except for a few things like textiles and motor vehicle components.

The effect of Japanese capital on the major social forces which are building up Indonesia is likely to be felt more at the macro-level of the state and overseas debt than the factory. The industrial working class as a whole, not to mention that section of it which works in Japanese factories, is still too small to move anywhere near centre stage. Rather, working-class experience of Japanese imperialism will more likely add to a cross-class experience, from peasants through to capitalists, and feed the potentially most explosive force in Indonesia. Resentment against imperialism runs deep in this society, and in spite of twenty years of Suharto's New Order, there is still little certainty that bourgeois nationalism has triumphed over revolutionary nationalism.

While the Indonesian government might publicly claim to oppose this new imperialism from its northern neighbour, in reality cooperation with the Japanese at both the state and private corporate levels has been extremely close. The parallel with South Korea is obvious. Both ruling classes must present themselves as continuing the struggle against imperialism, not least Japanese imperialism, and both tread a thin line between suppressing and helping to fuel the growth of revolutionary nationalism. The part Japanese capital plays in this is through the conspicuousness of its presence, particularly the enormous wealth it flouts among desperately poor Indonesians. Preventing resentment against that from spilling into resentment against both it and its local collaborators will not be easy.

The real problem, as far as the Indonesian masses are concerned, is not that they will be side-tracked by the Japanese presence into bourgeois nationalism, but that their revolutionary organisations have been destroyed. More frequent outbursts of rebellion, often with revolutionary intentions, are thus likely to founder for their inability to build into a revolutionary movement. The Japanese will probably prefer this to the writing which seems to be appearing on the wall in the Philippines, and switch back into Indonesia.

PHILIPPINES

History of Struggle

The Filipino people have a much longer history of being ruled by an alliance between imperialism and the local ruling class than any other in ASEAN. In fact, a large proportion of present day local ruling class individuals and institutions originate out of Spanish colonialism, which dominated the country until 1898. But becoming an American colony at that time did more than shift the locus of the foreign partner in the ruling alliance. It qualitatively altered its dynamic and internal balance. The period of classical American colonialism, which lasted until the end of the Second World War, was the period of American capitalism's rise to world dominance, and the history of the Philippine class struggle was profoundly influenced by that fact.

American capital, which imposed a regime of free trade on the country, was preoccupied with the development of export crops. Throughout the period, almost 90 per cent of exports comprised sugar, coconut products, abaca and tobacco. But the most important was sugar, which in 1934 contributed 65 per cent of exports and 30 per cent of national income. The planters, millers and traders were known as the 'sugar barons', and they comprised Americans, Spaniards, religious corporations and Chinese merchants. However, in this as in other export industries, the Americans were less involved in crop cultivation than in processing for export, and the primitive capitalism which developed here was no better from the workers' point of view than the more fully feudal system in food production was from the tenants' point of view. In fact, all industries revealed various mixtures of the most backward forms of bourgeois social relations with those of Spanish feudalism (Bello *et al.*, 1982; Ofreneo, 1980).

While there were some important peasant uprisings in the prewar period, the immediate postwar crisis saw the largest escalation in organised struggle by workers and peasants, under considerable influence from the Communist Party. Although the US granted the Philippines nominal independence in 1946, the Americans retained an overbearing presence throughout the country's political, military, economic, social and cultural institutions. Because the Philippines never went through any 'emergency period' or armed struggle for independence as was required almost everywhere else in Southeast Asia, the transition from colonialism to neo-colonialism was so much less noticeable. To this day, almost regardless of what the Japanese might do or the support they might give the local ruling class, US imperialism is so overwhelming that the revolutionary struggle has its sights set firmly and almost exclusively on the US.

The Americans continued to enforce free trade onto the weak republic, and their goods flooded the Philippine market (76 per cent of imports in 1946–55), while the 'parity rights' they claimed in the exploitation of natural resources ensured that development would be confined to the traditional export sector. Lawlessness reigned everywhere, with almost all large landowners using private armies to terrorise militant peasants. By 1950 the US was forced to intervene with a carrot and stick programme of moderate reform combined with heavy handed repression.

In the countryside, the Americans recommended a break-up of the feudal estates to allow greater capitalist development, but the local (ex-Spanish) ruling class was adamant. Yet more moderate land reforms, which transferred some feudal into bourgeois property, did allow for capitalist penetration of agriculture beyond export crops. The main forms in which this occurred were through the foreign companies, which sold the inputs of high-tech agriculture to the various contractors who were directly engaged in farming: fertilisers, chemicals, tractors, new seed varieties and so on.

It was at this level, after reparations payments had smoothed the way for them, that the Japanese *sōgō shōsha* first saw opportunities in the Philippines. Capital penetrated not simply traditional crops, but was important in creating new ones, like bananas, which became a major export to Japan. In the log and timber industry, the situation became quite outrageous: very little forest management or reforestation was even contemplated, and notorious wastefulness resulted from such practices as abandoning logs with defects. In 1966–68, forest products contributed 27 per cent of Philippine exports, 80 per cent of which went to Japan.

For a while it seemed that manufacturing would fare better, since the free trade regime was effectively undermined by the import and foreign exchange controls the government had imposed to contain the foreign exchange crisis of the late 1940s. This *de facto* framework for ISI produced a much more advanced (light) manufacturing sector than in Indonesia and, more important, raised a group of local capitalists with strong interests in ISI.

However, by the late 1960s, light industry had more or less exhausted its potential, and the crisis in industry coincided with an agricultural crisis – rural poverty and landlessness was increasing, as was the inability of agriculture to feed the population – as well as a political crisis. Stagnation and growing unemployment led to widespread demonstrations and struggles, all fuelled by growing US involvement in Vietnam. The ruling class was bitterly divided: nationalists advocated ISI in intermediate and capital goods, while foreign-linked capital, expressing itself mainly through the World Bank and the Marcos regime, called for export-oriented industrialisation.

Marcos had defeated his even more rightwing predecessor in the election of 1965. And, in the most corrupt and violent elections in postwar history, he secured a second term, breaking even the ruling class convention to take turns in appropriating the spoils of government. Conflict within the ruling class degenerated to violent vendettas among private armies. And so with the blessing of the World Bank and the US government, Marcos declared martial law in September 1972.

This was an event of epochal significance in Filipino history, since it signalled the same shift that occurred in Indonesia and Singapore in 1965, in Thailand and South Korea a few years later, and in Malaysia in the 1950s. It brought the same package of measures: an authoritarian regime to ensure cheap disciplined labour, incentives for foreign capital in export industries (for example FTZs and tax concessions), and building infrastructure for foreign capital's importing and exporting.

For the Japanese, martial law solved a major problem. The atrocities committed during the Pacific War had left deep scars on relations between the two ruling classes. Even though a Treaty of Amity, Commerce and Navigation had been signed in 1960, it had to be shelved because of its rejection by the Senate. By abolishing Congress, Marcos solved the problem and ratified the Treaty by proclamation in 1973. Not that Japanese capital had been absent from the Philippines before then. In every area except DFI, it had all but overshadowed even US capital. But large volumes of trade, yen loans and contracts for government projects all made the Japanese presence very visible, and they needed to be legitimated and complemented by direct investments.

Opening the Floodgates

The 'rush' into the Philippines began in 1973, peaked in 1974, and then fluctuated until the assassination of Benigno Aquino in 1983 almost entirely choked it off. Thereafter it once again varied with the political climate, falling off sharply when it seemed that Cory Aquino's regime was to be short-lived. Although the timing of the political changes which opened the floodgates was different, the parallel with Indonesia is striking. If one excludes the oil and gas investments in Indonesia (or equates them with steel sintering and iron ore and copper mining in the Philippines), even the amounts invested were comparable, as were their main targets in manufacturing: textiles and motor vehicles. But there the parallel ends, since the enormous US investments in semiconductors for export recall parallels with Malaysia. Today, the Philippines' leading exports are garments and semiconductors.

Japanese DFI in the Philippines was mainly an expression of the raw materials crisis faced by Japanese capital in the 1970s. Table 7.6, which shows the equity investments approved by the Board of Investment since 1968, confirms the enormous weight of foreign capital, from the US and to a lesser extent Japan, *vis-à-vis* Filipino capital, particularly after 1983. It also shows that 45 per cent of the total equity invested by Japan to the end of 1987 entered in the rush period of 1974–82. The largest productive investments from Japan were in

Table 7.6   Equity investments in the Philippines, by date of approval and country of origin (P million)

	1968–73	1974–82	1983–85	1986	1987	1968–87	Jan.–June 1988
Filipino	1 983	16 390	6 704	1 553	4 933	31 562	2 910
Wholly-owned	n/a	n/a	3 048	726	2 833	n/a	n/a
Joint ventures	n/a	n/a	3 656	826	2 100	n/a	n/a
Foreign	1 329	10 097	9 328	1 594	3 427	25 775	5 130
Wholly owned	n/a	n/a	5 764	574	982	n/a	n/a
Joint ventures	n/a	n/a	3 564	1 020	2 446	n/a	n/a
US	692	3 010	4 825	458	800	9 784	1 680
Japan	113	1 873	1 110	455	591	4 141	670
Europe	n/a	n/a	1 560	338	545	n/a	n/a
Taiwan	n/a	n/a	31	7	186	n/a	2 080
Hong Kong	n/a	n/a	279	149	570	n/a	225
TOTAL	3 312	26 487	16 032	3 146	8 360	57 337	8 040

Note: The P800 million for the US in 1987 is the North American total, and figures for Hong Kong, Taiwan and Europe before 1983 were not available to me.
Source: To 1986, Board of Investment; 1987, as cited in Montez and Koike, 1988, pp. 212–3; 1988, *FEER*, 1 September 1988, pp. 49–50 and *JS*, November 1988, p. 52.

basic metals (36 per cent of the total accumulated by September 1981), chemicals (11 per cent), transport machinery (9.7 per cent), mining (6.3 per cent) and textiles (4.7 per cent). However, since borrowing rather than equity is the main source of finance for large-scale investments in mining and resources, Japanese MOF figures, which include loans, are more relevant. Of the accumulated total of $913 million invested by the end of fiscal 1986, 43 per cent was in mining, 13 per cent in transport machinery, 9 per cent in basic metals, 8 per cent in chemicals, 4.2 per cent in agriculture and forestry, 2.8 per cent in food and 2.3 per cent in textiles. Clearly, the priorities of Japanese capital in the Philippines have not moved away from raw material extraction and processing plus motor cars (Lindsey, 1987; Nihon bōeki shinkōkai, 1988c, p. 61; Ōkurashō, 1988a).

Links with Local Ruling Class

Since DFI is essentially a political process bringing together capitalist classes from different countries, it is better to highlight some of the details behind these statistics in their proper political context, the Filipino business groups. In fact the joint ventures are striking for the degree to which they have allied the Japanese transnationals with the leading local business clans. In a classical study, Tsuda Mamoru concluded: 'the Japanese conglomerates are the "pushing forces" for the export of Japanese capital to the Philippines while the Filipino big business stratum and the government itself are the "accommodating" or even the "pulling forces"' (Tsuda, 1978, p. 155).

Tsuda's study, which was written in the midst of the 1970s rush, showed that both parties possessed the highest levels of economic power and concentration in their own countries. Out of a total of 385 joint ventures, he identified 105 major ones which accounted for 96 per cent of total Japanese investments. However, 93 of these involved only 77 leading Japanese firms and 93 per cent of total investments, while 81 involved affiliates of the big six Japanese *zaibatsu* and 85 per cent of total investments. On the Filipino side, Tsuda identified 25 leading partners who were involved in 69 of the 105 major joint ventures, the 69 accounting for 85 per cent of total Japanese investments. In 58 major joint ventures members of the big six Japanese *zaibatsu* and the 25 leading Filipino clans came together, and these comprised 78 per cent of total investments (*ibid.*, pp. 141–53).

The most important of these 25 Filipino clans and the numbers of joint ventures they were involved in were: Ayala (11), Philippine government (11), Yuchengco (7), Dee Chiong (7), Dee-Owyong (6), Soriano (5), Disini-Velayo (6), Sycip (5), Del Rosario (5), Silverio (5), Yulo (5), Puyat (5), Laurel (5), Jose Fernandez, present Governor of the Central Bank (5) and Tan-Lee (4). There were ten other partners with three major joint ventures each and 21 with two each (*ibid.*, pp. 98–142).

Although these can be identified as having either Spanish, Chinese of Malay lineages, ethnic divisions are not important in the Philippines and are typically overshadowed by rivalries among families. The state, notably in the Marcos years when 'crony capitalism' reached its height, tends to favour particular clans and not, as in Malaysia and Indonesia, indigenous capitalists. Even during the heyday of the national bourgeoisie in the 1950s and early 1960s, Chinese capital was penalised not so much for its ethnic ties as for its lack of Filipino citizenship (for example, following the Retail Nationalisation Act of 1954), a legacy of US colonialism. Once naturalised, Chinese capitalists thrived along with the others. And because the Chinese had also long been pressured to become Catholic, religion also failed to divide the Filipino ruling class. The only

Table 7.7   Major Chinese business groups in the Philippines, 1987

Group	Core companies	Other activities
Yuchengco	Rizal Commercial Banking Corp. Malayan Insurance	Plantations, trade
Palanca[a]	La Tondeña (brewing) Lepanto Consolidated Mining (copper mining)	Real estate, glass
Lucio Tan	Fortune Tobacco Allied Banking Asia Brewery	Hogs, steel structures
Leonardo Ty	Union Ajinomoto (seasonings) Manila Paper Mills	Electrical, car sales
Gokongwei	Universal–Robina (foodstuffs)	Cosmetics, real estate hotels, shopping centres
Chung	Philippine Blooming Mills (iron and steel)	Tobacco, fats
Yao	Columbia Tobacco	Chemicals
Sy	Shoemart	Shopping centres, property, supermarkets

Note: [a]Now controlled by San Miguel.
Source: Inoue, 1987, p. 197; interviews

significant division is between local and foreign capital, and within local capital the related division between national and comprador capital.

While most of the leading Filipino business clans owe their existence to ties with American capital, by the mid-1980s a few had emerged on the coattails of Japanese manufacturers. The shift to export-oriented production that came with Marcos increased the importance within manufacturing of high-tech industries relative to those which had relied on local advantages, such as food and tobacco. The trend was further boosted by the stagnation which followed the second oil crisis, by the financial panic of 1981 among the Chinese groups, by the balance of payments crisis of 1983 and the mounting debt crisis thereafter, by the collapse of commodity prices and the negative growth in the mid-1980s, and finally by the political crisis in which Marcos and the clans closest to him were ousted by the military and Cory Aquino was allowed to succeed him. Table 7.7 shows the main Chinese groups which emerged from that shakeup.

The largest of these by far is the Yuchengco group, which survived even the fall of Marcos with whom it had close ties. It also has long standing links with Japanese capital, and three of the top six group members are joint ventures with Japanese interests: Rizal Commercial Banking Corporation (10 per cent owned by Sanwa Bank but also 30 per cent owned by Continental Illinois), Philippine Fuji Xerox (40 per cent owned by Fuji Xerox) and Pan Malayan Insurance (30 per cent owned by Tokio Marine and Fire Insurance). The group includes at least 70 companies, but they are heavily concentrated in finance and insurance and to a lesser degree in trade, agriculture, lumber, oil exploration, construction and cement. Like many other 'rent collectors' in Southeast Asia (Yoshihara, 1988), the Yuchengco group does not have a high-tech industrial base, whose importance is acutely felt in times of crisis and which increases the leverage of Japanese capital. But the influence of the Yuchengco group extends well beyond its member companies, which have themselves spread into Hong Kong, Taiwan, the US, the UK, Australia and Indonesia. The group also has close ties with other leading Chinese families, such as Sycip, Chester Babst and Dee Chiong, while its founder, Alfonso Yuchengco, was a recent Ambassador to China (Inoue, 1987, pp. 192–8; Tsuda, 1978, pp. 121–3; Shūkan tōyō keizai, 1988; Jetro Manila, 1986; Yoshihara, 1988, p. 191; Montez and Koike, 1988, pp. 188–92).

Most of the remaining Chinese groups also have some or other link with Japanese capital. For example, Lucio Tan, close friend of Marcos who miraculously survived the purge to become one of the country's richest men today, through his Century Park Sheraton Hotel joined with All Nippon Airways in the Maranao Hotel in 1976. A more important tie-up was in 1974 between Gokongwei and Kawasaki Steel (and Nippon Mining) in the country's fourth largest mining company, Philex, which has been involved in everything from oil exploration to copper concentrates, gold, silver and magnetite iron ore.

The Kawasaki group at this time accounted for almost a third of the total value of Japanese investments in the country. They included a motor cycle factory opened in 1974 with del Rosario, the wholly-owned Philippine Sinter Corporation, still the most forbidding Japanese presence in the Philippines, the 40 per cent share in the government's P300 million Philippine Shipyard and Engineering Corporation (PHILSECO), the 30 per cent share in Dolomite Mining (with the Tuazon group) and its wholly-owned Philippine Mining Service.

Both of Kawasaki's giant projects were controversial outcomes of Japan's restructuring out of heavy industry. The steel sintering plant was set up to export the pollution this industry causes and has known connections with the military, as became clear in the Mindanao-wide strike in May 1985. PHILSECO is inside the military retirees reservation, PHILVIDOC (Philippine Veterans Investment and Development Corporation), where it mends ships right next to the US Subic naval base. So far, it has only serviced commercial vessels. The key figure behind the project was Benjamin Romualdez, the brother of Imelda Marcos. According to its marketing vice president, PHILSECO's higher labour productivity than the other shipyards is 'because of the work ethic transfer that we have set up in the company' (*BD*, 10 November 1986, p. 13). Kawasaki's current plans include investment in pineapple pulp drying via debt–equity conversion.

The only Japanese projects worth more than PHILSECO and the steel sintering plant either have less Japanese money or are in the hotel industry: the Maranao Hotel of Lucio Tan and All Nippon Airways; the Manila Garden Hotel belonging to a Japan Airlines consortium (93 per cent) and the Ayala clan; Mitsubishi's 20 per cent share in Ayala Corporation; Marubeni's 2 per cent share in the state-owned Philippine National Construction Corporation (PNCC); and the Marubeni consortium's 32 per cent share in Philippine Associated Smelting and Refining (PASAR), the government's copper refinery.

However, apart from Yuchengco, none of the Chinese groups is as reliant on Japanese capital as Leonard Ty is on Union Ajinomoto. One of the giants of the Philippine manufacturing industry, Ajinomoto commenced production in 1962 and employs over a thousand workers today. Ty's other joint-ventures with Japanese partners include Hitachi–Union (although Hitachi withdrew from it in June 1985) and Rinnai Philippines, which makes gas equipment. The greatest leverage possessed by Japanese capital tends to be in the manufacturing industries requiring higher technology, particularly motor vehicles and electronics. But here the Philippine partners are more typically the older Spanish or indigenous groups: Ayala, Soriano, Del Rosario and Silverio (*FEER*, 17 March 1988, pp. 76–7; 15 December 1988, pp. 112–6; 22 December 1988, pp. 50–1; Tsuda, 1978; Shūkan tōyō keizai, 1988; Jetro Manila, 1986; Yoshihara, 1988; Jetro, 1982; *JEJ*, 2 and 9 January 1988, p. 25; Montez and Koike, 1988, pp. 11–20; 192–6).

Ayala is the largest and oldest conglomerate in the country, accumulating wealth and power hand in hand with the US colonial exploitation of coffee, indigo, sugar, spinning, dyes and coal. The core company which holds the whole show together is Ayala Corporation, of which the Ayala family owns 45 per cent, employees and members of the public a further 35 per cent and the Mitsubishi group 20 per cent. Ayala has also extended its financial empire into Hong Kong, Brunei, the US, Spain, Palau, Vanuatu and Liberia. In the Philippines the group embraced 36 companies in 1984, the most important of which are joint ventures with American capital.

Ayala's most rapid rise to the number one position among Philippine business groups was based on real estate, principally development of the Makati area, the business centre of Manila. More recently, it moved into manufacturing and agriculture, although until 1983 most manufacturing investment went into shares in San Miguel, the citadal of the Soriano family with which it is related. While Ayala has many joint ventures with Japanese companies (mainly in the Mitsubishi group), its greatest debt to the latter is the development of Ayala Corporation into a top-class *sōgō shōsha* (Inoue, 1987, p. 262–71; Tsuda, 1978, pp. 118–20; Yoshihara, 1988, pp. 164–5; Montez and Koike, 1988, pp. 181–4).

The Soriano family has an almost equally long history, but its manufacturing base is stronger than Ayala's even if this is in low-tech lines like brewing and agribusiness, or in cooperation with foreign capital, as in copper mining and soft drinks (Coca Cola). That the Soriano brothers retain American citizenship reflects a real alliance between the clan and US capital, with a large proportion of the over 40 group members having links with American companies.

Japanese capital has equity ties with only two group members, one of which is their number two: Atlas Consolidated Mining and Development Corporation. Although Mitsubishi Metal's share in this, the largest copper mining firm in Southeast Asia with over 6000 workers, is only 2 per cent, the Japanese company's influence on it is bolstered by the power of marketing, technology and finance. The largest Soriano company, San Miguel, is relatively independent and even brews beer in Bermuda, Hong Kong, Indonesia and Papua New Guinea. The other core group member linked to Japanese interests is the country's 31st ranking company, Far East Bank and Trust, which is 18 per cent owned by Mitsui Bank, 18 per cent by America's Chemical Bank, and 23 per cent by the Gokongwei group. Its principal shareholder was 'Jobo' Fernandez, Governor of the Central Bank for Marcos and now for Aquino (Inoue, 1987, pp. 272–9; Jetro

Manila, 1986; Tsuda, 1978; *FEER*, 19 May 1988, p. 86; 26 May 1988, p. 95; Montez and Koike, 1988, pp. 184–8).

The most important Filipino allies of Japanese capital are not actually in the top three families, but ones which have tried to enter high-tech industries such as motor vehicles and electronics. The largest car maker in the country, Canlubang Automotive Resources (renamed Philippine Automotive in 1987), was a joint venture between Mitsubishi Motors and the Yulo clan of Canlubang Sugar Estate. Starting in 1972, it moved into the leading position in 1985 when GM closed down, around which time it also became a wholly Japanese owned operation. In 1974, after Marcos had launched the Progressive Car Manufacturing Programme (PCMP) to increase local content, Mitsubishi and Yulo (and Nissho Iwai) opened a second joint venture, Asian Transmission, partly to supply Canlubang, but to export 70 per cent of its production in return for its preferred pioneer status. Even today, like the engines assembled out of Japanese parts by Mitsubishi Krama Yudha in Indonesia, the transmissions are simply put together in the Philippines. Although the distributor of Mitsubishi cars, Apex Motor Corporation, is wholly Filipino owned, even it began as the exclusive Mazda distributor through the good offices of Nissho Iwai. Shock absorbers have been supplied since 1977 by Apex Motor Manufacturing, a joint venture with Kayaba and Nissho Iwai. But the recession has hit the car industry very badly, and total car production was slashed from 34 328 in the peak year of 1978 to a mere 5543 in 1987. So far only two companies besides Mitsubishi have been accepted into the Car Development Programme (CDP) of late 1987: Nissan and Toyota.

Nissan vehicles had been assembled under licence since 1972, but the crisis of the 1980s stepped imports of knockdown sets, and the Japanese parent stepped in more aggressively at the height of Marcos' power and corruption in 1983. Teaming up with Imelda Marcos through the Domingo M Guevarra family, Pilipinas Nissan was set up to assemble cars and Columbia Motors to assemble trucks and buses. After the exile of Marcos, interests connected with Aquino's family stepped in to fill the gap. Nissan now sees the Philippines as one of its three major sources of components in ASEAN, with eight affiliated companies, compared to nine in Malaysia and sixteen in Thailand.

The company with the longest experience in the Philippines is Toyota, which nurtured the development of the Silverio empire almost from its real beginnings in the late 1950s. Ricardo Silverio established Delta Motor Corporation (DMC) to assemble Toyota vehicles under licence, soon claiming the largest share of the market and making his company one of the country's leaders. From the late 1960s a host of joint ventures with Japanese partners started up, particularly in auto parts, including Delta International (1969), Delta Electric Motor (1973), Porcelana Mariwasa Noritake (1974), Goko Tools & Dies (1975), Nippondenso (1976), Daikin (1976), Tokai Densai (1976) and Delta Hi-Steel (1978). However, excessive jaunts into the unproductive sector combined with the crisis of the early 1980s led to the takeover of DMC in 1984 by its creditor bank for failing to pay debts of $77 million. Nevertheless, Ricardo Silverio, ex-Marcos crony, remains the single most important Japanese ally in the car industry and *vice versa*. As Tsuda (1978, p. 127) commented: 'The Silverio family is a relatively new industrial elite which grew from its close tie-ups with Japanese capital'.

In order to take part in the government's new CDP, Toyota has bought the old Delta facilities. Its partners in the new venture are Mitsui & Co and Metropolitan Bank, which is majority owned by George Ty, tycoon of one of the leading Chinese business groups. Since the local market cannot absorb the output of even the limited number of companies in the CDP, there is plenty of capacity for a major shift into exports, particularly of components.

Japanese companies dominate this field as fully as they do car assembly. In addition to the Mitsubishi, Kayaba and Silverio-allied ventures already noted, a company with a very sharp eye for cheap labour, Yazaki Sogyo, opened its large factory jointly with the Torres family in 1973. Today it uses 2600 workers to make its wire harnesses. Among the other smaller parts makers in the country is Friction Materials, which makes brake linings. In motor cycles, Suzuki Philippines is wholly owned by the parent in Japan, Honda has ties with the Ayala (BPI Trust) and Silverio (Delta International) families, while Kawasaki's partner is Jesus del Rosario (*Weekly Executive Update*, 21 August 1986, p. 5; Jetro Manila, 1986; Shūkan tōyō keizai, 1988; *Business Day*, 22 and 27 August 1986, p. 13; 1 October 1986, p. 9; *JEJ*, 5 December 1987, p. 21; *AS*, 25 November 1987, p. 11; *FEER*, 9 June 1988, p. 104; 10 November 1988, p. 79).

If the Silverio family has a counterpart in the electrical industry then it is the del Rosario family, which has long-standing links with Matsushita. It was also Hitachi's partner in Hi-Eles Industrial (1976) and Mitsubishi Electric's partner in International Elevator & Equipment (1969). But it has ties with Japanese capital in other industries too; for example, it leads the local group which owns 60 per cent in

Kawasaki Motors (1974) and it owns 70 per cent of Delsa Chemicals & Multi-Products (1980).

Matsushita's local partner, Precision Electronics Corporation (PEC), was founded by Jesus del Rosario, the brother of Manila's ambassador to Tokyo and the leading member of the family empire. Its rise to prominence in the 1970s echoes that of the Gobel group in Indonesia, which depended even more heavily on Matsushita. At one time employing 1100 workers, PEC has become the largest consumer electronics company in the country, with exports rising from 15 to 40 per cent of sales.

Matsushita is one of a small number of Japanese companies which have recently made new commitments in the Philippines: a \$2.4 million floppy disk drive (FDD) factory in cooperation with PEC. While Matsushita, the world's largest FDD maker, supplied the technology for this its first disk drive factory outside Japan, the project was financed by PEC profits. The only foreign exchange it brings in thus comes from exporting its entire production, which was anticipated to reach \$22 million in 1988. The new factory employs 95 young women workers, who are said to be as skilled as any in Singapore. With three group members making parts in the Philippines, the Matsushita group is even considering the Philippines as a re-export base similar to Taiwan, Malaysia and Singapore (Jetro Manila, 1986; Tadem, 1983, pp. 4–5; Shūkan tōyō keizai, 1988; *JEJ*, 5 December 1987, p. 7; Nihon bōeki shinkōkai, 1987a, p. 147; *Business Day*, 19 September 1986, p. 1).

Because Japanese capital had a very close relationship with Marcos, it formed many joint ventures with the government, which boosted the number of public corporations from 23 to 243 in the period 1972–84. Most prominent among such joint ventures were PASAR, PNCC, PHILSECO and Sharp (Philippines). Although the Aquino government's privatisation programme has attracted many US and Japanese bargain hunters, the programme seems to have lost steam and might even be quietly forgotten, well before the really big prizes, like Philippine Air Lines and the Manila Hotel, come up for sale. Government corporations will apparently remain one of the institutional forms in which the Japanese and Filipino ruling classes combine (Jetro Manila, 1986; *NKS*, 17 November 1987, p. 8; *FEER*, 5 November 1987, pp. 84–5; 7 July 1988, pp. 88–93).

Since the basic moving force behind the Japanese swoop on the Philippines in the 1970s was the crisis of the heavy and basic materials industries, the chief targets were raw materials and food rather than cheap labour. Although most of the main projects were in cooperation with the large Philippine business groups and families, there were a few others. In some of these, such as Sumitomo's 3000 worker Davao Fruits in 1971 (with Jesus Ayala, a prominent adviser of the Aquino government) and Pacific Metal's 728 worker Rio Tuba Nickel Mining (1973), the two attractions of the Philippines came together. However, there were also a number of major joint ventures in which cheap labour was the sole attraction, mainly in textiles and electronics: Sanyo's 500 worker factory to make black & white TVs and fridges (1971), Tomen's 1400 worker synthetic fibre plant (1971) and three large sewing factories, belonging to Sega Menswear's with 1000 workers, Tosanya with 800 workers and Toshin with 1200 workers (their sole overseas ventures and all in 1973 in the Philippines) (Shūkan tōyō keizai, 1988).

Japanese foreign investment in the Philippines must not be seen as an invasion from the outside, but as a political process in which the leading members of two ruling classes have come together. In cases involving high-tech production, particularly motor vehicles and household electronics, the Japanese possess an upper hand which leaves their Filipino partners simply to provide workers and a few accessories. In raw materials, however, it is the Japanese capacity to spend which has led their Filipino allies to sell off the nation's resources. Although the alliance with Japanese companies has been crucial in both broad areas and has richly rewarded the local partners, it has not had anything like the across-the-board significance of the alliance with the US. In addition to supplying over half of all DFI, the latter keeps, not simply the Philippines, but the Asia-Pacific region as a whole, safe for all foreign investors by means of its overbearing military presence in the Philippines. Only Japanese government aid compares as a broad source of support for the regime and its leading members.

Crisis of the 1980s

What ended Japanese capital's rush into the Philippines was not its dislike of the Marcos dictatorship, since it has always worked amicably with dictators like Marcos so long as they kept the lid on things. What the Japanese do not find comforting are popular movements which challenge dictatorships, and it was the rise of the National Democratic Front and the New People's Army under the leadership of the Communist Party of the Philippines which began to dampen their enthusiasm from the early 1980s.

Well before but also for some time after the display of people's power at EDSA in February 1986, which led even the military to abandon Marcos, most foreign capitalists shared this extreme caution about putting more money into the Philippines. That was one of the factors behind the declining rate of economic growth, from 3.5 per cent in 1981 to minus 7.1 per cent in 1984 and recovering to a mere 1.5 per cent in 1986. In 1982 it had even seemed that the Philippines might surpass Malaysia as the top production base for US semiconductor companies, with exports of $1 billion compared to Malaysia's $1.35 billion. However, by 1986, Japanese and American companies in Malaysia had pushed exports to $2.74 billion, while in the Philippines exports fell to $919 million (*FEER*, 7 January 1988, p. 42; 25 August 1988, pp. 72–3).

The Japanese were particularly put out by Marcos' fall, involved as they had been to a still unknown degree in all sorts of shady operations with him (Tsuda and Deocadiz, 1986). But there has been a growing recognition outside Japan that the Aquino regime is potentially more stable and hospitable than its predecessor. In 1987 GNP grew by 5 per cent and semiconductor exports, a good barometer of US capital's confidence, surged by 22 per cent to $1.12 billion. Aquino had been willing to remove most of the remaining legacies of the ISI period, and more fully even than Marcos tow the line of free trade and free movement for international capital. The Omnibus Investment Code of August 1987 was also the most attractive package of export incentives for foreign capital in the country's entire neo-colonial history. But then the $28.6 billion overseas debt, the servicing of which absorbed 40 per cent of the 1988 budget and the interest alone on which absorbed some 44 per cent of export revenues, signalled that this was also the country's worst ever crisis (Araneta, 1987; Guinigundo, 1987; Sagalla, 1988; *Business Journal*, March 1988, pp. 6–7).

Once it became clear that Aquino had rejected non-capitalist solutions to the Philippine crisis, the local ruling class became more vulnerable to the demands of foreign capital. As had occurred under similar circumstances elsewhere in ASEAN, the balance of power shifted heavily towards the latter. It is ironic that this should have happened after the fall of Marcos. In November 1986 Aquino visited Japan to beg for more foreign investment, receiving a most enthusiastic response from the heads of the *sōgō shōsha*, whom she saw separately. The 60 per cent devaluation of the peso against the yen since 1983, the lowest wages in Southeast Asia and an English-speaking labour force were almost irresistible. As pointed out by Ebashi Masahiko, JETRO's Philippines watcher, 'there is tremendous sentiment that may intensify into investment fever' (*Asiaweek*, 19 October 1986, p. 63).

At one point there were signs that this might happen. The two leaders of Japan's top two industries currently being internationalised, Toyota and Matsushita, came off the fence and boosted their commitments in the Philippines. The top *shōsha*, which had ushered in the mining and manufacturing companies in the 1970s, were all expressing interest: Marubeni in textiles, biotechnology, agribusiness and tourism; Sumitomo in fisheries; C Itoh in tourism; Tomen in coffee; and Nissho Iwai in auto transmission parts and textiles (with Ramie Textiles, the 2000 worker subsidiary of San Miguel) for export to Japan and elsewhere. In late 1986 two officials from Yamaha visited the Cavite Export Processing zone, where the company decided to produce skiing equipment for export to Japan and the US. Yamaha has links with the Yupangco family, which is related by marriage to Vice President Laurel. A few months later another giant company with many years of experience in the country, Ajinomoto, took a 50 per cent share in California Manufacturing, and in direct response to the rise of the yen and the Taiwan dollar, Uniden decided to transfer its production of electrical components from Taiwan to the Philippines from early 1988.

This latter caught the headlines for some time, since it involved the transfer of the company's mainline production and exporting operations to the Philippines, where Uniden now has two affiliates. Starting monthly wages of their women workers are a mere ₱1900 ($94), one third of what they had been in Taiwan. In the words of Muto Hiromi, the company's senior managing director, 'We will never move the plant from the Philippines. We believe it is the last site for labor-intensive manufacturers like us to operate abroad.' Another company of the same mind is Takahashi Denki, the wire harness maker which moved to the tax-free Mactan district in May 1988: 'In a year or so we will shift half of our Japanese production facilities to Mactan' (*JEJ*, 10 December 1988, p. 8). A month earlier, Asahi Glass had launched a feasibility study to set up in the Philippines its fourth Asian production base in cooperation with Republic Glass. If that comes through, it will be the first new giant project since the fall of Marcos (*JEJ*, 31 October 1987, p. 4; 20 February 1988, p. 18; 16 April 1988, p. 19; 13 August 1988, p. 6; 17 December

1988, p. 22; *Philippine Development*, November–December 1986, pp. 2–5; *Business Day*, 24 May and 24 July 1985; and 15 September 1986:24; *Manila Chronicle*, 19 November 1986, p. 4).

Conclusion on the Philippines

In spite of Aquino's successful referendum on the new constitution and the congressional elections which swept her supporters to office in mid-1987, the kidnapping of Mitsui's Wakaoji a few months before and the attempted coup a few months afterwards confirmed the fragility of her position. Many members of the ruling class had adopted a wait and see attitude, coming to her support only after it was clear that the balance of power still favoured her. As past Japanese ambassador Sawaki had said in 1985 (*Business Day*, 15 August 1985, p. 5): 'The trouble is there is nobody who is qualified enough to succeed Mr Marcos.' Indeed! The Japanese ruling class as a whole still fears that no one can keep the lid on in the Philippines, and the bubble of interest expressed in 1986–88 is losing air. Having being caught with their fingers in the till during the EDSA uprising, they do not want to get too close to any other ruling class faction whose hold on the country might be uncertain.

Other foreign capital, particularly from the NICs where profit margins are tight and differences in wages are critical, has been less cautious and has been pouring into the country. In the first half of 1988, total approved foreign equity investments soared by 369 per cent over the same period in 1987 to $248 million, the largest share coming from Taiwan in agribusiness (shrimps and prawns) and petro-chemicals. The latter had been in the works since 1977, and at last the time for it seemed ripe. Even more significant is that the foreign share of the total approved equity investments leapt from 38 per cent to 64 per cent (Table 7.6). Although the amount from Japan jumped by 142 per cent, it was still only 13 per cent of the total, indicating Japanese capital's continued ambiguity. Following its July survey, the Japan Bond Research Institute upped its risk-rating score for the Philippines to a mere 3.9 out of 10, the highest since 1984, but still low compared to 9.9 for Singapore, 8.3 for South Korea and Thailand, 7.4 for Malaysia and 6.0 for Indonesia. However, by the end of the year, when it seemed that foreign capital had helped GNP grow by 6.5 per cent, the *Nihon Keizai Shinbun* (3 November, p. 11) pointed out that 'it is beginning to be noticed that following Malaysia and Thailand, the next site for the relocation of Japanese factories will be the Philippines' (*JEJ*, 3 September 1988, pp. 1, 5; 17 September 1988, p. 8; *NKS*, 30 October 1988, p. 7; 3 November 1988, p. 11; *FEER*, 1 September 1988, pp. 49–50; *JS*, November 1988, p. 52).

The Aquino government has done everything possible to unite the various ruling class factions and institutions, particularly within the military and between the military, the Church and the leading bourgeois families. Its limited success has been the main reason for the reluctance of Japanese companies to make new investments. But while capitalists remain cautious, the Japanese government is providing unprecedented amounts of aid to the regime, having agreed with the US that the Philippines is the most strategic area in Asia.

Although it may seem that Japan's importance in the Filipino class struggle is insignificant compared to that of the US, the Aquino government relies more heavily on it than did Marcos, the President herself even attending Hirohito's funeral. However, the main source of Japan's current leverage is in finance and trade rather than investment. As in Indonesia, it is at this macro-level that the Filipino masses will be affected most by the Japanese presence and will in turn affect it. Neither of those two ASEAN countries, which receive most of Japan's aid and most of whose aid comes from Japan, has a sizeable working class raised in Japanese factories.

The larger Filipino industrial working class is a major force in that country, and it is increasingly organised under the umbrella of the National Democratic Front. But the latter's growing confrontation with the Aquino regime will only be indirectly affected by the activities of private capitalists, whether local, American or Japanese. Of the three, the Japanese are the most adept at breaking grassroots organisation, and their importance might increase if their 'sentiment' does translate into 'investment fever'. At the national level, next to the repressive might of the US military, Japanese money will make the second most important contribution to the struggle, because it alone will be able to meet the growing fiscal crisis of the Philippines government.

CONCLUSION

There is no question that the crises in both the Philippines and Indonesia, which reached their height in 1983–86, greatly reduced the independence from foreign capital of their ruling classes. Both governments have virtually gone begging for foreign investment, but the leading capitalists in the region, from Japan, have remained cautious. The Japanese government, lacking the politico-military experience to manage the empire its capitalists have been buying, still relies on the leading capitalist power in the region, the US. So while Japanese capitalists hesitate, the government founders with its limited colonial experience trying to operate a neo-colonial system which even the US can no longer manage. Simply pressing on in the old way, by offering financial aid to complement American military aid, and by letting capitalists confine themselves to their global strategy of finding cheap parts and assembly sites for their faltering machine industries, is proving a manifest failure in countries like Indonesia and the Philippines.

Conclusion: Trade and Japan's New Imperialism

To grasp the connection between Japan's countless DFI projects throughout the world and the new imperialism requires looking at them through a different window, one with a global view. I have selected trade to serve this purpose, because the rise of the yen resulted from the problem first manifesting itself at this level, and because it is a window through which the realities of capitalism are normally the least visible. In the case of Japan's new imperialism, however, this window is singularly illuminating.

Trade connotes bartering, exchanging different things to meet mutual needs. But when capitalists sell products, they do this in order to realise the surplus value which was extracted from workers, not to meet mutual needs. And when buying and selling across national boundaries is not just between different firms, but between different branches of the same firm, the notion of trade becomes quite meaningless. Trade statistics might record prices for goods which are purely nominal, reflecting not what nations exchange, but the accounting strategies of TNCs to minimise taxes.

It is important to know when what is called trade is in fact simply a book-keeping entry within a corporation. However, there are reasons, even in such cases of 'transfer pricing', for examining national trade statistics. The most important is the occurrence of unequal change, which can be grasped better at the macro-level of international trade than the micro-level of the company.

There are three main ways in which Japanese capital benefits from buying and selling across national boundaries, two relating to imports and one to exports; together they constitute the imperialism of trade. First, Japanese capital obtains raw materials at the least cost in rent, by using its market power to force the lowest possible prices onto the owners of the raw materials, or by getting a share in that ownership and rent through DFI. This type of trade occurs heavily between Japan and the ASEAN countries. Second, Japanese capital gets cheap supplies of labour-intensive manufactures (including components), and benefits from the unequal exchange that results from their pricing. Both import strategies, buying raw materials and labour-intensive manufactures, result from the international separ-

244

ation by the TNCs of their production sites from their sites of circulation. The former are located where costs are lowest and the latter where effective demand is highest. The most important part of the world with which Japan trades in this way is Asia.

Finally, by selling abroad, Japanese capital 'realises' the surplus value created by Japanese workers. This kind of trade has as its object the marketing of Japanese made goods. It involves the opposite kind of separation between production and circulation: low-cost production at home and selling in high-purchasing power countries abroad. North America and Europe are the key areas for exporting consumer goods in this way, while Asia is the main target for exporting investment goods. To understand why these three activities constitute the imperialism of trade, I need to explain briefly why labour intensive products tend to sell at prices which are below their value and why raw materials sell at prices above their value.

UNEQUAL EXCHANGE AND RENT

I start with the Marxist distinction between surplus creation and surplus distribution. The former, Marx showed, could only be grasped in value terms, as the difference between the socially necessary time workers put in (the value they create) and the socially necessary time required to make what they can buy with their wages (the value they get back). The notion of socially necessary emphasises that employers impose certain requirements on their workers – average skill and average speed – and that they must keep up with the technologies of rivals. Otherwise, they lose profitability and eventually go bankrupt.

The distribution of the surplus, however, occurs through the price mechanism. It must be expressed in values, to show how much surplus is created, and prices, to show how much is distributed to each industry. So long as all workers put in the same working day and get the same wage, labour intensive industries create more surplus value than capital intensive industries. Now if prices correspond to values so that the surplus created corresponds to the surplus distributed, then capital in the most labour intensive industries will earn the highest rate of profit and *vice versa*.

These different rates of profit will then signal movements of capital from low to high profit industries, and the resulting falls and increases in their supplies will shift their price structures. The shortages in the low profit industries will lead to price rises (above value), while the abundances in the high profit industries will pull prices down (below value). The points at which the prices settle are where capital ceases to move from one industry to another, that is, where the rate of profit (the surplus distributed in relation to total outlay) is the same in all industries.

The prices at which labour intensive and capital intensive products exchange are thus *not equal* to their values. Equilibrium prices ensure an equal *distribution* of the surplus, each industry getting an amount proportional, not to the surplus created (not to its outlay on labour), but to its *total* outlay. Unequal exchange is thus the norm: at equilibrium prices which yield the same rate of profit (the same rate of surplus distribution), labour intensive industries surrender more value than they receive in return, while capital intensive industries receive more than they surrender.

The most insightful extension of this reasoning to international trade was by Arghiri Emmanuel (1972). He distinguished two types of unequal exchange in trade between the advanced and the underdeveloped capitalist countries: that resulting from their respective specialisations in capital and labour intensive industries (a simple extension of the above to trade), and that resulting from the lower wages of workers in the underdeveloped countries.

Both claims were very controversial. Emmanuel had argued that surplus creation was greater in the underdeveloped countries, not just because they specialised in labour intensive products, but because their wages were lower. Surplus created, he argued, could vary for two distinct reasons: first, according to the degree of labour intensity of an industry, which determines the total new value created by workers, and secondly, according to the degree to which workers in the industry are paid for the new value they create (the rate of surplus value).

Orthodox Marxism rejected both of Emmanuel's arguments for the same basic reason. It claimed that since productive forces in the underdeveloped countries were backward, the value created in a working day was less than that created in the advanced countries with their higher technologies. So although long hours were put in by workers in the underdeveloped countries, and although their workers received a pittance, neither the total value created nor the surplus left after wages were paid compared with the advanced countries, simply because the time put in was not *socially necessary*. The use of backward technology meant that a lot of time was wasted.

The power of the orthodox critique rested heavily on the conditions of the 1960s. Before the massive DFI of the 1970s by the advanced powers in the underdeveloped countries, the value created in the latter was not very great. Even though real wages (the physical quantities of goods they bought) were abysmal, the *value* of these wages (the time needed to make the goods with backward technologies) was relatively high. So the level of surplus creation in the underdeveloped countries was low. For this reason, capital could only find opportunities for accumulation in raw material related industries, as explained above.

By the late 1980s, however, Japanese and other advanced capital had brought a large amount of the most up to date plant and equipment into underdeveloped countries, and the value created in a working day has come to approach that in the advanced countries. Both labour intensive production and lower wages now translate into higher levels of surplus creation in the underdeveloped countries. There is thus growing reason to believe that unequal exchange has become widespread.

However, a totally different kind of unequal exchange which has in the past operated in favour of underdeveloped countries, namely rent, is now becoming rarer. Rent from raw materials used to compensate for backward technologies because raw materials, such as natural rubber, while themselves requiring no socially necessary time to make (though some must be added to extract them), nevertheless can do the same jobs as substitutes (synthetic rubber) which do take time to make. Since using them yields a higher rate of profit than their more costly substitutes, capital is naturally keen to get hold of them. With their prices exceeding their value (the time needed to make them), their sale secures a distinctive share of the total surplus created, called rent. They receive in exchange more value than goes into them. The scarcer they become, or the more costly are their synthetic substitutes, the higher their prices and the more rent they command.

However, precisely because of rising rent due to greater scarcity, a point is reached where production of substitutes becomes profitable, and a growing share of world demand is met by substitutes. These were the kinds of forces which raised and then pulled down the oil and other commodity prices, drastically reducing the rent received by ASEAN countries in the mid-1980s.

ASEAN AND THE STRUGGLE OVER RENT

Wherever productive forces have been backward, capital's chief opportunities for accumulation have been in rent-related industries. That was why nineteenth century imperialism targeted countries rich in raw materials, and why they eventually became capitalist themselves. Their urban centres functioned as clearing houses for trade in raw materials, and after these were separated from their hinterlands in the struggles for decolonisation, they became the Asian NICs. But capital accumulation in the hinterlands continued for some time to be based on trade in raw materials.

Table 8.1 shows that apart from the Philippines, which exports more manufactured than non-manufactured products, the ASEAN countries in 1985 still relied overwhelmingly on non-manufactured exports. But even the relatively high figures for the Philippines and Thailand are illusory, since the bulk of the manufactured exports are either processed raw materials or components of one sort or another made by TNCs for export. That they do not reflect an overall development of the productive forces is confirmed by the uniformly high shares of imports occupied by manufactures: Indonesia (74.4 per cent), Malaysia (76.4 per cent), Thailand (66.3 per cent) and the Philippines (68.0 per cent) (ASEAN Promotion Centre, April 1988, pp. 20–1).

The weights of the different commodities in ASEAN trade depend heavily on supply and demand, which can fluctuate violently and cause dramatic changes in rent. From 1980–86, commodity prices fell 31 per cent in real terms, the only comparable decline this century occurring in the Great Depression in 1925–32. Since 1985–86, there has been a partial but uneven recovery, and this has greatly altered the export structures of some countries. In general, the demand for industrial materials has increased in response to the revival of accumulation in the advanced countries, but food prices have not improved much. However, even within these broad categories there are variations. Tin prices were more than halved when the International Tin Agreement collapsed in October 1985, and by mid-1988 they were still only 60 per cent of their previous price-support level. The price of oil also continues to languish (falling to $11.50 a barrel in October 1988) as producers fail to deal with over-supply. Natural rubber and wood pulp prices, on the other hand, are at record levels. And partly because of the devastating drought in 1987, large production declines of commodities like rice have lifted their prices

Table 8.1   Top six exports of ASEAN countries, 1970–85

Indonesia

1965		1980		1985	
Rubber	31.4	Crude Oil	63.3	Crude Oil	44.4
Crude Oil	24.8	LNG	13.2	LNG	19.6
Petroleum		Wood	8.3	Plywood	5.1
Products	13.7	Rubber	4.9	Rubber	3.9
Tin	5.6	Coffee	3.0	Coffee	3.0
Coffee	4.5	Tin	2.0	Petroleum	
Palm oil	3.9			Products	2.4
Manufactures	–	Manufactures	3.8	Manufactures	13.7

Malaysia

1960		1980		1985	
Rubber	38.3	Petroleum	23.8	Petroleum	23.0
Tin	20.6	Rubber	16.4	Electronic Parts	11.8
Logs	10.0	Logs	9.3	Rubber	7.5
Iron ore	3.6	Tin	8.9	Logs	7.2
Palm oil	3.1	Electronic Parts		LNG	6.2
Wood	2.1	Wood	8.1	Palm Olein	6.0
Manufactures	–	Manufactures	4.2	Manufactures	27.2
			17.3		

Thailand

1965		1980		1985	
Rice	33.6	Rice	14.6	Textiles	12.2
Rubber	16.4	Tapioca	11.2	Rice	11.6
Tin	9.0	Rubber	9.3	Tapioca	7.7
Jute	8.6	Tin	8.5	Rubber	7.0
Maize	7.8	Textiles	7.2	IC	4.3
Tapioca	6.2	Maize	6.5	Maize	4.0
Manufactures	6.0	Manufactures	34.7	Manufactures	41.0

Philippines

1960		1980		1985	
Copra	24.8	Sugar	10.8	Semiconductors	15.3
Sugar	23.9	Coconut Oil	9.8	Coconut Oil	7.6
Wood	16.4	Copper	9.4	IC	3.8
Abaca	7.5	Semiconductors	8.7	Sugar	3.7
Coconuts	3.4	Gold	4.1	Copper	3.6
Copper	3.3	Wood	3.1	Bananas	2.4
Manufactures	3.2	Manufactures	33.4	Manufactures	69.8

Source: *JS*, November 1987, p. 51.

somewhat. But palm oil prices fell by over 50 per cent in 1985–87 (*FEER*, 9 June 1988, pp. 90–4; 5 January 1989, pp. 36–8).

With logs and rubber as the main gainers, and oil, tin and palm oil as the main losers, the main effects on the structures of ASEAN exports can be illustrated in Malaysia. In 1985–87, the shares of petroleum tumbled from 23 to 13.9 per cent, of palm oil (including processed) from 10.4 to 7.2 per cent and of tin from 4.3 to 1.9 per cent, while those of rubber rose from 7.5 to 8.7 per cent and logs from 7.2 to 9.5 per cent. Meanwhile, exports of electronic parts climbed from 11.7 per cent to claim number one position with a share of 15.3 per cent. If parts, electrical appliances and other electrical machinery are included, the share of electrical machinery soared from 17 to 24.3 per cent (*Quarterly Bulletin*, Bank Negara, March–June 1988, pp. 84–90).

The main effect of the crisis of commodity prices on Thai exports has been further to erode the weight of rice, which by 1987 had fallen to 7.6 per cent, and to slash that of tin to a mere 0.8 per cent. ICs, on the other hand, climbed to 5.0 per cent and textiles soared to 16.2 per cent (*Quarterly Review*, Bank of Thailand, December 1987, pp. 54–5). In the Philippines, the structure of exports remained unchanged, mainly because the rape of the country's resources had long since reduced the share of any one of them, apart from coconut oil, to relative unimportance. The same unchanged structure of Indonesian exports resulted from the opposite cause: so great is the dominance of oil and gas that even the current depression could not remove them from their top positions.

JAPAN'S IMPORTS FROM ASEAN

Japan is the number one trading partner of both Muslim countries in ASEAN, in 1986 accounting for 44.8 per cent of Indonesia's exports and 29.2 per cent of her imports, and 22.5 per cent of Malaysia's exports and 20.5 per cent of her imports. Japan was also Thailand's number one source of imports (28.2 per cent), but taking only half that share of Thai exports she was second to the US. The Philippines' trade remains dominated by the US (35 per cent of exports and 24.8 per cent of imports), but Japan is the second largest trading partner, with 17.8 per cent of exports and 17.0 per cent of imports (ASEAN Promotion Centre, April 1988, pp. 18–19).

The dominant features of present day Japanese trade with ASEAN, an almost exclusive concentration (weakening slightly in 1982–88) on importing natural resources and exporting manufactures, still reflects the structure of Japanese capital accumulation

Table 8.2   Japan's main imports from ASEAN, 1982–87

	Indonesia		Malaysia		Thailand		Philippines	
	1982	1987	1982	1987	1982	1987	1982	1987
Raw Materials	98.5	88.4	86.6	91.0	75.8	70.6	88.9	79.3
Foodstuffs	2.5	6.3	1.7	1.9	30.0	43.7	27.0	40.4
Textile Materials	0.0	0.1	0.4	0.6	0.1	0.1	0.5	2.0
Metal ores and scrap	2.7	3.4	3.7	2.3	1.5	0.5	45.3	25.5
Mineral fuels	81.9	75.1	37.9	37.6	0.0	0.1	0.0	1.8
Other raw materials	11.4	3.5	42.9	48.6	44.5	26.2	16.1	9.6
Rubber	0.5	0.7	3.0	1.9	38.2	19.7	0.0	0.0
Wood	10.7	2.4	36.0	43.8	0.8	1.4	13.2	5.9
Manufactures	1.5	11.6	13.4	9.0	24.2	29.4	11.1	20.7
Chemicals	0.1	0.4	0.4	1.5	2.7	2.7	2.1	3.7
Machinery	0.1	0.1	1.7	1.9	0.4	6.5	3.8	2.6
Other	1.3	11.2	11.2	5.6	21.5	20.2	5.2	14.4
Non-ferrous metals	0.8	2.8	9.0	2.4	9.9	2.5	0.6	5.5
TOTAL VALUE ($ billion)	13.2	8.4	3.5	4.8	1.1	1.8	2.0	1.4

Source: ASEAN Promotion Centre, April 1988, pp. 29–37.

before the oil crises. The basic materials industries required the importation of natural resources for processing and then re-exporting them as finished products. The ferocious appetite for things like logs – fed by high rates of accumulation – was a major cause for one of the greatest ecological tragedies of Southeast Asia: deforestation. Table 8.2 shows that ASEAN's function in the Japanese trading scheme, even in the mid-1980s, has been almost exclusively to supply raw materials.

If we look at particular commodities, the same overwhelming reliance by ASEAN on a few resources required by Japanese capital appears. In the first six months of 1988, Indonesia's top exports to Japan were LNG ($1.6 billion), crude and raw oils ($1.5 billion), heavy fuel oils ($288 million), intermediate aluminium products ($172 million), shrimps ($172 million), naphtha ($157 million), copper ore ($125 million), intermediate nickel products ($114) and tropical lumber ($74 million). Malaysia's top exports to Japan in the same period were liquefied gas ($534 million), crude oil ($312 million), natural rubber ($68 million), palm oil ($49 million), intermediate tin products ($46 million), copper ore ($37 million), kerosine ($34 million), tropical lumber ($32 million), shrimps and prawns ($24 million) and prepared elements ($21 million). Heading the Philippines' list were bananas ($193 million), copper ore ($146 million), shrimps and prawns ($107 million), iron ore ($93 million), intermediate copper products ($63 million), tropical lumber ($44 million), pineapples ($38 million), gold ($18 million), ferro-alloys ($17 million) and naphtha ($11 million). In Thailand, apart from the conspicuous influence of Minebea, the story was the same: natural rubber ($262 million), shrimps and prawns ($111 million), poultry ($78 million), precious and semi-precious stones ($75 million), squid ($69 million), sugar ($46 million), bearings ($38 million), jewelry ($31 million), gypsum ($26 million) and intermediate tin products ($26 million) (Nihon bōeki shinkōkai, 1988c, pp. 33–6).

Most of these imports into Japan are handled by trading subsidiaries of the giant *sōgō shōsha*, and in many cases the purchases are made from one or other of the DFI ventures which flooded Asia in the 1970s and still extract the resources. They either help the Japanese buyer get the cheapest possible deal, or if they have substantial involvements they too get away with a share of the rent. However, rising prices do not necessarily indicate increases in total rent, since the only really substantial and sustained price rises since 1978 have been for resources which have been massively depleted. While the rent on the remaining supplies might well rise, when these are close to exhaustion, as has happened to timber and to a lesser extent certain fish almost throughout Southeast Asia, the total rent falls.

The share of forests to total land area in Southeast Asia has plunged over the years: in the Philippines from 60 to 27 per cent in 1960–85 and in Thailand (now a net importer of timber) from 66 to 29 per cent in the same period. Following a recent flood disaster due to deforestation, the Thai government finally banned commercial logging in January 1989. In 1979 Indonesia and Malaysia produced 58 per cent of the world's hardwood logs and 85 per cent of world exports, but at current rates of logging even Malaysia's reserves will only last some time into the 1990s (Sahabat Alam Malaysia, 1987, p. 12; *FEER*, 22 December 1988, p. 14; 12 January 1989, pp. 34–41; 2 February 1989, pp. 26–7).

Japan gobbles up half the world's tropical timber exports. But because of mounting restrictions due to excessive deforestation, each of the Philippines, Indonesia and Malaysia has in turn risen to and then fallen from the position of supplying about half the Japanese demand for logs. The Philippines supply peaked in 1969, but restrictions soon followed and exports were finally banned by the Aquino government. The Japanese had been smuggling huge quantities of logs, by grossly understating the value of the shipments in the Philippines relative to the value of what was unloaded in Japan. A serious conflict over the issue developed in 1985–86 when the Philippines government instituted a system of having the logs remeasured in Japan by a Japanese-based inspection agency. The Japanese government regarded this attempt to stop the smuggling as an infringement on Japanese sovereignty (*Business Day*, 15 January 1986, p. 2).

The Indonesian supply of logs to Japan peaked in 1974 but fell rapidly in 1981–85 when exports were finally banned, although Japan now simply imports Indonesian plywood instead. However, the Japan Plywood Manufacturing Association has felt threatened by the success of the Indonesian export incentive scheme, and has appealed to GATT. The dispute has escalated into a bitter conflict, with an Apkindo (Indonesian Wood Panel Association) official criticising Japan's 'colonial type thinking' of been willing to import only raw materials and not processed products. Today, Malaysia occupies the top position, but so far there are no signs of the supply being cut off, only of its depletion (*JEJ*, 19 March 1988, p. 16; Sahabat Alam Malaysia, 1987, p. 254 ff.).

A similar tale could be told of the Japanese appetite for shrimps and prawns, which the giant corporations and the vested interests that benefit from the 'trade' have stimulated to 2.6 kgs a year per person. Since 1963, when only 17 per cent of Japan's needs were met by imports, the latter have surged a hundred-fold to thrust Japan into the top position with 33 per cent of the world's share.

A detailed study on the shrimp trade by the Pacific Asia Resource Centre (*Ampo* Vol. 18, No. 4, 1987) has shown how long a road exists, from the pittance received by the Indonesian fisherpeople who catch the shrimps ($3.20 a kg in 1984) or the workers on the large joint venture boats ($1 a day), to the Japanese consumer ($16.84 a kg). It runs from the sub-contractor, through the coordinator, the packer-exporter, the trading company, primary and secondary wholesalers, to the retailer or restaurant, each one taking a slice of the rent. The Japanese and joint venture companies dominate less through the catching of fish (80 per cent of imports are netted by local concerns) than through their monopoly of the freezing and packing process, so that the share of the rent that accrues to Indonesians is minimal. 'The bulk of the profits', concluded the PARC research team, 'seem to have been enjoyed by the cold-storage firms, the exporters, the Japanese sales outlets and the local large coordinators' (ibid., p. 6).

From the local peoples' point of view, the problem is not just that the Japanese get away with the lion's share of the rent, but that the resource ceases to be available to them. In some cases, the supplies have been almost totally exhausted, and there is neither a livelihood for the fisherpeople nor the protein for the wider community. I talked to some of the people who had been displaced into a slum in Bataan (Philippines) by this process, and was told that it was the joint venture boats and the coalition of interests in Japan and the Philippines who were responsible. The Irian Jaya Sea, once among the most fertile waters of Indonesia (the sea would turn yellow with eggs), today yields under ten kgs of prawns a day to a local wooden trawler.

Fish supplies also become inaccessible to local people when the Japanese bid up the prices to levels no one can afford. So even when cultured prawns begin to replace those caught at sea, as they have in Taiwan, the cost remains prohibitive, not least because of the expensive feed, imported from Japan (or Taiwan). Cultured prawns have also left a bitter trail of pollution, usually from the seawater seeping away onto farmland from the ponds. Other problems are shortages of fresh water, which is sucked from underground wells to control the salinity in the ponds (*FEER*, 20 August 1987, pp. 62–5).

Either way, prices have become too high for local people to enjoy their traditional sources of protein. In Sri Lanka, shrimp curry was once a popular dish, but it is rarely eaten nowadays because exports have driven up prices. Malaysians can no longer afford to buy *Panaeidae* prawns because their popularity in Japan has converted them into an export product. And the pickled mullet roe (*karasumi*) or sea bream, to name two of my favourites, are no longer found in the fish shops of New Zealand.

Japanese capital responded to the oil crises of the 1970s by restructuring out of the basic materials industries and by relocating many of them in Asia close to where the resources themselves were to be found. But even with the shift into machinery, resource-poor Japan continued to require the importation of vast quantities of food, fuels and materials still needed in Japan. Trade and DFI in ASEAN therefore remained inseparable: the search for profitable investment outlets and for supplies of raw materials preserved the previous structure of trade and investment between Japan and ASEAN.

CHEAP MANUFACTURES FROM THE NICS AND ASEAN

However, *endaka*, industrial restructuring and the internationalisation of the machine industries has brought about a major shift in

Table 8.3   Changing structure of Japan's trade, 1980–88 (%)

	1980	1985	1986	1987	Jan.–June 1988
Food	10.4	12.0	15.2	15.0	14.2
Raw materials	16.9	13.9	13.9	14.7	15.1
Fuels and mining products	49.8	43.1	29.2	26.2	22.6
Manufactures	22.9	31.0	41.8	44.1	48.1
Chemicals	4.4	6.2	7.7	7.9	7.9
Machinery	7.0	9.6	11.6	12.8	14.3
Gold	0.5	1.6	5.5	2.3	2.3
Other	10.9	13.6	16.9	21.1	23.6

Source: *JS*, October 1988, p. 51.

Japan's trade. Although a lot (indeed an increasing amount) of food is still imported from Asia and elsewhere, the restructuring of the Japanese economy since 1985 has radically reduced the importation of basic materials and raised that of manufactures. Table 8.3 shows that the effect of *endaka* was primarily to substitute manufactured for basic material imports.

The giant corporations now need from ASEAN, not simply basic materials and cheap labour for the assembly industries, as they did during the 1970s, but components as well. In the 1970s most of these projects, apart from textiles, had looked heavily to the domestic markets and meshed with governments' ISI strategies. Instead of exporting finished products to Asia, Japan exported parts and assembled them with cheap labour. But now Japanese parts are too expensive, not just for the assembly plants in Asia, but also for use in Japan and the advanced countries. Since 1980, not simply have manufactured imports skyrocketed, but the emphasis has shifted markedly towards the importation of components, as revealed by Table 8.4.

The main shift in Japan's trade resulting from *endaka* is thus on the import side and on the side of component imports. But there has also been a mounting trend away from the developed to the underdeveloped countries as sources, with the NICs and ASEAN scoring the greatest increases. Among ASEAN countries the most dramatic changes have been the rising manufactured imports from Thailand and Malaysia, but also from Indonesia, although in each case most of what are called manufactures are processed raw materials. Table 8.5 shows the trend away from the advanced to the underdeveloped countries as sources of components for the Japanese machinery industries.

Table 8.4 Annual rates of increase in Japan's imports of machinery components, 1979–87

	1979–83	1983–87	1986–87
Total imports	3.4	4.3	18.3
Manufactured imports	4.5	17.7	25.0
Machinery components			
imports	11.2	17.6	31.3
Electrical	11.6	16.5	30.0
General	7.8	17.2	33.6
Transport	19.7	18.3	30.9
Precision	5.0	15.1	30.2

Source: *JS*, May 1988, p. 91.

Even NICs trade with Japan contains many of the vulnerabilities that characterised the colonial past. They all still rely heavily on exporting food, raw materials and either light manufactures, such as textiles, or relatively unsophisticated finished goods (like fridges) and components (like transformers). Nearly a fifth of South Korea's exports to Japan still comprise foodstuffs, while in the case of Taiwan it is a full third. Half of Singapore's exports to Japan are mineral fuels, while Hong Kong still specialises in textiles, watches and jewelry. On the other hand, Japan's exports to each of these countries are overwhelmingly sophisticated consumer and producer goods. However, as Table 8.6 shows, the share of manufactured to total exports to Japan of each of the NICs has risen since 1975, and machinery has increasingly substituted for textiles.

Each country has its own special function for Japan, although there have been changes over time. South Korea started as a supplier of textiles but is now also a source of iron and steel and machinery (electric and transport). Taiwan's role has been similar, although this has been complemented by key role in raw materials (such as shrimps) and reveals a longer and larger focus on electrical machinery. Hong Kong was once little more to Japan than an offshore textile factory, but like Taiwan today also concentrates on electrical and precision machinery. Singapore is still a clearing house for raw material exports (re-exports) from the ASEAN hinterlands, but it has also become a supplier of chemicals (particularly petrochemicals) and electrical machinery.

The growth of manufactured imports from the Asian NICs, in particular South Korea and Taiwan, has been the most spectacular

Table 8.5   Change in sources of machinery component imports, 1979–87

	General 1979	1987	Electrical 1979	1987	Transport 1979	1987	Precision 1979	1987	Total 1979	1987
Advanced	91.1	78.2	70.4	69.4	93.9	95.0	83.4	84.5	83.1	79.3
US	53.2	48.4	61.0	57.1	64.3	69.5	55.3	59.2	58.2	57.7
West Germany	15.2	10.3	2.4	3.5	7.1	10.7	9.1	8.9	8.4	7.7
Britain	5.3	4.3	1.2	3.4	13.5	4.9	5.2	6.0	5.2	4.2
Underdeveloped	8.8	21.7	29.5	30.3	6.0	5.0	16.6	15.0	16.8	20.5
Asian NICs	6.7	15.3	22.6	27.5	3.2	3.9	11.1	13.7	12.4	17.1
South Korea	1.4	5.5	12.2	15.3	1.1	1.7	2.3	5.5	5.4	8.3
Taiwan	2.0	4.2	9.0	9.9	0.9	2.1	4.3	4.8	4.6	5.9
Singapore	2.6	3.4	0.9	1.6	1.1	0.1	2.2	1.3	1.7	1.8
Hong Kong	0.7	2.2	0.5	0.8	0.0	0.0	2.4	2.2	0.7	1.2

Source: *JS*, May 1988, p. 91.

feature of Japanese trade with Asia since the rise of the yen. Table 8.7 shows that it has been accompanied by an even more spectacular fall in the American share and rise in the EC share of Japan's manufacture imports.

Since the rise of the yen, South Korea has moved from the third to the second and Taiwan from the fifth to the fourth largest source of Japan's manufactured imports, claiming 9.4 and 6.4 per cent respectively in the first half of 1988 (Nihon bōeki shinkōkai, 1988c, p. 17). When one looks through a list of the top three sources of Japan's manufactured imports, the dominance of the US, South Korea and Taiwan is striking. South Korea and Taiwan are most prominent in electrical machinery, between them accounting for about a quarter of the total. Imports from Germany, currently in number three position, are mainly motor cars, while those from China (in fifth position) resemble ASEAN: largely processed raw materials or light manufactures such as textiles.

GYAKU YUNYŪ (RE-IMPORTS): THE RAGE IN JAPAN

Because of the extraordinary degree to which the *sōgō shosha* dominate the handling of imports to Japan, capital absorbs most of the advantages stemming from low-cost production in Asia. The *shōsha* are notorious for their capacity to extract surpluses in the world of distribution, in typical merchantilist fashion by buying cheap and selling dear. So even when local suppliers have no links with Japanese

Japan's New Imperialism

Table 8.6 NICs manufacturing exports to Japan (shares of total exports to Japan) 1975–88

	1975	1985	Jan.–June 1988
South Korea (mfg total)	61.4	64.4	78.1
Chemicals	2.4	4.9	4.6
Machinery	12.9	12.2	14.6
Iron and steel	0.9	10.4	14.4
Textiles	32.0	22.9	20.1
Non-ferrous metals	0.2	0.4	1.0
Country weight[a]	6.8	6.6	9.4
Taiwan (mfg total)	45.8	57.6	67.3
Chemicals	2.4	3.5	3.3
Machinery	12.2	13.8	19.7
Iron and steel	1.2	4.1	9.8
Textiles	11.9	10.7	9.7
Non-ferrous metals	0.4	0.8	2.1
Country weight[a]	3.1	4.9	6.4
Hong Kong (mfg total)	80.3	84.4	85.0
Chemicals	2.6	3.6	1.6
Machinery	7.9	14.3	18.1
Iron and steel	0.0	0.0	0.1
Textiles	30.6	33.3	19.8
Non-ferrous metals	0.6	0.3	0.4
Country Weight	1.7	1.6	1.8
Singapore (mfg total)	21.7	28.5	48.7
Chemicals	8.3	9.4	15.3
Machinery	8.9	12.1	19.0
Iron and steel	0.3	0.0	1.4
Textiles	1.0	0.4	0.5
Non-ferrous metals	0.2	0.4	0.6
Country weight[a]	0.7	1.1	1.2

Note: [a]Share of Japan's manufacturing imports from that country to Japan's total manufacturing imports.
Source: Nihon bōeki shinkōkai, 1988c, pp. 134–44.

capital, the *shōsha*'s capacity to force low prices ensures that unequal exchange in its favour is maximised.

OEM contracts also typically see Japanese companies as the prime beneficiaries, since well advertised brand names guarantee passage through the labyrinthine Japanese distribution system and high profits at the end. The popular press almost daily runs some or other major article on how lucrative the Japanese market is supposed to be. However, we have seen that Japanese workers do not have the buying power to absorb the outputs of Japanese factories, and that if

Table 8.7   Shares of Japan's manufacture imports, 1985–88

	1985	1987	Jan.–June 1988
US	35.5	26.8	26.3
EC[a]	18.6	23.0	22.9
Germany	7.0	9.0	8.6
UK	3.9	4.0	4.3
France	2.7	3.7	4.0
Southeast Asia	19.1	23.7	23.9
NICs[b]	13.0	17.6	17.6
ASEAN	4.6	4.7	4.8
China	4.4	4.5	4.8
Other	22.4	22.0	22.1

Notes: [a]after 1985 includes Spain and Portugal.
[b]excludes Singapore.
Source: Nihon bōeki shinkōkai, 1988c, p. 16

there are big spenders in Japan then they belong to the upper classes. But for consumer goods imported from Asia, cheaper because of the lower wages in the region and because of the higher yen, the Japanese working class does possess immense spending power. Even if it means a fall in the quality of some goods, workers can raise living standards by buying NICs and ASEAN. Japanese capital has realised this and is getting in on the spoils, importing left, right and centre under whatever scheme it can. So while the upper classes are buying imports from America and Europe, particularly cars from Germany and gold and diamonds (originally) from South Africa – gold and passenger cars have been the top consumer import items since 1987 – the working classes are shopping for bargains.

The top items for the latter are black-and-white TVs, portable radios and electric fans, with imports from the NICs by August 1987 respectively claiming 66.5, 58.4 and 56 per cent of domestic consumption. Tokyo now has many 'NICs Shops', specialising in goods from the region, and if precious metals enter this picture it is in such press headlines as 'NIC good importers find Tokyo gold mine'. One of them in Yurakucho is called NICSSONS! (*JEJ*, 26 December 1987, p. 2; 16 April 1988, p. 1; *JEJ*, 12 March 1988, p. 1; *NKS*, 27 November 1987, p. 23).

A number of large supermarket chains are aggressively importing NICs products. Daiei, Seiyu, Ito-Yokado and Jusco have been the most active, but so have some leading department stores like Mitsukoshi. Jusco has brought in South Korean playback-only videocassette recorders, 14-inch colour TVs, fridges and bicycles. A spokesperson proudly claimed that 80 per cent of its Japanese brand radiocassettes were made in the NICs and brought in under OEM contracts (*NKS*, 18 January 1988, p. 17; *JEJ*, 26 December 1987, p. 2; *JJTI*, No. 5 1987, pp. 20–2).

OEM contracts, particularly in the electronics industry, are becoming a major cost-cutting strategy for the Japanese TNCs. For example, in South Korea Toshiba gets fridges and washing machines from Samsung; NEC has a tie-up with Goldstar to supply fridges and electric stoves and with Daewoo also to supply electric stoves; Matsushita gets fridges from Goldstar; and in 1989 Canon will get memory chips from Samsung. To complement its use of South Korean metal moulds, Hitachi is boosting its supply of labour-intensive products (parts for radiocassettes and small TVs) from the NICs. Indeed Hitachi is 'shifting its business style from one led by exports to an import-dependent one' (*JEJ*, 29 January 1988, p. 24; 20 August 1988, p. 13; *NKS*, 4 November 1988, p. 13). Toshiba and JVC are bringing in low-end stereos, while the OEM contracts of many major companies for colour TVs are soaring. One has to guess how many from the numbers of imported colour TVs, which rose to 347 471 in 1987, since as the *Japan Economic Journal* pointed out:

> As South Korean-brand TVs are still not very popular among Japanese consumers, it is likely that many of the TVs imported from that country are sold under Japanese brand names (5 March 1988, p. 3).

In 1988 the South Korean share alone of Japan's domestic market for colour TVs and VCRs was about 10 per cent. One of the big Japanese players in both products is Crown Corporation, which gets supplies from Goldstar, Samsung and Daewoo (*JEJ*, 11 June 1988, p. 17; *NKS*, 31 October 1988, p. 1).

Lest one exaggerates the strength of the recent trend, it is well to remember that US firms still have even more OEM tie-ups with Korean *chaebol*, such as Kia cars to Ford, Daewoo cars (Pontiac LeMans) and car parts to GM, and Hyundai small motors to GE. But neither are OEM contracts being limited to the NICs or even to Asia: in January 1988 NEC Home Electronics awarded a contract to a Spanish firm (Electronica Bertran SA) to make 25-inch colour TVs for the European market. A year before JVC had signed a contract with a producer in Britain, the other favourite (low cost) production

Table 8.8   Recent (including planned) cases of re-imports by Japanese
companies, 1987

Company	Production site	Commodities re-imported
Toyota Motors	US	Selica convertibles
Nissan Motors	Taiwan	Pressed parts
Honda Motors	Italy	Sports bikes
	US	Large bikes, small cars (Accord Coupé)
Mitsubishi Motors	Thailand	Pressed metal moulds
Suzuki Motors	South Korea	50 cc motor cycles
Toyota Body Parts	Taiwan	Pressed parts
Showa Manufacturing	Indonesia	Motor bike shock springs
Yushin	US	Car mechanical parts
Matsushita Electric	North America	Colour TV
Hitachi Manufacturing	North America, Taiwan	Colour TV
Sony	US	Colour TV
Canon	Taiwan	Desktop calculators
Sharp	Thailand	Electric stoves, fridges
Mitsubishi Electric	US	TV phones
Oki Electric	US	Car phones
Aiwa	Singapore	Stereo headphones, Mini-Combo[a]
Nippon Colombia	Taiwan	Mini-Combo[a]
Akai	Taiwan	Mini-Combo[a]
Sapporo Beer	US	Carbonic acid, fruit juice drinks
Yamanouchi Seiyaku	Taiwan	Anti-coagulant for blood tests
Pokka	Singapore	Canned drinks
Japan Pepsico	China	Pepsi Cola
Kagome	US	Carbonated drinks

Note: [a]A Mini-Combo is a miniaturised stereo combination system.
Source: *NKS*, 21 December 1987, p. 37.

site in Europe. Most of the majors are beginning to re-import from
their subsidiaries in the North America. For example, Hitachi gets
colour TVs from its Canadian plant, Matsushita colour TVs from the
US and Toshiba electric ovens and 46-inch colour TVs from its
Tennessee plant (Ishida, 1987, pp. 57, 220; *JEJ*, 9 January 1988, p.
10; 5 March 1988, p. 3; 12 November 1988, p. 22).

Japanese capital is therefore not just pushing imports from the
NICs, but also from Japanese subsidiaries everywhere. Table 8.8 lists
some of the most prominent cases of *gyaku yunyū* in 1987. Major

examples of the same thing in 1988 include the decision by Fujitsu to import such high-tech products as magnetic disks and optical communications equipment from its Oregon and Dallas subsidiaries on a full-fledged basis (*NKS*, 26 September 1988, p. 11).

The car industry represents the most advanced combination of Japanese capital's world-wide low-cost production strategy with a careful targeting of its domestic market. At the upper end is the US made Honda Accord, whose left hand drive sells it at a premium for being 'free spirited'. Mazda's two-door sports coupe developed with Ford, the Probe, falls into a similar category, as does Mitsubishi's 2600cc Magna re-imported from Australia. The real top end of this market is of course held by such foreign concerns as Daimler–Benz and Jaguar Japan, but even here Japanese capital is getting in on the act, for example, through a wholly owned subsidiary set up by Nissho Iwai to market Benz and BMW cars (*JEJ*, 20 February 1988, p. 3; 13 August 1988, p. 18; 12 November 1988, p. 22).

The first spectacular onslaught on the bottom end of the car market occurred on 15 August 1988 when Mitsubishi and Hyundai brought in 150 Pony Excels, to test the water. It may take some time to penetrate the Japanese market, partly because the prices were not as cheap as expected. In the meantime, Mitsubishi still has the satisfaction of the price advantage its own cars get from importing transmissions, gears and other parts from Hyundai. Carefully monitoring the process are Daewoo and Kia, which are planning to follow suit with their LeMans and Festive respectively. Perhaps right at the tail end of the vehicle market are Honda's plans to import its Thai-made 100cc motorcycles, to complement the larger bikes from its Italian and US plants (*NKS*, 25 October 1988, p. 3; *JEJ*, 8 August 1987, pp. 1, 14; 13 February 1988, p. 19; 27 August 1988, p. 2).

Almost all the Japanese car makers are also using overseas made parts for their vehicles at home: low cost ones from Asia and sophisticated functional ones from the US. But so far only Nissan has dared to procure entire vehicles from a foreign supplier, for a foreign market and on an OEM basis: three types of fork lifts from Britain for the European market (*JEJ*, 5 March 88, p. 3).

Even what might be called traditional imports from Asia have been expanding at rates which have frightened some capitalists in Japan. Sweaters and knitwear imports have already forced the Japanese textile trade balance into the red, and capital in the industry has laid dumping charges against South Korean exporters. Half of the total imports come from South Korea, with most of the rest from China,

Taiwan and Hong Kong. While Japanese capital can hold its own in the highly capitalised areas of the industry, it can no longer compete in the more labour intensive garment sector. By the end of 1988 South Korean sweaters were claiming well over a third of the Japanese market (*NKS*, 6 November 1988, p. 11; *JEJ*, 10 September 1988, p. 4; 29 October 1988, p. 2; *FEER*, 31 December 1987, pp. 40–1).

Imports of certain basic materials, particularly steel and cement, are also sending shivers down the backs of capitalists in those industries, let alone those of workers. In both steel and cement, once again, the competition is coming from South Korea, notably Ssangyong Cement Industrial which accounts for 80 per cent of Korea's exports. In 1983–87, the share of the Japanese cement market claimed by imports shot up from 0.2 to 4.0 per cent, and the trade balance moved into the red in 1986. The Japanese steel industry, already in crisis because of falling exports, is particularly concerned about competition from South Korea, which accounts for 44 per cent of imports. In 1988 Japanese steelmakers took the extraordinary step of raising their prices by 25 per cent in an attempt to induce Chinese importers to switch to Korean steel, so that the Korean supply would be absorbed and not enter Japan (*JEJ*, 12 March 1988, p. 4; 23 July 1988, p. 5; 23 April 1988, p. 8).

Even the export drives of capital in the NICs are shifting from the US to Japan, so that South Korea and Taiwan have become to Japanese imperialism what Brazil and Mexico are to US imperialism. Japan is starting to take the idea of an Asian free-trade block, 'centred on itself and built on the yen, very seriously indeed' (*The Economist*, 17 September 1988, p. 25; *JEJ*, 12 March 1988, pp. 1–2, 5–6).

INTRA-COMPANY TRADE: THIRD COUNTRIES

While in the past the bulk of sales by Japanese overseas subsidiaries were in the local markets (ISI) and did not appear in trade statistics, the pattern is now shifting to DFI for export, either back to Japan (*gyaku yunyū*), or to third markets. Table 8.9 confirms the growing trend for Japanese companies to export to their subsidiaries overseas, for the latter to add some local content and then to export to third countries. These were the two fastest increasing tendencies of all those involving intra-company trade within the TNCs in 1980–86.

The new trends are strongest in Asia, which to Japan is still more a

Table 8.9   Intra-company trade of Japanese TNCs ($ million)

	1980	1983	1986
World exports	1 896 700	1 680 600	1 993 800
Total exports of Japanese TNCs	279 581	305 381	–
(Share of world exports)	(14.7%)	(18.2%)	–
From firms in Japan	189 177	221 483	–
From parent to overseas subsidiaries	33 739	48 703	97 871
From parent to unrelated overseas firms	138 355	157 070	208 331
From unrelated firms to overseas subsidiaries	17 083	15 710	–
From overseas subsidiaries	90 404	83 898	91 330
To parent in Japan	23 606	19 913 ⎫	41 740
To unrelated firm in Japan	37 297	28 631 ⎬	
To third countries	29 502	35 353	49 590

Source: Tsūshō sangyōshō, 1988a, p. 195.

supplier of low cost products than a market for them. Selling in the domestic market and allying with ISI, which used to be the strategy of Japanese subsidiaries in Asia, is now shifting to the advanced countries, mainly because the most threatening protectionism is now in the advanced countries rather than the underdeveloped ones. Table 8.10 confirms that DFI in America looks overwhelmingly to the domestic market in comparison to that in Asia, and that the electrical and precision machinery industries in Asia are the most export-oriented of all. Table 8.11 shows that the Asian subsidiaries have become even more export oriented since the rise of the yen.

The new export-orientation of Japanese overseas subsidiaries is not confined to Asia, even though it is strongest there. Since the rise of the yen, it is even extending to the US, which has become a cheaper production site than Japan. Although there are few statistical measures of the changes in the export-orientation of Japanese subsidiaries in the US, press and magazine reports provide numerous cases. For example, since mid-1988 Mazda has exported its US made MX-6 (Capella in Japan) to Taiwan, while Toyota and Fuji are planning to follow suit in 1989. Honda will export its US Accord to

77

Table 8.10   Markets of Japanese overseas subsidiaries, by industry and region, 1983 (%)

	Local	Japan	Other	North America	Asia	EC	¥ billion
In the USA							
Textiles	98.7	0.1	1.3	(0.0	38.3	0.0)	26.8
Iron and Steel	97.2	3.3	0.2	(0.0	0.0	100.0)	80.3
Machinery: General	94.2	0.8	4.9	(0.0	0.0	0.0)	6.2
Electrical	95.8	1.9	2.3	(4.7	94.9	0.0)	922.0
Transport	95.9	0.2	3.9	(0.0	65.9	23.8)	192.7
Precision	99.6	0.2	0.3	(0.0	0.0	0.0)	7.3
In Asia							
Textiles	62.6	5.3	32.1	(6.1	18.7	4.8)	399.7
Iron and steel	91.5	7.5	1.1	(35.2	39.0	0.0)	167.1
Machinery: General	72.1	15.2	12.7	(24.3	5.2	3.9)	73.9
Electrical	37.3	21.0	41.7	(45.0	23.9	13.5)	535.1
Transport	86.6	5.5	7.9	(15.1	24.3	32.0)	350.5
Precision	16.8	30.5	52.7	(7.2	62.3	7.2)	37.7

Source: Itsuki, 1988, p. 345.

Table 8.11   Markets of Japanese subsidiaries in Asia, 1978–86 (%)

	1978	1980	1983	1986
Local	67.4	63.9	66.9	54.7
Export	32.6	36.1	33.1	45.3
Back to Japan	8.9	9.8	10.8	15.8
To third countries	23.7	26.4	22.3	29.5

Source: Tsūshō sangyōshō, 1988a, p. 192.

South Korea in association with Daelim Motors, which sells Honda motorcycles and has technical tie-ups with Honda, as a way round the South Korean government's ban on imports of Japanese vehicles (*JEJ*, 28 May 1988, p. 20; 25 June 1988, p. 24; 30 July 1988, p. 19).

HIGH TECH EXPORTS TO ASIA: NOT JUST A MARKETPLACE

Although the major markets for Japanese exports have been in Europe and America, Asia is rapidly becoming more important.

Table 8.12   Japan's trade balances with Asia, 1980–88 ($ million)

	1985	1986	1987	1–6, 1988
Indonesia	−7 947	−4 649	−5 437	−3 524
Malaysia	−2 162	−2 137	−2 604	−1 053
Philippines	−306	−132	62	−166
Thailand	1 003	639	1 157	1 069
Singapore	2 266	3 113	3 960	2 665
South Korea	3 005	5 183	5 154	2 002
Hong Kong	5 742	6 087	7 311	4 385
Taiwan	1 639	3 161	4 218	2 423

Source: Compiled from Nihon bōeki shinkōkai, 1985b–1988b.

Particularly where Japanese subsidiaries focus on manufacturing, such as in the NICs or increasingly in ASEAN, Japanese companies like to complement their labour intensive imports with capital intensive exports. Almost without exception, when the emphasis on a country shifts from supplier of raw materials to supplier of labour-intensive manufactures, its importance as an export market increases and its current account surpluses with Japan turn into deficits. So in Asia, Japan runs trade deficits with Indonesia, Malaysia and to a lesser extent the Philippines, but surpluses with the NICs and Thailand (Table 8.12). In each case the rise of the yen increased the surpluses and, because it was accompanied by a fall in commodity prices, cut the deficits.

The single most important structural change in Japan's exports since the rise of the yen has been an easing in the share absorbed by the US and many Third World countries, but a radical increase in exports to Asia, particularly to the NICs, and to the EC (Table 8.13). Also, apart from places which are used as cheap production sites, the poorer the country, the greater has been the decline in Japanese exports to it since the rise of the yen. For example, in 1986–87, exports to the Middle East fell by 6.3 per cent and to Latin America by 7.7 per cent, while the 18.5 per cent rise in exports to Asia concealed the falls which took place to the poorer countries: −16.3 per cent to China, −17.2 per cent to Burma, −19.8 per cent to Bangladesh, −6.8 per cent to India, −13.0 per cent to Sri Lanka, −5.5 per cent to Vietnam, and −30.4 per cent to Brunei (a country rich only in oil). However, exports to all the NICs and ASEAN countries soared, mainly because their accumulation strategies make them dependent on Japanese imports, whose value was simply inflated

Table 8.13   Shares of Japan's exports, by region, 1980–88

	1980	1985	1986	1987	1–6, 1988
US	24.2	37.2	38.5	36.5	33.0
EC	13.8	11.8	14.7	16.4	18.6
Asian NICs	14.8	12.8	14.4	17.2	18.4
China	3.9	7.1	4.7	3.6	3.3
Others	43.4	31.1	27.8	26.3	26.7

Source: Compiled from Tsūshō sangyōshō, 1987–1988b.

with the rise of the yen: South Korea (25.3 per cent), Hong Kong (23.9 per cent), Taiwan (44.5 per cent), Singapore (31.3 per cent), Philippines (30.0 per cent), Thailand (45.5 per cent), Malaysia (26.9 per cent), and Indonesia (12.3 per cent). In January to June 1988, exports to the number one DFI target these days, Thailand, skyrocketed by 96.3 per cent over the same period the year before (Nihon bōeki shinkōkai, 1988b, pp. 354–5).

The close link between increasing Japanese DFI in manufacturing (particularly machinery) in Asia and Japanese exports to the region results from the dependence of each country on Japan for technology, machinery and equipment. Table 8.14 shows that the overwhelming majority of imports from Japan belong to the heavy and chemical industries, and within them to the categories of machinery and equipment. Within the light industries imports reflect a particular focus of Japanese DFI, for example, clothing and watch making in Hong Kong, electronics in Malaysia and Singapore, and motor vehicles in Thailand. However, the more even distributions within the heavy and chemical industries, except in the Philippines which relies more on the US than on Japan, tend to reflect an across-the-board dependence on Japanese capital.

The continued expansion of Japan's trading surplus with Asia since the rise of the yen reflects the changes in the production and circulation structures of Japanese capital. The weight of production in Japan for export to the US has fallen, but much of this has been replaced by expanded production in Asia for export to the US. Table 8.15 shows how the trade surpluses of the NICs with the US have grown in just one year since the rise of the yen.

There have been some signs that the NICs surpluses with the US will ease from 1988, not least because the pressure has resulted in such changes in Taiwan as a 40 per cent currency revaluation since

Table 8.14 Composition of Japanese Exports to Asia, by industry, 1987

	South Korea	Hong Kong	Singapore	Taiwan	Thailand	Indonesia	Philippines	Malaysia
Food and materials	3.1	2.9	1.9	4.0	2.8	1.5	4.3	2.8
Light industry	11.3	22.9	11.7	9.3	6.7	6.5	18.5	8.5
Textiles	4.9	12.2	3.7	6.3	2.5	2.4	7.9	3.5
Heavy industry	84.5	72.5	84.1	85.1	89.4	90.9	76.0	87.4
Chemicals	12.7	6.6	5.0	12.0	12.7	10.9	12.7	7.3
Metals	12.4	7.2	10.0	14.6	19.7	15.8	13.9	13.7
Iron and steel	9.3	4.2	5.6	10.2	16.1	12.1	10.4	9.7
Machinery	59.4	58.7	68.5	58.4	57.0	64.2	49.5	66.5
General	25.4	13.5	17.8	20.8	22.7	30.6	17.2	19.7
Electrical	25.7	28.4	39.5	26.8	12.7	12.6	15.8	31.2
Transport	5.2	5.3	8.4	8.1	20.1	19.6	15.0	13.0
Precision:	3.0	11.6	2.7	2.7	1.5	1.4	1.5	2.6

Source: Jetro, 1988, pp. 195–217.

Table 8.15   NICs overall trade balances and trade balances with the US, 1986–87 ($ billion)

| | Overall Balance | | | Balance with US | |
	1986	1987	1988 est.	1986	1987
South Korea	3.1	6.3	5.5	7.3	9.5
Taiwan	15.6	19.0	14.0	13.6	16.0
Hong Kong	0.1	0.1	1.7	8.1	9.4
Singapore	−3.0	−3.9	–	3.2	1.5

Source: Nihon bōeki shinkōkai, 1988b, p. 28.

late 1985 and the cutting of tariffs on some 4800 import items in 1987. But some of the signs are illusory: just as Japan could substantially cut its surplus with the US by importing American gold in 1986, Taiwan's central bank has cut its surplus by similar purchases in 1988 (*FEER*, 28 April 1988, pp. 64–5; 31 March 1988; p. 69).

Instead of simply exporting directly to the US, Japanese capital is carving out a triangular trading block in which it increasingly exports to its Asian factories the capital goods, industrial components and semi-processed materials needed for re-export to the US. The *Far Eastern Economic Review* estimated that if one added to Japan's direct exports to the US its indirect exports (via the NICs), then the total share was over 50 per cent (26 November 1987, p. 100).

The strategy is designed to get round the conflict with the US and the costs of the higher yen, and has in a sense been working. But the contradictions are appearing elsewhere. Japan's trade in invisibles has been in chronic deficit until 1986, but the surpluses from the early 1990s will be round the $5 billion mark and add a new source of friction. Already in fiscal 1987, Japan's net income from dividends and interest on its overseas investments leapt by over 75 per cent to $16.6 billion, the largest in the world (*JEJ*, 16 April 1988, p. 14). Moreover, the direct heat might have shifted a bit from Japan to Asia, particularly Taiwan, South Korea and Hong Kong, but Japanese capital has by no means escaped the radiation.

Pressure in the US has been intensifying to restrict imports from the NICs, to abolish the preferences they receive, further to revalue their currencies and to secure easier access to their markets for US exports. In the first half of 1987 alone no fewer than 30 actions against South Korean imports (anti-dumping investigations and restrictions) were initiated, seventeen of them by the US. In 1988 the attention shifted to the US announcement that it would remove the four NICs from the generalised system of preferences (GSP) duty-free import programme from 1989. The sudden surge of textile and garment imports from the NICs reminded the US government that GSP had been intended to help developing countries break out of dependence on apparel and textile exports, not flood the American market with them. Since exports to the US accounted for 42 per cent of South Korea's and 74 per cent of Taiwan's growth in 1980–86, a growth which fed the demand for Japanese imports, closing the US market to NICs goods directly affects Japan. In Europe matters have taken an equal turn for the worse. In September heavy anti-dumping duties were imposed on South Korean video-cassette recorders, and in November a dispute with Hyundai Merchant Marine over pricing further exacerbated relations with the EC (*JS*, October 1987, p. 65; May 1988, p. 61; *FEER*, 25 February 1988, pp. 68–73; 3 November 1988, p. 91; *JEJ*, 6 February 1988, p. 22).

On the other hand, there is mounting pressure within Asia for protection from the Japanese export drive and for freer access to the Japanese market. The demand is for direct access to Japan without the help of the trading companies and other intermediaries that gobble up the lion's share of the surplus. And while 1988 also saw some reduction of Japan's trade surplus with a country like South Korea (by 34.2 per cent in the first eight months), the amount is still substantial and the friction unabated. Access to Japan's construction market is only one major bone of contention. But the surpluses in January to August with Taiwan and Hong Kong increased by 27.1 per cent each and with Singapore by 45.2 per cent (*NKS*, 6 September 1988, p. 5; 8 October 1988, p. 7; *JEJ*, 30 April 1988, p. 7).

The politics of trade towards the end of 1988 centered more and more on the contradictory forces generated by each country trying to increase the protection of its own market while simultaneously pressing for free trade in the markets of its neighbours. In the case of Japan, in response to the proposed European Single Market of 1992 and the recent Canada–US Free Trade Agreement, serious attention is being given to the idea of a Japan–US free trade agreement, which the US has become interested in as a trump card to play against the Europeans. Meanwhile, Japan is also clamouring for an Asian free trade block, while itself continuing to resist pressure from Asia for free access to Japan (*NKS*, 19 October 1988, p. 7; 2 November 1988, p. 7; *JEJ*, 20 August 1988, p. 1; 13 August 1988, p. 23; *FEER*, 2 June 1988, pp. 60–3).

Accusations of dumping and of unfair protectionism have been flying around constantly for years (*Exim Review*, October 1987, p. 11). Three very typical reports could be from any local newspaper, but in fact came from the *Star* before its closure by the Malaysian government, *Business Day* before its voluntary closure in protest at the Aquino government, and the *Japan Economic Journal*, the mouthpiece of Japanese capital:

> Japan's practice of shutting out our manufactured goods is a sore point in its trade relations with Malaysia (25 April 1986).
> Textile mills have expressed the fear that Japanese garments suppliers are dumping their off-season products in the Philippines (17 January 1986).
> [The] Japanese have been more concerned with their relations with the U.S. and even Europe. Japanese proclamations of the importance of Asia . . . come across as mere lip service, if not empty promises, largely because Japan has tended to take the region for granted and adopted a condescending attitude toward it (13 August 1988, p. 23).

The purpose of free trade for an imperial power is not the same as it is for a colony. In both cases, exports serve as a way of realising the surplus value in something locally made but for which there is no local buying power. But from the imperial power's point of view, exports also help preserve the world division of labour and the technical backwardness of the colonies, because they ruin infant industries wherever the imperial power 'dumps' its cheaply made products. The only 'ruin' that free trade from the underdeveloped world to the advanced world can cause is not to the productive forces, but to the livelihoods of workers. When Japan is flooded with cheap imports from Asia, these are in labour intensive industries and serve to undermine the living standards of the Japanese working class. They cannot put a break on technical progress by forcing less technically advanced capital into bankruptcy, which is the effect of the free trade Japan is urging on Asia.

CONCLUSION

Under pressure from growing inter-imperialist rivalry and crisis at home, Japanese companies have been buying themselves an empire in Southeast Asia, not in a systematic planned way, but piecemeal as their eye for profit leads them to relocate their factories to wherever it seems labour productivity in the particular industry or branch concerned can be maximised. This is a relatively new way of going about such a task, which when undertaken by more experienced players, was normally preceded by a politico-military control which ensured the environment would remain hospitable.

The main problems Japanese companies face therefore tend to be political: from conflicts with their upper class allies to having mobs burn down their factories. Even in the US, the veneer of benevolence has been exposed as Japanese companies show their true colours:

> After an initial honeymoon, particularly in U.S. communities with high unemployment, Japanese manufacturers consolidated their reputations as creator of needed jobs. Now this aura of effortless success is disappearing in a series of bitter disputes over employment practices (*TBT*, October 1988, p. 42).

Needless to say, they have found this disturbing, if not bewildering. They have not appreciated that capital is a social relation, and that internationalising it is not like going shopping for bargains, but extending to the peoples of the world the peculiar Japanese way of exploiting human beings. This works rather well in Japan, because so many supporting institutions have long existed to mesh the profit-making activities of particular companies into coherent ruling-class strategies. For example, in Japan the companies have an authoritarian education system and police force, a highly centralised state apparatus, a rich feudal past which has nurtured ingenious mechanisms of social control, and a system of industrial relations which has developed under the wings of all of these. Bourgeois social relations in Japan have come to be synonymous with this whole package, and Japanese companies will have more and more difficulty attempting to internationalise their operations simply by taking their money and machinery abroad.

Direct foreign investment is a relatively open political move, in which capital extends to new places its ways of exploiting workers and tries to accomodate these to possibly less supportive environments. In the heydays of British and American imperialism, the lack of a supporting environment was solved respectively by means of direct rule or by militarily threatening direct rule. Neither of these is available to Japanese capital, which must rely almost entirely on the local governments of the countries it enters. The only opportunity it has systematically to work in this area is through 'aid'.

In my original breakdown of the subject matter for this book, I had set aside a chapter on aid and lending to complement a chapter on trade. However, I found that this was not a subject which could be telescoped into one chapter, and it seemed better to limit myself to the more manifestly 'economic' aspects of Japan's new imperialism. Aid is about the politics of imperialism at the state level in an age of neo-colonialism, something the Japanese are not at all good at, the subject of another study.

However, to put Japanese DFI in its proper context in each country, it is important to see its relationship to aid. Although DFI is the particular form in which the many Japanese capitals tie up with their counterparts in Asia, there is another level in which a related outcome is achieved. At the state level in which 'aid' is the characteristic cement, the concern is not normally with particular money-making projects (although a lot of aid has lined many individual's pockets), but with improving the general environment for the particular capitals to get on with their business.

The problems addressed by 'aid' normally fall into the two categories of what have long been variously referred to as accumulation and legitimation. The former concerns the supporting infrastructure on which capital accumulation depends, but which is too costly or cumbersome for particular capitals to risk: road, ports, power, communications, and so on. Legitimation is about keeping the lid on the political struggle, by means of the whole range of mechanisms through which people are made to comply with with their exploitation.

Both of these tasks are normally undertaken by the state, through which the interests, which have most to gain from this infrastructure and secure lid, have to work. However, when the state does not command the necessary resources and when the strongest interests in its success lie with foreign capital, then either aid or direct rule from the outside is necessary. The two dominant powers in Asia, Japan and the US, have divided between themselves a way of avoiding direct rule. The US worries mainly about keeping the lid on things, not very ingeniously through a heavy emphasis on military aid, while the Japanese get on with aiding the building of an infrastructure to make business more profitable for its capitalists.

The transition to 'NIC-dom' is from this point of view a transition from a colonial state not equal to the task and in need of massive aid, to one which can increasingly on its own provide a money making

Table 8.16   Direct investment in Asia as a percentage of total capital
receipts

NICS	%	ASEAN	%
Singapore	73	Indonesia	19
Taiwan	62	Malaysia	10
Hong Kong	62	Thailand	12
South Korea	55	Philippines	7

Source: Asian Development Bank, as cited in *National Business Review*, 18
March 1988, p. 37.

environment for foreign capital. Table 8.16, which shows the shares
of direct investment relative to total capital receipts since World War
Two in Southeast Asia, confirms that most money that went into the
NICs did so to make more money (DFI), while in ASEAN the
overwhelming proportion of foreign capital has gone into improving
the making money environment (various forms of aid).

It is in practice increasingly unlikely for this transition to be made,
mainly because the foreign powers which 'give' the aid do not in fact
do that. They lend it at rates of interest which, although claimed to be
concessionary, concede little, and the debt burden on aid recipients
becomes too crushing. Indonesia and the Philippines, currently the
main recipients of Japanese and other aid, are also the two whose
debt crises have reached catastrophic levels. Because the imperialist
powers which finance the infrastructural developments do not actually suspend their money-making activities in the underdeveloped
world, aid after all becomes simply a *different* way in which foreign
capital makes money.

What my research on Japanese DFI in Southeast Asia has shown is
that the *basis* of foreign capital's continued domination of the region
and its across-the-board capacity to gain most from all the many types
of investment, trade and lending stems ultimately from its technological power in the production place. In the key industries examined,
cars and electronics, Japanese companies have possessed almost total
control over the joint venture partners through their technological
edge, usually expressed in terms of supplying sophisticated parts for
assembly or in subcontracting out the manufacture of simple parts.
Yoshihara referred to this as 'technologyless' industrialisation:

Most of the major components are supplied by the Japanese
companies, and some which are produced locally are made under

the technical supervision of the Japanese companies. The South East Asian capitalists are essentially the distributors of Japanese cars, with the differences that they have assembly plants. Technologically, however, they are almost 100 per cent dependent on their Japanese licensers, and, under the present set-up, it would be impossible for them to become technologically independent and start exporting their products. Their technological dependency is not temporary but, being structural, is semi-permanent (1988, p. 112).

But Southeast Asian capitalists do not need to become technologically independent to export Japanese cars, or parts for Japanese cars, Japanese fridges, TVs, microwaves, audio equipment, floppy disk drives or even CD players. On the contrary, the high yen in Japan and growing inter-imperialist rivalries have forced Japanese capital to shift many of its Asian subsidiaries from production for the domestic market to production for export. This has not just meant switching market places, but restructuring the production process from one geared to conditions in particular countries to one geared to the global strategy of producing where costs are low and selling where buying power is high. As Yoshihara notes, all that is required of the Southeast Asian capitalists is that they become compradors, receptacles for these and other projects which Japanese capital has shifted from Japan itself (ibid., pp. 111–12).

Even the authoritarian industrial regime which used to single the Japanese working class out for the task of producing cheaply became insufficient with the rise of the yen. An extra tightening of the screws at home, which is leaving a growing number of unemployed and creating an expanding underclass, had to be complemented by new sources of cheap labour if Japanese capital was to survive the intensified inter-imperialist rivalry. But displacing the problem to Asia not simply preserved Japanese capital's deal with its own middle class and labour aristocracy, it also created conditions for finding common ground with its imperialist rivals and so attenuating the tensions.

So while there are alliances among the different upper classes of the world, these are not of the same order. At the highest level and providing the context for all others is the 'Japamerica' (Kato, 1988) axis, which is closely complemented by the tie-up with Europe, the importance of which rises each day with the approach of the single market to be established in 1992. These alliances are cemented by centuries of political-economic and cultural domination, the racism of which often even threatens admission of the Japanese ruling class. However, with the growing incapacity of the US to provide an 'ultra-imperialism' to stabilise and service the world for imperialist plunder, including suppressing rivalries amongst the great powers and waging war against the rebellions of the victims, a new multi-polar imperialist system is emerging, with the Soviet Union increasingly as a one-and-a-half faced partner. This new system is simultaneously more powerful *vis-à-vis* the peoples of the underdeveloped world, but also potentially more capable of explosive rivalries. So far, it seems that the common bond in turning to Asia for the productive activities no longer profitable within their own borders has contained the latter tendency.

Japanese, US and European capital therefore go to Asia having already settled their differences and consolidated their combined strength, the companies from different countries competing with one another much as those from the same countries compete. Asian capital, whether NICs or ASEAN, can only submit to this technological might and ally with it on the best terms its other resources allow. Under certain circumstances, for example, during the 1970s, the resources possessed by ruling classes in oil rich countries like Indonesia were considerable. But because their greater bargaining power was not rooted in any advance of their own productive forces, they have lost ground almost as quickly as they gained it. New technologies which produce many cheap substitutes for a wide range of raw materials have eroded the traditional sources of Asian capital's independence.

NICs capital is not really any better off in this regard than ASEAN capital, since a wide technological divide also separates it from the imperialist powers. But from the point of view of the latter, the difference is important. And the difference lies mainly in the conditions which have made NICs labour *more productive than ASEAN labour*, for example, the existence of an all-round supporting infrastructure, including things like an education system which allow the use of technologies excluded from ASEAN.

It is this that gives the NICs a technological foot in the door ahead of ASEAN, but it does not necessarily give them what they need to join the imperialist club, technological independence. We have seen that even the South Korean *chaebol* do not have that. So rather like a labour aristocracy which can win higher wages than the mass of workers because it possesses a higher lever of skill than the mass, NICs capital wins better deals from the great powers than ASEAN capital because it gives access to more productive workers. But just as the labour aristocracy still has more in common with other workers who sell skills, as opposed to capital which buys skills, so does capital in the NICs and ASEAN share a common antagonism towards the possessors of the technology that trickles their way only when it is no longer the leading edge in advanced capital's arsenal.

From the worker's point of view, the dilemmas presented by capitalism in its present phase of internationalisation are more complicated although no different in kind from what they always have been. The dilemma of the system has long been recognised: it is always worse not to be exploited by capital than to be exploited, because unemployment means the loss of livelihood. And to be exploited means finding an employer who can stand up to the competition of rivals through access to the necessary technologies. Workers employed by technically backward capitals can only retain their jobs if they comply in the extra-low wages needed to compensate. And so the hierarchy of power among capitals, stemming from their different technical capabilities, translates into a hierarchy of wages and conditions among workers. And when the former assumed an international division, so did the latter.

However, although such a relatively tight international division of the world's capitalist and working classes did develop before the current worldwide crisis that began in the mid-1970s, there have been major changes since then. The most important have stemmed from the use, in countries with traditionally low wages because of their traditionally low technologies, by TNCs of their most up-to-date and efficient techniques. These are not transferred to the ruling class of the underdeveloped country, but simply used there by the corporations in order to combine advanced capital's power, technology, with backward capital's power, low wages.

The effect of this new weapon's use by Japanese, US and European capital is to erode the conditions which gave their own working classes the privileged working and living conditions which used to win their loyalty. Now, factories are being shut down in the advanced countries when their TNCs take sophisticated plant and equipment to low-cost labour sites in Asia, and a powerful new pressure is homogenising the class structure at the bottom to complement the alliances at the top.

This tendency – it is no more than that – towards forcing the same conditions on workers in TNC factories wherever they are, is one of the factors behind the vastly improved networks that are emerging among workers all over the world. For so long the peoples of Asia and elsewhere in the Third World have had to confront a virtually solid imperialist world, in which both labour and capital cooperated in their exploitation. Now, by taking rather than transferring their leading technologies to the Third World, advanced capital has as it were let the enemy into its very citadel.

I believe that the future of the entire Asian people lies in transcending the racism which Japanese capital practices and which it in turn provokes against its own people. If Japan's new imperialism means spreading the practices it cruelly imposes at home onto the peoples of Southeast Asia; and if that in turn means bringing back to Japan the wages, conditions and joblessness it exploits in the region; then Japanese capital will itself have created the conditions for unity among all the peoples of Asia. It is to that end that I wrote and to which I dedicate this book.

Appendix: Comparison of Foreign Investment Incentives

Item	Indonesia	Malaysia	Philippines
I. Tax		Income Tax 40%	
1. Corporate Income tax Rate	−Rp10mil 15% Rp10–50mil 25% Rp50mil +35%	Development tax 5% Excess Profit tax 3% (for profit more than M\$ 2 mil only)	− P100 000 25% P100 000 + 35%
2. Tax Incentive: Exemption from corporate tax	None	Yes 5 years granted to pioneer status (certain cases up to 10 years, but so far no case approved)	Yes (new law of July 17, 1987) 8 years for registered pioneer company, 5 years for non-pioneer company (newly registered)
Exemption from or reduction of taxes on imported capital goods/raw materials	Capital goods: Yes Raw Materials: Yes/No by commodity (as from April 1985)	Both for capital goods which are not produced in Malaysia and for materials used to produce export goods	(New law of 17 July 1987) Import duty 100% exempted on machinery and parts imported by registered companies for 5 years from 17 July 1987. Subject to prior approval of Board of Investment, etc.
Other Tax Incentives	Import duty exemption and surcharge restitution for the importation of machinery, spare parts & raw materials if the production is intended entirely for export. Deferment of payment of value	Investment Tax Allowance for 5 years (max 100% of capital outlay). Accelerated depreciation allowance for modernisation capital outlay	New law of 17 July 1987. 1. Incentive to investors in registered pioneer company: tax deduction up to 30% will be approved during 1 Dec. 1986–31, Dec. 1988. Tax deduction up to 20% for investment in less developed

Singapore	*Thailand*		*Korea*	
33% (reduced from 40% effective from 1987)	Listed co. Unlisted co.	30% 35%	– Won 50 mil. Won 50 mil.	20% + 30%
Yes 5–10 years (depending upon merit of the pioneer enterprise). Post Pioneer Incentive: Reduction of income tax to 10% for 5 years	Yes (3–8 years)		Yes (5 years)	
Yes (Almost all imports are duty free)	Yes Exemption or 50% reduction of import duty and business tax for the importation of machinery & equipment. Up to 90% reduction of import duty and business tax for the importation of components and raw materials		Yes for capital goods; yes for raw materials for domestic use for first 6 m/s after operation only. Yes for exports (to be refunded later)	
20% of corporate income can be exempt provided that the equal amount is deposited as R & D reserve. Investment Allowance 50% (depending upon the importance)	Corporate income taxes can be exempted for 3 to 8 years by BOI. If the J/V company suffers losses during the exemption period, it can carry forward the losses and deduct them as expenses for up to 5 years after the end of the exemption period.			

Item	Indonesia	Malaysia	Philippines
	added tax for the importation of the capital goods required for the production of goods or services. Import duty exemption and surcharge restitution for the importation of capital goods which are used for manufacturing capital goods in Indonesia provided that such an industry is contained in the DSP (priority list)		area during 1 Jan. 1989–31 Dec. 1990 2. Incentives to Registered Enterprises: Accelerated depreciation (double speed) for increased capacity, modernisation, etc. Tax deduction up to 50% for additional direct labour cost related to expansion for the first 5 years
II. Foreign Equity 1. 100% foreign ownership	Not allowed	Possible if J/V exports more than 50% or employs more than 350 people. Majority must be given to Malaysian shareholders if domestic market oriented	Allowed for a limited area
2. Transfer of Equity	Local share: 51% within 10 years	70% by 1990 (Bumiputra 30% Non-Bumiputra 40% as a guideline for total Malaysia, not for individual companies)	60% within 30 years
III. Land Property 1. Ownership by J/V	Not allowed	Not allowed	Limited; foreign equity share must be less than 40%

Singapore	Thailand	Korea
Income tax exempted up to 5 years on the increased income generated by the expanded business	5 years tax exemption for withholding tax originating from overseas remittance of goodwill, royalties or fees. Exclusion from taxable incomes of dividends derived from promoted enterprises during income tax holiday	
Allowed for a limited area like technology, industry or export oriented industry	Allowed under some conditions (e.g. 100% export company)	Allowed for a limited area (80% of total industrial fields has been opened to foreign participants)
Not restricted	General shift to Thai majority	Not restricted
Allowed	Limited foreign equity share must be less than 49%	Limited; foreign equity share must be less than 50%

Item	Indonesia	Malaysia	Philippines
2. Leasehold (period)	Yes (30 years). The right of exploitation is granted only for Indonesian partners	Yes (60, 66, 90, 99 years)	Yes (25 years in general)
IV. Others			
1. Wholesale and retail activity for J/V	Prohibited	Allowed	Retailing is prohibited
Import tax on commercial documents (tender documents, technical brochures, shipping documents, spec. list, etc.)	Imposed	None	None
3. Work Permit	It takes time and money to obtain work permits due to policy of indigenisation	Difficult to obtain work permit except Key post person and technicians	Free but obliged to have trainees over 2 and transfer the jobs to the trainees within 5 years
4. Export Incentives	Refund of import duties paid for materials to be used for export	1. Export credit refinancing scheme 2. An abatement of adjusted income for export 3. Export allowance of 5% based on FOB value of export sales is granted to trading companies which export products manufactured in Malaysia 4. Double deduction of export credit insurance	1. Refund of import duty paid for materials used for re-export. 2. 5 years income tax exempt for export oriented foreign companies

Singapore	Thailand	Korea
Allowed (99 years)	Yes (30 years)	Yes (unusual)
Wholesale only	Allowed	Allowed
None	None	None
Only workers of salary less than S$1,500/day are required to obtain work permit	Free	Free
Requirement: To export more than 20% of total sales exceeding S$100 000/year. Incentive: 90% of profit generated from exports is tax deductible. Income tax is reduced to 4% (from 33%) for 3 years after the exemption period of corp. tax	Exemption of Income Tax for at least 5 yrs Exemption of Export Tax. Exports are granted tax coupon in the range of 0.2–8.0% of export value. Exporters have the right to pay import duty, corporate income tax, business tax, etc., by utilising tax coupon. Minimum export requirement reduced to: 50% (–2 years) 80% (3rd year+). 100% tax exempted	Duty refunds on imported raw materials incorporated into exports. Various tax deductions. Due to the favourable balance of payment in 1986, the US requested Korea to open up the domestic market. So, special incentives for exporters will be gradually reduced

Item	Indonesia	Malaysia	Philippines
		premium 5. Double deduction for promotion of export 6. Industrial building allowance	
5. Status of Trading companies	Representative office (prohibited from doing business)	Branch & J/V trading (off-shore trade & domestic business allowed to J/V trading only)	Branch
6. Minimum allowable foreign equity investment	US$1 000 000 × foreign share	NA	NA

Singapore	Thailand	Korea
	on imported spare parts & replacement machinery	
Branch	Branch, 100% owned subsidiary and J/V trading (indent business allowed to J/V trading only)	Branch
NA	NA	US$50 000

Source: *Himpunan Bulletin*, Vol. XI, No. 5 (Sept.–Oct. 1987), pp. 26–33.

References

JAPANESE SOURCES

AOKI, SATOSHI (1987) *Nippon kūdōka: haishin no daikigyō* [Deindustrialising Japan: Betrayal by Large Companies] (Tokyo: Shin Nihon shuppansha, 1987).

CHŪSHŌ KIGYŌCHŌ [Small and Medium Enterprise Agency] (1987/88) *Shōwa 62/63 chūshō kigyō hakusho* [1987/88 Small and Medium Enterprise White Papers] (Tokyo: Ōkurashō insatsukyoku, 1987/88).

CHŪSHŌ KIGYŌ JIGYŌDAN [Japan Small Business Corporation]. (1988) *Kigyō tōsan chōsa geppō* [Monthly report on the Survey of Company Bankruptcies], no. 113, August 1988.

HAYASHI, KENTARŌ (1988) 'Nihon dokusen: 21 seiki e no takokusekika senryaku' [Japanese Monopoly: Transnationalisation Strategy for the 21st Century], *Keizai*, no. 294, October 1988.

FUJIMORI, HIDEO (1988) Keizai kyōryoku shirīzu dai 138 go [Economic Cooperation Series, no. 138] *Hatten tojōkoku no genchika seisaku* [Local Content Policy in the Developing Countries] (Tokyo: Ajia keizai kenkyūjo) [Institute of Developing Economies], 1988.

FUJITA, KAZUO (1987) 'Sangyōbetsu bunseki: denki' [Industry Analyses: Electrical], *Keizai*, no. 283, November 1987.

ICHINOSE, HIDEFUMI (1989) 'Gendai shihonshugi no teikokushugiteki honshitsu' [The Imperialistic Character of Present Day Capitalism], *Keizai*, no. 297, January 1989.

IGUSA, KUNIO (ed.) (1988) *Asean no keizai keikaku: rekishiteki kadai to tenbō* [ASEAN Economic Plans: History and Prospects] (Tokyo: Ajia keizai kenkyūjo, 1988).

IKEMOTO, YUKIO (1988) 'Rijunritsu, kigyō shūchū to shitauke kankei' [Industrial Concentration and Subcontracting System: A Case Study of Siam Motors Group], *Ajia Keizai*, September 1988.

IMAMIYA, KENJI (1989) 'Saikin no kawase o meguru shomondai to ensōba' [All the Problems of the Recent Exchange Rate and Yen Market], *Keizai*, no. 297, January 1989.

INOUE, HIROSHI (1988) 'Nihon kigyō no takokusekika to minshuteki kisei' [The Multinationalisation of Japanese Companies and their Democratic Control], *Keizai*, no. 294, October 1988.

INOUE, RŪICHIRO (ed.) (1987) *Ajia no zaibatsu to kigyō* [Asian Business Groups and Companies] (Tokyo: Nihon keizai shinbunsha, 1987).

ISHIDA, MASARU (1987) *Nikkan sangyō masatsu* [Japan-Korean Industrial Conflict] (Tokyo: Keirin shobō, 1987).

ISHII, TAKEMOCHI (1986) Nikkei sangyō shirīzu [Nikkei Industry Series], *Mekatoronikusu* [Mechatronics] (Tokyo: Nihon keizai shinbunsha, 1986).

ITSUKI, TAKETOSHI (1988) 'Ajia no sekai no kōjōka to NIES' [The NIES and Asia's World-Factories], *Keizai*, no. 295, November 1988.

288

IWASAKI, IKUO (1988) 'Shingapōru no kanjikei kigyō shudan' (Chinese Business Groups in Singapore), *Ajia Keizai*, March 1988.

IWAMOTO, NAOMI (1988) 'Pāto hanazakari no kage de' [Thanks to the Blooming Partimers], *Keizai*, no. 292, August 1988.

KAMIO, KYŌKO (1988) 'Kyūzō suru zaitaku tere wāka' [Rapidly Increasing domestic Tele-workers], *Keizai*, no. 292, August 1988.

KANO, YOSHIKAZU (1987) *Jūnengo no Nihon sangyō* [Japan's Industries Ten Years On] (Tokyo: Tōyō keizai shinposha, 1987).

KATŌ, TETSURŌ (1988) *Japamerika no jidai ni* [Towards the Age of Japamerica] (Tokyo: Kadensha, 1988).

KAWASHIMA, TAKAO (1987) 'Nihon kigyō no taigai shishutsu: sono rekishiteki suii' [The Overseas Shift by Japanese companies: Its Historical Change], *Keizai*, no. 283, November 1987.

KEIZAI (1988) Tokudaigo [Special Enlarged Issue]. *Nichibei keizai kankei no genkyokumen* [On the Present Relationship between Japan and the US], no. 295, November 1988.

KEIZAI KIKAKUCHŌ [Economic Planning Agency]. (1987a/88a) *Shōwa 62/63 nen keizai hakusho* [1987/88 Economy White Paper] (Tokyo: Ōkurashō insatsukyoku, 1987/88).

KEIZAI KIKAKUCHŌ CHŌSAKYOKU [Research Bureau of the Economic Planning Agency] (1987b) *Kokusaiteki senryaku o susumeru kigyō kōdō* [The Corporate Activity of Firms Pursuing International Strategies] (Tokyo: Ōkurashō insatsukyoku, 1987).

KEIZAI KIKAKUCHŌ CHŌSAKYOKU (1987c) *Nihon keizai no genkyō* [The State of the Japanese Economy] (Tokyo: Ōkurashō insatsukyoku, 1987).

KEIZAI KIKAKUCHŌ SŌGŌ TŌKEIKYOKU [General Statistical Bureau of the Economy Planning Agency] (1987d) *21 seiki e no kihon senryaku* [Basic Strategy Towards the 21st Century] (Tokyo: Tōyō keizai shinposha, 1987).

KEIZAI KIKAKUCHŌ SŌGŌ TŌKEIKYOKU (1988b) *Shitsugyō (Sono kōzō to shinkokudo)* [Unemployment: Its Structure and Gravity] (Tokyo: Ōkurashō insatsukyoku, 1988).

KISO KEIZAI KENKYŪJO [Institute of Fundamental Political Economy] (ed.) (1987) Kōza: Kōzō tenkan [Lectures: Structural Change], vol. 1, *Kokusai no naka no Nihon* [Japan amidst Internationalisation] (Tokyo: Aoki shoten, 1987).

KISO KEIZAI, KENKYŪJO (1987b) vol. 2, *Kawaru rōdō to seikatsu* [Changing Work and Livelihood] (Tokyo: Aoki shoten, 1987).

KITADA, YOSHIHARU and AIDA, TOSHIO (1987) *Endaka fukyōka no Nihon sangyō* [Japanese Industry under the High Yen Recession] (Tokyo: Ōtsuki shoten, 1987).

KUDŌ, AKIRA (1987) 'Ijō endaka to sangyō kōzō no chōsei' [Industrial Restructuring and the Unusual Value of the Yen], *Keizai*, no. 274, February 1987.

LA INTERNATIONAL (1987a) Rinji zōkan (Kokusai keizai), tsūkan 270 go [Special Issue (International Economy), no. 270]. *Shingapōru tokushū* [Special Issue on Singapore] (Tokyo: Kokusai hyōronsha, 1987).

References

LA INTERNATIONAL (1987B) Rinji zōkan (Kokusai keizai), tsūkan 277 go, *Thai tokushū* [Special Issue on Thailand] (Tokyo: Kokusai hyōronsha, 1987).

LA INTERNATIONAL (1988) Rinji zōkan (Kokusai keizai), tsūkan 296. *Mareshia tokushū* [Special issue on Malaysia] (Tokyo: Kokusai hyōronsha, 1988).

MARUYAMA, KEIYA (1987) 'Nihonteki keiei no kaigai iten' [Japanese Management's Shift Overseas], *Keizai*, no. 283, October 1987.

MARUYAMA, KEIYA (1988) 'Nihonteki keiei no kaigai iten: Jiyasto in taimu o chūshin' [Japanese Management's Shift Overseas: Focus on Just in Time], *Keizai*, no. 294, November 1988.

MATSUI, MIKIO (1988) Nikkei sangyō shirīzu [Nikkei Industry Series] *Jidōsha buhhin* [Auto Parts] (Tokyo: Nihon keizai shinbunsha, 1988).

MIAMI, JIRŌ (1987) 'Chiiki kōsai: ASEAN, Hong Kong' [Regional Association: ASEAN and Hong Kong], *Keizai*, no. 283, November 1987.

MINAMI, JIRŌ (1988) 'Kanmin kyōryoku ni yoru kigyō shinshutsu no jittai' [The Reality of Corporate Relocation due to Public-Private Cooperation], *Keizai*, no. 294, October 1988.

MONTEZ, M.F. and KOIKE, KENJI (eds) (1988) ASEAN nado genchi kenkyū shirīzu no. 2 [Field Research Series on ASEAN and Others, no. 2]. *Fuiripin no keizai seisaku to kigyō* [Philippine Economic Policy and Companies] (Tokyo: Ajia keizai kenkyūjo [Institute of Developing Economies], 1988).

MORI, YASUO (1987) 'Kaigai ni mukau chūshō kigyō' [Small Companies Looking Abroad], *Keizai*, no. 283, November 1987.

NIHON BŌEKI SHINKŌKAI [JETRO]. (1982a/1985a/86a/87a/88a) *1982/ 1985/86/87/88 Jietoro hakusho, tōshihen: sekai to Nihon no kaigai chokusetsu tōshi* [1985/86/87/88 Jetro White Paper, Investment: The World and Japan's Direct Foreign Investment] (Tokyo: Nihon bōeki shinkōkai, 1985/86/87/88).

NIHON BŌEKI SHINKŌKAI [JETRO]. (1985b/86b/87b/88b) *1985/86/ 87/88 Jietoro hakusho, bōekihen: Sekai to Nihon no bōeki* [1985/86/87/88 Jetro White Paper, Trade: The World and Japan's Trade] (Tokyo: Nihon bōeki shinkōkai, 1985/86/87/88).

NIHON BŌEKI SHINKŌKAI (1987c) Jietoro bōeki shijō shirīzu 274. *Kankoku* [Korea] (Tokyo: Nihon bōeki shinkōkai, 1987).

NIHON BŌEKI SHINKŌKAI (1988c) *Nihon no seihin yunyū dōkō, 1988 nen 1–6 gatsu* [The Trend of Japan's Manufactured Imports, Jan.–June 1988] (Tokyo: Nihon bōeki shinkōkai, 1988).

NIHON BŌEKI SHINKŌKAI (1988d) Jietoro bōeki shijō shirīzu 285 [Jetro Trade-Market Series, no. 285] *Fuiripin* [The Philippines] (Tokyo: Nihon bōeki shinkōkai, 1988).

NIHON FUJIN DANTAI RENGŌKAI [Japan Federation of Women's Associations] (1987) *Fujin hakusho 1987* [1987 White Paper on Women] (Tokyo: Horupo shuppan, 1987).

NIHON GINKŌ CHŌSAKYOKU [Research Bureau of the Bank of Japan] (1986) *Nihon keizai o chūshin to suru kokusai hikaku tōkei* [Comparative International Statistics Centering on the Japanese Economy], June 1986.

NIHON KYŌSANTŌ CHŪŌ IINKAI SHUPPANKYOKU [Publishing

Bureau of the Central Committee of the Japan Communist Party]. (1987) *Dokusen shihon no arata na senryaku* [Monopoly Capital's New Strategy] (Tokyo: JCPm 1987).

NHK TOKUSHŪ [NHK Special Edition] (1988) Kinkyū ripōto [Urgent Report], *Sekai no naka no Nihon: Ajia kara no chōsen* [Japan in the World: The Challenge from Asia] (Tokyo: Nihon hōsō kyōkai shuppankai, 1988).

NIHON KEIZAI SHINBUNSHA (ed.) (1987) 90 pun kaisetsu [90 Minute Explanation], *Kankoku keizai 50 no pointo* [50 Points on the Korean Economy] (Tokyo: Nihon keizai shinbunsha, 1987).

NIHON KEIZAI SHINBUNSHA (ed.) (1988) *Shin Nihon keizai: subete ga kawari hajimeta* [Restructuring of Japan's Economy] (Tokyo: Nihon keizai shinbunsha, 1988).

NIHON NŌRITSU KYŌKAI [Japan Productivity Association] (ed.) (1987a) *Ajia NICs ni okeru kigyō senryaku* [Company Strategy towards the Asian NICs] (Tokyo: Nihon nōritsu kyōkai, 1987).

NIHON NŌRITSU KYŌKAI (1987b) *Hokubei ni okeru kigyō senryaku* [Company Strategy towards North America] (Tokyo: Nihon nōritsu kyōkai, 1987).

NIHON YUSHUTSU YUNYŪ GINKŌ KAIGAI TŌSHI KENKYŪJO [Foreign Investment Research Centre of the Japan Export Import Bank] (1986) *Kaigai chokusetsu tōshi ni kansuru ronbunshū* [A Collection of Essays on Foreign Direct Investment] (Tokyo: Nihon yushutsu yunyū ginkō, 1986).

NIHON YUSHUTSU YUNYŪ GINKŌ KAIGAI TŌSHI KENKYŪJO [Foreign Investment Research Centre of the Japan Export Import Bank] (1987) Nikkei bunko (375), *Kaigai tōshi no chishiki* [Information on Foreign Investment] (Tokyo: Nihon keizai shinbunsha, 1987).

NIHON YUSHUTSU YUNYŪ GINKŌ KAIGAI TŌSHI KENKYŪJO [Foreign Investment Research Centre of the Japan Export Import Bank] (1988) *Wagakuni taiō chokusetsu tōshi no dōkō* [The Trend of Japan's Foreign Direct Investment in Europe] (Tokyo: Nihon yushutsu yunyū ginkō, 1988).

NIHON ZAIGAI KIGYŌ KYŌKAI [Japan Overseas Enterprises Association] (1988) *Taiō tōshi masatsu* [Investment Conflict in Europe] (Tokyo: Nihon zaigai kigyō kyōkai, 1988).

NINOMIYA, ATSUMI (1987) *Endaka resshima to sangyō no kūdōka* [Japan's High Yen and the Hollowing out of Industry] (Tokyo: Rōdō junposha, 1987).

NISHIMURA, MITSUGU (1988) 'Takokuseki kigyō no sozei kaihi no shuhō to Nihon no kokusai kazei seido' [TNCs Method of Tax Avoidance and Japan's International Tax System], *Keizai*, no. 294, October 1988.

NOMURA SŌGŌ KENKYŪJO [Nomura Research International] (1987) *Nichi-Bei-Kan kigyō no keiei senryaku: 21 seiki o kirihiraku chikyūkei kigyōgun* [Managerial Strategies of Japanese, American, and South Korean Firms: Global Corporate Groupings Opening up the 21st Century] (Tokyo: Nomura sōgō kenkyūjo jōhō kaihatsubu, 1987).

OGAWA, YŌICHI (1986) Nikkei sangyō shirīzu [Nikkei Industry Series] *OA kiki* [OA Equipment] (Tokyo: Nihon keizai shinbunsha, 1986).

292   *References*

ŌKURASHŌ [Ministry of Finance] (1987a/88a) 'Shōwa 61/62 nendo ni okeru taigai oyobi tainai chokusetsu tōshi todokede jisseki' [Actually Reported Internal and External Foreign Investments for the fiscal year 1986/87], 28 May 1987 and 31 May 1988.

ŌKURASHŌ [Ministry of Finance] (1985b/87b) *Zaisei kinyū tōkei geppō* [Monthly Bulletin of Monetary and Financial Statistics], Taigai minkan tōshi tokushū [Special Issue on Private Overseas Investment], nos. 404 and 428, December 1985 and December 1987 (Tokyo: Ōkurashō insatsukyoku, 1985/87).

RŌDŌSHŌ [Ministry of Labour] (1986) 'Nihon-Amerika oyobi Nihon-Nishidoitsu no shōhi kōbairyoku heika (suihei)' [Estimates of the Consumer Buying Power Par Value between Japan, America and West Germany], November 1986.

RŌDŌSHŌ [Ministry of Labour] (1987a) 'Saikin no kinrōsha setai no kakei dōkō ni tsuite' [Concerning the Recent Trend of the Budgets of Workers' Households].

RŌDŌSHŌ [Ministry of Labour[(1987b/88b) *Shōwa 62/63 nenkan rōdō hakusho* [1987/88 Labour White Paper] (Tokyo: Nihon rōdō kyōkai, 1987/88).

RŌDŌSHŌ [Ministry of Labour] FUJINKYOKU [Women's Bureau] (1988) *Fujin rōdō no jitsujo* [The Realities of Women's Work] (Tokyo: Ōkurashō insatsukyoku, 1988).

SASAKI, KEN (1986) *Nihonkei takokuseki kigyō* [Japanese Style Multinational Companies] (Tokyo: Yūhikaku, 1986).

SASAKI, NORIAKI (1987) *Oshiyoseru shitsugyō: zaikai no 21 seiki senryaku to sangyō kūdōka* [Mounting Unemployment: Deindustrialisation and the Financial World's Strategy for the 21st Century] (Tokyo: Shin Nihon shuppansha, 1987).

SATŌ, ISAO, KAWAKAMI, SABURŌ and TORIYAMA, HIROSHI (eds) (1987) *Nichibei jidōsha sensō: 1990 nendai e no savaivaru o kakeru* [The Japan–America Auto War: Betting on Survival in the 1990s] (Tokyo: Daiyamondosha, 1987).

SATŌ, YŌSUKE (1987) 'Sangyōbetsu bunseki sen'i' [Industry Analyses: Textiles], *Keizai*, no. 283, November 1987.

SEKAI KEIEI KYŌGIKAI [World Management Association]. (1987) *Ajia taiheiyō shokoku aida ni okeru kaigai seisan kaigai chōtatsu* [Overseas Production and Supplies among the Asian and Pacific Countries] (Tokyo: Sekai keiei kyōgikai, 1987).

SEKAI (1988) Rinji zōkan [Special Issue], *Nihon yūtakasa dēta bukku* [Data Book on Affluent Japan], no. 510, January 1988 (Tokyo: Iwanami shoten, 1988).

SHIGA, HIROKO (1988) 'Hakken rōdō wa kyaria o ikaseru ka?' [Is Dispatched Labour to Fetch and Carry?], *Keizai*, no. 292, August 1988.

SHIMADA, KATSUMI (1986) *Kaigai chokusetsu tōshi nyūmon* [An Introduction to Foreign Direct Investment] (Tokyo: Gakumonsha, 1986).

SHIMOKAWA, KŌICHI (1985) Nikkei sangyō shirīzu [Nikkei Industry Series] *Jidōsha* [Automobiles] (Tokyo: Nihon keizai shinposha, 1985).

SHIMURA, YUKIO (1986) Nikkei sangyō shirīzu [Nikkei Industry Series] *Denchi buhhin* [Electronics Parts] (Tokyo: Nihon keizai shinbunsha, 1986).

SHŌJI, HIKARU and MIYAMOTO KENJI *Nihon no kōgai* [Japan's Pollution] (Tokyo: Iwanami shoten, 1975).
SHŪKAN TŌYŌ KEIZAI (1973–88) Rinji zōkan/dēta banku [Special Issue/databank]. *Kaigai shinshutsu kigyō sōran* [Japanese Multinationals, Facts & Figures] (Tokyo: Tōyō keizai shinposha, 1973–88).
SUEHIRO, AKIRA and YASUDA, OSAMU (eds) (1987) Ajia kōgyōka shirīzu 3 [Industrialisation of Asia Series, no. 3]. *Tai no kōgyōka: NAIC e no chōsen* [The Industrialisation of Thailand: The Challenge to become a NAIC] (Tokyo: Ajia keizai kenkyūjo [Institute of Developing Economies], 1987).
SUGINO, MIKIO (1987) 'Sōgō shōsha no shinshutsu to konnichiteki yakuwari' [The Overseas shift by the Trading Companies and the Present Day Role], *Keizai*, no. 283, November 1987.
TADA, KENZŌ (1986) Nikkei sangyō shirīzu [Nikkei Industry Series] *Tekkō* [Steel] (Tokyo: Nihon keizai shinbunsha, 1986).
TAKEUCHI, HIROSHI, MACHIDA, YŌJI and KIUCHI, AKIRA [1987] *Endaka fukyō: gekihen suru Nihon keizai shinchizu* [The High Yen Recession: The Rapidly Changing New Economic Map of Japan] (Tokyo: Yūhikaku Livret, 1987).
TAKIZAWA, KIKUTARŌ (1982) *Chūshō kigyō no kaigai shinshutsu* [Overseas Advance of Small and Medium Enterprises] (Tokyo: Yūhikaku, 1982).
TOKUMASU, HAJIME (1987) Nikkei sangyō shirīzu [Nikkei Industry Series]. *Zōsen, jūkikai* [Heavy Industries] (Tokyo: Nihon keizai shinbunsha, 1987).
TSŪSHŌ SANGYŌSHŌ [Ministry of International Trade and Industry] (1987a/88a) *Shōwa 62/63 nenkan tsūshō hakusho* [1987/88 Trade and Industry White Paper], (Tokyo: Ōkurashō insatsukyoku, 1987/88).
TSŪSHŌ SANGYŌSHŌ (1987b/88b) *Shōwa 62/63 nenkan tsūshō hakusho* [1987/88 Trade and Industry White Papers], kakuron [details] (Tokyo: Ōkurashō insatsukyoku, 1987/88).
TSŪSHŌ SANGYŌSHŌ SANGYŌ SEISAKUKYOKU KOKUSAI KIGYŌKA [International Company Division of the Policy Bureau of MITI] (1984c/86c/87c/88c) *Dai 12–13/14/15/16/ Waga kuni kigyō no kaigai jigyō katsudō* [Overseas Business Activities of Our Country's Firms, nos. 12/13/14/15/16] (Tokyo: Keibun shuppan, 1986/87/88.
TWU, JAW-YANN (1988) *NICS: Kōgyōka Ajia o yomu* [NICs: Reading on Industrialising Asia] (Tokyo: Kodansha gendai shinsho, 1988).
UTSUMI, AIKO and MATSUI, YAYORI (1988) *Ajia kara kita dekasegi rōdōshatachi* [Migrant Workers from Asia] (Tokyo: Akaishi shoten, 1988).
WONGHANCHAO, WARIN and IKEMOTO, YUKIO (1988) ASEAN nado genchi kenkyū shirīzu, no. 1 [Field Research Series on ASEAN and Others, no. 1] *Tai no keizai seisaku: rekishi genkyō tenbō* [Economic Policy of Thailand: Past, Present and Future] (Tokyo: Ajia keizai kenkyūjo [Institute of Developing Economies], 1988).
YAMAUCHI, ICHIZŌ (1985) Nikkei sangyō shirīzu [Nikkei Industry Series] *Kaden* [Home Electrical Appliances] (Tokyo: Nihon Keizai shinbunsha, 1985).
YAWATA, SHIGEMI and MIZUNO, JUNKO (1988) Keizai kyōryoku

294 *References*

shirizu dai 142 go [Economic Cooperation Series, no. 142]. *Nikkei shin-shutsu kigyō to no kigyō aida bungyō kōzō to gijutsu iden: Tai no jidōsha sangyō o jirei to shite* [The Structure of the Division of Labour and the Transfer of Skills within Japanese Subsidiary Companies: The Case of the Thai Auto Industry] (Tokyo: Ajia keizai kenkyūjo [Institute of Developing Economies], 1988).

YONEKURA, AKIO (1988) 'Nihon kigyō no takakuteki na seisan kyōtenka' [The Multiplication of Production Sites of Japanese Companies], *Keizai*, no. 294, October 1988.

YOSHIOKA, MASAYUKI (1986) Nikkei sangyō shirīzu [Nikkei Industry Series] *Sen'i* [Textiles] (Tokyo: Nihon keizai shinbunsha, 1986).

ENGLISH SOURCES

AMIN, MOHAMED and CALDWELL, MALCOLM (eds) (1977) *Malaya: The Making of a Neo-Colony* (Nottingham: Spokesman Books, 1977).

AMIN, SAMIR (1974) *Accumulation on a World Scale: A Critique of the Theory of Underdevelopment*, 2 vols (New York: Monthly Review Press, 1974).

AMPO (1977) Special Issue, 'Free Trade Zones and the Industrialisation of Asia', vol. 8, no. 4 and vol. 9, nos. 1–2 (1977).

AMPO (1980) Special Issue on Transnational Enterprises in Indonesia, vol. 12, no. 4 (1980).

AMPO (1986) Special Issue, 'The Challenge Facing Japanese Women', vol. 18, nos. 2–3, 1986.

AMPO (1987) Special Issue, 'The Life and Times of the Shrimp: From Third-World Seas to Japanese Tables', vol. 18, no. 4, 1987.

ARANETA, CARMELITA R. (1987) 'The Import Liberalisation Program', *CB Review*, November 1987.

ASEAN PROMOTION CENTRE ON TRADE, INVESTMENT AND TOURISM (ASEAN Centre) (1987a) *Influence of the Yen Appreciation on Japan's Direct Investment* (Tokyo: ASEAN Centre, 1987).

ASEAN PROMOTION CENTRE ON TRADE INVESTMENT AND TOURISM (1987b) *Japanese Investment in ASEAN* (Tokyo: ASEAN Centre, 1987).

ASEAN PROMOTION CENTRE ON TRADE INVESTMENT AND TOURISM (1988) ASEAN–Japan Statistical Handbook (Tokyo: ASEAN Centre, 1988).

ASIA PACIFIC MARKETING SERVICES LIMITED (1987) *Asia's 7500 Largest companies, 1988* (Oslo: A. Sokinomisk Literatur, 1987).

BANGKOK BANK MONTHLY REVIEW (1981) 'Japanese Investment in Thailand', May 1981.

BELLO, WALDEN, KINLEY, DAVID and ELINSON, ELAINE (1982) *Development Debacle: The World Bank in the Philippines* (San Francisco: Institute for Food & Development Policy, 1982).

BRENNAN, MARTIN (1982) 'Class, Politics and Race in Modern Malaysia', *JCA*, vol. 12, no. 2, 1982.

BCAS [*Bulletin of Concerned Asian Scholars*], Special Supplement, 'October 1976: The Coup in Thailand', vol. 9, no. 3, July–Sept. 1977.

CALDWELL, MALCOLM (ed.) (1975) *Ten Years' Military Terror in Indonesia* (Nottingham: Spokesman Books, 1975).

CHEE, PENG LIM and LEE POH PING (1979) 'The Role of Japanese Direct Investment Malaysia', Institute of Southeast Asian Studies, 1979.

CHOONHAVEN, KRAISAK (1984) 'The Growth of Domestic Capital and Thai Industrialisation', *JCA*, vol. 14, no. 2, 1984.

CUMINGS, BRUCE (1981) *The Origins of the Korean War* (Guilford: Princeton University Press, 1981).

DOBASHI, KENJI (1986) 'Japan's Emerging Direct Investments in Asian NICs', *Asian Perspectives*, June–July 1986.

DORE, RONALD (1986) *Flexible Rigidities: Industrial Policy and Structural Adjustment in the Japanese Economy* (London: Athlone Press, 1986).

ELLIOT, DAVID (1978) *Thailand: Origins of Military Rule* (London: Zed Press, 1978).

EMMANUEL, ARGHIRI (1972) *Unequal Exchange: A Study of the Imperialism of Trade* (London: New Left Books, 1972).

FRANK, A.G. (1967) *Capitalism and Underdevelopment in Latin America* (New York: Monthly Review Press, 1967).

FOSTER-CARTER, AIDEN (1987) 'Korea: From Dependecy to Democracy', *Capital and Class*, no. 33, Winter 1987.

FUJITA, KUNIKO (1988) 'Women Workers, State Policy, and the International Division of Labor: The Case of Silicon Island in Japan', *BCAS*, vol. 20, no. 3, July–Sept. 1988.

GORDON, ALEC (1978) 'Some Problems of Analysing Class Relations in Indonesia', *JCA*, vol. 8 no. 2, 1978.

GORDON, ALEC (1979) 'Stages in the Development of Java's Socio-Economic Formations 700–1978 AD', *JCA*, vol. 9, no. 2, 1979.

GORDON, ALEC (1982) 'Indonesia, Plantations and the "Post Colonial" Mode of Production', *JCA*, vol. 12, no. 2, 1982.

GUINIGUNDO, DIWA C (1987) 'Structure and Direction of Philippine External Trade: Some Basic Issues', *CB Review*, May 1987.

GUILATCO, LINDA (1977) 'Japan in the Philippines: 1974–1977', *Ampo*, vol. 9, no. 3, 1977.

HALIM, FATIMAH (1982) 'Capital, Labour and the State: The Case of West Malaysia', *JCA*, vol. 12, no. 3, 1982.

HALLIDAY, JON and MCCORMACK, GAVAN (1973) *Japanese Imperialism Today* (Penguin Books, 1973).

HARIAN PERINTIS (1986) *Malaysia: Commerce & Industry, 1986/87* (Kuala Lumpur: Harian Perintis, 1986).

HEWISON, KEVIN J. (1981) 'The financial Bourgeoisie in Thailand', *JCA*, vol. 11, no. 4, 1981.

HEWISON, KEVIN J. (1986) 'Capital in the Thai Countryside: The Sugar Industry', *JCA*, vol. 16, no. 1, 1986.

HIGGOTT, RICHARD and ROBISON, RICHARD (eds) (1985) *Southeast Asia: Essays in the Political Economy of Structural Change* (London: Routledge & Kegan Paul, 1985).

HIMPUNAN USAHAWAN INDONESIA–JEPANG [Indonesia–Japan

Entrepreneurs Association] (1984) *A Decade of Himpunan Usahawan Indonesia–Jepang 1974–1984: The Role and Contribution of Indonesia–Japan Joint Venture Companies* (Jakarta, 1984).

IBON RESEARCH (1982) 'Japan in Northern Luzon', *Ampo*, vol. 14, no. 3, 1982.

IBRAHIM, KHALID (1987) 'Corporate Restructuring: The PNB Experience', in K.S. Jomo *et al.*, *Crisis and Response in the Malaysian Economy* (Kuala Lumpur, Malaysian Economic Association, 1987).

INOGUCHI, TAKASHI and OKIMOTO, DANIEL I. (1988) *The Political Economy of Japan*, vol. 2, The Changing International Context (Standford: Standford University Press, 1988).

JETRO (1982) *Directory: Affiliates & Offices of Japanese Firms in the ASEAN Countries* (Tokyo: Jetro, 1982).

JETRO (1988) *White Paper on International Trade: Japan 1988* (Tokyo: Jetro, 1988).

JETRO JAKARTA (1987) *List of Foreign Investment Projects in Indonesia, 1967–86* (Jakarta: Jetro Jakarta Centre, 1987).

JETRO KUALA LUMPUR CENTRE (1986) *Japanese Related Companies in Malaysia* (1986).

JETRO MANILA AND THE JAPANESE CHAMBER OF COMMERCE & INDUSTRY OF THE PHILIPPINES (1986) *Business Directory: Japanese Capital-Affiliated Domestic Corporations and Wholly Owned Japanese Enterprises in the Philippines* (Manila, 1986).

KAJI, ETSUKO (1986) 'Herded into the Labour Market', *Ampo*, vol. 18, nos. 2–3, 1986.

KHONTAI (1980) 'Japan's Shibato Company: Defrauding Sugarcane Growers in Thailand', *Ampo*, vol. 12, no. 3, 1980.

KHOR, KOK PENG (1983) *The Malaysian Economy: Structures and Dependence* (Kuala Lumpur: Marican & Sons, 1983).

KIM, C.I. and KIM, HAN-KYO (1967) *Korea and the Politics of Imperialism, 1876–1910* (Berkeley: University of California Press, 1967).

KIM, IL-HWAN (1987) 'Direct Foreign Investment in Korea', *Monthly Review of the Exchange Bank of Korea*, October 1987.

KIM, JOONG-HYUN (1987) 'The Machine Tool Industry in Korea', *Monthly Review of the Exchange Bank of Korea*, April 1987.

KITAZAWA, YOKO (1976) 'Japan Indonesia Corruption', parts I and II, *Ampo*, vol. 8, nos. 1 and 2 (1976).

KITAZAWA, YOKO (1979) 'Development and Dependence: Japanese Inroads into the Brazilian Economy', *Ampo*, vol. 11, no. 4, 1979.

KITAZAWA, YOKO (1982) 'Integrating the Pacific Basin: Japanese and Australian Capital Restructure Southeast Asia and the Pacific', *Ampo*, vol. 14, no. 1, 1982.

KITAZAWA, YOKO (1983) 'The Japanese Economy and the Third World', *Ampo*, vol. 15, nos. 3–4, 1983.

KITAZAWA, YOKO (1987) 'Setting Up Shop, Shutting Up Shop', *Ampo*, vol. 19, no. 4, 1987.

KUZNETS, PAUL W. (1977) *Economic Growth and Structure in the Republic of Korea* (New Haven: Yale University Press, 1977).

KWAG, DAE-HWAN (1987) 'Korea's Overseas Investment', *Monthly Re-*

view of the Exchange Bank of Korea, September 1987.

KWON, YONG-SOO (1986) 'The Automobile Industry in Korea', *Monthly Review of the Exchange Bank of Korea*, November 1986.

LEK, KIAT-LUECHA (1977) 'Thailand: One Year after the October 6 Coup', *Ampo*, vol. 9, no. 3, 1977.

LIM, MAH HUI (1980) 'Ethnic and Class Relations in Malaysia', *JCA*, vol. 10, no. 1/2, 1980.

LIM, MAH HUI and TEOH, KIT FONG (1986) 'Singapore Corporations Go Transnational', *Journal of Southeast Asian Studies*, vol. VII, no. 2, 1986.

LINCOLN, EDWARD J. (1988) *Japan: Facing Economic Maturity* (Washington, DC: The Brookings Institution, 1988).

LINDSEY, CHARLES W. (1987) 'The Philippine State and Transnational Investment', *BCAS*, vol. 19, no. 2, 1987.

MATSUI, YAYORI (1979) 'Malaysia: Japan Exports Pollution in Return for Copper', *Ampo*, vol. 11, no. 1, 1979.

MCCORMACK, GAVAN and GITTINGS, JOHN (1977) *Crisis in Korea* (Nottingham: Spokesman, 1977).

MINISTRY OF INTERNATIONAL TRADE AND INDUSTRY (MITI) (1987) *Statistics on Japanese Industries, 1986–87* (Tokyo: International Trade and Industry Association, 1987).

MIRZA, HAFIZ (1986) *Multinationals and the Growth of the Singapore Economy* (London: Croom Helm, 1986).

MORGAN, MALCOLM (1977) 'The Rise and Fall of Malayan Trade Unionism', in Amin and Caldwell, op. cit. 1977.

MORRIS-SUZUKI, TESSA (1984) 'Japan's Role in the International Division of Labour – A Reassessment', *JCA*, vol. 14, no. 1, 1984.

NAHM, ANDREW C. (ed.) (1973) *Japanese Colonial Rule: Studies of the Policy and Techniques of Japanese Colonialism* (The Centre for Korean Studies, West Michigan University, 1973).

NAKANO, KENJI (1978) 'Japan's Petrochemical Promiscuity', *Ampo*, vol. 10, nos. 1–2 (1978).

NAKANO, KENJI (1978) 'Behind the IHI Shipyard Disaster in Singapore', *Ampo*, vol. 10, no. 4, 1978.

NG, C.Y., HIRONO, R. and AKRASANEE (1987) *Industrial Restructuring in ASEAN and Japan: An Overview* (Singapore: Institute of Southeast Asian Studies, 1987).

OFRENEO, RENE E. (1980) *Capitalism in Philippines Agriculture* (Quezon City: Foundation for Nationalist Studies, 1980).

OKADA, OSAMU (1980 'Taiyo Fishery Co., Inc.: Japan's Largest Commercial Fishery', *Ampo*, vol. 12, no. 3, 1980.

PANGLAYKIM, J. (1983) *Japanese Direct Investment in Asean: The Indonesian Experience* (Singapore: Maruzen Asia, 1983).

PARK, SOON-PONG (1987) 'The Electronics Industry in Korea', *Monthly Review of the Exchange Bank of Korea*, June 1987.

PARK, PYEONG-KYU (1987) 'The Iron and Steel Industry in Korea', *Monthly Review of the Exchange Bank of Korea*, February 1987.

PHONGPAICHIT, PASUK et al. (ed.) (1986) *The Lion and the Mouse? Japan Asia and Thailand*, proceedings of an international conference on

Thai-Japanese Relations organised by the Faculty of Economics, Chulalongkorn University, April 1986.

PRASARTSET, SUTHY (1981) *Thai Business Leaders: Men and Careers in a Developing Economy* (Tokyo: Institute of Developing Economies, 1981).

PRESTOWITZ, CLYDE V. (1988) *Trading Places: How America Allowed Japan to Take the Lead* (Tokyo: Charles E. Tuttle, 1988).

ROBINSON, W. (1985) 'Imperialism, Dependency and Peripheral Industrialisation: The Case of Japan in Indonesia', in *Southeast Asia: Essays in the Political Economy of Structural Change* (ed.) Richard Higgott and Richard Robison (London: Routledge & Kegan Paul, 1985).

ROBISON, RICHARD (1986) *Indonesia: The Rise of Capital* (Sydney: Allen & Unwin, 1986).

SAGALLA, LAMBERT B. (1988) 'The Omnibus Investment Code of 1987: Major Innovations and Comparability with Member Countries of the ASEAN', *CB Review*, February 1988.

SAHABAT ALAM MALAYSIA (1987) *Forest Resources Crisis in the Third World* (Penang: Sahabat Alam Malaysia, 1987).

SARAVANAMUTTU, JOHAN (1983) 'Malaysia's Look East Policy and Japanese Expansionism', *Ampo*, vol. 15, nos. 3–4, 1983.

SHORT, KATE (1979) 'Foreign Capital and the State in Indonesia: Some Aspects of Contemporary Imperialism', *JCA*, vol. 9, no. 2, 1979.

SONO, HARUO (1981) 'Japanese Automobile Capital and International Competition', parts 1 and 2, *Ampo*, vol. 13, nos. 1–2, 1981.

STENSON, M.R. (1970) *Industrial Conflict in Malaya: Prelude to the Communist Revolt of 1948* (London: OUP, 1970).

STENSON, MICHAEL (1976) 'Class and Race in West Malaysia', *BCAS*, vol. 8, no. 2, 1976.

STEVEN, R. (1983) *Classes in Contemporary Japan* (London: Cambridge University Press, 1983).

STEVEN, R. (1986) 'Equal Pay for Work of Equal Value: Marxist Theory', *Race Gender Class*, no. 4, December 1986.

STEVEN, R. (1988) 'The High Yen Crisis in Japan', *Capital and Class*, no. 34, Spring 1988.

STEVEN, R. (1988) 'Japanese Foreign Direct Investment in Southeast Asia: From ASEAN to JASEAN', *BCAS*, vol. 20, no. 4, Oct.–Dec. 1988.

SUNOO, HAROLD HAKWON (1978) 'Economic Development and Foreign Control in South Korea', *JCA*, vol. 8, no. 3, 1978.

SUZUKI, MOTOYOSHI (1986) 'Theory and Some Empirical Evidence of Japanese Foreign Investment in Thailand', MA Thesis, English Language Program, Faculty of Economics, Thammasat University, April, 1986.

SZYMANSKI, ALBERT (1981) *The Logic of Imperialism* (New York: Praeger Publishers, 1981).

TADEM, EDUARDO (1983) 'The Japanese Presence in the Philippines: A Critical Re-Assessment', Third World Studies Centre, University of the Philippines.

TAMBUNLERTCHAI, SOMSAK and MCGOVERN, IAN (1984) 'An Overview of the Role of MNCs in the Economic Development of Thailand', Proceedings of the Conference on The Role of Multi-National Corporations in Thailand, July 7–9, 1984, Thammasat University (eds)

Nongyao Chaiseri and Chira Hongladarom.

TONO, HARUHI (1984) 'Asian Women as Victims of Overseas Expansion: A Case Study of Toray', *Ampo*, vol. 16, nos. 1–2, 1984.

TSUCHIYA, TAKEO (1979) 'Mitsubishi Shoji: A Century-old Conglomerate Goes Transnational', *Ampo*, vol. 11, no. 1, 1979.

TSUCHIYA, TAKEO (1980) 'Mitsui: Japan's Advance Guard in the Third World', *Ampo*, vol. 12, no. 1, 1980.

TSUCHIYA, TAKEO (1983) 'Japan's Overseas "Aid" Paves the Way for a New "Greater East Asia Co-Prosperity Sphere"', *Ampo*, vol. 15, nos. 3–4 (1983).

TSUCHIYA, TAKEO (1984) 'The Japanese Sphere of Influence: Multinational Investment in Asia', *Ampo*, vol. 16, nos. 1–2 (1984).

TSUDA, MAMORU (1978) *A Preliminary Study of Japanese-Filipino Joint ventures* (Quezon City: Foundation for Nationalist Studies, 1978).

TSUDA, MOMORU and DEOCADIZ, LEO A. (1986) *RP-Japan Relations and ADB: In Search of a New Horizon* (Manila: National Bookstore and Business Day, 1986).

THIRD WORLD STUDIES CENTRE, UNIVERSITY OF THE PHILIPPINES (1978) 'Japanese Interests in the Philippines Fishing Industry', *Ampo*, vol. 10, nos. 1–2, 1978.

THIRD WORLD STUDIES CENTRE, UNIVERSITY OF THE PHILIPPINES (1981) 'TNC Control of the Philippine Banana Industry', *Ampo*, vol. 13, no. 3, 1981.

UTRECHT, ERNEST (1977) 'Japanese Private Investments in Singapore', *Ampo*, vol. 9, no. 3, 1977.

UTRECHT, ERNEST (1978) 'Japanese Private Investments in Thailand', *Ampo*, vol. 10, no. 4, 1978.

UTRECHT, ERNEST and CALDWELL, MALCOLM (1979) *Indonesia: An Alternative History* (Sydney: Alternative Publishing Cooperative, 1979).

UTSUMI, AIKO (1988) 'Will the Japanese Government Open the Legal Door?' *Ampo*, vol. 19, no. 4, 1988.

WALLERSTEIN, IMMANUEL (1979) *The Capitalist World Economy* (London: Cambridge University Press, 1979).

WARREN, BILL (1980) *Imperialism: Pioneer of Capitalism* (London: New Left Books, 1980).

WATANABE, SOITSU (1986) 'Trends in Japan's Direct Investment Abroad for FY 1984', in Nihon yushutsu yunyū ginkō, op. cit. 1986.

YAMADA, NOEL (1980) 'The Poisoning of Cagayan de Oro: Kawasaki Steel in the Philippines', *Ampo*, vol. 12, no. 2 (1980).

YAMAKA, JUNKO (1978) 'Overview of the Japanese Fishing Industry', *Ampo*, vol. 10, no. 4, 1978.

YAMAKA, JUNKO (1984) 'Fisheries in Asia and the Pacific: Japan's Involvement and its Problems', *Ampo*, vol. 16, nos. 1–2, 1984.

YAMAKA, JUNKO (1985) 'More Pollution Export by Japan: Nuclear Waste Dumping Exposed in Malaysia', *Ampo*, vol. 17, no. 1, 1985.

YOSHIHARA, KUNIO (1978) *Japanese Investment in South East Asia* (Honolulu: The University Press in Hawaii, 1978).

YOSHIHARA, KUNIO (1988) *The Rise of Ersatz Capitalism in South-East Asia* (Singapore: Oxford University Press, 1988).

Index

300